P9-CKS-434

Marketing Research Kit

FOR

DUMMIES®

by Michael R. Hyman, PhD
and Jeremy J. Sierra, PhD

WILEY

Wiley Publishing, Inc.

Marketing Research Kit For Dummies®
Published by
Wiley Publishing, Inc.
111 River St.
Hoboken, NJ 07030-5774
www.wiley.com

Copyright © 2010 by Wiley Publishing, Inc., Indianapolis, Indiana

Published by Wiley Publishing, Inc., Indianapolis, Indiana

Published simultaneously in Canada

No part of this publication may be reproduced, stored in a retrieval system or transmitted in any form or by any means, electronic, mechanical, photocopying, recording, scanning or otherwise, except as permitted under Sections 107 or 108 of the 1976 United States Copyright Act, without either the prior written permission of the Publisher, or authorization through payment of the appropriate per-copy fee to the Copyright Clearance Center, 222 Rosewood Drive, Danvers, MA 01923, (978) 750-8400, fax (978) 646-8600. Requests to the Publisher for permission should be addressed to the Permissions Department, John Wiley & Sons, Inc., 111 River Street, Hoboken, NJ 07030, (201) 748-6011, fax (201) 748-6008, or online at http://www.wiley.com/go/permissions.

Trademarks: Wiley, the Wiley Publishing logo, For Dummies, the Dummies Man logo, A Reference for the Rest of Us!, The Dummies Way, Dummies Daily, The Fun and Easy Way, Dummies.com, Making Everything Easier, and related trade dress are trademarks or registered trademarks of John Wiley & Sons, Inc. and/or its affiliates in the United States and other countries, and may not be used without written permission. All other trademarks are the property of their respective owners. Wiley Publishing, Inc., is not associated with any product or vendor mentioned in this book.

LIMIT OF LIABILITY/DISCLAIMER OF WARRANTY: THE PUBLISHER AND THE AUTHOR MAKE NO REPRESENTATIONS OR WARRANTIES WITH RESPECT TO THE ACCURACY OR COMPLETENESS OF THE CONTENTS OF THIS WORK AND SPECIFICALLY DISCLAIM ALL WARRANTIES, INCLUDING WITHOUT LIMITATION WARRANTIES OF FITNESS FOR A PARTICULAR PURPOSE. NO WARRANTY MAY BE CREATED OR EXTENDED BY SALES OR PROMOTIONAL MATERIALS. THE ADVICE AND STRATEGIES CONTAINED HEREIN MAY NOT BE SUITABLE FOR EVERY SITUATION. THIS WORK IS SOLD WITH THE UNDERSTANDING THAT THE PUBLISHER IS NOT ENGAGED IN RENDERING LEGAL, ACCOUNTING, OR OTHER PROFESSIONAL SERVICES. IF PROFESSIONAL ASSISTANCE IS REQUIRED, THE SERVICES OF A COMPETENT PROFESSIONAL PERSON SHOULD BE SOUGHT. NEITHER THE PUBLISHER NOR THE AUTHOR SHALL BE LIABLE FOR DAMAGES ARISING HEREFROM. THE FACT THAT AN ORGANIZATION OR WEBSITE IS REFERRED TO IN THIS WORK AS A CITATION AND/OR A POTENTIAL SOURCE OF FURTHER INFORMATION DOES NOT MEAN THAT THE AUTHOR OR THE PUBLISHER ENDORSES THE INFORMATION THE ORGANIZATION OR WEBSITE MAY PROVIDE OR RECOMMENDATIONS IT MAY MAKE. FURTHER, READERS SHOULD BE AWARE THAT INTERNET WEBSITES LISTED IN THIS WORK MAY HAVE CHANGED OR DISAPPEARED BETWEEN WHEN THIS WORK WAS WRITTEN AND WHEN IT IS READ.

For general information on our other products and services, please contact our Customer Care Department within the U.S. at 877-762-2974, outside the U.S. at 317-572-3993, or fax 317-572-4002.

For technical support, please visit www.wiley.com/techsupport.

Wiley also publishes its books in a variety of electronic formats. Some content that appears in print may not be available in electronic books.

Library of Congress Control Number: 2010922048

ISBN: 978-0-470-52068-0

Manufactured in the United States of America

10 9 8 7 6 5 4 3 2 1

WILEY

About the Authors

Michael R. Hyman, PhD, is the Stan Fulton Chair of Marketing at New Mexico State University in Las Cruces, New Mexico. He earned his undergraduate degree at the University of Maryland and his master's and doctoral degrees at Purdue University. Back in the day, he fancied himself a Texan — he was a faculty member at the University of Houston and then later at the University of North Texas — but he has since become a loyal green-chile-eating, motorcycle-riding, non-tie-wearing New Mexican.

Mike has taught marketing research at the undergraduate, masters, and doctoral levels for more years than he cares to admit (30 and counting). Although they occasionally suggest that his exams are overly challenging, students never complain that his research courses are poorly structured or lack sufficient rigor.

Roughly 20 years ago, Mike toyed with the idea of leaving academia for full-time consulting. For almost three years, he consulted extensively with major hospitality industry clients. After straddling the university-consulting fence during this period, he decided — with the help of several perpetually annoying colleagues — that he was best suited to university life. Although he still accepts the occasional consulting gig, he has never regretted that decision. Nonetheless, he learned more about "real world" marketing research during those three years than during all his years of schooling.

Golfing and fishing are Mike's only "Type B" activities. When not teaching, spending time with his family, playing poker, or following the exploits of his beloved New York Yankees (a remnant of his misspent youth), he's usually preoccupied with some writing project. His roughly 70 academic journal articles, 45 conference papers (10 which won a "best paper" award), 2 books, 15 other academic works, and 20 nonacademic works attest to this writing compulsion. He's also a sucker for professional service requests; among other activities, he's been talked into serving on 13 journal editorial boards, reviewing an excessive number of manuscripts and books each year, serving as a journal editor, and coordinating two different doctoral programs.

Jeremy J. Sierra, PhD, is an Assistant Professor of Marketing at Texas State University — San Marcos. He teaches a wide array of marketing courses, including Marketing Research, which he has taught the past four years. Prior to joining the marketing faculty at Texas State, he taught at Northern Arizona University. He earned his MBA. and PhD from New Mexico State University and his BS in Hotel and Restaurant Management from California State Polytechnic University, Pomona. Before entering academia, Jeremy accumulated ten years of experience in the hospitality industry, where he acquired his knack for cost controls, customer relationship management, and in-store design. His industry experience ranges from entrepreneurial restaurant establishments to high-end resorts (for example, Scottsdale Princess and Scottsdale Plaza Resort) and golf club environments (for example, Frenchman's Creek Country Club in Palm Beach Gardens, Florida).

Jeremy's research interests include advertising effects, consumer behavior, marketing ethics, and services marketing. Jeremy's research is published in the following journals: *Journal of Academic Ethics; Journal of Advertising; Journal of Business and Management; Journal of Current Issues & Research in Advertising; Journal of Marketing Education; Journal of Marketing Theory and Practice*; and *Journal of Services Marketing*. Jeremy has presented numerous conference proceedings, including two "best paper" awards, and has received a research grant from the Research Enhancement Program at Texas State. He is an avid golfer and an ardent Nebraska football fan, and he also is hopeful that this book will make you a better marketing researcher.

Authors' Acknowledgments

Mike: To read about every person who ever inspired me, and as a result this book, would be at best a mind-numbing experience. That said, certain people were more directly and indirectly influential in its creation and therefore especially deserving of acknowledgment.

My wife, Stacey, and sons, Aaron, Derek, and Evan, should be commended for their tolerance with my oft-uttered "Daddy would love to spend time with you now, but he's got to work on his book." Of course, the boys' college funds will benefit from their patience, so I prefer to rationalize their considerateness as "enlightened self–interest." Regardless, they are my primary motivation for awakening each morning. (Translation: They arise at 6 a.m. and make enough noise to wake the dead.)

My parents, Aaron and Selma, reinforced my genetic predisposition toward workaholism with a perpetual Get-Out-of-Jail-Free card. They always forgave any personal transgression — such as forgetting to call on their anniversary — when I could attribute it to my preoccupation with a school or work-related project. In essence, they encouraged the type of self-absorption requisite to a large writing project like this book.

Robin Peterson, a partner in crime and the best golfing buddy on the planet — when he doesn't almost flip our cart — effectively discouraged me from dwelling on his many non-lucrative book-authoring efforts. Sadly, he often failed to convince me that I would benefit more from an afternoon of golf than an afternoon of writing. Now that this book is finished, he will ensure that I renew my support of the golf ball industry.

Unlike the drama junkies who inflict discord and dysfunction on many academic departments, my colleagues at New Mexico State University are truly wonderful people. No one could find better co-workers and friends than Pookie Sautter, Jerry Hampton, Kelly Tian, Kevin Boberg, Bruce Huhmann, Michelle Jasso, Collin Payne, Mihai Niculescu, Pat Gavin, and Virginia Espinosa. By making my life so easy, they allowed me the time and energy needed to write this book.

I would be remiss if I failed to thank the many students throughout the years who enrolled in my marketing research course. They taught me more about teaching than all other sources combined and had an enormous influence on the quality of this book.

Finally, I also would be remiss if I failed to thank my Wiley editorial teammates for their trust and patience. When I initially panicked over the magnitude of this project, Mike Baker repeatedly reassured me that Jeremy and I could complete it. Natalie Harris, Jessica Smith, and Christy Pingleton ensured that the text never drifted into obtuse esoteric academese (like the last phrase). Thanks also to Jenny Swisher and the Media Development team for their help in setting up the DVD.

Jeremy: For brevity, I would like to acknowledge a few essential people (although there are a host of others) that have helped me along the way. For her love, companionship, and support, I would like to thank my wife, Dian; she is the best co-pilot a guy could ask for. To my Mom who showed me persistence growing up, although I never asked her what it was. To my Dad who would hit countless fly balls to me and throw hours of batting practice; these were his ways of communicating that in life, your toughest competitor is yourself. To my Grandma, for her love and support throughout my life, especially during my 11-year, 3-degree process. I also would like to acknowledge and thank my mentors, colleagues, students, and former professors for their insight about marketing. Finally, to the underdog, which I usually side with unless they're playing Nebraska: You inspire and make the world a better place. Keep the upsets coming.

Dedication

Mike: To Aaron, father and son.

Jeremy: To my wife and family, the underdog, and the loving memory of my Mom.

Publisher's Acknowledgments

We're proud of this book; please send us your comments at http://dummies.custhelp.com. For other comments, please contact our Customer Care Department within the U.S. at 877-762-2974, outside the U.S. at 317-572-3993, or fax 317-572-4002.

Some of the people who helped bring this book to market include the following:

Acquisitions, Editorial, and Media Development

Project Editor: Natalie Faye Harris

Acquisitions Editor: Mike Baker

Copy Editors: Jessica Smith, Christy Pingleton

Assistant Editor: Erin Calligan Mooney

Editorial Program Coordinator: Joe Niesen

Technical Reviewer: John Hall

Media Development Producer: Jennifer Swisher

Editorial Manager: Christine Meloy Beck

Editorial Assistant: Jennette ElNaggar, David Lutton

Art Coordinator: Alicia B. South

Cover Photos: © Chris Thomaidis/Stone/Getty

Cartoons: Rich Tennant (www.the5thwave.com)

Composition Services

Project Coordinator: Kristie Rees

Layout and Graphics: Carl Byers, Ashley Chamberlain, Yovonne Grego, Mark Pinto, Christine Williams

Proofreaders: John Greenough, Toni Settle

Indexer: Potomac Indexing LLC

Publishing and Editorial for Consumer Dummies

    Diane Graves Steele, Vice President and Publisher, Consumer Dummies

    Kristin Ferguson-Wagstaffe, Product Development Director, Consumer Dummies

    Ensley Eikenburg, Associate Publisher, Travel

    Kelly Regan, Editorial Director, Travel

Publishing for Technology Dummies

    Andy Cummings, Vice President and Publisher, Dummies Technology/General User

Composition Services

    Debbie Stailey, Director of Composition Services

Table of Contents

Chapter 9: Writing Good Questions **153**

Chapter 10: Designing Good Questionnaires **187**

Introduction

• •

*I*f you're reading these words, it's unlikely that you're thinking "Marketing research . . . I'd rather watch paint dry than read about, let alone conduct, marketing research. What could be duller?" Perhaps we're a bit biased, but we believe that marketing research is exciting because it's an important source of information that can help you make better business decisions. It touches every aspect of marketing practice.

Many undergraduate students believe that successful marketing practitioners merely need to learn a few broad principles and to apply their common sense. Although we generally disagree with that assessment, it's particularly false for marketing research. A marketing study is only as good as the quality of its weakest of many components. In other words, the devil is in the details — and we're your friendly neighborhood demons.

About This Book

Among others, our main goals for this book are to make you an informed consumer of marketing research and to prepare you to conduct a basic survey — most likely a customer satisfaction survey — for yourself or your organization. To accomplish these goals, we must show you what is and isn't proper for good marketing research. That way, you'll know what should be done and what should be avoided (like slivovitz, haggis, tripe, and overeating on Thanksgiving).

If we achieve these goals, the probability that you'll perform and acquire useful marketing research is far higher. You may conduct research yourself, or you may hire someone to conduct research on your behalf. Either way, it's a waste of time, effort, and money to conduct a study and then discover that it was carried out incorrectly and is worthless for making better marketing decisions.

In this book, we discuss the many skills associated with conducting a successful marketing research study, such as the following:

✔ Identifying a research problem
✔ Developing a series of research questions related to that problem

✔ Writing good questions and designing a good questionnaire that will explore those research questions

✔ Fielding a survey and avoiding common survey research errors

✔ Designing a qualitative study — like a focus group — that will explore your research questions

✔ Collecting respondents' data, entering it into a computer spreadsheet, analyzing it, and interpreting the results

✔ Writing a report that can help your organization or encourage a loan officer to lend you (and perhaps your associates) money for a business venture

Conventions Used in This Book

Here are some conventions that we use in this book:

✔ Whenever we introduce a word or phrase that may not be familiar to you, we put that word in *italics*. You can bet that there's a nearby definition, explanation, or vivid example.

✔ We use **bold** for key words in bulleted lists and the action part of numbered steps.

✔ On occasion, we include URLs for Web sites that we think may interest you. Those Web addresses appear in `monofont`, which distinguishes them from the rest of the text.

When this book was printed, some Web addresses may have needed to break across two lines of text. If that happened, rest assured that we haven't put in any extra characters (such as hyphens) to indicate the break. So, when using one of these Web addresses, just type in exactly what you see in this book, pretending as though the line break doesn't exist.

What You're Not to Read

We wrote this book to help you easily find and understand what you need to know about marketing research. Because you may be too busy to read every word, we've designed the book so it's easy to recognize less critical text.

Unless you're super-compulsive or short on reading material, you can skip the following:

- ✔ **Text in sidebars:** The shaded boxes that appear occasionally are called sidebars. They include asides and additional but noncritical detail.

- ✔ **Text associated with the Technical Stuff icon:** Skipping this interesting but advanced text should be okay if your goal is to conduct a basic customer satisfaction survey.

Foolish Assumptions

This book presents such a broad range of information that we can't presume we know exactly why you're reading it. Here are some good — and perhaps not so good — guesses:

- ✔ You're thinking about starting a business and you need credible market analyses — of customers, competitors, and the business environment — to convince investors or a loan officer that this business is likely to succeed.

- ✔ You already own (or co-own) a business and you want marketing research that can help you decide how to grow (or at least maintain) that business.

- ✔ You want to know the ways that marketing research can improve marketing-related decisions.

- ✔ You want to improve your financial or nonfinancial success. For example, you want to boost your market share, improve consumers' responses to your brand, or increase your gross margin percent.

- ✔ You don't know your targeted customers or competition as much as you'd like to know them.

- ✔ You're a student enrolled in a marketing research course and you want a readable and affordable text without 10,000 footnotes.

- ✔ You're not a math, statistics, or econometrics whiz.

- ✔ You'd rather read this book than our academic journal articles.

We also hope we're safe in assuming that you know your PC's DVD tray isn't a cup holder. Seriously, we assume you know how to use a word processor (to create questionnaires and write reports) and spreadsheet software (to analyze the data you collect).

How This Book Is Organized

We've grouped the chapters in this book into five parts, each one focusing on a particular aspect of marketing research. The following sections provide an overview of the content in each part.

Part I: Marketing Research: Learn It, Live It, Love It

This part begins by introducing marketing research and the approaches used to create a research plan. We summarize the research process and the basic types of research you may conduct: exploratory, descriptive, and causal. We then discuss the ethical do's and don'ts for research doers and research consumers. The part concludes with how to choose, work with, and assess the efforts of marketing researchers you may hire.

Part II: Surveys: A Great Way to Research

This part begins with an overview of the different types of surveys and the relative strengths and weaknesses of each type. Next, we discuss strategies you can use to boost the reliability and validity of respondents' answers as well as to increase response rates and control research-related costs. We then introduce attitude research, including information about question forms such as Likert and semantic differential scales. We also explain guidelines for question and questionnaire do's and don'ts, including a brief overview of formatting issues and constant sum, ranking, and purchase-intention scales. We round out the part with chapters on sample type and sample size.

Part III: More Methods to Meet Your Needs

This part discusses the types of secondary data and how to use them; we emphasize important online sources and sites with links to multiple sources. Also, we discuss qualitative and observational research, with an emphasis on in-depth interviews and focus groups. Finally, we introduce experiments, including multiple examples of experiments you may run (for example, identifying effective price points, promotional efforts, and shelf/floor space organization).

Part IV: Collecting, Analyzing, and Reporting Your Data

In this part, we begin by discussing strategies for increasing respondent involvement, avoiding respondent bias, and inputting data. We then discuss how to analyze survey and internal (for existing businesses) data using Microsoft Excel or a comparable spreadsheet program. We conclude with the art of creating research reports.

Part V: The Part of Tens

Our two Part of Tens chapters provide quick and useful insights about critical marketing research do's and don'ts. Chapter 20 offers ten essential tips for business operators. Such readers may find it useful to peruse this chapter first. Chapter 21 describes ten statistical methods that a marketing research supplier may use to analyze data. Because it focuses on uses, examples, and potential misuses for each method, the chapter is meant more for research consumers than research doers.

Also included in this part is an appendix that discusses the DVD. This appendix shows computer hardware and software requirements for accessing the DVD. It also provides a list of the DVD's content.

Icons Used in This Book

In the margins of this book, you find the following icons — mini-graphics that denote paragraphs containing certain types of information. Here's a list of icons we use and what they mean:

This icon highlights information that's so important you'll definitely want to read it (and perhaps return to it later).

Although interesting, this information isn't critical to using or conducting marketing research. Of course, we find it fascinating — and you may too!

Based on our experience and knowledge of marketing research literature, we believe this information may prove especially helpful. These tidbits may save you time or money, or may just be nuggets of insider information.

Our warnings are meant to save you from defective studies and practices that mislead you into costly marketing mistakes.

This icon denotes information that can be accessed on the DVD.

Where to Go from Here

We designed this book with four sets of readers in mind. You may consider the following reading game plan if one of these groups describes you:

- **Research doers:** If you're a research doer, you may want to read this book in the following sequence: Part I, Part III, Part II, and Part IV. Without understanding the big picture (Part I), you can't put any of our remaining discussion in the proper context. Although survey research is popular, and you're likely to conduct a customer survey eventually, you'll benefit from considering the alternatives first (Part III). After you decide to field a survey, you'll benefit from discovering how to write a good questionnaire (Part II) and how to analyze the data you collect from it (Part IV). Of course, if you ultimately decide that you should find and hire a low-cost marketing research supplier, you can return to Chapter 5.

- **Research consumers:** Other than Chapter 5, you should focus on the remaining four chapters of Part I — which provide an extensive overview of marketing research — and the two Part of Tens chapters. We meant those last two chapters predominantly for research consumers. Also, Chapter 19 indicates what you should expect from any report summarizing the results of a marketing study. Obviously, being an informed consumer requires extensive knowledge about product features, so you'll benefit from reading additional text as it pertains to a study you're considering.

- **Students:** Sadly, there's no shortcut for students, because much of our text addresses topics included in most marketing research courses. In essence, we suggest that students read our book from beginning to end. Look on the bright side: If you buy this book — rather than borrow it from a library — you'll get your money's worth!

- **Need a customer survey yesterday:** If you have an immediate need to field a survey, analyze its data, and make a marketing-related decision, you'll want to focus on Parts II and IV of this book. (That said, you should at least skim Chapter 11 to avoid a totally useless respondent pool.) You always can return to the remaining text at a later date.

Part I

Marketing Research: Learn It, Live It, Love It

The 5th Wave

By Rich Tennant

"We're still analyzing the data from our door-to-door survey."

In this part . . .

This part introduces you to marketing research and tells you how to begin the process of creating a research plan. In Chapters 1 through 3, we summarize the research process and the basic types of research you may conduct. In Chapter 4, we discuss the ethical do's and don'ts for research doers and research consumers. Chapter 5 shows you how to choose, work with, and assess the efforts of marketing researchers you may hire.

Chapter 1

Seeing What Marketing Research Can Do for You

*M*arketing research is more than those annoying people who call you during dinner to ask you a series of questions. It's also more than those oddly cheerful people at the mall — with clipboard and pencil in hand — who want to ask you seemingly innumerable questions rather than let you shop.

Marketing research is about knowing, understanding, and evaluating. As human beings, we want to know what's happening in our world and understand why those things are happening. We also want to identify the best choice from the alternatives available to us and then measure the success of that choice. Marketing research is both an intellectual and artistic activity. To solve marketing problems, you must obtain the necessary information and interpret it properly, which requires careful thought as well as creativity and artistry.

In this chapter, we define marketing research, compare it to marketing information systems, discuss when it should be pursued or avoided, detail its components, and explain its value in making informed and appropriate business decisions. This chapter gives you a better understanding of the systematic and objective nature of marketing research and how it can help you make better marketing-related decisions.

What Is Marketing Research?

Although professors and textbook authors have proposed many different definitions of marketing research, an appropriate and simple definition is this: *Marketing research* is the systematic and objective process of generating information to help you make marketing-related decisions. For a more comprehensive definition, it's hard to go wrong with the latest one proposed by the American Marketing Association (AMA), the largest association of marketing practitioners and academicians in the world.

Although powerful, marketing researchers can't replace managers. Think of it this way: A hammer can't bang its own nail, and a computer can't write its own report. Similarly, a marketing research study can't *make* a decision for you or anyone else. The results of a marketing research study should be one of many inputs into a marketing-related decision. With the information in this book, you'll better recognize the extent to which you should trust different kinds of research and which type of study you should use to make different marketing-related decisions.

Marketing research can be any of the following three things:

✔ It can be fast, in the sense that it can be completed quickly.

✔ It can be good, in the sense that the results can reflect reality accurately.

✔ It can be cheap, in the sense that the researcher can choose a less costly design among comparable research designs.

Unfortunately, each research project can be only two of these three things. If a research project is good and fast, then it won't be cheap. If it's good and cheap, then it's impossible to conduct it quickly. Finally, if it's fast and cheap, then it's unlikely to produce accurate findings.

The American Marketing Association (AMA) definition of marketing research

Every few years (or so it seems) the American Marketing Association (AMA) revises the definitions of key marketing terms. Recently, the AMA adopted the following definition of marketing research:

Marketing research is the function which links the consumer, customer, and the public to the marketer through *information — information used to identify and define marketing opportunities and problems; generate, refine, and evaluate marketing actions; monitor marketing performance; and improve understanding of marketing as a process. Marketing research specifies the information required to address these issues; designs the method for collecting information; manages and implements the data collection process; analyzes the results; and communicates the findings and their implications.*

The AMA definition highlights the continuous process of marketing research. Marketers must constantly seek the opinion and insight of their stakeholders. Without sound market data and analysis, it's almost impossible to design effective products and marketing strategies that appeal to the needs and wants of targeted consumers. Sound marketing analysis is a byproduct of appropriate and timely data collection. Thus, trustworthy measurement bridges marketing research and effective business decisions.

Comparing Marketing Research to Marketing Information Systems

Differentiating marketing research from marketing information systems is essential because the data provided by each varies and the manner and context in which those data are used also vary.

Marketing information systems have four components:

- **Internal data:** This type of data is generated from accounting records and data on sales, costs, and inventories. Because this type of data is organized according to accounting needs rather than according to marketing needs, it may be necessary to convert that data into a form that's more readily suited to marketing purposes.

- **Marketing intelligence:** This intelligence comprises observations and data from existing publications or companies, such as syndicated data services that are dedicated to providing such data. (We talk more about these sources in Chapter 13.) By observations we mean managers' or business owners' observations of and interactions with sales force members, distributors, suppliers, or other managers or co-owners.

- **An analytical system:** This system is developed by marketing scientists who create empirical models meant to help managers make better decisions. Because such a system relies on sophisticated statistical methods and computer algorithms, the mangers who use one often don't understand its inner workings. Fortunately, not understanding what's under the hood is no more a problem for managers than it is for automobile drivers. Of course, most drivers must take their car to a mechanic when it breaks because they don't know how to fix it; similarly, most managers must ask a marketing scientist to fix an analytical system that no longer produces useful information.

✔ **Marketing research:** This is a component of the information system that's triggered by observations or trends revealed by the ongoing data-collection process. For example, the first three components of a marketing information system may reveal a sales decline in one geographical region, but it's unlikely they include the information needed to create marketing strategies and tactics to reverse that decline. However, a marketing study of consumers, retailers, and wholesalers may suggest the cause of the decline, which in turn may suggest ways to reverse it.

Marketing research — which we discuss throughout this chapter and book — and marketing information systems differ in two main ways:

✔ **Why they're used:** Marketing research is conducted to answer an immediate, one-time question like "In the last year, why have our restaurant's customers reduced their purchases of appetizers by 25 percent?" It's inspired by a problem or an opportunity that managers or current or potential business owners suddenly or gradually recognize.

In contrast, marketing information systems generate marketing information on a routine basis, which can be weekly, monthly, or quarterly. Marketing information systems generate ongoing reports in a standardized format that managers and business owners can use for benchmarking or tracking trends. For example, these reports can alert a restaurant operator that dessert sales have been higher the first weekend of each month for the past six months.

✔ **How much data is collected:** Marketing research uses only those data sources that are relevant to the research problem. If marketing research is needed to better understand attitudes among various consumer groups, a survey-based study is appropriate. Of course, sane study participants with real lives will answer only a limited number of questions, preferably on a single occasion.

In contrast, an information system gathers great quantities of data, and if the system is working properly, it allows its operators to sift and organize that data in ways that allow managers to recognize patterns and trends.

Even though a marketing research study deals with much less data than a marketing information system, these data sources complement one another. In fact, an information system may alert a manager to a problem and indicate that marketing research is required to better understand that problem.

An example: Seeing marketing information systems in use

Among other service providers, restaurant operators may benefit from a marketing information system. Suppose a restaurant's sales have been declining during the last two months and the operator wants to know why. Before conducting a customer survey, the operator can evaluate internal data, which in this case can include the following:

✔ A menu-item analysis to identify items that are and aren't selling well.

✔ A promotions analysis to assess coupon redemptions and happy-hour purchases.

To further explain declining sales, the operator can then use marketing intelligence gained from *primary* (distributors and frequent patrons) and *secondary* (industry magazines) sources. Although eyeballing raw data can help you detect trends, a structured system for analyzing the data can reveal otherwise hidden patterns. An analytical system can provide a comprehensive assessment of the data and suggest actions to reverse slumping sales. Finally, with a better understanding of the research problem, the operator can engage in meaningful marketing research, through which patrons' opinions, suppliers' ideas, and employees' insights can be sought and obtained.

Using Research for Problem Identification and Problem Solving

Marketing research is divided into two basic domains:

✔ Problem-identification research
✔ Problem-solving research

Identifying the correct problem is a prerequisite for solving that problem. Without proper identification, you're likely solving the wrong problem. In the following sections, we explain the differences between the two basic marketing research domains and provide examples of each.

Looking at problem-identification research

Problem-identification research (see the chapters in Part II) attempts to assess market potential, market share, company/product image, market characteristics, current/future sales, and business trends. Such research helps marketers understand their marketing problem and identify marketing opportunities.

You can use problem-identification research to determine the types of information covered in the following sections.

Market potential

If you're planning to launch a new product or introduce a new-and-improved version of a current product, you need to know your market potential. Without a reliable forecast of total sales for this type of product, it's impossible to know how consumers will respond to price changes, from which stores they're likely to buy the product, or to which types of advertising they'll respond favorably.

For example, inspired by years of watching late-night infomercials, suppose that you've invented a new consumer product that you've named The Study Mate. The product is meant to help students multi-task more efficiently based on unique sounds made by the device. Before you invest $2 million on Study Mate inventory and your own infomercials, you want to ensure — as much as possible — that enough people will order it at your $29.99 selling price. After all, you're placing your children's college fund at risk! Although The Study Mate has no direct competitors, consumers can listen to their iPods or to Internet radio to achieve a similar effect. To forecast likely first-year sales, you need to determine whether students will purchase this product as a replacement for other sound-producing devices. Focus groups and survey data can help with this determination.

Market share

The market share you care about is the percent of total product sales — either in units or in dollars — captured by your product versus your competitors' products. In essence, all market share calculations follow this simple ratio: us ÷ (us + competitors).

Here's an example: If you're a restaurant operator who's interested in forecasting your future share of dining-out dollars for similar restaurants, the calculation is straightforward. These are steps you'd follow to gain the information you need:

1. Consult published trade figures for trends in total dining-out dollars spent in your community.

2. Calculate the percent of dining-out dollars now spent in restaurants like yours.

3. Survey your customers about their predicted near-term dining-out expenditures (or expected changes in their recent dining-out expenditures).

Based on their current expenditures, forecasted changes, and community trends, you can forecast your future share of dining-out dollars.

Although market share alone is a poor predictor of company success (because the calculation omits costs), it provides a sense of competitive viability and strategy feasibility. For example, if earning a profit requires capturing 80 percent of a well-established market, you're best off selling apples on a street corner!

Brand image

It's important to determine your customers' perceptions of your brand, retail availability, customer service, and the like. If you're a retailer, such information can help you decide your store's décor, merchandise displays and assortments, and credit policy.

For example, suppose that your retail store has been successful for so long that it has become a community landmark. Nonetheless, new competitors have entered your market and are slowly eroding your sales. Your store's and your new competitors' mix of products and the prices are comparable, but your old customers are still shifting their purchases to these new stores. Perhaps your customers see your store as dated and out-of-touch with current shopper preferences. To improve your store's image with current and potential new customers (which you believe will lead to an increase in loyal clientele), you decide to publicize your donations of time and money to local worthy causes. However, you're unsure how your customers will respond to the causes you've chosen to support. To reduce your uncertainty, you can conduct a survey to assess their attitudes about which causes you should support.

Brand image can be influenced in many ways. Through surveys (see Chapters 8 through 10) and focus groups (see Chapter 14), for example, you can determine which advertising strategies are likely to favorably influence consumers' perceptions of your brand.

Market characteristics

Each market — whether defined geographically, socioeconomically, behaviorally, or in other ways — has key characteristics that you must consider when developing your marketing strategies. Most efforts to develop a general strategy that's meant to appeal to all consumers are doomed; for example, Hispanics in San Antonio are likely to have far different preferences and purchase tendencies than Hispanics in Los Angeles. The better you understand the characteristics of your targeted customers, the more likely you are to develop successful marketing strategies.

Sometimes, businesses fail because their owners don't fully understand their target markets. Understanding nationwide cultural trends is insufficient; to meet and exceed customer needs — and thus remain competitive in the marketplace — you must target consumers who identify with different subcultures. To this end, you can use survey and census data to better understand the subcultures you're targeting.

Consider this example: Say you've noticed a dip in sales during the last quarter. You believe that fewer consumers think of your brand as "their brand." Perhaps your ads no longer recognize the unique characteristics of your targeted customers, especially their ethnicity. If true, you may consider including ethnic cues in your ads (such as flag colors and ethnic verbiage). However, you're unsure which cues would be most effective. To reduce your uncertainty, you can conduct an experiment in which consumers evaluate ads with different ethnic cues. You can then run the best-liked and best-recalled ads in a new ad campaign.

Sales

As every Internet marketer knows, it's insufficient to simply attract customers; you also must make the sale. Without accurate sales forecasts, it's impossible to set appropriate production levels. The better you understand which factors influence sales, the more accurate your predictions of future sales.

Suppose, for example, you've been selling a successful regional beer for almost 15 years. Now you want to start selling your beer nationally. However, you're uncertain whether your beer can compete with national brands. To assess your beer's national viability, you can do the following:

- Conduct blind taste tests to assess whether consumers find your beer as tasty as those national brands
- Survey beer drinkers to assess their beer preferences and purchases
- Conduct a virtual (online) focus group (see Chapter 14) with beer vendors nationwide to locate regions with growing sales and weak (in terms of sales, not alcohol content) beer brands

Business trends

To enhance their long-run success, companies must monitor their business environments constantly. Social trends, like increased social networking and efforts to simplify everyday life, can affect advertising efficacy and overall consumption levels. Regulatory changes can alter the cost of doing business. Beating your competitors to the punch by recognizing such trends helps you gain an immediate — and possibly sustainable — competitive advantage.

For example, suppose you've noticed that more and more companies are developing group postings on social media Web sites. You know that your target market — younger adults — is inclined to visit such Web sites often and take the information found there more seriously than your expensive ads. Through focus groups and direct interviews, you can determine the best ways to use these social media sites to your advantage and ride latest communication wave.

Becoming familiar with problem-solving research

After you identify your problem, you then need to research how to solve it (see the chapters in Part III). That subsequent *problem-solving research* focuses on issues such as *marketing mix* (marketing decisions related to the product and its price, promotion, and distribution) and *segmentation* (division of customers into meaningful subgroups). The following sections present the areas in which problem-solving research can help you.

Segmentation

Market segments are groups of customers with similar backgrounds or product preferences. Problem-solving research may determine the best characteristics for grouping customers, forecasting potential sales to different customer groups, and understanding the lifestyles of heavily targeted customers (to design ads meant to attract them).

Consider this example: As a store owner, you're trying to update the theme and ad campaign for your store. Because peer and cultural influences affect consumer purchases, you can collect data about these influences to help identify the most promising store theme and ad campaign for attracting new customers. Qualitative and quantitative data can help you better understand who or what influences your consumers.

Product research

Problem-solving product research includes testing concepts for possible new products, looking for ways to modify existing products (for example, by changing the packaging or repositioning the brand so it competes more effectively with newer products), and test marketing. (We discuss test marketing further in Chapter 16.)

Suppose, for example, you're on the verge of choosing a location for a new retail store. Do you select the location that has more or less square footage? You know that effective space utilization is a critical aspect of retail success. To understand how big is too big, you can observe people as they wander through comparable brick-and-mortar stores. You may discover, as is true of many modern electronic devices, that smaller is better (although we prefer large-screen televisions to handheld video players). After all, not everyone shops for everything at big-box stores.

Pricing research

Setting the ideal price — typically the one that maximizes long-run profits — is critical for new and existing products. Problem-solving research can answer these types of pricing questions for new products:

- Should you set a high initial price that extracts maximum dollars from price-insensitive customers but reduces total units sold? Or should you set a low initial price that attracts the largest possible number of customers and secures long-run sales?
- Will customers who are seduced by a new brand return if you lower the price of your established brand?
- Can you increase the overall profit of your product line if you increase the price of your top-of-the-line model?
- How sensitive are your most frequent customers to small increases or decreases in the price of your product?

As an example, say your chain store operation is entering a new geographic market and you're trying to decide whether an everyday-low price or a frequent price-promotion strategy will work best. To discover which strategy will attract the most customers in this new market, you can survey potential customers.

Promotional research

Promotional problem-solving research can answer these types of questions:

- Are we spending the right amount on advertising?
- Does our advertising compliment our couponing and other temporary price-reduction efforts?
- Are our ads effective in attracting new customers and retaining current customers?
- Should we start placing ads online or should we continue to spend most of our promotional dollars on radio and newspaper ads?

Say, for example, you own a store that sells prerecorded movies and music. Unfortunately, an economic downturn has hurt your sales, so you have excess inventory that you need to unload. You know that consumers generally spend more on bundles of goods; for example, they'd prefer to buy a bundle of five CDs by a popular artist rather than three individual CDs. However, you don't know whether bundling will work with your customers, because many have had to tighten their financial belts. By experimenting with different bundles and prices, you can develop a price promotion strategy that helps you reduce this unwanted inventory.

Distribution research

Your customers can't buy what retailers don't carry, so identifying the best way to get your product into your customers' hands is critical. Distribution research can determine the best path — through wholesalers and retailers — from your production facilities to your customers' shopping bags. It also can answer questions about the ideal mix of retailers to carry your product, the recommended retail price (because customers won't buy excessively marked-up goods), and the location of inventory centers.

For example, suppose you want to compete on low price, but your supply chain is long; that is, your product makes several stops before it reaches retailing outlets. As a result, you must set a high-selling price to cover the cost of these middlemen. To combat this problem, you're thinking about selling directly to your customers over the Internet and through home shopping networks. To ensure that your customers will buy directly, you can survey them about their online and shopping network preferences and behaviors.

The Most Appropriate Research at Each Stage of the Product Life Cycle

The *product life cycle* (PLC) models sales (vertical axis) over time (horizontal axis) and offers a visual depiction of a product's or product category's life (see Figure 1-1). The PLC can be used as a forecasting tool and provides insight into marketing strategies and tactics. It assumes that products move through the following five stages:

1. **The precommercialization stage.**

   This stage occurs before a product is launched. During this stage, many types of qualitative studies (see Chapters 14 and 15) and test markets (see Chapter 16) may be more suitable than quantitative studies. For example, focus groups, concept tests, ad copy tests, and simulated test markets can offer unique insight into preferred product functionality, potential customers' willingness to buy, and nonfunctional value (such as the appeal of a well-known brand name).

2. **The introduction stage.**

   Because concerns at the introduction stage relate to launching a product, research can help you make decisions about time of commercialization, range of distribution outlets, advertising and promotion strategies, pricing, competition, and buyer behavior.

3. **The growth stage.**

   Although the growth stage is a prime time for businesses, products that reach this stage face a new set of issues, such as new (and possibly improved) competitors, higher costs from expanded production, more diverse consumers as markets broaden and new markets are entered, and the difficulty of maintaining a consistent message across various marketing media.

4. The maturity stage.

Concerns at the maturity stage entail maintaining or growing market share for a product. At this stage, you're unlikely to grow industry sales, so increasing your sales means capturing competitors' sales. As a result, lifestyle and segmentation research — to identify key consumer groups and to assess their attitudes and behaviors — can help you reposition your product so it becomes more attractive to a different or larger share of the market.

5. The decline stage.

In the decline stage, you're basically trying to milk the product. Typically, buyers in a product's decline stage are very sensitive to price. To squeeze every last dollar of profit out of an old product, you should determine peoples' sensitivities to its price (the change in demand related to changes in price) and what you can do to reduce its cost.

Although it's a great tool, the PLC is an idealized model, so the sales trajectories of some products don't conform. For example, many high-tech consumer products may not reach the maturity stage before manufacturers introduce a newer version, thereby beginning a new PLC. Frequently purchased consumer products, like soft drinks, may remain in the maturity stage for many years. In addition, some products that reach the decline stage, like vinyl records, may reverse sales declines due to changing consumer preferences.

Just as certain strategies prove more effective at various PLC stages, different types of research are more typical at different PLC stages (see Figure 1-1). The planning and research methods necessary for product development and launch differ somewhat from those necessary for ongoing products.

Rather than gather data and react, which often occurs with mature products, research to support product introduction is proactive in assessing the opinions and preferences of consumers and business operators. For example, focus groups and in-depth personal interviews, which provide extensive psychological and behavioral insights, would be more effective than traditional mass surveys for precommercialized products. (We discuss these research methods more in Chapter 14.) Test marketing, which can help to fine-tune the product and the strategy for selling it (see Chapter 15), also is critical to product development and pre-product-launch decisions.

Although no research program can guarantee successful product commercialization, sound and appropriate research maximizes the likelihood of success.

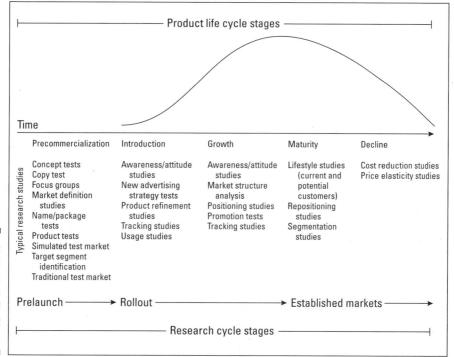

Figure 1-1:
Typical
research
methods
for each of
the different
PLC stages.

Making the Big Decision to Do (Or Not to Do) Marketing Research

We cover the various marketing research types and approaches in detail in Parts I and II of this book. For now, consider the value of knowing the answers to these research questions:

✔ In an already fierce competitive environment, is it sensible for a well-established, low-price apparel retailer to reposition itself as a high-end boutique?

✔ Can a local restaurateur capture and maintain market share in a business environment crowded with corporate franchises?

✔ When relevant, should ad agencies persuade their clients to use an overt or a discreet warning label to create a socially responsible reputation among consumers?

Marketing research can help you answer such questions. Understanding the difference between a situation that merits research and one that doesn't is critical to making an appropriate decision about conducting a study.

Here are some of the things that marketing research does for you and your business:

- ✔ **It provides important behavioral information.** More specifically, it provides the information that you use to reach your consumers, customers (remember that the person who buys a product may or may not be the person who uses that product), and the general public. It can reveal the attitudes and behaviors of those people.

- ✔ **It generates, refines, and evaluates your marketing activities.** It can provide marketing-related insights about the things you should be doing as well as about ways to modify and improve the things you're already doing. As a result, marketing research should improve your business operations.

- ✔ **It helps you benchmark and monitor your company's performance.** Although marketing information systems also can help in this regard, marketing research can determine your company's performance in terms of consumer attitudes toward product and service quality, sales volume, and the like. (Refer to the earlier section "Comparing Marketing Research to Marketing Information Systems" for more information.)

- ✔ **It helps you understand marketing as a process,** even if you only gain basic insights into how your market functions. Ultimately, those insights may be turned into better decisions.

Unfortunately, misguided conventional wisdom is rampant in marketing. For instance, some folks believe marketing research can solve all their business problems. Don't fall victim to this type of thinking. One value of marketing research is its ability to examine erroneously held ideas about customers, competitors, and the environment — in essence, all areas related to effective marketing.

In the following sections, we provide some helpful information to assist you in determining when and when not to conduct marketing research.

When you should do marketing research

You should plan to conduct marketing research if it can help you make a better decision; that is, a decision based on external evidence and careful analysis rather than a spouse's or friend's intuition. Specifically, the goal of marketing research is to help managers and business owners select the best among alternative viable courses of action.

You'll likely want to conduct marketing research in the following circumstances:

- ✔ **When you want to better understand your customers:** If you more thoroughly understand your customers, you're more likely to create products and services that they prefer and will purchase. That ability should boost your sales and profits. For instance, it may help to know if ethnic background influences purchase intentions, how gender relates to Web browsing behavior, and what products your customers would rather shop for online.

- ✔ **When you need to discover what went wrong in your business:** You may conduct the best research, have the best people working on a marketing problem, seemingly develop the best marketing strategy, and then still fail miserably. It's often worthwhile to determine what caused the failure that you initially thought would be a success.

  For example, a restaurant owner may believe, based on worldwide culinary trends and casual conversations with customers, that fried frog legs would make a nice addition to his menu. However, after changing the menu, his customers may instead protest to *save Kermit and his friends*. Marketing research can indicate what went wrong in this case.

- ✔ **When the additional information meaningfully reduces uncertainty associated with selecting the best course of action:** It's one thing to have a hunch that a certain business decision will lead to higher sales; it's another to base that decision on research results. When using your gut to make a decision, subjectivity and uncertainty about the outcome are higher than the systematic and objective approach that marketing research affords.

- ✔ **When its value exceeds the estimated costs:** Wild guesses about value versus cost often are faulty, so examine our DVD examples and Excel template, which show a Bayesian approach to assessing research value. This quantitative method provides you a more objective way to calculate whether research value exceeds research costs.

You must anticipate when your marketing ship is starting to drift off course and you need appropriate research to right its course. If bankruptcy is inevitable, marketing research will be of little help. It's too late then!

We're not proposing marketing research as a cure for all marketing problems; instead, we're proposing that it's only appropriate in some situations. You may find this odd and wonder why we aren't stronger advocates. Is marketing research so faulty that we can't advocate its use at all times? No! Marketing research can be valuable if it's conducted correctly and when it's appropriate; when those conditions don't prevail, you're best off avoiding marketing research.

You should never assume that marketing research will be perfect. It can't be. In fact, for any given decision, you may be better off flipping a coin or consulting a palm reader. After all, it's possible that a given study will be very far from perfect. (Consider, for example, Coca-Cola's *New Coke* fiasco and all the seemingly sound research that Coca-Cola conducted before introducing the new version of its original soft drink.) However, over the course of many decisions, if you help marketing researchers understand the basic business environment and give them ample time and resources to conduct appropriate studies — or you conduct your own marketing research — then, on average, you'll make better decisions.

When you shouldn't do marketing research

Sometimes it's best not to conduct marketing research. If you mistakenly conduct or commission research studies when they're unnecessary, you'll eventually conclude that marketing research is of little value, overpriced, and irrelevant — and that would be the most incorrect conclusion you could draw!

When is it ill-advised to conduct marketing research? Here's a partial list of circumstances when you shouldn't spend the money needed to complete a marketing research study:

- ✔ **You and your staff or other owners can't agree on the information that's needed.** In this case, it's impossible to provide researchers with the guidance they need to conduct a useful study. If researchers don't know what they need to discover, the results of their studies can't help you make a better decision. Hence the importance of well-defined research questions that are acceptable to all relevant parties.

- ✔ **You don't have the necessary resources to conduct a proper study.** If you own your home and want to add on a room, would you hire a contractor to start the job if you only had enough money to tear a hole in the side of your house and pour a concrete slab? Of course not! Similarly, you shouldn't try to conduct a marketing research study unless you can afford a complete and proper study.

  As consultants, we were often asked by clients to conduct studies for one-third of the amount that we originally quoted. We know that studies can't be executed properly with an inadequate budget. As a result, we'd refuse to conduct the studies. We'd suggest alternatives, including other research suppliers, but we wouldn't participate in research that would be untrustworthy due to an insufficient budget. Neither houses nor businesses should be built on sand, especially in earthquake zones!

- ✔ **Your study will be poorly timed.** Perhaps it's premature to conduct the study; for example, maybe your market hasn't yet matured sufficiently. In that case, the research information will be so dated by the time you need to make a decision that it's no longer trustworthy.

✔ **You'll alert your competitors.** Conducting a study can alert competitors about a new product that you may launch or a new configuration for an existing product you may try. As a result, you're giving competitors an opportunity to develop a "me too" product, which will cost you much of the advantage associated with introducing a product without competitors' prior knowledge.

✔ **The information you need already exists.** You don't need to reinvent the wheel. If you can find secondary sources (which we discuss more in Chapter 13) or previous studies that pertain and are timely, it's nonsensical to spend the money needed to conduct a new marketing research study.

✔ **You want a scapegoat or excuse for poor performance.** Unless you live for office politics, have colleagues or co-owners who want your scalp, or can't face your own mistakes, you should worry about your future successes rather than finding excuses for your previous failures. We're not saying a postmortem meant to help avoid future failure isn't worthwhile; rather, we believe that the blame game isn't worth playing. Save those games for troublesome siblings!

Because research is meant to assist rather than replace managerial decision-making, you can't blame previously conducted research for your faulty decisions. In a pinch, remind disappointed business associates that the value of a decision isn't based on the outcome. You can determine whether to trust the results of a research study, and thus make a more informed decision, but that decision still can produce a marketing failure.

✔ **You've already made your decision.** It's nonsensical to pay for marketing research that confirms an already-made decision. After you've made a decision, you've eliminated all uncertainty about that decision (but obviously not the outcome of that decision). Paying for confirmation of an already-made decision is perhaps good for massaging your ego, but it's a true waste of money.

✔ **The cost of the study outweighs its benefits.** If the benefits don't exceed the cost, it's senseless to conduct marketing research. After all, why pay more for something than it's worth? The value of research is to decrease uncertainty, to increase the likelihood of a correct decision, and to improve marketing performance. The costs are equally clear: the direct cost of doing research, the cost of any delay in implementing a decision, and the cost of potentially tipping rivals to your actions.

It may not be obvious when the cost outweighs the benefits, so the DVD accompanying this book contains a detailed discussion and an Excel template for formally assessing research cost versus benefits.

Chapter 2

Following the Stages of the Marketing Research Process

....

....

*A*lthough it isn't subatomic physics, neurosurgery, or analytic philosophy, marketing research — if conducted correctly — requires careful attention to its intricacies. Think of marketing research as a chain that's only as strong as the weakest link, where those links are stages in a process.

A professional baseball player can slump for several weeks during the season yet win the batting championship if he hits .500 for a month. Because their regular season lasts six months, players can overcome a slow start and play to the back of their baseball cards by season's end. Similarly, students who perform poorly on a first exam still can earn a good grade in the course by performing exceptionally on subsequent exams. Baseball and school accomplishments are compensatory; it's possible to recover from mistakes. Not so with marketing research.

Once you've failed to identify the correct marketing research problem, your subsequent research efforts are wasted. If you don't know what you need to know, you can't uncover the answer to your research problem. An improperly designed and fielded study can't provide trustworthy data for subsequent analysis. Faulty data analysis is meaningless at best. An inability to communicate study results clearly to decision-makers — for example, possible investors in your new business venture — greatly increases the likelihood of a poor decision.

To avoid any weak research links, we guide you through the stages of the research process, from defining your research problem to presenting your findings. This chapter is meant to help you develop the tools you need to conduct your own research or to oversee the efforts of supposedly well-trained researchers. May the research force be with you!

Working Your Way through the Stages of Research

Research is a multi-stage process that's often somewhat iterative — conclusions from one stage of the process can create new ideas for other stages in the process, and the linkages are both forwards and backwards. Also, stages can occur concurrently.

Stage 1: Identifying the problem

If you can't define the problem properly, it's impossible to find the appropriate solution. Unfortunately, the problem isn't always obvious, often because the cause of the problem isn't readily apparent. Hence, the "Iceberg Principle" comes into play: The dangerous parts of many marketing problems may be obscured because they're below the surface. Your job (and that of the marketing researcher, if involved) is to identify the appropriate problem despite the fact that it may be submerged.

Defining problems is basically a six-step process. Here's a rundown of those steps:

1. **Ascertain your objectives.**

   You and your business associates — the loan officer at your friendly neighborhood bank, for example — may have different yet equally reasonable objectives. For example, you may be more interested in growing your business, whereas your associates may want immediate increases in sales or profits. Clearly, the goals and types of market research projects may vary markedly based on whether a short-term or a long-term increase is sought.

2. **Understand the problem background.**

   To avoid — or at least minimize — the "iceberg" problem we note earlier, you should step back and gain perspective. An informal gathering of background information about the environment in which your business operates can help in that regard.

   When trying to understand the business environment you confront, a good researcher will "pick your managerial brain." Fortunately, bragging about or sharing your situation and your efforts to cope with it with someone who's informed and interested is relatively painless.

3. **Isolate/identify the problem, not the symptoms.**

   Symptoms can be confusing. You may be so caught up in the symptoms that you don't recognize the disease! Good marketing research can help you to structure and understand the true problem.

Consider the following example. A new mobile telephone with basic computing and Internet capabilities is selling poorly. Distributors claim that poor sales are symptomatic of competitors' lower prices for similar products. Based on the distributors' beliefs, the company conducts a detailed analysis of competitors' products, paying special attention to pricing. In fact, the analysis reveals that the true problem is the distributors' lack of product knowledge and concomitant inability to explain the product's value to potential customers.

4. Determine the unit of analysis.

Depending on the research problem, the appropriate unit of analysis can be persons, households, spouses, or organizations (see Chapter 11). Without identifying the appropriate unit of analysis, you can't draw a suitable sample or perform suitable data analyses. In consumption studies, for example, households rather than persons are the appropriate unit of analysis. To understand major purchases — an automobile or home — an examination of spouses' decision-making processes is critical. Marketers who don't understand those processes are flying blind in their efforts to provide the best possible product.

5. Determine relevant things to ask about.

Although you may want to assess non-quantifiable issues, important issues typically are quantifiable. In essence, this step of the process entails determining what to measure and how to measure it. (We discuss measure type — nominal, ordinal, interval, ratio — in Chapter 18.)

The dependent and independent variables (which we discuss more in Chapter 16) determine the focus of your study, especially in forecasting contexts. As the words denote, the dependent variable *depends on* one or more independent variables. If you want to forecast next month's sales (the dependent variable in this case), then you should identify things this month that predict those sales accurately (the independent variables in this case). For example, realtors can predict home-buying behavior during the next quarter or the next year by looking at things that relate to future home-buying behavior, such as growth in disposable income, growth in investment income, and consumer sentiment.

6. Translate the marketing problem into researchable objectives.

Because researchers must create researchable objectives concordant with their problem definition, often they want to express those objectives in the most rigorous terms — something called a hypothesis. A *hypothesis* is a formal, testable statement that can be refuted by empirical data. Whereas you may have a belief or hunch about your customers, a hypothesis about your customers is a formal statement of that belief or hunch that can be tested by marketing research. To generate one or more hypotheses for formal testing, start with a purpose. This helps to generate some research questions that can be answered by exploratory research, your experience, and basic marketing theory.

Often, exploratory research (which we discuss more in Chapter 14) is a necessary prelude to developing hypotheses. Perhaps you don't understand the underlying process sufficiently to develop a formalized, testable statement, in which case exploratory research is a preliminary step. Different types of exploratory research include reviewing secondary data, running pilot studies, conducting in-depth interviews with people who have requisite experience, and implementing case studies.

Stage 2: Designing the study

The *research design* of a study is basically the master plan for the research that follows. This stage specifies the basic methods you or the researcher will use to conduct the study.

Here are some basic questions you should ask when considering research design:

- ✔ **What types of questions need answering?** You must decide the questions that need answers and whether the answers can be provided by some combination of surveys, experiments, or analyses of secondary data. If you're uncertain about those questions, preliminary exploratory research may be necessary.

- ✔ **What's the data source?** If you conduct a survey, your initial design issues relate to your questionnaire and data-collection method, which are intertwined. (Chapter 10 focuses on questionnaire design, and Chapter 6 focuses on alternative survey data-collection methods.) For example, complex questions and questionnaire structures are ill advised for surveys administered via telephone.

  If secondary data are needed — to conduct a site location analysis, for example — you need to determine the timeliness and compatibility of existing sources. In essence, you have to ask this question: Is the available data a square peg that you're trying to stuff into the round hole of your research needs? (We discuss assessment of secondary data sources in Chapter 13.)

- ✔ **Can you get accurate answers by simply asking people?** Often, people are unaware of their reasons for doing things or are incapable of responding meaningfully to questions posed to them about their attitudes and behaviors. When that's the case, asking people directly won't work. Alternatively, you may be able to discover answers to your research questions indirectly through observation, which we discuss more in Chapter 15.

- ✔ **How quickly is information needed?** You must decide how quickly your research study must be completed. Again, marketing research can be relatively accurate, relatively fast, and relatively inexpensive, but it can only be two of those three simultaneously (see Chapter 1). If you needed to know yesterday, the expense for a study of sufficient quality increases markedly.

✔ **How should survey questions be worded?** Wording survey questions so that answers accurately reflect people's attitudes and behaviors is both an art and a science. Chapter 9 provides much of the detail you need to write good survey questions.

✔ **How many questions can be asked at one time?** Respondents don't have infinite patience, especially when you call them at home or intercept them at the mall. Thus, the survey data-collection method you choose depends on the number of questions you need to ask. (We compare and contrast these various methods in Chapter 6.)

✔ **Are descriptive findings sufficient, or will an experiment be necessary?** Surveys are helpful for assessing people's attitudes and preferences for current products, and they're somewhat useful for self-reports about previous consumption (assuming you ask well-designed questions, which we discuss in Chapter 9). However, they aren't especially good for predicting people's reactions to new products.

For example, a survey about alternative features for electronic book readers administered to people who have never used such devices is unlikely to produce accurate forecasts of future reader purchases. An experiment in which different people use different readers with different features may provide far more predictive data. (We discuss experiments in Chapter 16.)

✔ **If you're running an experiment, what will be tested?** If an experiment is needed, you must determine what treatment or condition the researcher will test. You need to decide what circumstance you'll place one group of people in and how you'll compare their responses to the responses of a different group of people placed in a different circumstance.

For example, if you want to identify the most effective among several alternative print ads you may run in a local newspaper, you must determine how you'll expose people to those ads. You want people to respond naturally to these ads, but to show them only the ads and then ask them what they think is an artificial task likely to produce untrustworthy results.

Stage 3: Selecting a sample

If you have only 25 customers to whom you may offer a new service, you can survey all of them without compromising your retirement plan. However, if you have 100,000 customers, surveying all of them is neither cost effective nor necessary. Instead, you can select a representative sample to ask about this possible new service.

Although Chapter 11 provides a more detailed discussion about sampling, here are several basic questions you should ask about sample selection:

- ✔ **Is a sample necessary?** If the population is small and reasonably accessible, you can query every person in the population — in which case you're taking a census rather than drawing a sample.

- ✔ **Who or what is the source of the data?** Are the groups of interest — your sampling unit — individual consumers, households, or organizations? A *probability sample* — one that you can comfortably generalize to the groups you want to query — requires drawing respondents from a representative list (or sample frame). Such lists are available from commercial suppliers, but you need to identify the supplier and the characteristics of your respondent pool. Regardless, the next step is to identify the unit of analysis and to identify a sample whose constituents are consistent with that unit of analysis.

- ✔ **Can the target population be identified?** Typically, there's no one correct population to sample; sampling from any one of several alternative populations is acceptable. Suppose you want to access consumer preferences for a reformulated soft drink. You can sample from any population of consumers who consume soft drinks heavily, such as high school students, college students, or young professionals. In this case, convenience and cost should dictate your population choice.

    Suppose that your target population is ill defined. Even if you assume that potential new customers are similar to your current customers, it's nonsensical to ask current customers what would cause them to switch to your store. In this case, you can pay a commercial supplier for a list of people with demographics similar to your current customers. Then you'd disqualify current customers through a brief telephone screening questionnaire. (We discuss screening questionnaires in Chapter 10.) Alternatively, if you want to survey current customers as well, you'd use that brief telephone questionnaire to sort respondents into receivers of your current customer questionnaire and receivers of your potential new customer questionnaire.

- ✔ **How accurate must the sample be?** Many questions about sample size relate to accuracy and the way in which the sample is drawn from a larger population. For many commercial studies, researchers are required to use commercially available lists, and those lists may be deeply flawed. Mike once purchased a list for a study of people who had recently moved. Despite promotional materials and assurances from the list provider to the contrary, that list included people who hadn't moved in 57 years! After a careful analysis of this $4,000 list, Mike discovered he would have been as well off contacting people randomly via telephone.

- ✔ **Is a probability sample necessary?** Researchers may need to assess whether a probability sample is necessary. For some research purposes, convenience sampling — a type of non-probability sampling — is much less costly and may be appropriate. We discuss the different types of samples and when to use them in Chapter 11.

✔ **Is a local sample sufficient?** The need for only a local or regional sample rather than a national sample may affect the methodology you use. For example, if your research requires a national or international sample and you're concerned about cost, you'll probably opt to collect respondent data via the Internet or snail mail. For a local sample, the telephone or other data-collection technology may suffice.

✔ **How large a sample is necessary?** Knowing the scope of the sample is useful, if only to keep data-collection costs within budget. Because the cost of data collection is a large share of total study cost, staying within budget becomes impossible once data-collection costs soar.

Stage 4: Gathering the data

When conducting research, arguably the most important stage is the data-collection stage. Research questions can't be answered, consumer needs can't be met, and your business can't benefit from pertinent findings without data. In essence, research data represent the gold nuggets vital to business riches. You must have a sound game plan for the data-collection process.

Here are some basic questions about data gathering:

✔ **Who will gather the data?** If it's an independent field service, then you'd like some control over the way in which interviewers query respondents. Chapter 17 discusses fieldwork in more depth.

✔ **How long will data gathering take?** You must decide on a time horizon for completing your study, because that horizon may dictate many aspects of your study, such as data-collection method, sample size, extensiveness of preliminary qualitative and secondary research, and so forth.

✔ **How much supervision is needed?** The needed field service supervision depends on the data-collection method. For example, telephone surveys often are fielded by data-collection services with supervisors who monitor — some may say eavesdrop on — many calls placed from extensive telephone banks. Supervising such fieldwork is fairly straightforward. For personal interviews, immediate oversight is impossible, so the type of supervision differs markedly. Supervising personal interviews typically entails verifying that at least 10 or 15 percent of interviews were conducted as indicated by field service workers.

Stage 5: Analyzing the results

Data without analysis is rubbish. Although universities offer statistics courses in which hand tabulation is required, the software packages available in the real world trump the use of such archaic computation methods. The use of statistical and spreadsheet software makes analyzing data efficient and fun (at least for Jeremy). Because good business decisions depend on trustworthy empirical analyses, you must learn to use the software needed to perform such analyses. Although advanced statistical analysis software — such as Statistical Package for the Social Sciences (SPSS) and Statistical Analysis Systems (SAS) — is available, you also can run your analyses with Microsoft Excel.

We explore the use of Excel for data analysis in Chapter 18, and provide additional guidance and templates on the DVD.

Here are some basic questions to ask about data processing and analysis:

- ✔ **Will standardized editing and coding procedures be used?** How will the data be edited and coded? (For survey research, *editing* means clearing the data file of impossible and inconsistent responses. *Coding* means creating a data file in which numbers rather than words represent respondents' answers.) Extensive expertise is required to edit and code open-ended questions (see Chapters 9 and 17). Alternatively, if you want to create a data file of responses to close-ended questions — for example, the type of questions that are scaled 1 to 7 — minimal expertise is required.

- ✔ **How will the data be categorized?** The ability to analyze data depends on how they're grouped. Subject to the type of data, the way they're grouped or categorized enables certain types of statistical analysis. For example, nominal data like gender or ethnicity enables descriptive statistics like total number and percentage in each group. Interval data — for example, attitudes measured on a 1 to 7 (unfavorable to favorable) scale — can be grouped by their relationship to a calculated mean score.

Categorization in this context is more than a statistical notion; it has practical implications. Perhaps you want to compare current customers to non-customers. Alternatively, you may want to compare frequent customers, infrequent customers, and non-customers. Assessing differences between groups of current customers may provide marketing insights unavailable from assessing a monolithic group.

- ✔ **What data analysis software will be used?** Commercial packages like SPSS and SAS enable almost any type of statistical analyses (and then some). SPSS uses drop-down menus and is relatively user friendly; SAS is a syntax-based package, which some statisticians prefer, but it isn't as user friendly (at least to us). Prices for these packages, depending on the configuration, can run into thousands of dollars. Although they're ideal for seasoned marketing researchers, you can run worthwhile analyses with Microsoft Excel.

For example, you can run standard descriptive statistics, cross-tabulations, correlations, and difference tests in Excel; our DVD includes templates for running such analyses.

✔ **What's the nature of the data?** If the data are qualitative, you're looking at people's open-ended and rambling responses to questions. If the data are quantitative, you're looking at close-ended data, which are far easier and more straightforward to analyze. Chapter 9 discusses the relative strengths and weaknesses of open-ended versus close-ended questions.

Stage 6: Communicating the findings and their implications

The value of a research study is only as good as the weakest link in the chain of the process. Even the best-conceived and best-conducted study is useless if the results of that study aren't presented meaningfully.

Understanding your audience is always a good idea if you're required to present your study. Chapter 19 discusses report creation in more detail. For now, the following are some basic questions to ask yourself about the type of report you should use:

✔ **Who will read the report?** Readership is critical because it determines the level of technical expertise. Marketing jargon and statistical analyses that may be decipherable by a venture capitalist may be a meaningless string of verbiage to the loan officer at your friendly neighborhood bank. Many audiences prefer well-constructed graphical displays to detailed tables and extensive exposition.

✔ **Do you want/need managerial recommendations?** If specific recommendations are required, then they should be included and justified in your report. If you're merely providing information that other people will use to draw their own conclusions, then providing recommendations is unnecessary.

✔ **Will presentations be required?** If so, how many presentations and to whom (for example, possible lenders or franchisees)? If presentations are required, you should determine the audience and number of presentations as part of the budgeting process.

✔ **What format will the written report take?** The degree to which a written report should be formal or informal may depend on corporate culture and the need to please the people who will read the report.

The more you understand such preferences and constraints, the more likely your report is to achieve its intended goals.

Anticipating Outcomes

Creating dummy tables — blank tables to be completed once data analysis results are available — helps guarantee that the most useable report is created. By providing dummy tables to report readers, you give them an opportunity to provide feedback about how helpful that particular set of tables, once completed, would be to their decision-making process.

Before beginning a study, consider these final, checklist-type questions to confirm the wisdom of conducting that study:

- **How much will the study cost?** You should confirm the cost of the study because that's a critical component to assessing its value. As we stress in Chapter 1, if the study costs more than the value of your reduced uncertainty about the best course of action, you shouldn't conduct that study.

- **Is the time frame acceptable?** Studies inherently require different times to complete, so you need to confirm that the time frame for completion is acceptable. In Chapter 6, we discuss likely completion times for different types of surveys.

- **Is outside help needed?** If outside help is needed, you should identify that outside help and make certain it's available. We dedicate roughly half of Chapter 5 to this issue.

- **Will the research attain your stated research objectives?** You must confirm that the research plan addresses your research objectives. To do so, return to your research problem and check that your objectives are consistent with it. Ensure that your objectives, if attained, are actionable; leave research for research sake to academics and other eggheads.

- **When should research begin?** Given budgetary and other concerns, you must confirm the starting date for the research and that the date corresponds with decision-making deadlines.

Chapter 3

Surveying the Types of Research You May Do

*J*ust as consumers have options at their local supermarket, such as the option of buying grass-fed or genetically-modified-corn-fed beef, you and your study participants also have research-related options. Depending on your research question, one type of study may be more appropriate than another type to acquire a trustworthy answer. Thus, it's important for you to understand the various research designs.

In this chapter, we discuss the various types of research that you can use to understand your customers, competitors, and business environment. Understanding these different types is pivotal to gathering the appropriate data that you ultimately can use to improve your marketing strategy.

Recognizing the Difference between Basic and Applied Research

Marketing research can be divided into two types:

✔ **Basic research:** *Basic research* is the type of research that academics may conduct; for example, it would include a university professor who surveys consumers and businesspeople, analyzes their responses, and writes an article for a professional journal.

✔ **Applied research:** *Applied research* is the type that research consultants, corporate research departments, or you may conduct. This type of research can help you choose among several viable courses of action.

Although we differentiate between basic and applied research, they can overlap; for example, Jeremy uses basic research methods to help answer applied research questions. In any event, it's generally safe to think of basic marketing research as being conducted by marketing professors and applied marketing research as being conducted by marketing research firms.

Many of the same marketing research methods, such as surveys, experiments, secondary data, observation, and qualitative research, can be applied to basic research or applied research. It's never that some methods are appropriate for one type of research but inappropriate for another. The application of these methods strictly depends on the problem at hand.

Basic: The research you probably don't care about

Basic marketing research helps expand the limits of marketing knowledge. Such research, often targeted for publication in scholarly journals, doesn't focus on finding solutions for a single company's current marketing problems. Instead, it's intended to develop new marketing knowledge that ultimately may help managers with their practical problems in the same way that cutting-edge medical research may eventually cure a disease or research on child behavior may help toy companies create a popular toy.

For example, here's a basic research question that would be perfect for a scholarly marketing journal: Do consumers experience post-purchase regret after buying something without researching it first? Without researching the alternatives, consumers may worry later that they should have purchased something else. However, if it's a product about which they care little, post-purchase regret, regardless of the poorness of choice, is unlikely.

Of course, different people care about different products to different degrees. For example, technophobes (like Jeremy), may not care much about buying a digital camera because their photography aspirations are limited to snapshots of families and friends. In contrast, photography buffs (like Jeremy's wife), may care greatly about purchasing and operating such equipment. This basic research question about consumers, post-purchase regret, and product involvement makes perfect sense for a scholarly marketing journal.

Applied: The research you want to do

Applied research, unlike basic research (which is discussed in the preceding section), is inspired by a real-life problem confronted by a real-life manager or business owner who must make a real-life decision in a timely fashion. Applied research can keep you from being swayed by faulty intuition and group think, or herd mentality (which also characterizes lemmings). If conducted correctly, applied research offers critical information for making important business decisions.

Here's an applied research question that a fast-food restaurant owner can confront: Should I add pasta dinners to my menu? Given current competition in the fast-food industry, pasta may be a great idea. Alternatively, the low-carb mindset and popularity of meat-based diets suggest otherwise.

Here's another example: Should a toiletry company add home teeth-bleaching kits to its product line, and if so, at what price? Dentists currently supply this service during office visits. Typically, such bleaching costs several hundred dollars and may take several hours. Also, dentists and other toiletry companies supply many competing home-based products at vastly different prices.

Exploratory, Descriptive, and Causal Research: Picking Your Approach

When performing marketing research for your business or organization, you can choose from three basic approaches:

- ✔ **Exploratory research,** which includes qualitative research, in-depth interviews, and observations. Exploratory research can clarify the research environment and thus help improve the design of descriptive studies. For example, a new store owner may want to identify which aspects of the store's design appeal most to customers (as a preliminary step to subsequent, more specific studies). Exploratory research often — but not always — is preliminary to more conclusive research (like the next two types).

- ✔ **Descriptive research,** which predominantly is survey-based research. Descriptive research can describe the environment by identifying the characteristics of things or phenomena that are associated with one another; for example, if males are more likely than females to purchase a certain product, or if the most frequent purchaser of a certain product is younger or older.

- ✔ **Causal research,** which chiefly relies on experiments to establish cause-and-effect relationships. Causal research seeks to control for external influences in an effort to assess a cause-and-effect relationship between two variables. For example, if the effect of warning label placement in a print ad is the basis for a research question, then a fictitious brand should be used to avoid predispositions toward an existing brand. If an existing brand is used in the test ads, the effect of label placement may be attributed to predispositions toward an existing brand rather than the placement of the warning.

Figure 3-1 shows each of these types of research and how they're related.

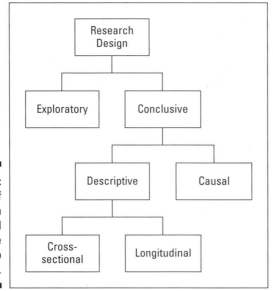

Figure 3-1:
Types of
research
designs, and
how they're
related to
one another.

Both descriptive research and causal research fall under the heading of *conclusive research.* Such research is meant to provide sufficient evidence for making more informed managerial decisions. Descriptive research may rely on *cross-sectional* (data collected at one time) or *longitudinal* (data collected over time) research designs.

Whether you choose to conduct exploratory, descriptive, or causal research depends on the level of certainty you have about your research environment. If you're very uncertain about your research problem and questions, or if you're unaware of the ways that your customers think about your product or the language they use to describe it, exploratory research can help to reduce your uncertainty.

Alternatively, if your research problem and questions already are well understood, you can design and perform a survey (which is in the realm of descriptive research) of reasonable quality. After you've conducted enough descriptive research to get a good sense for possible cause-and-effect relationships, you may want to conduct an experiment to test those relationships. For example, you may want to determine how much your sales would increase if you increased your advertising budget by $1 million.

Whether you do exploratory research or more conclusive research depends on your understanding of your research problem and related research questions. Here are some sample questions and the appropriate research approach:

✔ Exploratory research questions:

- Why are our sales declining?

- Would potential new customers be interested in our dessert menu?

- What, if any, is the nature of our customers' dissatisfaction with our brand?

✔ Descriptive research questions:

- What are the characteristics of our current customers?

- Who are our competitors?

- What features of our product do our customers prefer?

- How many people in town are aware that we sponsor a youth sports team?

✔ Causal research questions:

- Will our customers buy more of our product in a new package format?

- Which of two proposed advertising campaigns will be more effective?

- Does our latest advertising campaign convince our customers that our product is safe if used as directed?

Getting started: Exploratory research

Exploratory research often is initial research that's conducted to clarify and define the nature of a marketing research problem. In other words, exploratory research isn't meant to provide conclusive evidence upon which you can base a decision. Most researchers conducting an exploratory study would assume that subsequent, more conclusive evidence would be provided by one or more later studies.

Here are five common types of exploratory research:

✔ **Focus group:** A *focus group* is a type of qualitative research in which a group of people discuss their attitudes toward a product, an ad, an idea, and so on. An interactive group setting — coordinated by a paid moderator — encourages participants to speak freely with one another. Confusion about the need for further research is a major problem for managers enamored with focus groups. Some managers who order focus groups erroneously believe that these groups fully indicate consumers' thoughts and expectations, so they mistakenly fail to order the additional research that's needed. We discuss focus groups more in depth in Chapter 14.

✔ **Secondary or historical data:** *Secondary data,* which we discuss in Chapter 13, are collected for a purpose other than the research problem at hand. Such data often are economical in the sense that they're almost always less expensive to acquire than primary data. Such data can provide a quick source of background information.

 Given the growing prevalence of the Internet, this may be the dominant kind of research you do during the next 30 to 40 years. Data collected by the U.S. Census Bureau is an example of secondary data. The U.S. Government collects data from citizens that may help you to make better marketing decisions. Both the business literature targeted at academics and the literature targeted at practitioners may provide meaningful insight into the directions you may choose to take your organization.

✔ **Pilot study:** *Pilot studies* are initial, small-scale exploratory studies. If you intend to conduct a large and rigorous study, but you're concerned about possible design errors, a pilot study can help. It can provide feedback about the viability of the planned study, whether new procedures are required, and so on.

✔ **Experience survey:** An *experience survey* is a type of in-depth interview (discussed later in this chapter) in which knowledgeable people are asked about a particular research problem. These surveys typically are unstructured and detailed, so they require more than an hour to conduct. Fortunately, many experts are willing to talk about their expertise and their impressions of the problem or situation at hand. Such interviews offer a rare venue for experts to display their expertise to an interested person.

✔ **Case study:** A *case study* entails intensive investigation of one or more situations similar to the problem at hand. Often, case studies require the cooperation of a host site. For example, many marketing case studies require one or more companies' managers to provide case writers with detailed company and industry information.

To give you a better idea of how exploratory research (which we discuss in Chapters 13 through 15) works, here are two real-world examples:

✔ **Example 1:** The owner of a local hair salon is trying to design new ads for her business. She may turn to secondary data, in the form of existing competitor ads, to help design her own ads. Specifically, she can perform a content analysis of local newspaper and magazine ads run by her competitors in the last year. A careful analysis of these ads, along with her estimates of changes in the profitability of her competitors' salons during that time, can help her design her own new ads.

✔ **Example 2:** A pastry chef who currently works for a corporate bakery chain wants to open his own local dessert shop. However, with so many dessert shops in town, he's unsure about which type of desserts to offer. To research the decision, he spends a weekend at a local park asking people what types of desserts they enjoy and why. Based on these encounters, the pastry chef can develop a mock menu and formal questionnaire for further testing. Subsequently, he can create a final menu and related business plan to present to venture capitalists for funding.

Describing your market environment: Descriptive research

Descriptive research is intended to describe the characteristics of a population or phenomenon. A population could be potential customers for your product. A phenomenon could be the shifting economic reality, nationally or globally. The point of descriptive research is to provide some understanding (though not absolute) about the nature of a problem. For example, you can use it to differentiate among groups of consumers you want to attract or to understand the product features your customers prefer and how much they're willing to pay for each one.

Descriptive research results are more definitive — in large part because you better understand your research problem and associated research questions — than exploratory research results.

Take a look at the following two examples of descriptive research:

✔ **Example 1:** A survey of Weight Watchers customers may reveal that the typical customer is a woman who's roughly 40 years old, has at least some college education if not a college degree, is trying to juggle the demands of children and a job, and has a household income of roughly $50,000. Knowing that the company's typical customer has this profile would help its managers to more effectively modify and target products to people interested in purchasing Weight Watchers meals and services.

✔ **Example 2:** Economic trends are important for all businesses, especially businesses that sell luxury goods, like Tiffany & Co. Because Tiffany's recognizes that necessities (such as utilities, food, and fuel) take precedence over diamond ring and necklace purchases during difficult economic times, its managers may evaluate current customer demand for its products. Specifically, recent and previous customers can be surveyed to determine the types of luxury goods they want (if any) and the prices they're willing to pay.

Identifying relationships: Causal research

As the name implies, causal research is meant to identify cause-and-effect relationships. If you do X, then will the result be Y? Experimental settings are ripe for testing cause-and-effect relationships because the researcher creates a controlled testing environment. However, it's impossible to prove that a cause-and-effect relationship exists, because alternative explanations for a phenomenon may be true as well.

Experimenters try to control for all external explanations (as we discuss in Chapter 16), but they can't eliminate all external influences. Nonetheless, they try to ensure the following three conditions as evidence of causality:

- ✔ **Condition 1: An appropriate causal ordering of events (temporal sequence) must occur.** Event A always must precede Event B. If Event B ever precedes Event A, then Event A isn't the only possible cause of Event B.

- ✔ **Condition 2: You must have *concomitant variation,* which means A and B always vary together.** Variation is direct (and positive) if B increases when A increases, and if B decreases when A decreases. If A increases when B decreases, and vice versa, then there's a negative relationship between A and B.

- ✔ **Condition 3: Spurious relationships must be controlled for when concluding that a cause-and-effect relationship exists.** All alternatives and explanations for A seeming to cause B — as opposed to C causing B, or D causing B — are eliminated. For example, increased purchases of Arizona Cardinals apparel during January 2009 (effect) shouldn't be attributed to winter weather clothing needs (spurious variable) but rather to the team's Super Bowl appearance (cause).

Exploratory versus conclusive research: What's the difference?

How does exploratory research differ from conclusive (meaning descriptive and causal) research? The objective of exploratory research is to provide insights into the research environment and research problem; conclusive research, on the other hand, is meant to test specific hypotheses and to examine specific relationships among variables.

Because the information revealed by exploratory research is only loosely defined, the research approach must be flexible and unstructured. Such research relies on small samples and doesn't require drawing representative samples from a larger population of interest. Exploratory research tends to be qualitative rather than quantitative; in other words, it entails words instead of numbers.

In contrast, conclusive research incorporates well-defined information into the research design. In this sense, the research process is more formal because the questions are clearer. Such research depends on large and representative samples that can be projected to a larger population of interest. The data analysis is quantitative, or numbers oriented.

The findings, results, and outcomes are tentative for exploratory research but more definitive for conclusive research. Because exploratory research results help in designing sound conclusive research, the typical outcome of exploratory research is to suggest more research. Conclusive research findings can support more informed decisions.

Comparing Longitudinal Research and Cross-Sectional Research

Depending on your research question, you may need to gather data over time (longitudinal) or at one point in time (cross-sectional). As such, differentiating between these two types of research and understanding the value of each are essential. Whether you opt to conduct exploratory, descriptive, or causal research to answer your research questions, longitudinal and cross-sectional data can be gathered and analyzed.

Longitudinal research examines shifts over time. For example, it can assess the efficacy of a new ad campaign that's intended to increase sales. *Cross-sectional research* (conducted at a single point in time) can't serve this function because it can't indicate related shifts in two things over time.

Cross-sectional research provides a snapshot, whereas longitudinal research provides a series of snapshots that reveal movement. A flip book is an excellent analogy. Each page of the book contains a picture or snapshot; if you thumb the pages, whatever's depicted on each page seems to move across the scene. Longitudinal research is like thumbing multiple snapshots, and cross-sectional research is like a single snapshot.

For example, if you use longitudinal research to assess the effect of a new ad campaign on sales, you need to follow these steps:

1. **Measure awareness of the ad before, during, and after the ad campaign.**

2. **Measure sales during those same time intervals.**

3. **Determine whether sales increased as ad awareness increased.**

4. **If sales increased, determine whether profits increased more than the cost of the ad campaign.**

In contrast, *cross-sectional research* is designed to study differences among groups at one point in time. For example, a local chef who specializes in crepes may capture meaningful cross-sectional data during an annual community fair. During this event, the chef may sell his crepes and ask a similar number of the men and women who bought them to complete a short questionnaire about why they chose to buy his crepes. These questions may pertain to selling price, flavor, novelty seeking, healthfulness, and so on. Based on his analysis of these questionnaires, the chef can gauge whether men and women differ in their reasons for buying crepes; if they do, he can modify his marketing strategies accordingly.

Chapter 4

Believing In Marketing Research Ethics

*A*lthough many people believe that marketing ethics is an oxymoron, our goal is to convince you otherwise. We want to provide you with a basic perspective for making more ethical marketing research decisions. We tend to think about ethical issues in terms of rights and duties; so, in this chapter, we outline the rights of researchers, respondents, and research clients and their obligations to one another.

In the course of your research endeavors, you can be both the researcher and the research client. To keep all parties' respective roles straight, we present this chapter as if the researcher and the client are distinct parties.

A Solid, To-the-Point Ethics Checklist

We provide lots of detail on all things ethical in this chapter, but if you prefer a basic, upfront framework to help make more ethical marketing research decisions, Table 4-1 provides a simple checklist that we can really endorse. (Check the source of this checklist if you doubt our preference.)

Although "no" answers to all the questions in this checklist won't guarantee an ethical decision, the checklist still can assist you in making more ethical decisions. Furthermore, "yes" answers to any of these questions strongly suggest an unethical decision.

Table 4-1	A General Ethics Checklist
Questions	*Yes or No Answer*
(1) Does my decision treat me, or my company, as an exception to a convention that I must trust others to follow?	
(2) Would I repel customers by telling them about my decision?	
(3) Would I repel qualified job applicants by telling them about my decision?	
(4) Have I been cliquish? (If answer is "yes," answer Questions 4a to 4c. If answer is "no," skip to Question 5.)	
(4a) Is my decision partial?	
(4b) Does it divide the goals of the company?	
(4c) Will I have to pull rank (use coercion) to enact it?	
(5) Would I prefer avoiding the consequences of this decision?	
(6) Did I avoid any of the questions by telling myself that I can get away with it?	

General Ethical Checklist from Hyman, Michael R., Robert Skipper, and Richard Tansey (1990), "Ethical Codes Are Not Enough," Business Horizons, 33 (March–April), 15-22.

See the accompanying DVD for sample ethical dilemmas in marketing research and the related answers to these checklist questions.

Keeping in Mind a Researcher's Obligation to Respondents

Often, the success of marketing research depends on cooperative respondents. Just like Blanche DuBois in *A Streetcar Named Desire,* marketing researchers depend on the kindness of strangers who willingly serve as respondents. When a researcher abuses those respondents, he poisons the well for future researchers. After all, abusive treatment will discourage respondents from participating in future studies.

In the following sections, we show you how to maintain respondents' respect by receiving informed consent, avoiding deception, and recognizing privacy.

Obtaining informed consent

Consent means saying yes. *Informed consent* means you're saying yes with sufficient knowledge of the circumstances. To gain respondents' full cooperation, you should guarantee that everyone who decides to participate in a study is properly informed about that study, can make an informed decision about participation, and has granted a proper and informed consent to participate. These guidelines are especially relevant when studying children; for such research, it's necessary that you secure their parents' informed consent.

To gain consent from respondents, you can draft a letter that accompanies the questionnaire you provide. Your letter should include the following information:

- ✔ The study won't harm them psychologically or physically.

- ✔ There are no right or wrong answers.

- ✔ Respondents aren't required to answer any question that makes them uncomfortable, although they're encouraged to answer all questions that pertain to them.

- ✔ The goals of the study, but without revealing anything that would needlessly bias the responses. For example, a study meant to investigate the viability of boosting subscription fees may include a letter that states "This study is about consumer responses to different levels of service and associated fees."

At the end of your consent letter, include a statement that the respondent willingly agrees to participate in the study followed by space for dating and signing the letter. By doing so, respondents grant their consent to participate in the study.

See the accompanying DVD-ROM for an example consent letter that you can customize.

Avoiding deception

Everyone knows that lying is wrong, especially if you get caught! That said, you may need to temporarily disguise the true purpose of a research study to avoid biasing your respondents. In other words, you shouldn't state your true research goals in the cover letter for your questionnaire. If respondents are aware of your true interests — for example, determining whether customers would pay higher prices for your services — they may alter their answers to serve their own interests. After all, would any customer volunteer to pay higher prices?

Nonetheless, you shouldn't needlessly lie to respondents. They're volunteering their time and effort to answer your questions. Unfortunately, some researchers choose to deceive respondents; for example, they try to boost response rates by indicating that their questionnaire takes only 10 minutes to complete, when in fact it takes 30 minutes. Such deception often inspires respondents to retaliate with inaccurate answers. Another all-too-common lie is promising to keep respondents' answers confidential and then selling those answers to businesses searching for new customers.

Such ill-conceived efforts never remain secret, and once discovered they cause respondents to lose trust in the research process. That loss of trust lowers cooperation rates and boosts future data collection costs.

It may seem like you must walk a fine line to learn about respondents true thoughts and behaviors, but don't worry. The following sections show you the best ways to avoid deceiving respondents.

Protecting confidentiality and anonymity

Many respondents who agree to complete mail or online surveys are reluctant to answer personal background questions — especially if they believe their privacy won't be honored — so they don't answer them. Yet answers to these questions are often vital for data analysis purposes, especially when demographics are strongly related to consumers' behavior.

Unfortunately, respondents' violation-of-privacy fears aren't mere paranoia. In fact, researchers sometimes lie about protecting respondents' anonymity. They may promise that all answers will be kept anonymous, but then they may mark questionnaires with ultraviolet ink or ID numbers, or require respondent code names that would allow respondents to be linked to their questionnaires. This way, researchers can contact reluctant respondents and pressure them to answer those previously unanswered questions (which they'd enjoy as much as sibling children enjoy being asked about who broke the living room lamp). Obviously, researchers whose cover letters falsely promise that responses would be anonymous are acting unethically.

Note that confidentiality differs from anonymity. Researchers can promise they won't reveal that you answered a set of questions or responded to an experiment in a certain way. If they promise not to reveal or to link you with your responses, that's a guarantee of *confidentiality,* which is what attorneys and physicians grant their clients or patients. They know who you are, but they won't reveal anything that occurred as a result of your professional interactions with them or anyone else. In contrast, *anonymity* means that no one — not even the researcher — can link you to your responses.

Representing a study's sponsor truthfully

If you want to study your customers, you'll likely receive the most honest feedback when respondents believe that they're participating in a general survey, fielded by an independent marketing researcher, and your company happens to be included. Sadly, some unethical researchers misidentify the sponsor of a study to boost response rates.

It's always inappropriate to overtly misrepresent a study's true sponsor. For example, people are more willing to respond to surveys conducted by universities (those beacons of truth and beauty) than by commercial organizations (those bastions of social irresponsibility), yet you shouldn't pretend that you're conducting academic research.

To encourage respondents who otherwise would have opted out of a study, *field workers* — those people who collect your data — can pretend they're students working on their professor's research. After all, doesn't every marketing professor conduct a study about the viability of a new motel in Hobbs, New Mexico? (For more information on field workers, see the "Obligations of field services" sidebar in this chapter.)

We're not here to tell you that researchers should reveal their clients to respondents. To do so could cause appreciative customers to temper their negative feedback and hostile customers to be overly critical. Instead, you should provide the minimum detail about the research sponsor and goals needed to allow informed consent to participate in your study.

Bypassing "sugging" and "frugging"

Sugging and *frugging* are two related and obscene-sounding deceptive practices that you've probably encountered — even if you haven't been hip to the marketing lingo. Here's what these two terms mean:

- **Sugging:** Selling under the guise of research occurs when a firm sends a fake questionnaire to sell a product or service. Sometimes the questionnaire is a sweepstakes entry meant only to generate leads. Other times the marketer may ask more in-depth questions meant to refine a prospect's personal profile.

- **Frugging:** Fundraising under the guise of research is a major political problem because appeals for donations are confused with efforts to assess current voter beliefs and preferences.

Unfortunately, these practices, especially for telephone interviewing, have negatively affected researchers' abilities to collect survey data. The widespread usage of sugging and frugging have primed potential respondents to assume that any phone solicitation asking them to participate in a study will ultimately entail a request either to buy something or to contribute to a charitable organization. To avoid such unwanted telephone interactions, people either screen such calls or hang up automatically; as a result, response rates for telephone interviews have dropped precipitously and have needlessly increased survey costs.

The telephone isn't the only way in which marketers use these techniques. Marketers have recently begun sending sugging and frugging e-mails. See whether the e-mail in Figure 4-1 looks familiar. Clearly, this effort to collect marketing research data isn't a sincere one.

ShortSurveys.com

Do you currently have more than $5,000 in total credit card debt?	
○ Yes	○ No

What is your highest interest rate?
0-2.99% ▼

If you could, would you like to reduce your monthly credit payments by 60%?	
○ Yes	○ No

What is your zip code?
[____] Zip code

Submit

If you are unable to submit this survey, please click here.

Figure 4-1: Selling under the guise of research via e-mail.

Presenting a study's processes, procedures, and purposes accurately

When people agree to participate in a study, they should be fully aware of what participation entails. Misrepresenting data collection processes and procedures (to boost response rates and thus reduce research costs, for example) is unethical. In addition, respondents can't provide informed consent to participate in a study if they're unaware of its true purpose.

You can avoid common pitfalls (and outright lies) by putting your most truthful foot forward when discussing the following study details with respondents:

- ✔ **Time commitment required:** You must accurately represent the amount of time that participation will require from the respondent. To increase the likelihood of respondent participation, some researchers may tell a prospective participant that a questionnaire requires only 30 minutes to complete when they know that it takes an hour. (An hour is a huge time commitment for people who claim they're too busy to exercise regularly.) Failure to disclose any aspect of the research procedures, such as the use of follow-up questionnaires, also reflects inadequate concern for respondents' time.

- ✔ **Purpose of the study:** You should avoid grossly misrepresenting the purpose of your study. Yes, you may find it necessary to temporarily disguise the true purpose of a study to ensure unbiased responses (after all, telling people that they're participating in a study meant to help the IRS raise income taxes is bound to bias their answers). However, blatant lying is unethical. In essence, the issue is gaining informed consent, which is possible when you mildly misrepresent your study's purpose but impossible when you grossly misrepresent your study's purpose. Obviously, you can't proceed ethically without informed participant consent.

- ✔ **Use of results:** You must disclose how the results of your study will be used. A researcher who encourages respondents to believe that they're participating in an academic study when the results really will be used for a business purpose is being unethical.

Delivering upon promises of compensation

If you promise to compensate a person for participating in your study, do so. Anything else would be devious. If you promise respondents a magic decoder ring — or a summary of the research results — but fail to deliver, they'll doubt any future promise of compensation for study participation. By creating that doubt, you've greatly increased the data collection costs for future studies by businesspeople, researchers, and egghead academics.

You must solicit far more people — at far greater cost — to overcome the increased number of refusals created by an increasingly suspicious population.

Respecting respondent privacy

Personal privacy is a fleeting notion in today's turbo-charged, post-9/11 world. Many online consumers willingly trade information about their browsing and buying habits for purchase recommendations from intelligent software. (One simple and likely familiar example is Amazon's section "Customers who bought this item also bought . . . .") Regardless, enough people cherish their privacy that researchers shouldn't violate it cavalierly.

In the following sections, we indicate ways to show respondents that you respect their privacy while getting the data that you need.

Limiting requests for personal data

Respecting respondents' privacy doesn't mean you can't ever ask respondents for personal background data. Nonetheless, you only should ask such questions if the answers are vital to a study's success. It may be necessary, as part of a study, to understand key aspects of respondents' lives, so you may ask them about their education, their occupation, or their income.

For example, you may want to investigate whether a high-priced French restaurant would be successful in your neighborhood. In this case, it would be acceptable to ask respondents about their incomes because being able to relate dining-out preferences to incomes would help determine the likelihood of success.

Observing behaviors ethically

Observing people's behaviors without their consent is problematic. It's bad enough that many cities now rely on hundreds or thousands of video cameras to record everything from potential terrorist activities to traffic violations. How thrilled would you be to have strangers see a video recording of you buying condoms or adult diapers? Not cool.

A few common yet questionable observation methods include the following:

- **The use of hidden microphones and cameras:** If a researcher uses hidden microphones or video cameras, study participants won't be aware that their behaviors are being recorded. As a result, it's impossible for them to give fully informed consent because they're unaware of the full procedures and the implications of having agreed to participate in the study. (Refer to the earlier section "Obtaining informed consent" for more on the consent issue.)

- **Voice pitch analysis:** Despite increasingly powerful computers and sophisticated software, *voice-pitch analysis* may require careful assessment of recorded speech rather than real-time assessment of live speech. Obviously, recorded speech may be analyzed subsequently without the participant's consent.

- **Garbology studies:** *Garbology studies,* in which a researcher combs through people's trash to assess the things they've consumed, violate respondents' privacy (unless they've consented to sharing their trash for this purpose). After all, some adults don't want anyone to know they still eat highly presweetened cereals meant for children!

We don't mean to imply that you should never conduct studies that require hidden cameras and microphones or that involve voice-pitch analyses or garbage mining. Rather, you must take care when relying on these methods.

Mystery shoppers are an exception here. As we explain in Chapter 15, *mystery shoppers* are people hired by a store owner to report on a carefully specified buying experience. Although salespeople may think of mystery shoppers as hired scum, salespeople know they may be monitored in this way, so they've consented as a condition of employment.

Executing qualitative research correctly

Another privacy issue relates to *qualitative research methods,* which encourage respondents to project their opinions onto ambiguous pictures or scenarios. (Check out Chapters 14 and 15 for a full description of these methods.)

For example, respondents may be shown a picture of a person using a product and then asked to guess what that person is thinking. Of course, the respondent's guess would indirectly reveal what he thinks about the product. In essence, respondents are encouraged to expose their true feelings through a nonthreatening guise. Although the researcher knows that the respondents are revealing their true feelings, most respondents will be unaware they're doing so. This lack of awareness poses a thorny privacy issue that's difficult to resolve. At the very least, respondents exposed to qualitative research methods should be thoroughly debriefed. Given the mild deception typical of most marketing studies, it's unlikely any respondent will react badly being slightly mislead about the research sponsor or goals.

Combining information from various sources

A privacy issue is associated with merging data from multiple sources into a single comprehensive profile. You may be unconcerned if a healthcare provider has certain information about you, your mortgage lender has different information about you, and local government has still different information about you. The information about you in databases maintained by those separate organizations isn't worrisome because the incomplete picture it paints of you barely threatens your privacy. However, if some organization were to merge all that data into one aggregate and more powerful profile, you'd probably be concerned in a *1984* Big Brother way. If you work for a large corporation that now merges consumer data from multiple sources, try to discourage that practice.

Merging data from several sources is far more prohibited in Europe than in the United States. In fact, some European laws preclude this practice.

Taking responsibility for your respondents' well-being

You can have a laissez-faire attitude toward taking responsibility for your respondents' well-being. You can try to convince yourself that adult respondents can take care of themselves. However, that type of thinking fails to show the respect that respondents automatically earn by helping you find the answers to your research questions.

Inadequate concern for your respondents' well-being can take many forms, including the following:

- ✓ **Contacting them at an inconvenient time:** For example, calling people at dinnertime to conduct a 45-minute telephone interview is inappropriate.

- ✓ **Using incompetent or insensitive interviewers:** You should ensure that interviewers are properly trained. They should have a suitable demeanor, ask an appropriate number of probing questions, and generally interact well with respondents. In addition, always debrief your study participants if temporary deception was required.

- ✓ **Asking needlessly depressing questions:** Don't ask questions that can needlessly depress respondents. That's not to say you shouldn't ask questions about people's own funeral arrangements if you're conducting marketing research for a funeral home. Clearly, asking questions about one's demise is depressing, but it isn't *needlessly* depressing in this case. On the other hand, asking a die-hard Cubs fan about the Cubs' century-plus failure to win a World Series is needlessly depressing.

- ✓ **Querying excessively:** Avoid querying respondents excessively. When people are contacted to the point that they're no longer gracious about lending researchers their time and energies, response rates decrease, response quality decreases, and most marketing research becomes cost prohibitive.

Avoiding Abuse of Research Clients

Researchers are obligated to respect their respondents. (Flip to the preceding section "Keeping in Mind a Researcher's Obligation to Respondents" for additional discussion.) However, they also have obligations to businesspeople who buy their services.

A researcher should avoid abusing research designs, methods, or results, because a bad experience discredits marketing research and discourages businesspeople from relying on it when it's important.

Here are six ways in which researchers abuse clients:

- ✓ **Overcharging and double-billing:** Low-ball pricing, or winning a bid to conduct a research study knowing it can't be completed at the bid price and then immediately raising the price after winning the bid, is abusive and unethical.

✔ **Failing to maintain client confidentiality:** If a researcher collects information for a client, that client owns the information. Thus, the researcher has no right to provide that information to others.

✔ **Failing to avoid a conflict of interest when a researcher has multiple clients in the same industry:** What researchers discover when conducting a study for one client shouldn't be shared with other clients. In other words, one client shouldn't pay for research results provided to another client. For many reasons, General Motors wouldn't want to pay for Chrysler's research results.

✔ **Reusing data collected for another client, especially if it's proprietary:** Clients charged for data collection should be safe in assuming that they're paying for newly collected data. Even as a child, you knew better than to accept ABC (**A**lready **B**een **C**hewed) gum.

✔ **Conducting multiple interviews simultaneously:** Researchers conducting studies for two clients simultaneously may recognize cost efficiencies by conducting joint interviews for both clients. In other words, researchers may field a single questionnaire, making it longer and including key questions for both clients. However, this practice is unethical. Clients should be safe in assuming that researchers who bid on a project are bidding on a single study and that the effort to collect and analyze data is targeted specifically to their needs. (For a useful analogy, imagine how you'd feel if you discovered your main squeeze was playing footsie with someone else!)

✔ **Acting unprofessionally, not delivering what was promised, and missing deadlines:** Such behaviors are obvious abuses that require no elaboration. For example, what if we decided to be lazy and wrote *Insert Your Own Joke Here?*

In the following sections, we cover the main abuses you should do your best to avoid.

Making sure proprietary stuff stays proprietary

A researcher may, in the process of completing a study, develop a new data collection or analysis procedure. The client and researcher may agree that any newly developed methods are *proprietary* to the client. In other words, only the client has the subsequent right to use that procedure. If the researcher subsequently conducts a study for another client using the same procedures, the researcher has violated her obligation to the first client.

Even worse, if a researcher conducts a study in which collected data or newly developed methods are useful to competitors, and she subsequently solicits competitors about conducting a similar study, such solicitations represent a clear conflict of interest.

Conducting unnecessary research

Conducting unnecessary research merely to earn fees and cover overhead expenses — which is analogous to a physician performing unnecessary surgery or a dentist performing unnecessary dental work — is a major abuse that you should avoid.

If you conduct a study, that study ought to be necessary in the sense that it provides information to help someone select the best among several viable alternative courses of action. The research should reduce, in a meaningful fashion, uncertainty about the best course of action.

If you know in advance that a study can't succeed in this way, you can be sure that it's unnecessary research. From the outcome of the 2008 election, we suspect that John McCain's presidential campaign advisors conducted lots of unnecessary research.

Performing wrong or irrelevant research

Researching the wrong problem or an irrelevant one is equivalent to conducting unnecessary research. It's still unnecessary, but in this case it's both unnecessary and wrong. Such research gives the erroneous impression that it has provided relevant information. As a result, a client may delay a decision needlessly — and that delay may be costly.

For example, an apparel retailer may ask a local research firm to help it understand why its promotional efforts aren't increasing sales. However, the research firm, based on years of studying the local retailing environment, already knows that customers for the apparel carried by this retailer are very price sensitive. Thus, price promotions that lower prices 20 percent or more will be effective. Conducting the extensive consumer study the retailer requested, rather than merely disclosing this known information and suggesting other possibly worthwhile studies, is unethical.

Businesses may (unethically) conduct wrong or irrelevant research for political reasons as well. For instance, a company may know that consumers are misled by its advertising claims, yet those claims encourage additional sales. To avoid regulatory sanctions due to the misleading claims, the company can field a study that seemingly shows its claims are accurate. After all, it's far cheaper to field a study than it is to run expensive corrective advertising that can reduce sales.

Ignoring errors in ongoing studies

Continuing a study after spotting an error in the process is an abuse of clients. For example, suppose a researcher mails a questionnaire to 1,000 people — an expensive proposition — but then, after the questionnaires begin to return, he recognizes a major flaw in it. He fails to mention this flaw to the client. He just continues to accept the questionnaires, enters respondents' answers into a data file, analyzes those answers, prepares a report, and then presents it. Although no study is perfect, a researcher who spots a problem is obligated to correct it as soon as it's spotted.

Using unwarranted shortcuts

Questionable shortcuts designed to secure a contract or to reduce expenses are abusive of clients. Shortcuts typically entail using inappropriate research methods and failing to fully disclose important information about the research. Specifically, here are some of the most common yet unwarranted shortcuts taken by researchers:

- **Lax respondent checks:** Improper verification of respondents is unacceptable. Obviously, it's nonsensical to query people who are unqualified to participate in a study; for example, asking people who've never used a brand for advice about how to improve it can't yield meaningful insights.

- **Ignoring pretests:** Inadequate pretesting of questionnaires, which is likely to reduce their reliability and validity, is an unprofessional practice. Yes, the pretesting stage takes time, energy, and a bit of money, but it's necessary to ensure that the subsequent study is executed correctly.

- **Applying inappropriate analytical techniques:** Learning about sophisticated marketing research methods may be time consuming, and the software, computers, and other materials required to use these methods may be expensive. As a result, researchers may encounter financial pressures to apply inappropriate techniques merely to amortize their costs. Alternatively, they may be encouraged to think that if they have this research hammer, every research problem is a nail.

  Another way researchers apply inappropriate techniques is by using more-sophisticated analytical methods than are required to answer the research questions. Merely to impress a client is an inappropriate reason for using a sophisticated analytical technique. (Think Rube Goldberg here.)

Similarly, using overly technical language in reports is a problem. Dazzling clients with pompous explanations accomplishes little in the long run. You're obligated to communicate clearly and to provide each client with an honest assessment of the information they collected and how it can be used to make better decisions.

✔ **Exceeding uncertainty limitations:** Not meeting accuracy requirements — for example, by reducing the sample size to the point that random sampling error becomes an unacceptable threat or there are insufficient numbers of respondents in each category to make meaningful cross-category comparisons (see Chapter 12) — is unacceptable.

✔ **Hiding study limitations:** Misrepresenting the limitations of a study is an abuse. For example, you shouldn't hide errors caused by nonresponse or sampling error. You're obligated to sensitize your clients to the artificiality of an experimental design if a laboratory experiment is involved (see Chapter 16). (Contrary to rumor, you can't blame the marginal quality of prime-time network television programming on the responses of mice shown program pilots.)

Obligations of field services

Field services, which we discuss in Chapter 17, are research suppliers that specialize in collecting survey data. Whether retained by you or a marketing research supplier, they're obligated to avoid the following three practices:

✔ **Over-reporting hours worked:** Over-reporting hours worked is the same as overcharging because such services are compensated on an hourly basis.

✔ **Falsifying data:** Falsifying the data (or fudging the numbers) that researchers and businesspeople ultimately rely on being collected properly can cause severe damage, especially when a company's survival depends on a research-based decision. (Debacles involving former financial juggernauts such as Enron and Citibank come to mind when you think of data falsification.)

✔ **Using so-called professional respondents:** *Professional respondents* are people who participate excessively in studies. These respondents may be people who are retired and looking for an activity (other than mahjong and pinochle) or people who enjoy participating in research studies and would participate more regularly if given the option. Unfortunately, such people tend to differ from the general population. (These are the same people who as children sat in the first row and always raised their hand when the teacher asked a question.) Although cost considerations encourage their use despite their atypicality, field services should resist professional respondents because they aren't representative of the population.

Similarly, overstating the validity or reliability of any study is a problem. Managers ought to know to what degree the results of a study are reliable and valid, and thus know how much to weigh those results in their decisions.

✔ **Pretending to be an expert:** Having insufficient expertise to conduct research is related to the previous abuse. Say, for example, we have a longtime client who suddenly becomes interested in a type of research study about which neither of us is technically versed. Rather than indicate that we lack sufficient expertise to conduct this type of study, and perhaps suggest other researchers with such expertise, we may stumble along and attempt the study. Instead, if we lack the expertise to conduct a study, we shouldn't attempt it. After all, you wouldn't hire a podiatrist to perform open-heart surgery, right?

Recognizing Clients' Obligations to Researchers

Clients aren't free from obligations to researchers. Such obligations mainly entail following a proper proposal process. By proper research proposal process, we mean if you solicit proposals for research, anyone submitting a proposal should have a legitimate chance to win the research contract.

Occasionally, a businessperson who has already selected a research supplier wants to pick the brains of researchers working for other research companies, so she pretends there's an opportunity to win the research contract and solicits proposals. After those proposals are submitted, she makes them available to the researcher she's already selected.

Although this problematic process saves the chosen researcher much time and money (and perhaps some of those savings are passed on to the unscrupulous client), it's a total misuse of other research companies' time and money. Ultimately, legitimate clients bear the cost of creating such proposals, which needlessly drives up overall research costs for everyone.

Here's a list of ways to conduct a proper proposal process:

✔ **Avoid pseudo-pilot studies.** It's unfair to imply that an elaborate, multi-period study will be conducted — to secure a lower-cost bid — when, in fact, you intend to fund only a one-period study.

Unfortunately, Mike was involved in one such study. Several years ago, a big-city convention and visitors bureau supposedly was interested in conducting three years of quarterly studies on visitors. To conduct these studies, it was necessary to buy expensive computer hardware and software to assess tourists' attitudes toward different area attractions. Yet, rather than the 12 initially agreed-upon quarterly studies, which would have allowed for recovery of development costs plus a fair profit, the bureau cancelled the study after only one quarter. As a result, fees for the one-period study barely covered development costs. Had Mike known he'd be conducting only a one-period study, he would have charged a higher fee.

✔ **Keep proprietary methods confidential.** You're obligated not to disclose or use specialized techniques or models that are proprietary to the researcher because you're merely renting the researchers' abilities and tools. Those tools aren't your property unless you've purchased them.

✔ **Cancel research projects fairly.** Unless you have a good cause (they do happen), projects shouldn't be cancelled. Researchers often budget time and allocate overhead to projects, so unjustified cancelling of a project unfairly jeopardizes the researcher's financial well-being.

✔ **Don't support a political agenda.** Research shouldn't be conducted solely to support prior conclusions, or in other words, a political agenda. Marketing research is designed to help reduce uncertainty and to help you select the best option among viable alternative courses of action. If the course of action already is decided, then research is superfluous. Research as a mere political tool is a waste of everyone's time. If you solicit research, its conclusion and your actions should be undecided initially.

✔ **Conduct proper advocacy research.** *Advocacy research* is research conducted to support a legal claim. As an example, think about tobacco companies. They have an interest in demonstrating through empirical studies that the ads they ran didn't induce people to begin smoking; rather, they only induced people to switch brands. Clearly, these companies have a vested interest in research results that support this position. Even for research meant to assist *socially conscious tobacco companies* (the ultimate oxymoron), researchers are honor bound not to fudge their results; they should never compromise their integrity by pretending results differ from what occurred.

Remembering Clients' Obligations to Respondents

If you're the client, you never should try to convert respondents into sales prospects or lie to them about acting appropriately upon any dangerous or damaging results uncovered by the research you ordered. Although tempting, misrepresenting your motive or likely behavior in these ways is unethical. Instead, keep these two important guidelines in mind if you're a client:

✔ **Avoid creating prospect lists from respondent lists.** You shouldn't use respondents' attitudes and behaviors — as revealed by their responses to your questionnaire — to create a list of prospective customers. For example, if you ask a researcher to conduct a marketing study that requires identifying the names and addresses of people who are poten-tial first-time buyers of a product, it's inappropriate for that researcher to supply that information to you for selling purposes.

✔ **Act on dangerous results.** As a client, you're obligated to act on danger-ous results. Say, for instance, you ask for a study on how people use one of your company's products. If it's discovered that product owners use it improperly and, as a result, occasionally are injured, you're obligated to address that issue.

Recalling that Respondents Have Obligations, Too!

We believe that respondents have one obligation: If they opt to participate, assuming that they have been fully informed about the study and can give proper consent, they're obligated to be truthful.

Sadly, we've identified a group of people we call *mischievous respondents.* Such respondents, for whatever reason, decide to sabotage studies by giving bogus answers to questions or responding in an atypical way to experimental tasks. Participants trying to foul up experiments or surveys cost the people involved needless time, money, and energy. Mischievous respondents reduce the efficiency of the research process. Frankly, trying to have fun at research-ers' and businesspeoples' expense is inexcusable.

Possible ways to deal with mischievous respondents — like specially designed questions and statistical analyses to detect them — are discussed in Chapter 7.

Chapter 5

Working with Independent Marketing Researchers

In This Chapter

▶ Selecting an independent marketing researcher

▶ Discovering sources of reasonably priced researchers

▶ Being mindful of the qualities that your researcher should have

*A*lthough following our advice should help you design and execute trustworthy marketing research, conducting your own study poses a challenging task. These types of questions are bound to surface: "What do I want to discover about my business and my customers?" "How do I develop a good questionnaire?" and "How should I collect, analyze, and interpret the data I collect?"

Rather than approach these questions in isolation, you can seek partial or complete research assistance. The amount of assistance you bring onboard depends on your budgetary constraints and your comfort level with your research-related abilities. This chapter offers insights into finding and working with independent marketing researchers who can assist you.

Making the Choice to Solicit Outside Expertise

Five prominent components characterize survey research:

✔ Identifying research questions and understanding how to answer them (see Chapters 8 and 9)

✔ Questionnaire development (see Chapter 10)

✔ Drawing an appropriate sample (see Chapters 11 and 12)

✔ Data collection (see Chapter 17) and analysis (see Chapter 18)

✔ Interpretation of results (see Chapters 18 and 19)

If you've never conducted a survey, these five components may seem overwhelming. To cope, you may solicit help from local experts. When deciding the type and amount of assistance you prefer, you need to determine your budget and level of expertise required. For example, you may require only a little advice about conducting a few focus groups (see Chapter 14) but massive assistance in the design, execution, and analysis of an experiment (see Chapter 16).

Sources of Inexpensive Research Help

Marketing research expertise, like all expertise, takes years to acquire, so when hiring someone to help with your research, you should expect to pay for a blend of historical and current hours. Services offered by national marketing research firms are likely to exceed your budget and, more importantly, your needs. As we note in Chapter 14, marketing research companies often charge $10,000 or more for a small set of focus groups, and they may charge as much or more to conduct a modest survey.

Although corporations with global or national expansion plans and a healthy research budget easily can afford and seek such costly services, you and your company may have shallower pockets. Luckily, other effective and less expensive options are available to you.

Regardless of your preferred level of assistance or research budget, you can turn to local entities — such as universities and research firms — to help you design and execute a marketing study. We cover good sources for outside expertise in the following sections.

College and university students

Hiring students from a college or university is a great way to get help without spending a lot of money. Plus, the student pool is continuous, so this avenue is constantly available. In order from the most qualified to the least qualified, the most capable types of students are:

- ✔ Marketing students who have completed or are completing a marketing research course

- ✔ Psychology students with a background in survey and/or qualitative research (like focus groups, which we discuss in Chapter 14 and illustrate on the DVD)

- ✔ Journalism students who have completed or are completing a survey research course

Although such students are available, it's not always obvious how you'd recruit them to assist you. One possibility is to contact the faculty advisor for a local student chapter of a professional organization like the American Marketing Association. Such student groups thrive on working with local businesses; many students use their experiences helping local businesses as résumé builders.

Another possibility is to present your business problem to the chairperson of the marketing department in a college of business and to request that a student group — perhaps students currently enrolled in a marketing research course — conduct a research study inspired by this problem as a course-related exercise. Instructors often welcome the opportunity to engage students in a real-world learning experience.

The advantages of hiring students include the following:

✔ **They will work for little or no money.** College students may help you for résumé-building purposes rather than monetary compensation. If working on your research project is a course-related requirement, earning a good grade should be sufficient inducement to produce a high-quality report and a presentation of results. Members of a professional organization's student chapter often seek modest funds to support their attendance at national organization meetings.

✔ **Your research benefits from some faculty support.** Students who engage in a real-world research project — either for course credit or as members of a professional organization's student chapter — typically receive extensive advice from one or more faculty members. Although a quality guarantee is unlikely (faculty members usually resist taking responsibility for student work and undermining their pedagogy mission), instructor or advisor input in support of students' learning experiences should ensure properly conducted and relatively hassle-free marketing research.

Although hiring students saves money and provides guidance from faculty, the option also has its disadvantages, including the following:

✔ **They may not complete the study.** Because students may believe they're not obligated to complete a course-required project after they've received a course grade, studies that aren't finished by semester's end may remain unfinished. If students resist your pleas to complete your study, you could ask their instructor or advisor to intervene or complete it, which likely will require a modest non-tax-deductible contribution to that instructor's academic department. Because university budgets are tight, faculty members often are encouraged to attract supplemental funds for supporting their department's pedagogy and research missions.

✔ **They may not provide useful information.** Depending on students' abilities, their time frame for completion, and your data collection budget, the information they provide may be insufficient. So, it's important for you to clarify research requirements with students and their instructors or advisors at the onset of the project.

College and university research centers

Many universities have a business center for research. Often, these centers serve as clearinghouses for matching MBA or advanced undergraduate students to real-world clients. For example, the capstone course in Jeremy's MBA program required him (with another student) to develop a marketing plan for a local nonprofit organization. The client wasn't charged for the plan because completing it was a degree requirement.

These research centers also match faculty to real-world clients. Although we doubt we'll elicit much sympathy for low-paid university professors, such real-world projects allow them to supplement their salaries while supporting their business communities. For example, Mike created the telephone questionnaire shown in Chapter 6 for a local economic development study solicited through his university's research center; unfortunately, the study was cancelled due to budget constraints. (Yes, we know you feel his pain.)

Most colleges and universities have a community service agenda or mandate that encourages the business school — if they maintain one — to work with local businesspeople on marketing plans and research. For public institutions, such centers often are funded with state tax dollars, so availing yourself of their services is a way to recover part of your income taxes!

Here are some advantages of using a research center:

✔ **You gain access to faculty expertise.** If students primarily design and execute the research needed to address your marketing problem, they won't be flying solo; one or more faculty experts will oversee their efforts. For example, Jeremy had multiple faculty advisors for his MBA project. If a faculty member designs and executes your study — perhaps with students earning assistantship money from the research center — you'll be working with a marketing research expert.

✔ **You have year-round access.** Because semesters begin and end regularly, you have continuous access to student-based research help. MBA programs constantly search for real-world clients who can provide a challenging educational experience for students. Stereotypes of underworked faculty who take lengthy summer vacations notwithstanding, many faculty members are available year-round for supplemental research assignments.

✔ **You receive help for a relatively low price.** Little or no monetary compensation is required when students — with faculty oversight — conduct your research for course credit. A dinner for students upon study completion is a sufficient way to show thanks — and it's far less expensive than the fees charged by a commercial research firm for the same service. Although pricier than student teams, faculty members charge less than commercial suppliers — for example, student assistance at no additional cost — and university willingness to support a public service agenda.

Of course, you should consider the disadvantages of using a research center as well. The disadvantages include the following:

- **You may receive student-led research of spotty quality.** If students conduct your research, they're learning while doing; as a result, their work may be of uneven quality. That said, your research project provides an opportunity for business students to learn about the real world, so you're helping them while you're helping yourself.

- **You can't have it yesterday.** Commercial research suppliers have a profit motive, so they charge an amount proportionate to your speed-of-completion requirement; the sooner you want a summary of results, the more you'll pay for it. In contrast, students typically are given a semester — roughly four months — to complete a study, and faculty members working on supplemental projects are obligated first to their primary teaching and research assignments. In essence, research centers are a poor choice if you require information for an immediate decision.

College and university faculty

You may directly solicit a marketing professor for assistance with your next project. Faculty (like us) who are worried about funding their children's college funds may appreciate the opportunity to earn a few extra shekels.

Many professors also welcome high-quality experiential exercises for their students. A company manager or owner may ask a department chair for research assistance. The chair then may forward the request to a professor who's interested in gathering a group of students enrolled in his marketing research course to conduct a study for the company.

Beware of *joint academic-commercial research,* which is research meant to help a company while providing data (for proprietary reasons, probably disguised to protect the company's research investment) useful for academic research. Such research efforts automatically create a major conflict of interest because the company's and researcher's needs often diverge, which means neither party will be satisfied with the outcome. Unless you work for a corporation that's interested in state-of-the-art research and that's willing to allow publication of disguised research results, don't solicit faculty with this seemingly win-win proposition; they'll likely know better.

For example, when Mike was a naïve doctoral student (way too many years ago), one of his professors sold him on conducting joint academic-commercial research as a way to supplement a university salary while collecting data applicable to academic research. Although it seemed like a good idea in theory, in practice it proved unworkable because the clients' research needs superseded any academic data needs. As a result, the data Mike collected helped clients make better decisions but couldn't contribute to his academic research.

Some advantages of using college or university faculty to conduct your research include:

- ✔ **Access to their expertise:** Marketing professors have the skill set necessary to identify business problems and conduct sound research to solve and provide insight into these problems. Essentially, all those years of schooling should be good for something.

- ✔ **Expedited completion:** Faculty hired directly to conduct a study are independent contractors subject to the same motivations as other independent contractors. As a result, you can negotiate quicker study completion in return for increased compensation.

The one big disadvantage of using faculty for research is that time is money. Although they may charge less than commercial research firms, faculty members recognize the opportunity costs associated with consulting work and will bill their time accordingly.

Small local firms

Finances and logistics may encourage you to choose a smaller local research firm. To identify a firm that's compatible with your needs, you can ask for recommendations from local business fraternities, business school faculty, and fellow entrepreneurs. Alternatively, you can peruse classified ads and the Internet for prospective local firms.

By researching companies and communicating with them directly, you may discover that larger local ad agencies may have an underused in-house research staff; thus, they may be willing to perform research for you. In particular, if your research problem involves promotion-related research questions, ad agency researchers may prove ideal.

Advantages of going with a small firm are

- ✔ **Close proximity:** The geographic proximity of a local research firm should permit the face-to-face interactions that are unavailable from nonlocal research firms.

- ✔ **Lower cost:** Due to lower overhead, a local research firm will charge less than a national research firm.

- ✔ **Sincere service:** Because local firms depend on local business, they cherish positive word-of-mouth and work to avoid any negative claims against them. We aren't saying that a national firm won't meet your needs; rather, you'll have less leverage to ensure that outcome.

Disadvantages of a small firm are:

- ✔ **Limited options in smaller communities:** Although you'll likely have many options in a major city, your options may be limited in a smaller one. Fewer options mean less leverage when negotiating price and delivery time.

- ✔ **Myopic perspective:** Because a local firm's insights may be limited to your local community, research focusing on business expansion may require a research firm with a broader reach and perspective.

- ✔ **Limited expertise:** A local firm may lack the expertise to satisfy your research needs. Nonetheless, its owner or manager may attempt your study anyway (because revenue-earning opportunities are limited as well) but fail to execute it properly.

Qualities to Look for in a Researcher

To be an informed consumer of marketing research, you need to understand the indicators of a good researcher (no matter what type she may be), such as a slow-to-speak and quick-to-listen persona. No one knows the in-and-outs of your business better than you, so before marketing research is conducted, a good researcher will address all your questions and concerns. That way, the likelihood of a useful study is maximized.

You can get too close to a problem to recognize it. Fortunately, a good researcher can help you understand and structure your true problem. Recognizing your true problem is a prerequisite for selecting the best among viable alternative courses of action. In addition, a good researcher will conduct the appropriate research needed to address your problem and provide the information you need to make the most informed decision.

Sadly, many self-proclaimed marketing researchers are ill qualified to conduct marketing research. Although the American Marketing Association has considered accrediting marketing researchers, no process is currently in place. Researchers can acquire no certification— like a CPA — that verifies they understand the field and are sufficiently competent to conduct sound research. Beware of who you hire!

Marketing researchers who lack adequate training often try to match a technique they know well to whatever problem you face. Mike once worked with a self-proclaimed marketing researcher who knew about only one advanced marketing research technique: conjoint analysis (which we introduce briefly in Chapter 21). Regardless of the potential client or the problem, the solution was always, "We should run a conjoint analysis study for you." Sadly, this salesperson was unqualified to conduct marketing research properly and, as a result, clients didn't receive the research results they needed to make better decisions.

In this section, we tell you what qualities truly helpful researchers will possess. If your researcher fails to provide the kind of help we outline in the following sections, you should consider replacing her.

Helpful throughout the process

Throughout the many stages of the research process, it's important that the help you seek is available whenever it's needed. Whether they're correctly defining the research problem or interpreting the results of a study, good researchers are available and willing to listen to you before recommending a course of action. Think of a good researcher as your sturdy crutch down the path to research success!

Your researcher should help you:

- ✔ **Understand the real problem:** Good researchers can identify the correct problem. For example, a sales decline may be triggered by many possible causes. Before designing and fielding a study, a good researcher will consult extensively with you about the most likely causes. By relying on your expertise to focus the study, a good researcher can save valuable time and resources.

- ✔ **Select among viable alternatives:** Although it's possibly exciting from an academic perspective, a good researcher won't conduct research for research's sake. Instead, a good researcher recognizes that practical research should help decision-makers select among alternative viable courses of action.

- ✔ **Structure your research and subsequent analysis:** After the problem and alternative courses of action are identified, a good researcher should help you develop a research agenda that includes a timeline for data collection and data analysis. How and when you gather data dictates the type of analyses you can run. For instance, the quicker you know the results, the quicker you can replace any suboptimal marketing strategies.

Proper communication and analytical skills

Good researchers know their discipline so well they can effectively communicate — regardless of your level of marketing research and statistical expertise — the results of a study that can help you make a sound decision.

A good researcher won't resort to excessive jargon, and he won't ever utter the phrase "That's too complicated for you to understand."

A good researcher knows that anything worth communicating to you can be communicated effectively. We believe that communication skills, both written and oral, are as important as technical competence for developing and executing trustworthy marketing research.

Overlooking written and oral communication skills in a researcher could lead to a frustrating experience. Think of yourself as a pupil; if your questions aren't answered clearly by the researcher (teacher), your learning experience is compromised. You can screen for these skills during the research proposal stage.

Also, whether your data are quantitative or qualitative (see Chapter 3), a good marketing researcher will possess the requisite analysis skills, such as expertise in statistical and graphical presentation software for quantitative studies and expertise in theme analysis (in other words, identifying the basic themes revealed by respondents) for qualitative studies (like focus groups; see Chapter 14). Without sound analytical skills, your data won't be interpreted appropriately and your research effort will prove useless. You can assess these skills during the proposal stage. Don't be shy about asking for a list of satisfied customers.

A focus on partnership

Healthy interdependence characterizes a robust research partnership; that is, you and the researcher must trust and rely on one another to complete a successful marketing study. A good researcher, who's also a good partner, does the following:

- **Adheres to the project's specifications:** Good researchers don't deviate from the project's initial specifications, such as the timeline for data collection, sample size, analysis scheme, and so on, which are set prior to beginning the study. You must approve any deviation from such provisions; good researchers know this and won't take your research in a new direction without your consent.

- **Responds to your needs:** Good researchers listen and adhere to their customers' needs. Just as you try to meet your customer's needs, your researcher should do the same for you. Effective responders tend to be good listeners.

- **Uses your expertise:** To identify a true research problem, good researchers capitalize on their clients' business knowledge. For example, if your knowledge of social media (for example, Twitter and Facebook) is extensive and you believe advertising through these media will create a large customer following for your product, your researcher should apply that expertise to the design and execution of your advertising study.

✔ **Keeps you in the loop:** Researchers who design and field surveys, analyze data, and submit reports without regular client updates are insensitive to clients' needs. As you follow the research process, you'll gain a better perspective on what's required to conduct effective research. This new perspective will make you either a more informed marketing research consumer or an eventual marketing research doer.

✔ **Displays flexibility:** Marketing research, like business in general, can be unpredictable, so the researcher must be willing to adjust. Meeting times may need moving, data collection requirements may need altering, report delivery may need expediting, and so on. Whatever the circumstances, a good researcher is able to adapt to meet your needs.

Together, you and the researcher bring unique expertise critical to the design and management of your study. Such expertise must be applied to avoid misunderstandings about research deadlines, processes, outcomes, and perspectives.

Clearing up key issues before research begins

Prior to embarking on the research process, it's imperative that you and your researcher develop a relationship that encourages critiquing and questioning the forthcoming research. Such an open and respectful relationship is invaluable as the research process unfolds. Imagine instead that you have a research-related idea and are reluctant to mention it to your researcher because you believe he won't respect it.

Your research experience is more likely to prove fruitful when your researcher understands how you'll make your decision, the deadline for research completion, and what happens if the research findings encourage a strategy that fails. As such, before starting your study, a good researcher will assess three things:

✔ **Your decision-making process:** To provide the information you need to make the best possible decision, the researcher must understand your decision-making process. If the researcher provides information that you'll ignore because it's unrelated to your decision-making process, the researcher is wasting your time and money. Suppose, for example, that you're risk adverse. Rather than opt for the action with the highest expected return, you prefer to minimize the likelihood of a loss. In this case, a good researcher will present the research findings in a manner consistent with loss minimization.

✔ **Your decision time horizon:** If the researcher knows your deadline for making a decision, he can choose the optimal research approach from a reliability and budget perspective. For example, an expert researcher knows the time required to develop an effective questionnaire (one that will help answer your research questions), to collect data, to analyze that data, and to recommend a course of action. If the researcher is vague about a timeline for completion, consider the services of a different researcher.

> ✔ **The downside if your decision proves wrong:** A good researcher understands the impact of a wrong decision. For a corporation like IBM, a $10 million mistake is chump change, but for a small firm in a small town, a $10 million mistake could lead to bankruptcy and your selling apples on a street corner. A good researcher may pursue different types of research if the impact of a wrong decision is earning a bit less pocket money for shareholders rather than driving a company into bankruptcy.

Working through points of potential conflict

You may like your researcher very much, but be aware that conflicts can arise due to different, but equally valid, research orientations. For example, you may be proactive about a marketing study and resolute about an intuitive-based decision that you want the data to confirm quickly and at a relatively low cost; you expect no surprises. In contrast, your researcher may prefer to analyze and explore your business situation via research methods that cost you more time and money than you would prefer. Also, subsequent results may unveil aspects of your business that you didn't expect, leading to a reactive strategy adjustment.

Unfortunately, there's no magic solution to orientation-based conflict. If you've established a trusting relationship, trying to appreciate each other's perspectives is the only path to conflict resolution. It's also critical that you both remember the research benefactors: your business and its customers. Keeping these benefactors in mind should help minimize conflict between the two of you. But as married couples can attest, conflict at times is inevitable.

In Table 5-1, we list the main sources of potential conflict for you and your researcher. Try to anticipate these conflicts and resolve them before they can cause problems.

Table 5-1	**Potential Sources of Conflict between You and Your Researcher**
Your Orientation	*Your Researcher's Orientation*
Decision oriented	Technique oriented
Intuitive	Analytical
Want to confirm what you believe is true	Likes to explore
Time orientation: Need to know now and want to know about the future	Time orientation: Prefers to schedule work when convenient and wants to understand the past

(continued)

Table 5-1 *(continued)*

Your Orientation	Your Researcher's Orientation
Want to minimize costs	Believes you get what you pay for
Results orientation: Want certainty with no surprises	Results orientation: Loves surprises and prefers to speak abstractly about probabilities
Proactive	Reactive

High professional standards

Often, consultants overbook themselves; as a result, their rush to satisfy your deadline produces poor-quality research. Good researchers, on the other hand, won't overschedule themselves; as a result, they deliver sound and timely research. They're careful and conscientious. They also know that your expertise about your business environment can far exceed their own knowledge. To inform the research process, they try to acquire a sound understanding of that environment from you.

Good researchers avoid research with a covert purpose. For example, managers often solicit research in an effort to acquire evidence for already-made decisions. As we discuss in Chapter 1, it's a waste of time and money to conduct research for this purpose, and good researchers will refuse such projects.

Part II
Surveys: A Great Way to Research

The 5th Wave   By Rich Tennant

"Please answer the following survey questions about our company's performance with either, 'Excellent', 'Good', 'Fair', or 'I'm Really Incapable of Appreciating Someone Else's Hard Work.'"

In this part . . .

This part shows you how to put surveys to use in your marketing research plans. Chapter 6 presents you with different types of surveys and the relative strengths and weaknesses of each type, including online surveys. You also need to know how to avoid survey errors, which is covered in Chapter 7. Chapter 8 covers attitude research. Chapter 9 provides you with guidelines for writing good survey questions, and shows examples of poor or fixed questions. Designing good questionnaires, which we cover in Chapter 10, is vital to your survey success. And Chapters 11 and 12 tell you the best ways to settle on sample type and size.

Chapter 6

Different Types of Surveys You May Use

*W*hen appropriate, survey research provides an efficient and effective means for answering your research question. Obviously, there's no best method for collecting survey data; if one method dominated in all contexts, researchers would limit themselves to that method. In fact, each method has its own advantages and disadvantages, which make that method more or less suitable for a particular study.

Survey methods differ by the degree of person-to-person interaction. Face-to-face interviews — the most personal approach — typically are conducted at residences, offices, and shopping malls. Telephone interviews can be used to contact respondents at work or at home; and with cellphones, respondents can be reached while traveling. The ever-popular self-administered questionnaire — the least personal approach — can be delivered by conventional mail service or by evermore popular electronic means (via Web browser, e-mail, or interactive kiosk).

In this chapter, we summarize the different methods for collecting survey data and provide some detail about their relative advantages and disadvantages. We also give you tips on deciding which method to choose.

Conducting Face-to-Face Interviews

Although the classic door-to-door salesman — who sold products like encyclopedias and personal care items — has become an anachronism, using face-to-face personal interviewers remains an accepted way to collect survey data.

Respondents tend to relax when interviewed on their own turf — home or office — and thus tend to respond more fully and honestly.

In the following sections, we explain the general idea of face-to-face interviews and then delve in to intercept interviews.

Examining the general face-to-face setup

Face-to-face interviews typically are scheduled in advance, which establishes an interview completion date for a given study. Because the time needed to analyze interviewees' responses is reasonably predictable, you can anticipate accurately when you'll have study results.

The relative strengths of face-to-face interviews include the following:

✔ **They encourage respondent cooperation and discourage question nonresponse.** When respondents agree to participate in a face-to-face interview, they've committed their time to assist you. This time commitment tends to ensure genuine and thoughtful responses to your questions. This same commitment also reduces the likelihood that respondents will refuse to answer reasonable questions that are consistent with your stated research goals.

✔ **They permit versatile and extensive questioning.** With these interviews you spend more time with each respondent, so you can show visual materials — such as pictures, drawings, and videos — or demonstrate physical items like products. As a result, interviewers can explore consumer attitudes and preferences for alternative product configurations, packaging, advertising, and the like.

✔ **They produce high-quality data.** Miscomprehension is never impossible — as anyone who's attempted a serious conversation with a significant other can attest — but you'll often be able to spot when respondents fail to grasp a question. Because you can slowly repeat apparently misunderstood questions, respondents' misunderstandings are minimized. In reaction to superficial answers, you can ask probing questions that reveal deeply held attitudes and preferences along with seldom discussed behaviors.

Weaknesses of face-to-face interviews are:

✔ **They don't permit quick data collection.** Unless you have access to a well-trained staff of interviewers, you can't schedule and conduct lengthy face-to-face interviews overnight, especially if respondents are geographically dispersed. Given the need to drive between locations and the length of face-to-face interviews, an interviewer can complete only a few interviews per day with household members in a residential area — and even fewer interviews per day with business respondents in their offices. (If you've ever driven across a major U.S. city during a weekday, you know interviewer travel time is non-trivial.) Like Rome, a full complement of in-depth residential and office interviews can't be completed in a day.

✔ **Their need for skilled interviewers drives up costs.** As we discuss in Chapter 14, skilled interviewers require strong conversational skills; good face-to-face interviewers must be intelligent, articulate, and well trained. Such people must be compensated adequately for their time, which more than any other factor makes face-to-face interviewing the most expensive approach for collecting survey data.

✔ **They can be subject to response bias.** Despite confidentiality promises, respondents and their answers are known to interviewers. As a result, social desirability and other response biases (which we discuss more in Chapter 7) can degrade response quality. Notwithstanding extensive training, interviewers' subconscious body language and even the way they dress may sway responses into more conventional directions.

Performing intercept interviews

Surveying people in shopping malls is an all-too-familiar activity for many consumers. Yes, those annoying folks at the local mall with clipboards are conducting intercept interviews. Setting up an interview station near a facility's main entrance allows convenient access to a sample of visitors or customers. Your challenge is to get these people to stop and complete a ten-minute survey when their original reason for visiting the facility didn't include participating in your survey. To overcome reluctance to participate, you can offer monetary and other incentives as an enticement. For example, you can offer respondents a $5 gift card for the host shopping mall or local restaurant.

As fun as intercept interviews look for everyone involved, it's unlikely that you'll be allowed to intercept mall or store patrons without a mall security staff member asking you to leave. Research companies often purchase exclusive rights to interview mall patrons — and major retailers prefer that their customers spend time shopping rather than completing questionnaires from independent researchers. So, if you're interested in mall intercept interviews, you'll most likely need to hire the research company that's acquired the rights to conduct such interviews.

Although intercept interviews suffer from the same high potential for response bias as face-to-face interviews and high cost per completed interview, they also provide a method for collecting high-quality data, especially if physical items or special equipment are needed.

Here are strengths of intercept interviews:

✔ **They make relatively speedy data collection possible.** Assuming you have a popular location, multiple interviewers, and a reasonable-length questionnaire, you can complete hundreds of interviews in a few days.

✔ **They make versatile and extensive questioning possible.** As with face-to-face interviews in general, intercept interviews allow you to show visual materials or demonstrate physical items. In particular, they're especially well suited to testing foods and evaluating ads. The interactivity of such interviews can boost response rates and respondent interest in your study.

Weaknesses of intercept interviews include the following:

✔ **They're geographically inflexible.** Due to urban and local biases, your findings may not pertain to rural settings or distant regions. Relying on shoppers at a single local mall to help you test a regional or national marketing campaign is problematic.

✔ **Respondent cooperation is moderate at best.** Artifacts of this moderate cooperation level include limited questionnaire length and a higher number of incomplete interviews. Because most consumers visit malls to shop, they'll resist completing long and time-consuming questionnaires, which limits the number and types of questions you can ask each respondent. For example, respondents may ignore lengthy scenario-type questions; such questions typically require extensive reading and thought.

✔ **Callbacks or follow-ups are difficult.** Respondents may be reluctant to provide contact information (for fear of future solicitation), which limits your ability to verify answers later. Also, willingness to participate in an intercept interview is a momentary decision incompatible with the commitment required for participation in longitudinal studies (see Chapter 3 for more on longitudinal studies).

Conducting Telephone Surveys

Telephone surveys typically entail a call center with interviewers manning each telephone and a supervisor who randomly monitors interviews to ensure they're being conducted properly. National and state do-not-call lists notwithstanding, this method remains a popular one for collecting attitudinal, behavioral, and descriptive data. When questionnaire completion time is reasonable, this method is effective if you catch respondents at a time convenient to them.

Assuming you're administering your survey professionally — you aren't just paying your children's grade-school friends $5 per hour to interview people by telephone — questionnaire length is the predominant determinant of cost. Relative to a 50-item questionnaire, a 10-item questionnaire requires less time to administer, so interviewers will complete more interviews per hour. Because interviewer compensation is a major cost component — people tend to cost more than materials — shorter questionnaires cost less per completed response.

In the following sections, we explain the methods interviewers use in phone surveys, discuss the pros and cons of these surveys, and indicate a method for overcoming "as is" information found in telephone directories.

Reviewing the contemporary methods for conducting phone interviews

For telephone interviews, researchers rely on either paper-and-pencil or computer-assisted methods. Here's a quick breakdown of each:

- ✔ *Paper-and-pencil administration* means the interviewer reads through the interview and records the respondent's answers on paper. Eventually, those answers are entered into a computer file for data analysis. The additional data entry step — transferring written responses to a computer file — can introduce transcription errors, a type of administration error.

- ✔ *Computer-assisted administration* is a more accurate and somewhat more sophisticated approach. It differs from paper-and-pencil administration in that interviewers use a computer for survey administration and data recording. Because survey software can be programmed to ensure questions are asked in the proper order and only if appropriate (for example, skipping questions about pet food purchases for respondents without a pet), and also to avoid impossible answers (for example, accepting an answer of 6 on a 1-to-5 scale), administrative errors are minimized. (See Chapter 7 for more about administrative errors in survey research.)

Another way to conduct a telephone survey — one that we're sure you've experienced and come to dread — is the computerized and voice-activated interview. In essence, respondents speak to a machine, which is unlikely to garner thoughtful responses due to the interview's impersonal nature. Because we don't recommend this approach, we don't discuss it further.

Figure 6-1 contains a sample page from a telephone questionnaire, for a proposed study on spending priorities for a medium-sized city. You can see the complete questionnaire on the DVD. The survey, which was never fielded due to funding and political constraints, was meant to provide public input. (In Chapter 10, we provide more detail about the structure of this questionnaire.)

Community Attitude Questionnaire

Good evening. My name is _____ and I'm calling for the _____
_____ at _____ . We're conducting a survey about attitudes
towards_____ . You were scientifically chosen, so your answers—which
will be kept confidential—are important to the accuracy of our results. I shouldn't need
more than 15 minutes of your time. May I begin?

<Regardless of answer> Thank you.

<For cellular phone version only>
First, I'll need to ask you three qualifying question(s).

Do you have a land-line telephone in your residence?
_____ Yes <Terminate interview>
_____ No <Continue>

Is your residence in _____ ?
_____ Yes <Continue>
_____ No <Terminate interview>

Is your trash collected by _____ ? <Continue regardless of answer>
_____ Yes
_____ No

Wonderful! You're someone we want to interview. <pause> Now I'll read a series of
statements about _____ . For each statement, please say if you 'strongly
agree', 'agree', 'neither agree nor disagree', 'disagree', 'strongly disagree', or 'don't know'.
<Read list of choices again as needed.>

Statement	SA	A	NAD	D	SD	DK
Most residents have a strong sense of community	1	2	3	4	5	6
Decent housing is available for most residents	1	2	3	4	5	6
New subdivisions are being built in the right places	1	2	3	4	5	6
More low-income housing is needed	1	2	3	4	5	6
More middle-income housing is needed	1	2	3	4	5	6
Mixes of shops, restaurants, businesses, and residences within walking distance of each other should be encouraged	1	2	3	4	5	6
When near or at my home, I feel safe from crime	1	2	3	4	5	6
When at work, I feel safe from crime	1	2	3	4	5	6
Curbside pickup of recyclables is needed	1	2	3	4	5	6
More energy-efficient business buildings are needed	1	2	3	4	5	6
More energy-efficient residences are needed	1	2	3	4	5	6
Preserving open space is important	1	2	3	4	5	6
Local government does a good job promoting economic growth	1	2	3	4	5	6
Generally, the local workforce is well trained	1	2	3	4	5	6
Generally, wages and salaries are adequate	1	2	3	4	5	6
Working with _____ businesses should be encouraged	1	2	3	4	5	6
Working with _____ businesses should be encouraged	1	2	3	4	5	6

Figure 6-1:
Sample
page from
a telephone
question-
naire.

Reviewing the pros and cons

Strengths of telephone interviews include the following:

- ✔ **They allow speedy data collection.** Because you can use a professional data-collection service — with a bank of phones and interviewers — it's possible to collect data from hundreds of respondents in a few days.

- ✔ **They encourage respondent cooperation and discourage question non-response.** A friendly caller's voice can encourage cooperation. Although the interviewer knows the respondent's identity, telephone interviews are less personal than face-to-face interviews; thus, respondents may answer more honestly because they're unseen by the interviewer. Participant callback verification (to certify the interviewer's legitimacy) and caller ID reduce the threat of fake studies meant to collect personal data for fraudulent purposes.

- ✔ **They simplify fieldwork and interviewer supervision, especially if adapted to computer technology.** Computer-assisted telephone interviewing uses interactive computer software to gather data. Once programmed for a particular study, the software will display the correct question — based on the questionnaire and each respondent's previous answers — to ask in the proper sequence; the interviewer merely needs to read each question as displayed and enter the respondent's answer.

    Because it's automated, such software minimizes inappropriate question asking (due to errors in following question skipping and branching dictated by previous answers), data entry errors (by validating data as they're entered), interviewer training costs, and interviewer monitoring costs. The software easily can personalize complex questionnaires (based on respondents' profiles and previous answers) and suggest more standardized probing questions (which we discuss more in Chapter 7).

Weaknesses of telephone interviews are:

- ✔ **They offer only moderate questioning versatility.** Unless you've scheduled a longer interview in advance, you can't hold people on the telephone for more than 20 minutes. Also, the need to read questions and all possible answers (for close-ended questions) means it's difficult to ask complex questions. Certain response tasks, like responding to visuals, are impossible.

- ✔ **They can be subject to response bias.** Despite confidentiality promises, respondents and their answers are known to interviewers. As a result, response biases (which we discuss more in Chapter 7) can degrade response quality. Notwithstanding extensive training, interviewers' subconscious voice artifacts (like uhhs, ums, and long pauses) may sway responses into more conventional directions.

Noting the problems with telephone directories

Roughly 10 percent of the numbers listed in a telephone directory won't work or will be incorrect because people have changed their residence, changed their phone number, now only own a cellphone, and so on. In addition, the demographics and socioeconomics of people who choose to be unlisted will differ from those people who choose to be listed. As a result, phonebooks or other telephone directories are biased sample frames of people who own telephones. (For more on sample frames, see Chapter 11.)

People who opt to add their phone number to a do-not-call list are research-resistant, and likely will be annoyed if contacted by other means, such as e-mail or doorbell. Thus, it's appropriate and ethically sound to bypass such people. Persistent attempts to contact them will inflate your data-collection costs and produce negative word-of-mouth (spread virally through friends, family, and social media) about your research and company.

An ever-larger proportion of households are unlisted in telephone directories. Nationally, that proportion is roughly 30 percent, but in many cities the unlisted rate is more than 50 percent. That rate is especially high in California, with many cities having a rate greater than 50 percent. For example, roughly 60 percent of households have an unlisted number.

Why the big fuss about unlisted households? The problem is that listed and unlisted households differ from one another. Households with older heads are more likely to be listed. More than 50 percent of households with a person between the ages of 18 and 34 are unlisted, whereas roughly 40 percent of households with a person between the ages of 35 and 54 are unlisted. Among people who moved in the past two years, roughly 60 percent chose not to list their numbers. Unlisted households disproportionally tend to be unmarried persons and renters. Thus, raw telephone directories are unacceptable sample frames for telephone interviews.

Categorizing Self-Administered, Paper-and-Pencil Surveys

Self-administered questionnaires — the types that people complete without a live interviewer — come in many forms, including paper-and-pencil and electronic. Paper-and-pencil questionnaires can be delivered by mail or dropped off for retrieval at a scheduled time. The latter approach is common in international research because many people outside the United States are reluctant to respond to questionnaires unless there's a visible research sponsor. Paper questionnaires also can be delivered as magazine or newspaper inserts or as faxes.

Alternatively, self-administered questionnaires can be delivered electronically via e-mail, a Web site, or an interactive kiosk in a place like a shopping mall.

The wide range of approaches to self-administered questionnaires is shown in Figure 6-2.

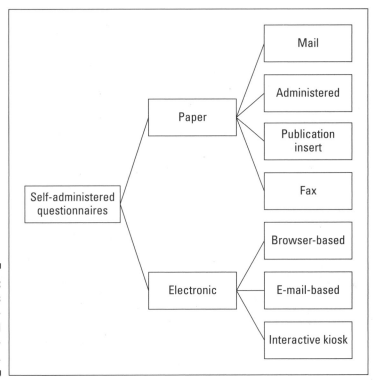

Figure 6-2: Types of self-administered questionnaires.

Your main choice is whether to use paper or electronic methods to capture self-administered questionnaire data. Depending on your research question, available resources, and timeliness needs, some options are superior to others. For example, it's cheaper and faster to survey many respondents with electronic methods. However, respondents tend to provide more thoughtful answers to a long for otherwise identical paper-and-pencil versus online questionnaire (because they're more likely to pause as needed, believe reading a paper document is less tiring than reading an electronic document, and so on).

Figure 6-3 contains a sample page from a self-administered questionnaire intended — but never used — for a survey to a state university improve attendance at its intercollegiate sporting events. You can see the entire questionnaire on this book's DVD. Because the questionnaire was meant for pre-event completion by event attendees, brevity was critical. In this context, attendees' patience for completing questionnaires would be minimal.

Questionnaire: _____ University Intercollegiate Athletics

Unless instructed otherwise, please circle the number next to your answer.

Q#1   On average, how many _____ **football** games did you attend each year **that you were a** _____ **student?**

Never attended a game
while a _____ student 1   1 to 2 games 3

                                                                          3 to 4 games 4

Less than 1 game 2   More than 4 games 5

Q#2   How many _____ **football** games have you attended **since you graduated from** _____ **?**

0 games 1   11 to 20 games 4

1 to 5 games 2   More than 20 games 5

6 to 10 games 3

Q#3   How many _____ **Homecoming Weekend football** games have you attended **since you graduated from** _____ **?**

0 games 1   11 to 20 games 4

1 to 5 games 2   More than 20 games 5

6 to 10 games 3

Q#4   How many _____ **football** games have you attended **with friends or family** since you graduated from _____**?**

0 games 1   11 to 20 games 4

1 to 5 games 2   More than 20 games 5

6 to 10 games 3

Q#5   How many _____ **basketball** games did you attend **when you were a** _____ **student?**

0 games 1   11 to 20 games 4

1 to 5 games 2   More than 20 games 5

6 to 10 games 3

Q#6   How many _____ **basketball** games have you attended **since you graduated from** _____**?**

0 games 1   11 to 20 games 4

1 to 5 games 2   More than 20 games 5

6 to 10 games 3

Figure 6-3:
Sample
page from
a self-
administered
question-
naire.

In the following sections, we introduce and offer advantages and disadvantages of mail and administered surveys. The former includes cross-sectional studies and mail panels; the latter includes publication inserts and fax surveys.

Mail surveys

Mail surveys come in two forms. In the *one-shot survey* (also known as a *cross-sectional survey*), potential respondents receive a questionnaire with a cover letter in the mail and are asked to respond to that single questionnaire. Alternatively — and we've personally participated in several such studies for the experience — respondents can join a *mail panel,* in which case they receive mail surveys on a routine basis.

Strengths of mail surveys include the following:

- ✔ **The questionnaire can be lengthy if you use proper procedures and incentives.** Because respondents can complete a mail questionnaire at their convenience and over multiple sessions, it can be longer than other types of questionnaires. Of course, respondents are unlikely to volunteer extensive time and effort to completing a questionnaire if they aren't compensated amply.

- ✔ **Because interviewers aren't present, interviewer-induced response bias isn't a concern.** Because their replies can be anonymous — and they may doubt a face-to-face or telephone interviewer's promise of confidentiality — respondents are more likely to answer personal and controversial questions extensively and truthfully.

- ✔ **It's a low cost method, especially if you're conducting a national survey.** First-class postage is the same regardless of distance. Hence, a national mail survey can be fielded at the same cost as a local mail survey. If you're mindful of weight when designing your questionnaire-related materials (such as the cover letter and stamped return envelop; see Chapter 10), it's possible to limit the outbound envelope to less than 2 ounces and the inbound envelope to less than 1 ounce. Even with rapidly increasing postal rates, that's still a data-collection bargain!

  Of course, you have to factor in more than postage costs. The direct expenses for creating a self-administered mail survey include planner salary, preparation costs for materials (like layout and photography), printing costs (for cover letters, questionnaires, and envelopes), mailing preparation costs (for folding, collating, stapling, inserting, addressing, and sorting), and premiums (which can be a pencil or a promise to provide a summary of the results). The indirect expenses include office space, office supplies, secretarial assistance, and utilities. In essence, low cost doesn't mean "no" cost.

Here are some weaknesses of mail surveys:

- ✔ **They don't permit quick data collection.** You can indicate clear deadlines for questionnaire return (and request questionnaire completion and return prior to those deadlines), but the multi-mailing procedure characteristic of mail-based surveys (see Chapter 7 for discussion of these procedures) means that you'll measure data-collection time in months rather than days or weeks.

- ✔ **They lack immediate human oversight, which can compromise data quality.** Poorly designed questionnaires will have low response rates, and people who choose to participate in your survey may answer questions selectively. Also, the potential for respondent errors is meaningful, especially in following your instructions for skipping questions that don't pertain to the respondent.

- ✔ **They preclude questioning versatility.** The highly standardized format can lead respondents to answer quickly or become bored with the process, resulting in poor-quality data, especially if you include many scaled questions. (Refer to Chapters 8 and 9 for more on scaled questions.)

Administered surveys

Administered surveys differ in the way that questionnaires are distributed to respondents. Typically, such surveys require managerial assistance. A researcher uses a company's managers to distribute and subsequently collect questionnaires from their employees. In essence, researchers use managers as highly persuasive solicitors. Because respondents receive the same questions in the same order, their answers can be aggregated and meaningful subgroup comparisons can be made either within or between time periods. Administered surveys are popular for studying employees within a single major corporation; for example, to assess their attitudes about customers. Although useful for studying a large sales force, administered surveys rarely are used in consumer research. Thus, you're unlikely to field an administered survey.

Publication inserts and fax surveys

Although you can use publication inserts and faxes to collect survey data, we recommend that you use other means. Publication inserts are ineffective because they're expensive and often yield biased samples. However, they can be useful for preliminary studies of hard-to-identify-and-access populations, such as spelunkers who subscribe to *Spelunker Today!* magazine. Fax technology is old, relatively expensive, and awkward; it has been superseded by other electronic delivery technologies. Both insert questionnaires and unsolicited faxes may be mistaken for junk material or may go unnoticed.

Opting for Self-Administered, Electronic Surveys

The questionnaire sample page shown in Figure 6-4 reveal some of the advantages of self-administered, electronic surveys. For example, radio buttons make it easy to answer attitude questions. Also, color can be used in browser-based surveys to improve both aesthetics and readability. To see the questionnaire in its entirety, please refer to the DVD.

In the following sections, we explore collecting survey data through Internet browsers, e-mails, and interactive kiosks. We discuss advantages and disadvantages of these data-collection techniques and present drawbacks of using Internet samples. Although you can use paper-and-pencil surveys to measure similar constructs and therefore answer comparable research questions (see the previous section "Categorizing Self-Administered, Paper-and-Pencil Surveys"), the digital-technology approaches discussed in this section greatly facilitate data collection.

Browser-based surveys

Browser-based surveys are self-administered questionnaires posted on a Web site. As with all self-administered surveys, you won't create any interviewer bias, you don't need interviewer supervision, and maintaining respondent anonymity is optional. (Asking respondents for contact information is unnecessary.) Respondents provide answers to questions that are displayed online by clicking on radio buttons, clicking on pull-down menus, or keying in answers.

Strengths of browser-based surveys include the following:

- ✔ **They permit speedy data collection.** After you click the Send button on your e-mail invitation, potential respondents should receive that invitation within minutes. You'll likely receive completed questionnaires within hours. Response time depends entirely on respondents; essentially, transmission time is trivial.

- ✔ **They're visually appealing and interactive.** As YouTube and most commercial Web sites clearly show, browser delivery permits sophisticated graphics and streaming media. Although pull-down menus and radio buttons can be considered graphics, the major benefit is the possibility of exposing respondents to product demonstrations (which for new products would be superior to detailed written descriptions) and alternative commercials you may run.

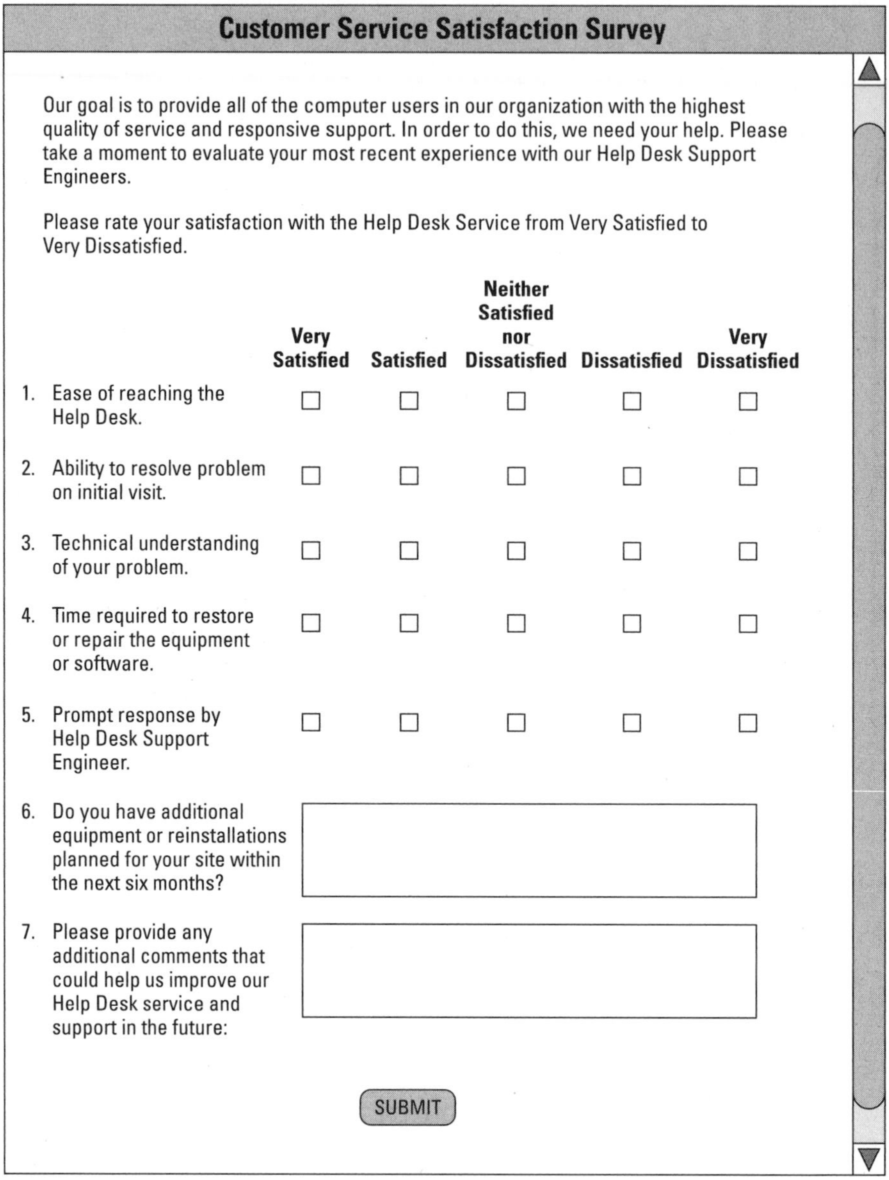

Customer Service Satisfaction Survey

Our goal is to provide all of the computer users in our organization with the highest quality of service and responsive support. In order to do this, we need your help. Please take a moment to evaluate your most recent experience with our Help Desk Support Engineers.

Please rate your satisfaction with the Help Desk Service from Very Satisfied to Very Dissatisfied.

	Very Satisfied	Satisfied	Neither Satisfied nor Dissatisfied	Dissatisfied	Very Dissatisfied
1. Ease of reaching the Help Desk.	☐	☐	☐	☐	☐
2. Ability to resolve problem on initial visit.	☐	☐	☐	☐	☐
3. Technical understanding of your problem.	☐	☐	☐	☐	☐
4. Time required to restore or repair the equipment or software.	☐	☐	☐	☐	☐
5. Prompt response by Help Desk Support Engineer.	☐	☐	☐	☐	☐

6. Do you have additional equipment or reinstallations planned for your site within the next six months?

7. Please provide any additional comments that could help us improve our Help Desk service and support in the future:

SUBMIT

Figure 6-4:
Typical appearance of a self-administered, electronic survey.

✔ **They provide powerful software infrastructure.** Because HTML and XML (two popular Internet languages) provide flexible software for creating questionnaires, you can present questions in a broad range of formats. As anyone who's left a field blank in an online application knows, the Internet software you choose can check that each field contains appropriate characters, thus minimizing question nonresponse. Finally, software can ensure that respondents receive appropriately customized questionnaires based on their profiles and previous responses; in particular, question skipping and branching dictated by previous answers can be followed flawlessly.

- ✔ **They have cheaper distribution and processing costs.** Pushing electrons around fiber-optic networks is far cheaper than sending multiple sheets of paper — possibly worldwide — through mail-delivery services. In addition, responses are returned as electronic files, which can reduce processing costs (by permitting automated data entry) and backup ease (by permitting duplication on multiple media in different locations).

Here are weaknesses of browser-based surveys:

- ✔ **The odds that respondents misinterpret some questions or misunderstand some instructions are far from zero.** Despite your best efforts to design a clear questionnaire, respondents may misinterpret some of your instructions and questions. Without an interviewer present to sense such confusion, it's likely you'll mistakenly include these meaningless responses in your data files and subsequent analyses.

- ✔ **Respondent cooperation varies if solicitation e-mail is seen as spam.** Spam filters are managed by Internet-service providers as well as by users' e-mail software. Depending on the restriction levels set at both levels, a solicitation e-mail may be identified as spam. Few people check their spam filters regularly for legitimate e-mails; as a result, many potential recipients may never see your solicitation.

  Many people maintain alternative e-mail addresses: one for chatting with close friends and family, one for conducting business, and one for commerce-related communications that are more likely to induce subsequent spam. If you send your solicitation to the third address category, it's more likely to be ignored as spam regardless of its merits.

  Finally, many people are overwhelmed by the quantity of e-mail they receive daily. To manage their e-mail deluge, they delete all messages from unknown parties automatically. In this case, the faulty spam filter is a human being.

- ✔ **Recontacting or following up with respondents is difficult.** Unless respondents submit their e-mail addresses with their questionnaires, it's impossible to know who to recontact or send follow-up questions to. As the seeming anonymity of the Web appeals to many respondents, urging them to identify themselves reduces response rates markedly.

  Some browser-based systems record IP addresses (the PCs Internet address), so it's possible to determine whether multiple responses were sent from the same PC. (Although multiple parties could have responded once from the same PC, it's best to assume that the same person responded repeatedly, and all but the first response should be deleted.)

- ✔ **They lack sample representativeness.** More than any other type of survey, browser-based surveys are subject to self-selection bias. In other words, people who "opt in" typically are far more enthusiastic about the topic in question, far more willing to provide their opinions, and far more likely to complete the questionnaire. (See Chapter 7 for more on self-selection bias.) Because some people lack Internet access, browser-based surveys tend to rely on relatively nonrepresentative samples of the population. A person without such access can't, by definition, respond to a browser-based survey.

Even for people with a PC and Internet access, limited PC power and computer sophistication can pose problems. If, for example, you want to test alternative ad executions, and those ads are either radio or television commercials, respondents must be able to receive streaming media content. For potential respondents with a primitive PC and narrow-band 56K modem, streaming video is problematic. In fact, it's likely that the software needed to view streaming media won't be installed on older PCs. Thus, people who use an older PC may avoid solicitations to participate in browser-based surveys.

To boost your cooperation rate, which is a more ethical approach than spamming, you can send potential respondents a query e-mail asking them to opt into your study. If they do, you can then send them an e-mail with specific instructions or a URL to visit.

E-mail-based surveys

Browser-based surveys require proactive respondents who will accept an invitation to participate and subsequently log on to a Web site. In contrast, e-mail surveys merely require reactive participants who will answer the questions posed in your e-mail (or your word-processed attachment) and return them to you.

Because they're both electronic self-administered data-collection technologies, browser-based and e-mail-based surveys share many relative strengths and weaknesses. One advantage specific to e-mail surveys is they can be sent and returned quickly. All that's needed are a potential respondent's e-mail address, a brief introduction to your survey, a questionnaire, and a process for entering them into an e-mail program. Most respondents will answer within a few days because fewer steps are required — relative to browser-based surveys — to respond.

However, you should consider these weaknesses of e-mail-based surveys:

  ✓ **They limit the types of questions and layouts you can use.** Extensive differences in the capabilities of respondents' PCs, Internet service providers, and e-mail software limit the types of questions and questionnaire layouts you can use. Some e-mail software can't handle complex graphics and attachments well. Some Internet service providers severely limit the sizes and types of files that can be sent as attachments. Even for e-mail surveys, PCs can struggle if bandwidth and monitor resolution are limited.

✔ **E-mails aren't secure, so hacking can occur.** Unlike browser-based interactions, which can be safeguarded through well-established encryption procedures, most e-mail correspondence is unencrypted. (Yes, you can find public encryption software, but few people use it, especially for mundane communications like surveys.) As a result, identity thieves can lift the personal information they need to ply their trade.

✔ **People are reluctant to open e-mail attachments from unknown sources.** Hackers can embed spyware, viruses, Trojan horses, and other malware into e-mail attachments. All that's necessary to install and activate such maleficent software is to open the attachment. As a result, most people won't open attachments accompanying unsolicited e-mails.

Interactive kiosks

Comparable to but far more technologically sophisticated than an electronic voting booth, an interactive kiosk provides a unique arena for capturing data. It can be set up near a facility's main entrance or in a central location. Data are captured via computer; this technological aspect of the process may prove appealing to potential respondents.

As with other electronic data-collection procedures, automated data collection minimizes human error and maximizes respondents' sense of anonymity. As with other self-administered survey techniques, self-selection bias can create a nonrepresentative respondent sample. Other relative strengths and weaknesses are explained in the following lists.

Here are strengths of interactive kiosks:

✔ **They're novel to most potential respondents.** The current novelty of this data-collection approach may pique the interest of respondents who otherwise would ignore the opportunity to participate in your study. The increased participation speeds data collection.

✔ **They provide nonaggressive solicitation.** Other forms of data collection require active solicitation of respondents through telephone, conventional mail, and e-mail requests. In contrast, participation in a kiosk-based study is entirely respondent motivated.

✔ **They allow on-the-fly data analysis.** Although you can conduct a pilot study, most self-administered questionnaires are created, distributed, and eventually returned for analysis (at least some percentage of them). As a result, you can't fix faulty or omitted questions spotted from early returns. In contrast, kiosks linked to the Internet can transmit responses immediately for analysis. If those responses suggest questionnaire modifications, you can make the necessary changes and upload a new and improved questionnaire for completion by subsequent respondents.

Weaknesses of kiosks include the following:

- ✔ **They're cumbersome to set up and break down.** Just as banquet rooms don't construct themselves (as Jeremy can attest through his hospitality industry work experience), the kiosk materials (for example, walls, chairs, technology) used for data collection will need to be delivered, set up, and hauled off, which can prove physically taxing. Also, venue operators — whose compliance must be obtained before installing a kiosk — typically are reluctant to offer floor space and disturb traffic patterns otherwise managed by careful facility design.

- ✔ **They're impersonal and unappealing.** After their curiosity about kiosk-based surveys has been satisfied, respondents may begin to shy away from them because they're impersonal and unappealing. As a result, it may become increasingly difficult to attract respondents without a very appealing incentive; so expenses related to the kiosk and data collection may end up exceeding your research budget.

Internet samples

You use *Internet sampling* when you want to collect data via the Internet; as such, it's considered unique among the ways to collect survey data. Internet surveys allow researchers to access a large sample rapidly and inexpensively, often through panels in which respondents are compensated for study participation. People need an adequate window of opportunity to participate in an online survey, so you must keep it open long enough for all solicited persons to have participated.

Depending on the technology for accessing respondents, Internet-based samples can be probability or nonprobability samples. Chapter 11 contains a detailed discussion about these different sample types.

We've conducted studies in which we've surveyed marketing professors in the United States. To do so, we first acquired a list of professors and their e-mail addresses from a publisher of this information. Next, we asked student volunteers to visit each university's marketing department Web page and find contact information for professors omitted from that list. Ultimately, we created our own list of 4,000 valid faculty e-mail addresses. Then, we sent an e-mail to the professors asking them to participate in our study. This type of sample frame (see Chapter 11) represents as a probability sample.

You can randomly select visitors to a Web site — who would comprise a convenience sample — via some pop-up technology that solicited a randomly selected person to opt into your survey. This type of sample is nonscientific because more frequent visitors would be overrepresented. Alternatively, you can identify a listserv or panel whose members would be qualified to participate in your study and make an appeal there. This process doesn't represent taking a census or a scientific sample because there's no list of population elements.

Although online surveys tend to rely on nonscientific opt-in samples, Internet samples may still be representative of a target population and allow you to access hard-to-reach respondents.

Logging Behaviors with Diary Panels

Diary panels consist of people who agree willingly to document their behavior longitudinally; these panels allow households to report their buying or media behaviors over a designated time. The two types of panels are purchase panels and media panels. The former pertains to purchase habits, and the latter pertains to media reading, viewing, and listening habits.

The benefit of a panel is that the same respondents complete diaries on a regular schedule, so it's possible to track changes in households' purchases or other marketing-related behaviors over time.

Panel samples comprise people who agree to participate in a study on a continuing basis. These people are compensated for their time either by having their names entered into a sweepstakes or by giving them small cash incentives for continued participation.

In the following sections, we discuss advantages and disadvantages of diary panels, pose questions that are answerable with diary panel data, and provide a sample diary page that shows the difficulty panelists may have in providing accurate data.

Strengths and weaknesses of diary panels

Strengths of diary panels include high response rates, efficient nominal data (see Chapter 18) collection, and vast response databases. Weaknesses include reliance on nonprobability samples, use of nonrepresentative samples, and potential response biases, to name a few. We now delve in to these advantages and disadvantages.

Here are strengths of diary panels:

- ✔ **They have high response rates.** Because panel respondents volunteer to participate in panel research, they're likely to respond to all questions; after all, they're being compensated! This limits the amount of missing data and increases the efficiency of the data-collection process.

- ✔ **They require you to collect demographic and socioeconomic data only once.** This is possible because you can chart the response track record of a given panel member. After respondents participate in an initial study, you can match their responses to their demographic and socioeconomic data for subsequently completed questionnaires.

- ✔ **They generate huge databases of responses.** This rich database allows you to assess subsamples based on demographics, lifestyles, product ownership, or other characteristics.

Weaknesses of diary panels include the following:

- ✔ **They rely on nonprobability samples.** Although research companies try to control the composition of their panel participants so they match the population on key demographic and socioeconomic characteristics, panel samples may be problematic because people who choose to participate in panels aren't representative of the general public.

- ✔ **People who choose to remain panelists tend to differ from most people.** For example, these folks enjoy compulsively recording all their household's purchases, so they must be "unusual." Given the idiosyncrasies of people who choose to continue as panelists, if diary panel companies aren't careful, their panel will become increasingly less representative of the general population. Therefore, it's necessary occasionally to retire some of the most diligent panelists.

- ✔ **They have high dropout rates.** Although many people agree to participate as diary panelists, they quickly decide, after completing detailed diaries several times, that it's not worth the effort. As a result, there's a high dropout rate. This dropout rate is problematic because it's impossible to track a household that vacates a panel.

- ✔ **Certain groups are underrepresented.** Although the companies that collect this data weight their samples appropriately when publishing results, minorities and lesser-educated people are underrepresented relative to their natural propensity in the general population. For this reason, panel data may be weak for tracking changes in such groups.

- ✔ **They create response bias.** People who know they're being observed tend to behave differently. For example, it's likely that people participating in a media panel will forget that they watched a *Gilligan's Island* or

Beverly Hillbillies rerun, but they'll always remember that they watched *Nova* or *Masterpiece Theater* on PBS. (We explain media panels earlier in the chapter.)

General recording errors will be commonplace with diary panels. It's a nuisance to make diary entries, so people often wait until the next day or later — when it's more convenient — to complete their diary entries for the previous days' reading, viewing, listening, or buying behaviors. As a result, they may misremember (a new word invented by the ex-pitcher Roger Clemens) the channel, the times, the programs, and so on.

✔ **It can be difficult to track rare behaviors.** Unless you have access to a large panel, sample size may be insufficient for tracking somewhat rarer behaviors, like buying pickled pigs' feet or listening to radio stations that play only classical music.

Questions answerable with diary panel data

Diary panel data can indicate both trial (buying something the first time) and repeat purchases. Although interested in trial purchases — after all, subsequent sales require a first sale — manufacturers are far more interested in repeat purchase rate because little profit is derived from one-time purchasers. People who try something but decide they don't like it won't account for many sales over time. In contrast, repeat buyers account for the lion's share of sales and profits.

You can use diary panel data to answer research questions about customer brand loyalty, customer demographics, and promotional strategies. Here are some examples on how diary panel data can be used to answer certain types of research questions:

✔ **Question 1: How loyal are your brand's buyers relative to your main competitors' buyers?** Purchase panel diaries track what people bought over multiple purchase occasions, so it's possible to determine the percent of panel households that bought your brand zero, one, two, and three times on the last three occasions. (We discuss purchase panel diaries earlier in the chapter.) For this reason, it's possible to determine the percent of households that buy each brand more and less frequently. If your competitors' customers are relatively more brand loyal — in the behavioral sense that they buy more repeatedly from a given competitor — you'd want to extend usage among existing buyers.

Your marketing options in this effort include in- or on-pack coupons, in-pack contests, and premiums in return for several proof-of-purchase seals.

✔ **Question 2: Are you and your competitors getting the same share of high-income customers?** As panelists provide their income when completing the initial profile questionnaire, you can compare the income profiles of your customers to the income profiles of your competitors' customers. If your share of high-income customers is meaningfully smaller than your competitors' share, and high-income customers represent a key market segment for your product, then you may refocus or revamp your advertising to reach those customers.

✔ **Question 3: Should you promote your brand with a coupon or a free sample?** Coupons are costly to manufacturers in terms of placement (because newspapers don't run coupons free of charge), redemption (because money is returned to consumers), and handling (because retailers and clearinghouses require compensation). Despite their expense, coupons are far less costly than distributing free samples.

Given the relative costs and efficiencies of each promotion, which promotional effort is best for your brand? To answer this question, you can run an experiment (see Chapter 16). In each of three different markets, you would provide panelists with a coupon, a free sample, or nothing. Then you'd use regularly collected panel data to reveal repeat purchase rates in those three markets over time. The best promotional scheme would generate the largest net increase in profits.

A sample diary page

Figure 6-5 consists of a single-day page from a radio-listening diary. At first blush, this page looks easy to complete. However, when you consider the difficulties associated with responding accurately, you'll realize the problems this diary page poses to respondents. Specifically, the diary requires panelists to indicate the time of day they started and stopped listening, the stations to which they listened, and where they were while they listened. Given people's propensities to channel surf (especially in the car), such record-keeping may be of dubious accuracy.

Also, it's easy to imagine how panelists would cope with the burden of maintaining a daily listening diary. Rather than record their listening behaviors as they occur, panelists would likely reconstruct during the weekend what they listened to throughout the week. As a result, this data may be less accurate than desired.

Wednesday										
Time			**Station**			**Place**				
			Call letters or station name Don't know? Use program name or dial setting.	(✓) Check one		(✓) Check one				
	Start	Stop		AM	FM	At home	In a car	At work	Other place	
➡ Early morning (from 5am)										
➡ Midday										
➡ Late afternoon										
➡ Night (to 5am Thursday)										

Figure 6-5: Page from radio-listening diary.

☐ If you didn't hear the radio today, please check here.

Factors to Consider When Choosing a Data-Collection Method

Although it may seem like an easy decision, selecting the best data-collection method for your research can be complex. For example, you need to consider factors such as your research questions, data timeliness, questionnaire complexity, sample makeup, data quantity, and respondent interest. We explore such topics in this section.

Here are some questions you should consider when choosing a data-collection method:

- ✔ **What's your available budget?** Personal interviews, for example, are far more expensive per completed interview than self-administered mail or online surveys. If your budget is limited, you may need to steer away from personal interviews.

- ✔ **How quickly do you need the data?** Turnaround time for telephone interviews, as you may recall from recent political elections, can be relatively quick — sometimes 24 hours or less. Alternatively, a self-administered mail questionnaire, with repeated waves of alerts, reminders, and questionnaire mailings, can require several months. (See Chapter 7 for more details about this multi-mailing procedure.)

  Of course, a quick batch of telephone interviews means a short set of questions administered by a field service with extensive telephone capabilities. If you're thinking about administering a questionnaire that takes 20 minutes to complete with a couple of college kids who need a few extra dollars and can use the phones in your back room (when available), you're looking at weeks rather than days of data collecting. In essence, you can complete a series of telephone interviews quickly if your information needs are limited or your data-collection budget is sufficient to cover a field service charging a premium for quick turnaround.

- ✔ **How complex is the structure or length of your questionnaire?** In today's time-starved, ADHD-impinged world, telephone questionnaires must be limited to 10 to 15 minutes unless you contacted the respondent beforehand and scheduled a time for a subsequent, far longer, telephone call. In contrast, self-administered mail or online questionnaires can be far more complex and include many more questions. The self-scheduling convenience of self-administered questionnaires, along with their visually rich delivery mechanisms, make them more suitable for such data-collection efforts.

- ✔ **Is it necessary to expose respondents to stimuli — for example, a test ad or a new-and-improved version of a soft drink?** If so, telephone interviewing isn't an option, but online (for testing ad copy) or personal (for taste testing a soft drink) data-collection procedures should work well. Online respondents with a reasonably powered PC and Internet connection easily can preview and respond to test commercials.

- ✔ **How important is collecting a representative sample?** Different data-collection methods lend themselves to greater or lesser sampling precision (which we discuss more in Chapter 11). Precision in this case means that the person you meant to respond to your questionnaire did, in fact, respond to it. If sampling precision is important, self-administered mail questionnaires are a poor choice; personal interviews, on the other hand, are an excellent option.

For example, if a publisher of marketing research textbooks mailed a questionnaire to the heads of various university marketing departments and asked them to forward it to a faculty member who teaches marketing research, any number of instructors may receive it because several instructors typically teach marketing research at most universities. Alternatively, the publisher may, due to dated public information about the teaching assignments of university faculty, send the questionnaire to someone who rarely teaches marketing research. Either way, the returned questionnaire would reveal little about current instructors' preferences for marketing research textbooks.

✔ **How important are data quality and quantity?** Personal interviews tend to produce the highest-quality data because interviewers can use thoughtful follow-up probing questions to ensure that respondents' answers are as complete as possible. In contrast, self-administered questionnaires produce data of lower quality.

✔ **Will respondents be interested in the topic?** If respondents are highly motivated, they'll respond thoughtfully to self-administered mail or online questionnaires. If, on the other hand, the topic is of lesser interest, strong encouragement may be necessary to get your questions answered. In this case, a personal or telephone interview may be more suitable.

✔ **Is obtaining respondent cooperation an issue?** For example, asking salespeople to complete a questionnaire or interview about unethical sales practices at their company may require an introductory statement followed by their signature of consent to participate in the survey. Using a manager to distribute a questionnaire about this topic is one way to increase respondent cooperation. (See our earlier discussion on "Administered surveys.")

Also, if the people you're trying to sample are less than 18 years of age, parental consent may be needed. This extra layer of consent may impede the data-collection process.

✔ **Is incidence rate an issue?** If a small percent of the population is qualified to respond, finding a sufficient and representative sample may prove difficult. For example, a hardware store owner who wants to survey recent purchasers of household paint may find that only 1 or 2 percent of people contacted bought such paint in the last 12 months. In such cases, a self-administered mail survey is less suitable than a telephone survey because the latter permits snowball sampling. (See Chapter 11 for more on such samples.)

Understanding the Problems with Commercial Lists

Although spamming and other junk electronic communications seem more worrisome now, being on a mailing list and receiving junk mail continues to annoy most people. Many commercially available lists used in applied marketing research started as standard mailing lists.

Commercial lists for rare or unusual populations abound. For example, you can find lists of affluent households, college department heads, exterminators, junk dealers, morticians, rabbis, taxidermists, and yacht owners. However, such lists tend to be problematic in the following three ways:

- **Representativeness:** *Representativeness* entails a predisposition to include or exclude certain members of a population. For example, telephone directories and mailing lists tend to exclude college students and military personnel because they change residences frequently.

- **Omissions and duplications:** *Omissions* are people who would qualify for the survey but aren't listed (such as those with unlisted telephone numbers and addresses), and *duplications* are people who are listed more than once (such as professionals and physicians with an office and home telephone number). Multiple listings mean that some people are more likely than other people to be surveyed, and these respondents will differ systematically from the general population. (Refer to the earlier section "Noting the problems with telephone directories" for more on how listed and unlisted populations differ.)

- **Recency:** *Recency* relates to dated lists with members who no longer qualify (such as physician lists that include recently retired physicians) or who are linked to old contact information. This problem has a reverse side: Commercial lists also tend to exclude recent additions to a population. In other words, it's likely that a list of million-dollar yacht owners still includes Bernie Madoff (despite his incarceration for fraud) but unlikely that a list of affluent households includes the latest Powerball lottery winners!

Chapter 7

Recognizing Errors in Survey Research

As with measurement error in general, sampling error should be minimized. *Sampling error* is created by the sampling process; it's the error that occurs when the sample drawn isn't representative of the population. Of course, you should consider the cost-to-benefit trade-off — for example, the cost of selecting a large sample or acquiring a more representative sample frame versus the increased accuracy of population estimates — when trying to reduce errors in survey research. (See Chapter 11 for more information on sample frames and populations estimates.) Even the U.S. government, with its seeming access to an infinite number of tax dollars, can't spend enough to collect perfect census data every ten years!

In a cost-to-benefit analysis, the three types of sampling errors to consider are random sampling error, systematic error, and nonresponse error. We discuss each of these in this chapter. We also delve in to administrative error and measurement issues, such as reliability, validity, generalizability, and scale sensitivity.

Respondent-Centric Survey Errors: Reviewing the Components

The main sources of error in surveys are random sampling error and systematic error. Random sampling error is, by definition, beyond your control. It's dictated by the luck of the draw, such as who in the population you selected or who you failed to select for participation in your study. In contrast, you can control systematic error to some extent. We cover the primary components of survey errors in more detail in the following sections.

Random sampling error

Random sampling error is the statistical fluctuation that occurs because of chance variation in the elements selected for the sample. If that definition makes your eyes glaze over, here's a simpler one to consider: Random sampling error is the difference between your sample results and the result of a census you conducted using identical sample selection procedures. It's probably obvious why such error is beyond your control: random means you don't influence which members of the population are chosen.

Given the nature of most marketing research samples, random sampling error should be minimal if you draw a sufficiently large sample. If you draw an insufficiently large sample, it's possible that your particular sample will be idiosyncratic in some way. (See Chapter 12 for more on the importance of sample size.)

You may believe that we're being overly dismissive of random sampling error. Here's why we believe otherwise: Thinking about typical errors in survey research, we contend that the procedure for selecting elements from a *sample frame* (the list of population members from which you'll draw a sample) introduces relatively little error — provided you have a sufficiently large sample. In fact, most survey research error is introduced by selecting the wrong sample frame or by *self-selection bias* (a nonrepresentative sample caused by greater or lesser participation in your survey by different categories of people, like males versus females or older versus younger customers).

As a result, we recommend that after you've identified an appropriate sample size you worry more about systematic error (discussed in the following section) than sampling error.

Systematic error

Systematic errors (also called *nonsampling errors*) are unrepresentative sampling results due to study design or execution flaws. For example, Figure 7-1 illustrates the problems associated with sample frame error. Circle D is ideal; the sample frame is complete and provides no sampling frame error. Circle C is acceptable; although incomplete, it's unbiased, which means certain types of population elements aren't excluded systematically. Because the frame is representative of the target population, any estimates made after sampling a sufficient number of elements should be reasonably accurate.

In contrast, Circles A and B represent problematic cases. The sampling frame in Circle A is incomplete, which means certain types of population elements are excluded systematically. As a result, the sample tends to overrepresent some population elements and underrepresent other population elements. Analyzing the data from this sample frame will produce biased estimates. Circle B is even worse; not only is the sample frame incomplete, but some listed entities aren't members of the target population. Circle B is the worst case scenario.

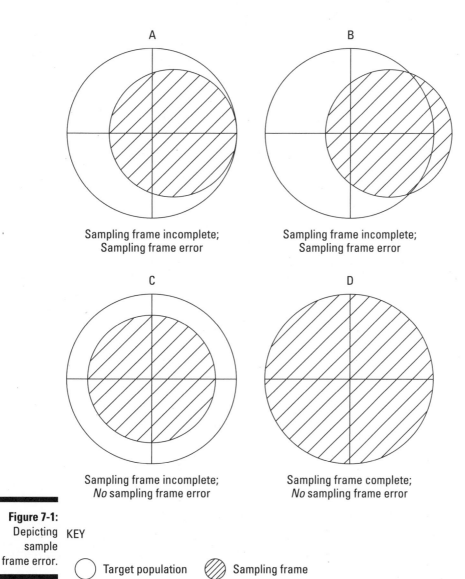

A

Sampling frame incomplete;
Sampling frame error

B

Sampling frame incomplete;
Sampling frame error

C

Sampling frame incomplete;
No sampling frame error

D

Sampling frame complete;
No sampling frame error

Figure 7-1:
Depicting
sample
frame error.

KEY

◯ Target population   ◲ Sampling frame

Understanding why respondents provide inaccurate information

Response bias occurs when respondents answer questions with a certain slant that consciously or unconsciously misrepresents the truth. Some respondents may choose to lie on a self-administered questionnaire (see Chapter 6) or during an interview (see Chapter 14): in contrast, other respondents may unknowingly provide inaccurate answers. Regardless of respondents' intentions, you're stuck with inaccurate data for analysis. In the following sections, we discuss ways respondents answer inaccurately.

Unwillingness to respond accurately (deliberate falsification)

A respondent's unwillingness to respond accurately to questions can be caused by many issues, including the following:

- ✔ **Invasion of privacy:** People may respond inaccurately because they're concerned about an invasion of their privacy. After all, they can't be certain how their responses will be used. Perhaps, for example, the IRS will compare their self-reported income to their tax return!

- ✔ **Time pressure and fatigue:** It's possible that respondents who are time pressured or fatigued will provide inaccurate answers. This problem may arise when you call someone in the evening or intercept a harried shopper who's been at the mall for several hours and is anxious to return home. It's also possible that respondents, who you've kept on the telephone for half an hour, are now fatigued or have other pressing matters to address. As a result, they'll be unwilling to answer your later questions as fully as your earlier questions.

- ✔ **Physical or social environment:** A respondent's social or physical environment may induce response errors. For example, if you ask a father with three screaming kids in the background (not that Mike's three young sons *ever* scream at each other), an excessive number of questions during a telephone interview, his responses may become increasingly curt or careless. Respondents in mall interviews may worry that their answers will be overheard by other mall patrons.

- ✔ **Questionnaire-specific issues:** The nature of the questionnaire — the way the questions are worded and how the questions are displayed — may induce an unwillingness to respond accurately. For example, questions with a seemingly liberal slant may anger politically conservative respondents. A polite response about a new government spending program is unlikely from Rush Limbaugh!

- ✔ **Mischievous respondents:** Mischievous respondents — people who, for whatever reason, decide to answer survey questions erroneously merely to foul up the research effort — may choose to answer inaccurately. We know from querying our marketing research students — who should be predisposed to respond otherwise because they're worried about their grades and impression management — that roughly 10 percent admit to responding mischievously at least once.

✔ **Social desirability bias:** *Social desirability bias* is caused by respondents' desire to gain prestige. (Although typically conscious, it also may be unconscious.) That desire may be triggered by self-enhancement needs or to impress other people (like interviewers and researchers). Here are two examples of what we mean by social desirability bias:

- **Example #1:** You can ask a college student to justify his recent purchase of an expensive automobile. Such a student doesn't have the salary or lifestyle to support that expenditure. Nonetheless, the student will try to justify that purchase to an interviewer. Rather than explaining that it was purchased on a whim or in an effort to impress friends, the student will offer bogus economic reasons — like "it gets great gas mileage"— for the purchase.

- **Example #2:** You can ask shoppers about their use of unit pricing information when buying groceries. Almost everyone recognizes that using pricing information, especially unit pricing information, should result in wiser shopping decisions. To appear as informed consumers, some shoppers may falsely admit to using this type of information.

Giving inaccurate answers unconsciously

As Don Rumsfeld famously said, "There are known knowns. These are things we know that we know. There are known unknowns. That is to say, there are things that we now know we don't know. But there are also unknown unknowns. These are things we do not know we don't know."

Unconscious misrepresentations belong to Rumsfeld's third category of unknowns; they're the incorrect answers that respondents don't know are incorrect answers. Although biases such as acquiescence, extremity, and auspices can distort responses to all types of surveys, the last four problems in the following list pertain only to studies conducted by moderators or live interviewers (see Chapter 14):

✔ **Acquiescence bias:** *Acquiescence bias,* or yeah saying, is a type of response bias due to some people's tendency to agree with all questions or to concur with a particular position. The problem with acquiescence bias is that people who tend to agree often limit their responses to the "strongly agree" end of questions with multi-point scales. When those extreme answers are averaged with other people's answers, those averages will be exaggerated.

✔ **Extremity bias:** Some people tend to use the extreme points of scales; they answer either "strongly disagree" or "strongly agree" to whatever you ask them. This response style produces *extremity bias.* Other people have the opposite tendency; they tend to see everything in shades of gray rather than as either black or white. As a result, they tend to avoid scale endpoints when answering questions. Both response styles distort data analyses, especially the ones that depend on grouping people by responses or average-of-responses calculations.

✔ **Auspices bias:** *Auspices bias* (also called *sponsor bias*) is caused by respondents being influenced by the organization conducting the study. For example, your authors generally respond more conscientiously to academic surveys than to commercial surveys because we're sensitive to our colleagues' needs to publish their research. In one case, we know we're helping a fellow researcher; in the other case, we're merely helping a company earn additional profit.

✔ **Interviewer bias:** *Interviewer bias* is as it sounds; it's a type of response bias caused by the presence of an interviewer. For example, males who are asked personal lifestyle questions by a female interviewer may be reluctant to answer accurately because they're embarrassed. As a result, questions like the following may lead to reluctant and inaccurate responses:

  • Are you sexually active? If yes, how often do you buy contraceptives?

  • Do you use recreational drugs?

Alternatively, younger people may respond differently and more enthusiastically to younger interviewers — to whom they relate better — than to older interviewers. Regardless, such bias affects the quality of the responses.

✔ **Subtle source of cues:** Interviewer error often is so subtle that the interviewer is unaware of it. As a result, interviewers must be trained to avoid nonverbal responses to people's answers, whether affirmative or negative. If you shake your head approvingly after a respondent answers each question, and then suddenly fail to shake your head after an answer, you've inadvertently given a subtle cue about "correct" answers. Skilled interviewers avoid giving such cues.

✔ **Appearance of incompetence:** As a respondent, you'd be discouraged from continuing to participate in a study if you sensed that the interviewer was clueless about proper procedures. You'd be reluctant to continue because you'd assume the interviewer is the public face of the study, and if the interviewer is incompetent, then it's likely that everyone associated with the study is incompetent. Rather than waste your time responding completely and carefully, you'd be far more likely to terminate the interview. Thus, it's important that the interviewer appear competent as a surrogate indicator of the research team's overall competence.

✔ **Insufficient or poor probing:** One truly important advantage of a personal or telephone interview is the interviewer's ability to probe further. If a respondent gives an interesting yet incomplete answer, the interviewer can ask the respondent to say more about that answer. If the interviewer's probes are ill-conceived, much of the value of a personal or telephone interview is eliminated. For example, car dealerships often send interviewers on post-purchase house calls to recent car buyers. Interviewers may ask buyers general questions about salesperson competence and degree of customer comfort during the purchase process.

Answers to broad questions likely will suggest important follow-up questions that allow respondents to clarify and amplify their earlier answers. Suppose an interviewer asked a respondent how she would compare her recent car-buying experience at Slick Willie's Car Emporium to her previous purchase experiences. She may answer, "My previous two experiences buying a car at Honest John's Auto Dealership were far superior because the salesperson listened carefully to me and satisfied all my important needs." A good follow-up question would be "What can Slick Willie's do to improve its relative performance?" In contrast, "Do you think your experience was influenced by your ethnic background or gender?" would be a poor question likely to infuriate or insult the respondent.

Being unable to respond accurately

Although some people may prefer to respond inaccurately to some questions, and response style biases and faulty interviewer behaviors may cause other people unknowingly to respond inaccurately, inarticulateness and ignorance also may cause inaccurate responses. We explain both of these causes in the following list:

✔ **Inarticulateness:** To an extent, articulateness is associated with the ability to respond accurately, and some people are more articulate than others. (And no, we're not comparing recent U.S. presidents in this regard!)

✔ **Ignorance:** Some people like to believe they're fonts of infinite knowledge; however, just because you ask them a question doesn't mean they'll know the answer. As anyone who's ever watched a TV game show can attest, people tend to be overconfident (even when ignorant) about knowing the correct answers to questions. For survey research, respondent ignorance to some types of questions may be attributed to many causes, including the following:

• **They can't answer knowledgably about other people.** Sometimes people respond inaccurately because they don't know the correct answer. For example, a respondent legitimately could be ignorant about another person's attitudes and behaviors. Marketing researchers often conduct surveys of households, yet they typically limit questioning to one person in the household. If they ask one person about the attitudes or behaviors of another person in the household — as they may in the case of a married couple — the answers they receive may be a product of ignorance rather than an knowledge and experience.

• **They can't predict their own behavior well.** Respondents may be ignorant in the sense that they can't predict their own behaviors well. Most people are poor predictors of what they'll eat for lunch tomorrow, let alone whether they'll buy a new refrigerator, automobile, or home in the next year. Asking people to predict their own behaviors is an iffy proposition, so if possible you should ask them about their recent behaviors rather than ask them to predict their future behaviors. People are far better at remembering their most recent behaviors, and surprisingly, their most recent behaviors are far better predictors for their future behaviors than any prediction they may make.

Tackling Nonresponse Error

Respondents can introduce error into your survey results in two ways: with their responses (which we cover earlier in the chapter) and with their decisions not to respond. If the people who choose not to respond differ systematically from those who choose to respond, your results will be non-representative of the population you want to understand.

Nonresponse error tends to vary by type of interview. For example, it's far less of an issue for personal interviews than for mail or Internet surveys; response rates for the latter types of surveys may be as low as a few percent.

In the following sections, we examine the reasons people don't respond to surveys and show you ways to encourage participation.

Understanding the reasons people become nonrespondents

Nonresponse error can be caused by many factors, including an inability to successfully contact some respondents; for example, those people who are excessively busy (like physicians and CEOs), rarely home, or reluctant to cooperate. People who are unenthused about the purpose of your research will pass on answering your questions. Respondents also may be preoccupied each time you contact them. There are many reasons potential respondents become nonrespondents; we tackle these reasons in the following sections.

Self-selection bias

People may choose, because of some personal or study-related characteristic, not to participate in your survey. This is called *self-selection bias*.

People who choose to cooperate in a study generally are more interested in it and its influence on the decisions of the sponsoring organization. As a result, organizations and companies often collect an overrepresentation of extreme opinions and underrepresentation of indifferent opinions.

For example, Republican voters are unlikely to participate in surveys sponsored by Democratic organizations and vice versa. As a result, operatives of both parties tend to receive partisan feedback that reduces the likelihood that they'll identify fruitful paths to acceptable political compromise.

Fear and anxiety

People who are fearful or anxious about participating in surveys are neither paranoid nor irrational. Despite researchers' claims about research goals and respondent anonymity and confidentiality, respondents can't be certain about all the purposes to which the survey data will be applied.

For example, a restaurant may place a questionnaire on each table that asks diners to indicate their names, e-mail addresses, likelihood of returning in the next month, and satisfaction with servers. Diners may be reluctant to complete this questionnaire because they're uncertain how their personal data will be used; if their experience was negative, they may want to avoid partial responsibility for the firing of poor servers.

If asked personal information, respondents may be concerned that it could fall into the wrong hands. Although Hollywood celebrities and cheating spouses have obvious motives for keeping the intimate details of their lives out of the news media, regular folks may worry that any personal information they reveal could lead to identity theft and other crimes against them.

Invasion of privacy

People may avoid your survey because they're concerned about invasion of privacy; they don't want others to know about their lives and their activities. This preference for privacy is why hotel bills just list "movie" rather than the movie's name. (No one submitting an expense account request wants the folks in the purchasing department to know he ordered blue movies.)

Asking respondents to document what they did on their last vacation (what happens in Vegas stays in Vegas) or what they plan to do during an upcoming weekend (which may entail a clandestine romantic getaway) may trigger privacy concerns for some respondents.

Hostility toward survey sponsor, topic of interview, or interviewer

Hostility toward sponsors, topics of interviews, and interviewers themselves are all reasons that people may refuse to participate in a survey. Here's a rundown of these issues:

- **Hostility toward a survey sponsor:** Most people won't help other people they dislike; similarly, most people won't give their time and effort to answer the questions of a disliked company or organization. For example, suppose a person is a disgruntled new graduate of Whatsamatta University. If she were contacted by a faculty member to participate in a survey, she may refuse based on her hostility alone.

- **Hostility toward the study topic:** Some studies may be about sensitive topics that some people choose to avoid. For example, an Atlantic City casino may field a survey that includes detailed questions about patrons' gambling behaviors and alcohol consumption. Patrons' answers may reflect their suspicion and hostility toward the casino that asked such questions.

✓ **Hostility toward the interviewer:** With a face-to-face interview, an interviewer's appearance or manner may cause respondents to become hostile. In addition, respondents may grow hostile to both the interviewer and the survey sponsor when the interviewer takes more time than was agreed upon. Instead of answering in overtime, people would rather interact with family, watch a greatly anticipated televised event, or take a much-needed nap. (If you're a telemarketer, never call Jeremy while he's watching Nebraska football!)

Encouraging respondent cooperation

People cooperate with survey researchers for the following four reasons:

✓ **To be supportive or helpful:** Respondents are more apt to being supportive or helpful when the interviewer is professional and polite and the research problem seems interesting. For example, a person who wants to be supportive of basic university research is more likely to participate in a survey conducted by a university professor.

✓ **To have a social interaction:** Think about retirees and the elderly, who may crave the opportunity to talk with someone for an hour, even if it's about laundry detergent or hand soap.

✓ **To satisfy their curiosity:** Some respondents may be curious about your research. In that case, they may be willing to sacrifice the time and energy needed to participate. Mike once spent 45 minutes on the telephone for a survey about cottage cheese. He couldn't believe anyone would field such an extensive survey on such a minor product. In large part, he chose to participate because he wanted to discover the kinds of questions the researchers had the field service ask respondents. (Fortunately, Mike now has better things to do.)

✓ **To be remunerated:** Respondents may be motivated by compensation for their time and effort. People who participate in surveys typically receive remuneration in advance, such as a dollar or a free pencil or pen. Alternatively, they may be given the opportunity to receive the results of the survey or to access those results online.

Keep these reasons in mind as you design and field your survey. If you do, you are likely to increase your participation rate.

Minimizing error by boosting your response rates

Unfortunately, people are losing or have lost faith in polls. They're inundated with regularly conducted polls that are reported on overzealously in the mass media. Requests to participate in surveys are a daily affair. As a result, many people have burned out on survey participation and reported findings. Potential respondents are no longer inclined to participate; nor are they willing to answer seriously when they do participate.

When response rates decline, the representativeness of survey results decline as well. Declining response rates are a major problem because they reduce research quality (by introducing error) and increase data-collection costs.

Because of this declining interest, it's important for you to maximize response rates and in turn the representativeness of your samples. It's critical for you to convince respondents of the important reasons to participate in your survey.

Figure 7-2 indicates the potential problems associated with nonresponse error. Circle A represents "zero" nonresponse error; the response rate for the planned sample is 100 percent. In Circle B, the response rate is less than 100 percent, but there's no nonresponse error because respondents don't differ systematically from nonrespondents. The problem comes with Circle C, where the response rate is less than 100 percent and respondents differ systematically from nonrespondents.

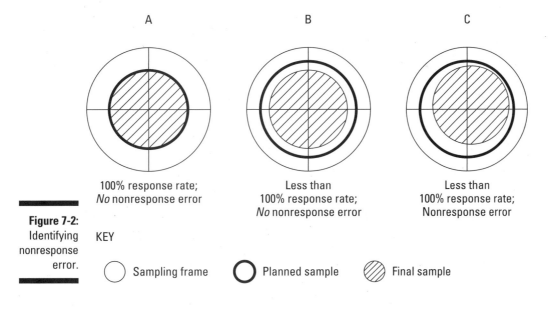

Figure 7-2: Identifying nonresponse error.

In the following sections, we show you how to boost your response rates for the different kinds of interviews and surveys you may conduct. (Browse Chapter 6 for more on these types of surveys.)

Face-to-face interviews

To boost response rates for face-to-face interviews, you can offer meaningful incentives (for example, money or a chance to win money or prizes), dress professionally (for example, pressed outfit, and shined shoes), and solicit potential respondents at the most convenient time of day (for example, a telephone interviewer calling at 6 p.m. on a Tuesday night — before dinner — is likely to garner a more favorable response than at 9 p.m. on a Sunday night).

Telephone surveys

Many potential respondents have encountered unscrupulous telemarketers pretending to conduct consumer research as part of a sales pitch. As a result, response rates for telephone interviews have dropped markedly in the last 20 to 30 years.

Answering machines and caller ID also have suppressed the response rates of telephone interviews. Even in 1983, the results of a study that involved more than 250,000 first-call attempts found that only 8.4 percent of those attempts produced a completed telephone interview. That extraordinarily low success rate is even worse today.

Even under ideal circumstances, completing a telephone interview is difficult. Figure 7-3 shows all possible outcomes to an attempted telephone interview. Only one of those outcomes — the one in the bottom right-hand corner — is a completed interview that's useful. All other outcomes are worthless.

When conducting telephone interviews, you can cope with first-call attempts that don't result in either a refusal or a successfully completed interview in the following two ways:

- ✔ **Call back potential respondents who aren't answering on different days and at different times.** Given the regularity of people's lifestyles and schedules, calling back at the same day and time is likely to result in another failed contact. Calling back on various days and at various times is a better option, assuming that person wants to participate in your survey. Three call-back attempts is the conventional number for telephone surveys. After three attempts, you should delete that potential respondent from further consideration.

- ✔ **Substitute other respondents for respondents who aren't home (or won't answer).** This procedure will cause the planned sample and the final sample to differ. However, if all members of the final sample are within the sample frame, your only concern is if some types of respondents were oversampled and other types undersampled. If that occurred, then potentially meaningful sample bias has been introduced. (Refer to Chapter 11 for more on sample bias.)

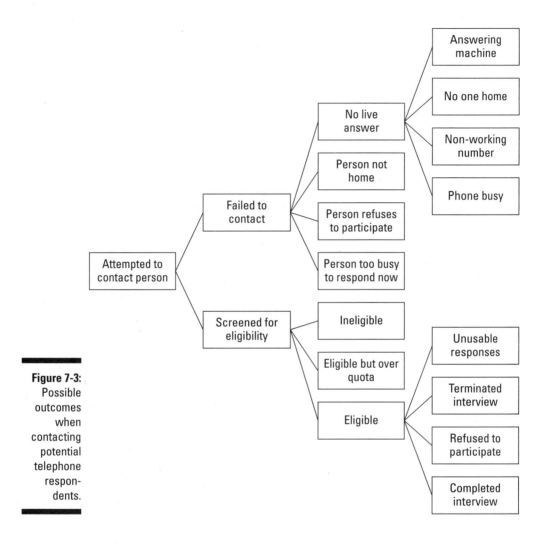

Figure 7-3:
Possible outcomes when contacting potential telephone respondents.

Mail surveys

Although survey researchers have explored many ways to increase response rates to mail surveys, here are some accepted ways to boost those response rates:

✔ **Create an effective cover letter for your survey.** Be certain that your cover letter is sales oriented, provides respondents with a good reason to respond to your survey, and mentions a token of appreciation. If that token is money, it can go to the respondent or a charity. Just mail the incentive as an advance to engender trust and encourage participation.

✔ **Ensure that your questions are interesting and not overly taxing to answer.** Neither a 10-page questionnaire about laundry detergent nor a 40-page questionnaire with detailed questions about every automobile sold in the United States is likely to garner a high response rate.

✔ **Send follow-ups.** Second and third mailings, reminder postcards, and letters that alert respondents that they'll receive a questionnaire shortly, are all useful for boosting response rates.

✔ **Reveal respected sponsor.** If the sponsor is well known — perhaps a prestigious university — response rates tend to be higher.

Consider the process that one sport-enthusiast magazine attempted to increase the response rate to its semi-annual survey of U.S. sport-equipment dealers. First, the magazine mailed an alert letter that indicated a questionnaire was coming to the respondent. Five days later, respondents received a questionnaire packet that included a cover letter, a questionnaire, a $1 bill, and a stamped return envelope. A second packet — which contained a reminder letter, a questionnaire, and a stamped return envelop — was mailed five days after the initial packet was mailed. A week later, a follow-up postcard, reminding respondents of the opportunity to participate, was mailed. One week after that, a second reminder postcard was mailed.

By using this procedure, the magazine achieved a 68 percent response rate, which is excellent for a mail survey. However, this result was achieved in 1987, when overall response rates were higher. Although an excellent procedure — and one that would boost your response rate meaningfully and cost effectively — the magazine would be unlikely to achieve such a stellar result today.

Administered surveys

To boost response rates for administered surveys (see Chapter 6), you must convince as many potential respondents as possible that it's important to participate in your survey. Asking a manager to distribute and endorse the survey is one way to increase your response rates because employees are reluctant to ignore a manager's request. Regardless of the distribution method, successfully conveying the importance of your research goals can increase response rates.

Online surveys

Because consumers frequently search online to shop and pass time, online surveys can be effective for data gathering. Because data are gathered online, respondents don't need to take pencil to paper, which in today's electronic communications age can be off-putting; thus, they may be more inclined to complete an online questionnaire than a pencil-and-paper questionnaire. Also, because shopping is just a few clicks away, a coupon or gift card for questionnaire completion should increase online response rates.

Managing Administrative Error

Administrative error is a type of systematic error that occurs when researchers don't attend to detail. Researcher carelessness and administrative error are related positively. Some examples of this error type include improper administration, data processing errors, a failure to record returned surveys, and a failure to double-check that surveys contained every page.

Administrative error, regardless of type, will undermine your research goals. As a result, your research question can't be effectively answered. Attending to the intricacies of your research will help reduce, if not all but eliminate, administrative error.

The following are factors that make a questionnaire (especially a mail questionnaire) unacceptable. Although painful, given the cost of data collection, you should discard such returned questionnaires.

- ✔ Major portions or key questions are unanswered, which make the entire questionnaire useless for data-analysis purposes.

- ✔ Evidence the respondent didn't understand the task or didn't take the questionnaire seriously; for example, the respondent answered 50 consecutive attitude questions identically (for example, a 4 on a 1-to-7 scale) or answered related questions in an obviously inconsistent way.

- ✔ You gave a respondent a survey with missing pages, so she couldn't answer a large fraction of the questions. If respondents are anonymous and it's impossible to recontact them and obtain responses to questions on those missing pages, then that questionnaire is unusable.

- ✔ The respondent is unqualified because she isn't a member of the target population. For example, a questionnaire about baby clothes sent to a resident of an assisted-living facility would be unlikely to yield meaningful data.

- ✔ Questionnaires returned after the cutoff date for study completion should also be excluded because of possible history effects. Events after the cutoff date may have influenced answers; as a result, those answers won't be typical of answers submitted before the cutoff date. For example, a person's pre- and post-9/11 responses to a questionnaire about homeland security likely would have differed markedly.

Interviewer cheating

Interviewer cheating is relevant only for face-to-face and telephone interviews. The interviewers for these types of surveys typically earn base pay plus a commission for each interview they complete. As a result, they have a motive for fabricating data. Most commercial research companies certify at least 10 percent to 15 percent of interviews to ensure that they were conducted in the manner specified by the client. Certification entails contacting respondents, verifying the survey was administered at the appropriate time and place, and double-checking several answers to questions.

Data processing errors

When transferring data from questionnaires to a computer file, it's possible that you or an assistant can enter numbers incorrectly. To ensure accurate data entry, commercial data entry companies typically process all data twice — creating two data sets that should be identical if errorless. These companies then compare the two sets. Whenever a discrepancy between the two sets arises, the original questionnaire is reexamined to determine which entry, if either, is correct. The odds of twice misentering the same data identically are minimal, so you shouldn't worry about missing those errors.

Errors in data analysis also may occur. For instance, you can inadvertently set your statistical program so that it recognizes missing values as zeros. If you do, your statistics will be erroneous because zeros are being treated as real answers! Data analysis often requires you to recode data, and when recoding it, errors may be introduced. (We discuss recoding more in Chapter 18.) When computer software is used to clean data by searching for discrepancies in answers, faulty programming logic can introduce errors. (See Chapter 17 for more on this topic.)

Looking at Reliability, Validity, Generalizability, and Sensitivity

A prerequisite of sound marketing research is your ability to measure whatever you intended to measure. To ensure your measures are effective, you must assess their reliability, validity, generalizability, and sensitivity. You can evaluate all these measure qualities through objective or subjective means.

Recognizing the difference between reliability and validity

Although they're used interchangeably in everyday English, reliability and validity have vastly different meanings to marketing researchers. For most marketing studies, researchers typically are searching for the differences between respondents and what causes those differences. These differences can reflect true variability, or they can reflect random or systematic error. *Reliability* addresses the random and systematic error component of measurement. *Validity* addresses the accurate-indicator dimension of differences within measures.

Reliability in a research context is the degree to which measures are free from random error and, therefore, yield consistent results. In other words, it's the repeatability of a measure: If you take that same measurement on the same object or person on multiple occasions, will you obtain the same number or score?

If you're a retailer, for example, you can measure customer emotions relative to changes in your store's *atmospherics,* which are the physical characteristics and related influences for creating a store image that attracts customers. If you change your store's background music from elevator music to contemporary music, will your customers feel better about their shopping experience and be more likely to return in the next month? To answer this question, you provide shoppers with a short exit questionnaire that asks them, "How pleasant was the background music you heard in the store today?" However, be mindful that people's moods and receptivity to music vary markedly from day-to-day, so the same person may judge the same music as very pleasant one day but slightly annoying the next day. To the extent this same measurement of the same person wouldn't elicit the same answer on different occasions, it's unreliable.

In contrast to reliability, *validity* is a more theoretical notion. When assessing the validity of a measure, marketing researchers try to determine the ability of a scale to measure the intended marketing construct. In other words, they want to determine whether the measure is measuring what it's supposed to measure.

Rulers — like the one you carried in grade school — provide reliable and valid measures. A ruler is reliable in the sense that if the same object is measured with the same ruler on consecutive days, the results would be similar; it's valid because it's designed to measure length and does that precisely.

Determining reliability and validity

Your marketing research goal is to obtain the best answer to your posited research questions in hope of identifying the ideal course of action. When answering your research questions, you need appropriate measures (questions on your survey). Appropriateness in this context has two related characteristics: reliability and validity, which we further discuss in this section.

The upper-left-hand corner of Figure 7-4 illustrates the circumstance under which a measure is valid and reliable. In this case, measurement needs to occur only once to determine the true value. Alternatively, the bottom-right-hand corner illustrates the circumstance under which a measure is neither valid nor reliable. In this case, it's unusable in any meaningful fashion; it's impossible to determine the true value by using a measure that's neither valid nor reliable.

The interesting circumstances are the ones on the diagonal: Cells B and C. Cell B (the upper-right-hand corner) illustrates the circumstances under which a measure is somewhat unreliable, in the sense that taking the same measure repeatedly would produce different values. From a theoretical standpoint, the measure reflects the correct underlying notion; it's measuring what it's meant to measure. In such a case, the solution is to take repeated measurements and then average them.

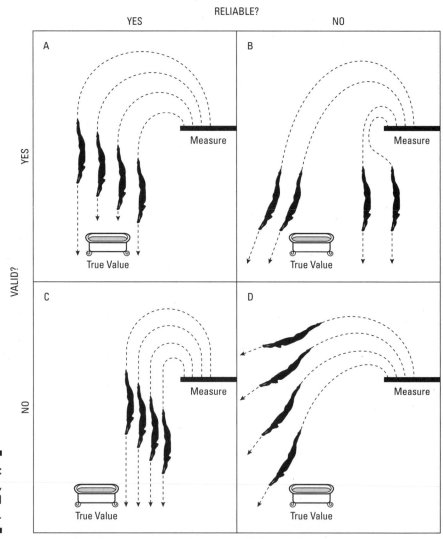

Figure 7-4:
Reliability,
validity, and
accuracy.

Cell C (the bottom-left-hand corner) illustrates the circumstances under which a measure is repeatable but not valid. It's possible that the measure is systematically biased; in that case, once the magnitude of that bias and its direction is known, all that's needed is a single corrected measure. If, for example, you wanted to measure respondents' social status but were limited to a measure of income — which should reflect social status but could be biased systematically — all that's needed is a single measure of income that's corrected for this bias.

The ideal of a reliable and valid measure is illustrated in Cell A. The unworkable situation is Cell D, in which a measure is neither valid nor reliable. With measures of the type shown in Cell B — valid but unreliable — the solution is to take repeated measures and then average them. With measures of the type shown in Cell C — reliable but not valid — the solution is to determine whether the invalid measure reflects the underlying construct of interest, determine the magnitude and direction of the bias, take the single measure, and adjust it accordingly.

Minimizing variation in responses

Researchers hope that differences in the number or score yielded by a measure relate to true differences among people on the characteristics of interest. However, there are unwanted causes of variation in responses related to reliability and validity. All but the first cause mentioned in the following list relate to reliability:

- ✔ **Stable characteristics of individual respondents:** For example, the responses of people with greater intelligence and educational achievement will be more stable than the responses of people with lesser intelligence and educational achievement. Obviously, you shouldn't try to control for these characteristics unless you're conducting a study for Mensa!

- ✔ **Short-term personal factors:** For example, completing a lengthy questionnaire or interview may fatigue respondents; once tired, they may begin to respond less thoughtfully, which can reduce the reliability of their answers. After you've taxed respondents beyond their ability to cooperate fully, your data-collection effort has become pointless.

  Careless — and hence unstable — answers are symptomatic of respondents who find the questionnaire or interview of little interest or who are ill that day. Although you can't control for interest or illness, you may be able to spot distracted respondents when conducting face-to-face and telephone interviews. You should politely terminate such interviews.

- ✔ **Situational factors:** People's responses to questions differ by their immediate situation. For example, a man may respond one way to a telephone interviewer who calls him at home three minutes before he must leave, and he may respond a different way if he doesn't plan to leave his home that day.

To minimize the effects of distracting situational factors in face-to-face or telephone interviews, try to create a rapport with respondents, perhaps through some pre-interview chit-chat about casual topics like the weather or sports. If you overhear likely distractions during a telephone interview, like screaming children or loud music, you should ask the respondent whether you may call back at a more convenient time.

✔ **Variation in administering the questionnaire:** The greater intimacy of face-to-face interviews may induce different responses than self-administered interviews. Interviewers who appear detached and unfriendly create disinterested or negative respondents who tend to provide unstable answers. In contrast, interviewers who appear engaged and friendly create interested and positive respondents who tend to provide stable answers.

✔ **Specific items included in the questionnaire:** There's an infinite number of ways researchers can ask the same question or try to measure the same underlying construct. However, the specific items chosen to measure a construct may cause some variation in people's responses due to the interpretation of the specific words or formatting chosen.

✔ **Lack of clarity in the measurement instrument:** Spoken language can be ambiguous and complex, so questionnaire items not of the absolutely simplest nature — like "What's your sex?" — invite confusion that may affect people's responses.

Today's popular alternative — "What's your gender?" — exchanges ambiguity for political correctness. Sex is a binary characteristic for all but the few hermaphrodites; in contrast, gender is a more continuous identity-related characteristic.

✔ **Mechanical or instrument factors:** For example, insufficient blank space on a self-administered questionnaire may encourage people to shorten their answers. An unprofessional-looking questionnaire may discourage people from providing complete answers.

✔ **Scoring/coding inconsistencies:** Efforts to code or score responses, especially if they're open ended, can introduce error.

Testing for reliability and validity

As emphasized earlier in the chapter, reliability and validity are essential for effective marketing research. We now discuss a host of ways you can test each one.

Testing for reliability

To assess the reliability, or repeatability, of your measures, you may use any of the five methods we explain in this section. As is often the case in marketing research, different approaches are more suitable to different circumstances.

All five approaches are good for assessing reliability. The first three approaches require collecting a larger sample, which would entail either more time or more expense (with advanced planning and a larger budget). Approach 4 is a relatively straightforward way to check for the consistency of multiple-item measures. Approach 5 is used to assess reliability when assessments or scores are assigned somewhat subjectively.

Here are the five approaches to consider:

- ✔ **Approach 1 – Repeated measurement:** *Test/retest reliability* means measuring a person at one time, re-measuring that same person at a different time, and finally comparing the answers. For example, if you're measuring an attitude and believe that attitudes are relatively stable, you'd expect similar answers on repeated measure administrations. Test/retest reliability is the degree of answer similarity.

- ✔ **Approach 2 – Differences in split samples:** You can ask 200 people the same question, randomly split those 200 people into two groups of 100 people, and then determine whether the answers from the first group are consistent (on average) with the answers from the second group. If they are, you've achieved *split-sample reliability*.

- ✔ **Approach 3 – Predictiveness:** *Alternative-forms reliability* relates to the infinite number of questions appropriate for assessing any underlying construct. For example, to assess customers' perceptions of a shoe store, you may create one set of questions to ask one set of people and a different but similar set of questions to ask a second set of people. Then you'd compare the responses of the first group to the second group. If you've created a reliable measure, the alternative forms ought to yield comparable responses.

- ✔ **Approach 4 – Consistency with other answers:** Another way to assess reliability is internal comparison. Some marketing constructs require multiple items for measurement. In such cases, a single item — like one used to assess income or the number of children in a household — is insufficient; assessing a notion like store image, which is far more complex, requires multiple items. To some extent, you can assess the reliability of those items by examining how the answers to each item relate to the scores on all other items. What you'd like is some consistency among responses to all the items. If one item tends to produce scores unrelated to the others, you'd know that item should be deleted from the set of items meant to assess the underlying construct. A reasonably consistent set of items is *internal-comparison reliable*.

- ✔ **Approach 5 – Consistency among coders:** If you're conducting a content analysis (see Chapter 15), or if you've asked respondents to answer open-ended questions (see Chapter 9), substantial subjectivity is involved in assigning scores to objects or people. To increase data reliability, you should use multiple coders who initially assign scores to objects or people independently. Upon completing their individual efforts, the coders then meet to reconcile coding differences, if any. (You may help coders resolve disagreements they can't resolve.) Coding consistency implies a sound coding scheme that's likely to produce reliable data.

Testing for validity

Here are the different types of validity you may come across and the ways you can assess them:

- **Content or face validity:** This type of validity merely assesses whether your questionnaire items adequately represent the underlying construct of interest. Typically, content or face validity is assessed by asking subject-matter experts whether or not the items make sense. For example, if you're designing a scale related to retailing, you may ask five retailers whether or not those items make sense; if they agree that the items make sense, you have achieved content or face validity.

- **Predictive validity:** This type of validity, also referred to as *criterion validity,* relates to whether a measure is predictive of something else you want to predict. It doesn't matter whether the measure makes sense from a theoretical standpoint; if a measure is predictive, it has predictive validity (although theoretically related measures tend to be more predictive). To the degree that one measure predicts another one, you've achieved predictive validity. For example, attitudes are scientifically dubious, yet they're somewhat predictive of people's behaviors. (We discuss this issue further in Chapter 8.) Thus, marketing researchers continue to collect attitude data from consumers.

- **Convergent validity:** If you have a strong sense that you're measuring the correct thing, you should be able to develop alternative measures, and the scores on those measures should be consistent.

Think about measuring IQ. There's an infinite number of ways to assess someone's intelligence. If psychologists have a good sense about the nature of intelligence, they should receive consistent scores on different IQ tests for the same person. The extent that scores are inconsistent suggests a lack of understanding about the underlying notion of intelligence. Thus, convergent validity indicates that the researcher understands the phenomenon in question and how to measure it appropriately.

- **Discriminant validity:** You want to be certain that your different scales measure different things — in essence, that you haven't confused measuring one thing with measuring something else. To the extent you can guarantee that your scale is measuring one thing and not something else, you've achieved discriminant validity.

Psychologists (and marketing academics) invent new measurement scales regularly. Although these new scales may have different names and rely on different questions, it's unclear whether they measure new things. For example, narcissism and self-esteem seem like different constructs, yet current scales for measuring them produce highly correlated scores. Less surprisingly, job-satisfaction scores correlate highly with willingness-to-leave-a-job scores. When scores on measures of two seemingly different constructs correlate excessively, it's unclear whether the theories used to develop those measures reflect a sound understanding of either construct.

✔ **Nomological validity:** Researchers like each measure to be related in a proper theoretical manner to other relevant marketing constructs. To the extent that a measure is consistent with measures of other marketing constructs, they've achieved nomological validity. Unless you're planning to write a marketing PhD dissertation, you can bypass this type of validity.

Valuing study generalizability

Generalizability is whether the results of a study can be generalized to a larger population or to a broader set of circumstances. For example, based on experiments that often rely on a few hundred subjects, researchers try to draw conclusions about how the general population, or at least a much larger population, may respond. The stronger the evidence that the responses of a few hundred people are generalizable to a larger population, the more comfortable researchers are with generalizing the results of an experiment.

The generalizability of a measure or study is achieved over time through multiple studies. These studies can be cross-sectional or longitudinal (see Chapter 2 for more). When generalizability is achieved (in a city, region, country), it offers researchers and those applying the findings, which is you, more confidence that the results will pay dividends.

Valuing measurement sensitivity

A measure can be reliable in the sense that it's repeatable; it can be valid, in the sense that it measures what was intended and is consistent with theoretical notions; and it can be generalizable, in the sense that the sample that was drawn is representative of the larger population in question. In contrast, *sensitivity* determines whether a measure accurately detects differences among people. A measure can be reliable, valid, generalizable, and relatively insensitive.

Imagine you feel ill and are a bit flush. You can take your temperature with a meat thermometer before heading for your doctor's office. However, you know that meat thermometers are designed to measure temperatures far in excess of human body temperatures, so you'd take your temperature with a thermometer sensitive to temperatures between 92 and 108 degrees Fahrenheit. The meat thermometer provides a reliable, valid, and generalizable but insensitive measure of a human being's temperature. Similarly, sensitivity is critical for researchers trying to classify people into different groups, as would be the case for segmentation analysis.

Sensitive measures are critical to assessing consumers' attitudes, emotions, and intentions. One sensitivity issue (which we discuss further in Chapter 9) is the number of response categories needed to differentiate people who have varying thoughts about something. For example, should you use 5-point, 7-point, or 9-point scales to assess people's attitudes about your product? Some people may find 9-point scales confusing — they may not know whether they rate a 6 and a 7 on a particular attitude — whereas 5-point scales may lack the sensitivity needed to differentiate people with truly different attitudes.

Chapter 8

Asking People about Their Attitudes

*I*n marketing research, understanding consumer attitudes is often paramount, as attitudes influence opinions and choices. Researchers can use both qualitative and quantitative methods to obtain consumer attitudinal responses. In this chapter, we focus on the latter and explore the effectiveness of using survey methods to capture consumer attitudes.

Although attitude measures are common in many marketing surveys, accurately measuring people's attitudes can be problematic. For example, asking people their attitudes about online gambling may produce socially desirable answers that don't reflect their true thoughts. In contrast, asking people their attitudes about different brands of toothpaste will — if you ask well-designed questions — produce meaningful responses. At best, people's answers to your attitude questions will reflect their beliefs and emotions. At worst, their answers — especially if you ask ill conceived or controversial questions — will be squirrelly. Regardless, you should strive to understand your customer's attitudes because they influence purchase behaviors.

In this chapter, we define attitude components and explore measurement methods that you can use to measure attitudes. No matter which method you use, accurately capturing your targeted consumers' attitudes is essential to your business success.

What's an Attitude?

An *attitude* indicates a person's like or dislike for a person, place, thing, or event. It represents a relatively enduring predisposition rather than a transient thought. Attitudes are a type of hypothetical construct, which is a nondirectly observed concept that researchers can use to explain something else. For example, the concept of intelligence can't be observed directly — despite widely held beliefs about the obvious stupidity of out-of-state drivers — yet marketers can use it to explain consumers' behaviors.

Attitudes don't have any physical correlates; you can't slice someone's brain open and point to the grey matter that contains their attitude about your product. Nonetheless, by assuming that attitudes exist and by measuring them, marketers (and psychologists) are better able to predict people's subsequent behaviors.

Because they aren't observable directly, hypothetical constructs must be measured by indirect means. In the case of attitudes, those indirect means are either verbal expression or overt behaviors. You can infer people's attitudes about something based on what they say, their responses to a self-administered questionnaire, or by how they act.

The problem with attitude as a hypothetical construct relates to causality. Marketers assume that attitudes can predict peoples' behaviors. However, the psychological literature also suggests that behaviors tend to influence people's attitudes. For example, buying a product repeatedly may induce more favorable attitudes toward that product because people are compelled to justify their repeated behaviors. Seemingly, attitudes are causes of behaviors, and behaviors are causes of attitudes. Because one thing can't be both a cause and an effect of another thing, attitudes are problematic from a scientific perspective. Nonetheless, as one of our professors used to say during lectures, "In the kingdom of the blind, the one-eyed man is king." (These lectures occurred before political correctness became de rigueur.)

Analogously, attitudes may be imperfect indicators of peoples' subsequent behaviors, but they provide a useful tool for predicting those behaviors. As one of the better tools, you shouldn't discard them.

Recognizing and Using the Three Attitude Components

Psychologists and marketers think of attitudes algebraically. Here's the formula they use to calculate an attitude score:

$$A_j = \Sigma\, w_i\, b_{ij}$$

Although people can have attitudes about anyone or anything, assume in this chapter that we're discussing products. In that context, the components in the attitude formula can be defined as follows:

- A_j is a person's attitude toward product j. This behavioral component comprises predisposition to action, intention, and behavioral expectation. In other words, the behavioral component of attitudes addresses issues about people's predispositions to act in a certain way, their intentions to act a certain way, or their expectations about acting a certain way. These intentions or expectations can be about things as simple as ice cream or as complex as a home or automobile.

- b_{ij} is a belief about product j on attribute i, which for an automobile model can be characteristics such as fuel economy, cargo space, and reliability. This cognitive component encompasses knowledge and beliefs. Beliefs, which also are referred to as *neutral cognitions,* comprise the cognitive component of attitudes. This component entails people's beliefs or knowledge about the world independent of their emotions about those beliefs. Cognitions are merely the facts of the world as people understand them. For example, you have certain beliefs about the fuel efficiency of your car, and you have different beliefs about the number of channels you receive on your television.

- w_i is the importance a person places on that i characteristic. In the context of automobiles, if a person cares little about fuel economy, the w_i on that characteristic for that person is a relatively small number. In contrast, if that person cares greatly about reliability, the w_i is a relatively large number. This affective component relates to a person's feelings or emotions toward an object. An *affect* is a person's emotional feelings toward an issue, object, event, person, or idea. An affect may be general (for example, you may love watching professional baseball) or specific (for example, you may love watching the Boston Red Sox lose to the New York Yankees, or any other team for that matter).

Reviewing the Classic Hierarchy-of-Effects Model

The *hierarchy-of-effects model* is one of the most enduring models of how advertising works. We present this model to stress the importance of measuring all three components of attitudes that we discuss in the preceding section. Without awareness, people can't have opinions on facts about your brand or feelings toward your brand or intentions to buy your brand. However, it's insufficient to measure only awareness. You must measure all three components to fully capture the explanatory power of this model.

Here's the breakdown of the basic model:

✔ **Step 1:** People become aware that a product exists. That awareness can be measured through aided or unaided recall. An *aided recall* question is "Do you recall seeing a TV commercial for Budweiser last night?" In contrast, an *unaided recall* question is "What TV commercials do you recall seeing last night?" The first question prompts you to recall the Budweiser commercial, so it's more likely you would recall having seen it. The second question provides no prompting, so it's more likely that you wouldn't recall seeing that Budweiser commercial.

✔ **Step 2:** After people become aware of a product, they discover the attributes of that product. These attribute discoveries — the b_{ij} in the previous section —represent factual knowledge.

✔ **Step 3:** After they learn about the product, people begin to form emotions toward it. As a result, people begin to like or dislike that product, which may become their first choice or part of the set of products they may consider on their next purchase occasion. This step relates to the affective component (w_i).

✔ **Step 4:** If people know of a product, including particular details, and have some emotional responses toward it, they may intend to buy it on their next purchase occasion. This step relates to the behavioral component (A_j).

✔ **Step 5:** Finally, people act on their intentions, or at least that's what this model forecasts.

Notice from Figure 8-1 that the three components of attitudes (knowledge [b_{ij}], affect [w_i], and intentions [A_j]), as presented in the previous section, are represented by the middle three steps.

As you can see, this hierarchy-of-effects model assumes that people progress through multiple stages when purchasing a product. A consumer first becomes aware, then she becomes knowledgeable, then she develops certain emotions, and finally she develops intentions to buy. She may have purchased the brand the previous time and — based on use-related experience — intends to purchase it on her next occasion to buy. As a result, marketers think about all users of a product: people who are aware of a brand, people who prefer that brand, people who last bought that brand, and people who are satisfied with that brand.

 Because people may be misinformed, you can and should measure their knowledge about your brand. To guide your marketing efforts, you also should measure people's liking of your brand. Finally, intentions can be an accurate predictor of eventual behaviors, so you should measure people's intentions to purchase your brand. Methodologically, you want to measure intentions as close to actual behaviors as possible, like measuring intentions to buy University of Nebraska football apparel at a shopping mall. In doing so, the intentions indicated should be more predictive of eventual behavior than if you asked people the same question in a telephone interview. Clearly, your goal is to predict the behaviors of potential customers accurately.

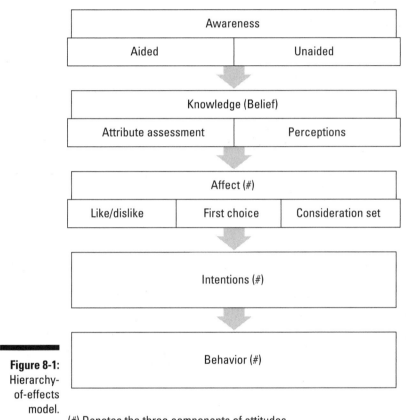

Figure 8-1:
Hierarchy-
of-effects
model.

(#) Denotes the three components of attitudes

Developing Sound Attitude Measures

Consumers' attitudes relate to many aspects of the goods and services they buy, from the tanginess of a certain brand of orange juice to the reliability of a certain brand of sand wedges (nothing like a golfing pun to brighten your day).

Like all psychological measures, attitude measures are subject to error. Specifically,

Measured value = True value + Measurement error

As we discuss in Chapter 7, reliability and validity are priorities for measuring things like attitudes. To the degree that reliability and validity are achieved, measurement error is reduced. Thus, sound attitude measures must be reliable and valid measures. To achieve reliability, a measure must be free from random error and must yield consistent results across contexts and samples. To achieve validity, the measure must assess what it's meant to assess.

Marketing theory is essential for understanding consumers because it offers a framework by which you can more accurately predict consumer responses to your business strategies and behaviors toward your product offerings. Through such a framework, attitudes can be identified and measured.

Understanding the importance of theory in measuring attitudes

Although many marketing-related theories are relevant to marketing research, they're especially relevant for designing attitudinal measures. Theories provide a framework for measuring attitudes properly; without a framework, it's unlikely the questions you ask truly will access the attitude you wish to measure. Before you can accurately measure a consumer's attitude, you must understand why it exists. Being able to define conceptually what the attitude represents and how it will be measured (operationalized) are important to achieving your marketing research objectives.

Consider *store loyalty,* which is a popular notion that retailers use to describe their customers. Marketers conceive store loyalty in one of two ways: as an attitude or as a behavior. When conceived as an attitude, store loyalty is typically measured in terms of multiple store attributes, such as merchandising displays, the assortment of goods, and value for the money.

However, store loyalty also can be conceived in strictly behavioral terms, such as the frequency that people visit a store. For example, if you tend to shop regularly at Macy's — if you patronized the store three of the last four weeks — you could be considered store loyal strictly based on your behavior; your attitudes toward Macy's aren't considered.

Identifying your conceptual and operational definitions

Specifying the conceptual and operational definitions for the attitude you want to assess are the first two steps in developing a sound measure. After you specify those definitions, you can use them to create the measure, collect data, and then analyze the quality of that measure.

Attitudes are concepts. A *concept* is a generalized idea about a class of objects, attributes, occurrences, or processes. Clearly, a concept is a mental construct rather than a physical construct. As the words indicate, a conceptual definition specifies the nature of a concept.

As a conceptual definition indicates the meaning of a concept, an operational definition is mechanical; it specifies what you must measure. In essence, operational definitions are measurement definitions, and conceptual definitions are theoretical definitions.

Here are related examples of each definition type, as well as a measure, associated with brands and a predisposition to purchase a given brand:

Conceptual definition: A predisposition to react favorably or unfavorably to a brand.

Operational definition: The likelihood that someone will buy Brand Y on the next purchase occasion.

Measure: On a scale from 1 to 10, where *1* means "definitely will not buy" and *10* means "definitely will buy," how likely are you to buy Brand Y on your next purchase occasion?

Operational definitions aren't limited to attitudes. For example, who should be included as a household member may seem a relatively straightforward matter, but Figure 8-2 suggests otherwise for U.S. Census–taking purposes.

Summary Table for Determining Who Is to Be Included as a Member of the Household (Control Card Item 14c)

	Include As Member of Household	
A. PERSONS STAYING IN SAMPLE UNIT AT TIME OF INTERVIEW		
Person is member of family, lodger, servant, visitor, etc.		
1. Ordinarily stays here all the time (sleeps here)	Yes	
2. Here temporarily – no living quarters held for person elsewhere	Yes	
3. Here temporarily – living quarters held for person elsewhere		No
Person is in Armed Forces		
1. Stationed in this locality, usually sleeps here	Yes	
2. Temporarily here on leave – stationed elsewhere		No
Person is a student – Here temporarily attending school – living quarters held for person elsewhere		
1. Not married or not living with own family		No
2. Married and living with own family	Yes	
3. Student nurse living at school	Yes	
B. ABSENT PERSON WHO USUALLY LIVES HERE IN SAMPLE UNIT		
Person is inmate of specified institution – Absent because inmate in a specified institution (see listing in Part C, Table A) regardless of whether or not living quarters held for person here		No
Person is temporarily absent on vacation, in general hospital, etc. (Including veterans' facilities that are general hospitals) – Living quarters hold here for person	Yes	
Person is absent in connection with job		
1. Living quarters held here for person – temporarily absent while "on the road" in connection with job (e.g., traveling salesperson, railroad person, bus driver)	Yes	
2. Living quarters held here and elsewhere for person but comes here infrequently (e.g., construction engineer)		No
3. Living quarters held here at home for unmarried college student working away from home during summer school vacation	Yes	
Person is in Armed Forces – Was member of this household at time of induction but currently stationed elsewhere		No
Person is a student in school – Away temporarily attending school – living quarters held for person here		
1. Not married or not living with own family	Yes	
2. Married and living with own family		No
3. Attending school overseas		No
4. Student nurse living at school		No
C. EXCEPTIONS AND DOUBTFUL CASES		
Person with two concurrent residences – Determine length of time person has maintained two concurrent residences		
1. Has slept greater part of that time in another locality		No
2. Has slept greater part of that time in sample unit	Yes	
Citizen of foreign country temporarily in the United States		
1. Living on premises of an Embassy, Ministry, Legation, Chancellery, or Consulate		No
2. Not living on premises of an Embassy, Ministry, etc. –		
a. Living here and no usual place of residence elsewhere in the United States	Yes	
b. Visiting or traveling in the United States		No

Figure 8-2: Operational definition of who's a household member.

Becoming Familiar with the Attitude Measurement Process

Depending on the research context and research question, you may gauge consumer attitudes in a variety of ways, which have all proven reliable and valid. This discussion introduces four different types of scales to assess people's attitudes about your product or service:

- **Ranking scales:** *Ranking scales* require respondents to place objects (or people) in a sequence, based on their attitudes about a characteristic of those objects (or people). For example, you can show respondents a list of six restaurants and ask them to rank those restaurants from best to worst on quality of service.

  Ranking tasks are best performed over a small number of objects (or people). If you asked people to rank 25 different makes of automobiles from their most preferred to their least preferred, they probably could indicate — with some degree of reliability — their most preferred, their second most preferred, and their least preferred. Any rankings between the two most preferred and least preferred automobiles are likely to be unreliable because people can't meaningfully differentiate among such a large set of nameplates. To make in-between rankings more reliable, you should limit the number of things that you ask respondents to rank; as a rule of thumb, limit the rankings to roughly a half-dozen things. (See Chapter 7 for more on reliability.)

- **Rating scales:** *Rating scales* require respondents to estimate the magnitude of a characteristic that an object (or person) possesses. A respondent's self-reported position on a scale is her rating of an object (or person) on one characteristic. For example, you can present respondents with a statement, such as "Car Y is the best value for the money," and then ask them to agree or disagree with that statement on a scale from 1 to 7, where 1 means "strongly agree" and 7 means "strongly disagree."

- **Sorting scales:** A *sorting scale* presents several concepts — represented either on printed cards or a computer display — that respondents must arrange into two or more piles or groupings. To a large extent, sorting is similar to ranking. The advantage to sorting — as a mechanical task — is that you can ask people to sort many more objects than they can accurately rank. Thus, sorting scales tend to be more reliable than ranking scales for large numbers of objects.

- **Choice scales:** A *choice scale* between two or more alternatives are a type of attitude measurement that assumes the chosen object is preferred over the other objects. It may not seem so initially, but choice scales are a type of attitude measure because you can infer people's attitudes from their choices. Marketers assume that the brand chosen as most preferred is the one about which the respondent has the most favorable attitudes. Similarly, the brand selected as least preferred is the one about which the respondent has the least favorable attitudes.

Strongly Recommended: The Popular Likert Scale

Likert scales comprise a series of statements that people respond to on scales with descriptors like the single example shown here:

I prefer watching a rented video at home than going to the movies

_____ Strongly agree
_____ Agree
_____ Neither agree nor disagree
_____ Disagree
_____ Strongly disagree

Likert-type *statements plus scales* (or items) are a popular way to measure attitudes. They're popular for several reasons, such as they're relatively easy to write and respondents are familiar with such questions. Even if they ignore your instructions, as most respondents do, they'll still be able to answer your questions properly.

A *Likert scale* is actually a set or series of Likert-type items. Although a single item doesn't constitute a Likert scale, many researchers misuse the term and refer to single survey questions as Likert scales. Nonetheless, Likert scales are multi-item sets of statements plus response scales that as a group cover the complete domain of a construct. For example, you can assess consumers' satisfaction with their current automobile with a single question like "How satisfied are you with your current automobile?" However, you would learn far more from a series of satisfaction questions about the automobile's reliability, fuel efficiency, roominess, handling, and so on. To determine overall satisfaction, you would sum satisfaction scores for each question to achieve a total satisfaction score.

Relative to each Likert-type statement, you can use Likert-type scales to assess level of agreement, importance, interest, quality satisfaction, and rarity, to name a few. Because you should label each scale point to maximize the likelihood that respondents' answers correspond as closely as possible with their attitudes, we provide possible descriptors for each scale point in Figure 8-3. (Of course, Likert-type scales can have more than five scale points.)

In the following sections, we show you how to construct your own Likert scales.

Agreement				
Strongly agree	Agree	Neither agree nor disagree	Disagree	Strongly disagree
Importance				
Extremely important	Very important	Important	Neither important nor unimportant	Unimportant
Interest				
Exciting	Interesting	Neither interesting nor uninteresting	Uninteresting	Boring
Quality				
Excellent	Very good	Good	Fair	Poor
Well above average	Above average	Average	Below average	Well below average
Satisfaction				
Completely satisfied	Somewhat satisfied	Neither satisfied nor dissatisfied	Somewhat dissatisfied	Completely dissatisfied
Very satisfied	Satisfied	Somewhat satisfied	Barely satisfied	Not at all satisfied
Rarity				
Extremely different	Different	Somewhat different	Barely different	Identical
Very similar	Similar	Neither similar nor dissimilar	Dissimilar	Very dissimilar

Figure 8-3: Descriptors for Likert-type items.

Constructing Likert scales

We now show three efficient matrix organizations for placing such items in a questionnaire. Although some researchers use non-matrix configurations — such as a series of items like the first Likert-type item in this section — a more efficient organization can reduce the paper, printing, and postage costs for self-administered mail questionnaires. Also, most browser-based survey providers (see Chapter 10) rely on matrix-type organizations for Likert-type items.

Numeric matrix organization

Including scale numbers under each of the scale descriptions — as shown in Figure 8-4 — will make it easier for you to transfer respondents' answers from a paper-based questionnaire to a spreadsheet (for analysis). Clearly, it's easier to enter a string of circled numbers into a spreadsheet than to look at checked boxes or blanks, mentally convert them into numbers, and then enter those numbers into a spreadsheet. Figure 8-4 shows several Likert-type items for assessing the store image of a supermarket. The statements appear on the left-hand side of the question table. The responses range from *strongly agree* to *strongly disagree,* and the response categories are summarized by numbers *1* through *5.*

Please circle the number that corresponds most closely to your level of agreement with each statement.

Statement	Strongly agree	Agree	Neither agree nor disagree	Disagree	Strongly disagree
Yummy Food supermarket has lower prices than competitors	1	2	3	4	5
Merchandise displays at Yummy Food supermarket are messy	1	2	3	4	5
Clerks at Yummy Food supermarket are unfriendly	1	2	3	4	5
Yummy Food supermarket is conveniently located	1	2	3	4	5
Yummy Food supermarket has a good assortment of foods	1	2	3	4	5

Figure 8-4: Examples of numeric Likert-type items.

Nonnumeric matrix organization

Instead of using numerals as a way to indicate responses, you can create Likert-type items that use blanks or boxes that require a check mark for the response categories. Figure 8-5 shows several Likert-type items with blanks rather than numbers for indicating responses.

Although many formats work for Likert-type items, we recommend a number format because it eases computer data entry and minimizes respondent confusion (see the preceding section "Numeric matrix organization").

Please place a check mark in the space that corresponds most closely to your level of agreement with each statement.

Statement	Strongly agree	Agree	Neither agree nor disagree	Disagree	Strongly disagree
Yummy Food supermarket has lower prices than competitors	___	___	___	___	___
Merchandise displays at Yummy Food supermarket are messy	___	___	___	___	___
Clerks at Yummy Food supermarket are unfriendly	___	___	___	___	___
Yummy Food supermarket is conveniently located	___	___	___	___	___
Yummy Food supermarket has a good assortment of foods	___	___	___	___	___

Figure 8-5: Examples of Likert-type items with non-numerical responses.

Reversed numeric matrix organization

Often, a Likert-type agreement scale runs from *strongly agree* to *strongly disagree*. But, it's best to make *agree* a larger number than *disagree* because respondents tend to equate *more* with *better*. Under this reversed scoring scheme, the higher the score, the greater the level of agreement. Figure 8-6 shows this popular organization for Likert-type items.

The ten items shown in Figure 8-6 — such as, "The commercial was comforting," "The commercial was not boring," and "The commercial was creative" — can be asked to assess people's impressions about a test commercial. If all ten items relate to the same basic underlying notion, such as the likeability of the commercial, you can sum people's scores on these items to derive an overall score.

Of course, a meaningful sum without recoding requires that you phrase all your questions in the same direction (positive or negative), which isn't the case for the items in Figure 8-6. Some of the descriptions — comforting, creative, exciting, meaningful, entertaining, and helpful for making a purchase decision — are positive. People who strongly agree with those items must like the commercial. In contrast, to strongly agree with the other descriptions — boring, absurd, mundane, and ineffective in showing the product's advantage over competitors' products — is to dislike the commercial. To compute a meaningful sum, you must reverse score one of the two description sets.

Reverse scoring codes all the answers as if the original questions were asked in the same direction. To score all ten items in Figure 8-6 in a positive direction, you'd enter a *2* for the second description (The commercial was boring) if the respondent circled *4;* similarly, you'd enter a *1* as a *5,* a *4* as a *2,* and a *5* as a *1.* (On a five-point scale, the midpoint is unchanged.) Reverse scoring allows a meaningful sum of scores on all items to derive an overall likeability score for the commercial.

Please circle the number that corresponds most closely to your level of agreement with each statement, which begins "The commercial was . . ."

Statement The commercial was . . .	Strongly agree	Agree	Neither agree nor disagree	Disagree	Strongly disagree
Comforting	5	4	3	2	1
Boring	5	4	3	2	1
Absurd	5	4	3	2	1
Mundane	5	4	3	2	1
Creative	5	4	3	2	1
Exciting	5	4	3	2	1
Meaningful	5	4	3	2	1
Entertaining	5	4	3	2	1
Helpful for making a purchase decision	5	4	3	2	1
Effective in showing the product's advantage over competitors' products	5	4	3	2	1

Figure 8-6:
Examples
of Likert-
type items
with scale
numbers
reversed.

Structuring Likert-type scales

In gathering accurate consumer responses, it's imperative that your survey questions are clear and concise. If questions are vague and difficult to follow, respondents' answers will be worthless. To help clarify question meaning, you should use verbal category descriptors.

Providing verbal category descriptions

When creating your Likert-type scales, you should provide verbal descriptions for each category, and those descriptions should be concise and specific. Don't assume that describing the endpoints of your scale is sufficient. For example, you may know that the midpoint on your five-point level of agreement scale means "neither agree nor disagree," but some respondents may believe it means "no opinion." Respondents must be clear on the meaning of each response category if their answers are to reflect their attitudes accurately. (The sample telephone and mail questionnaires in Chapter 6 illustrate the naming of each Likert-type item category.)

Determining the number of response categories

You need to choose the number of categories you'll provide for your Likert-type items. Discriminating between people — and in marketing, discrimination is a good word because it means trying to differentiate groups of people according to their needs and preferences — may mean spotting subtle differences. If you write questions with few response categories, you'll find it difficult to identify distinct groups of people.

Here's the rule of thumb: Scales should have at least four categories, but typically five to nine categories. If you offer more than nine categories, respondents won't be able to make clear distinctions, like discerning the difference between 15 and 16 on a 20-point scale. However, keep in mind that as the number of categories increases (up to nine), scale sensitivity increases, which in turn increases measurement accuracy.

Choosing a balanced or an unbalanced scale

You need to choose either a balanced or an unbalanced scale. A *balanced scale* has an equal number of positive and negative response categories; an *unbalanced scale* has an unequal number of those categories. Conventional wisdom dictates that you use a balanced scale unless you know that respondents tend to respond toward one scale endpoint or the other.

This unbalanced response problem is an issue for ethics research; due to social desirability bias, many respondents tend to answer toward the positive scale endpoint (see Chapters 4 and 7). Stretching the positive end of the scale makes it easier to differentiate among the people crowding that end.

Selecting odd or even number of categories

You need to decide whether to use an odd or even number of response categories. This is a somewhat arbitrary decision.

We recommend that you use an odd number of scale points only if respondents could be truly neutral or indifferent. By using an even number of scale points, you eliminate fence sitting. If you provide an odd number of categories with a middle neutral point, respondents can be cognitively lazy and respond *neutral* instead of carefully considering whether they're slightly more favorable or unfavorable toward that statement.

Deciding between forced and nonforced choices

You need to decide whether to force respondents to answer your questions. By force, we mean excluding a "don't know" answer option. Without a "don't know" option, people who have no opinion often circle the midpoint of the scale. In this case, a respondent is mistakenly equating lack of knowledge with indifference. However, if you believe that respondents could be unknowledgeable about a statement, you should include a "don't know" response option.

Formatting examples

As the preceding discussion indicates, you have many options when devising measurement scales. In this section, we show you several examples of scales that you may use. Remember that gathering accurate data is an essential goal of marketing research, so choose question formats that are easy for your respondents to understand.

Example #1:

How do you like the taste of Yummy Bread?

Like it very much 1
Like it 2
Neither like nor dislike it 3
Dislike it 4
Dislike it very much 5

The five response options in this first example are balanced. This example is a forced-choice question because respondents don't have the option of saying they don't know. It also has an odd number of response options and assumes the possibility of an indifference point for someone's attitude toward the taste of Yummy Bread.

Example #2:

Overall, how would you rate the taste of Shiny Smile toothpaste?

Extremely good 1
Very good 2
Somewhat good 3
Somewhat bad 4
Very bad 5
Extremely bad 6

As in Example 1, the scale in Example 2 is balanced and presents a forced choice, but Example 2 includes an even number of response options. This scale assumes that respondents can have either a somewhat positive or somewhat negative opinion about the taste of Shiny Smile toothpaste, but they can't be indifferent.

Example #3:

What's your reaction to this television commercial?

Enthusiastic 1
Very favorable. 2
Favorable 3
Neutral 4
Unfavorable 5

Unlike the previous two examples, this scale is an unbalanced scale because it includes three favorable statements and only one negative statement. It's a forced-choice item because respondents don't have the option of answering that they don't know. This example also includes an odd number of response options.

Example #4:

How would you rate the service at Burger Joint?

Very friendly 1
Moderately friendly. 2
Slightly friendly. .3
Neither friendly nor unfriendly 4
Slightly unfriendly. 5
Moderately unfriendly 6
Very unfriendly 7

Don't know 9

The scale in Example 4 is balanced because it contains as many positively worded as negatively worded response options. It's not a forced-choice item because it has a "don't know" option. This option is off the scale continuum (and thus offset from the substantive items and not numbered consecutively). By excluding the "don't know" response, the example includes an odd number of response options.

Semantic Differential (SD) Scales

The Semantic Differential (SD) scale is a popular scale that contains a series of bipolar rating items. (In other words, bipolar adjectives anchor the endpoints for each item.) Figure 8-7 shows a simple set of SD items for assessing people's attitudes toward bowling. Instructions for this type of scale would ask respondents to place a check mark or other type of mark on each line such that the proximity of that mark to each adjective reflects their attitude. The SD scale is popular mainly because respondents only need to make a choice relative to a set of two bipolar adjectives; in essence, SD scales are easy to read and quick for respondents to answer. However, we're much more concerned with measurement accuracy than response speed.

Data entry for this type of scale requires mental gymnastics. To enter respondents' answers into a database, you first need to assign a number to each scale point.

Place a check mark on each dashed line so that the relative position of that mark to each endpoint reflects your attitude about bowling.

Good exercise	—	—	—	—	—	—	—	Not exercise
Fun	—	—	—	—	—	—	—	Boring
Easy	—	—	—	—	—	—	—	Difficult
Popular	—	—	—	—	—	—	—	Unpopular

Figure 8-7:
An example of semantic differential items.

Although many people refer to SD scales as scales with bipolar ratings, the true SD scale assumes three underlying attitudinal dimensions that everyone, regardless of culture or language, uses to evaluate things in their social environment. These three dimensions are evaluation, power/potency, and activity; for example, good-bad for evaluation, powerful-powerless for power/potency, and fast-slow for activity. For a properly constructed SD scale, all your items should relate to one of these three dimensions. However, researchers have adapted SD-type scales in which items may be unrelated to one of these three underlying dimensions.

Reviewing the limitations of SD scales

Although SD scales are popular, and you're likely to encounter them and be tempted to use them, we don't recommend them for the following reasons:

✔ **Respondents tend to misuse them.** They don't always read the instructions and are unfamiliar with SD scales in general. Although you should include easy-to-read and easy-to-follow instructions throughout your questionnaire (see Chapter 10 for more on good questionnaire design) — and you should encourage that they be read, — you should assume that many respondents won't read your instructions. As a result, some respondents will circle one endpoint descriptor for each SD item instead of checking the appropriate box or marking the appropriate area on the line between bi-polar adjectives. When respondents circle one of the bi-polar adjectives, you shouldn't guess that they meant to check off the box or the area of the line closest to that adjective. In such cases, you should discard their response.

✔ **They're difficult to construct.** It's far more difficult to construct SD items than Likert-type items. If nothing else, you're limited to only a few words and it's difficult to summarize complex notions so concisely. Likert-type items permit many more — although not an infinite number of — words.

✔ **Negation doesn't necessarily mean the opposite.** Many of the bipolar adjectives in the previous examples show words that are *something* and then *not something*. Sometimes *not something* is the opposite, but other times it isn't. For example, *not black* includes all the other colors that aren't black, such as yellow, blue, green, red, and orange. Hence, the opposite of *black* is *white*. Unfortunately, negation misuse is a common problem for researchers who construct SD scales.

Likert scales are easier to construct. Also, respondents are far more familiar with them and are more likely to use them properly. That said, some marketers believe that profile analyses created from SD data provide valuable marketing insights. We explain why SD-based profiles are problematic in the following section.

Limitations of profile analysis

Figure 8-8 shows a profile analysis for three different beers. This figure summarizes responses of many people to SD items for three different beers: a regional brand, national beer #1, and national beer #2.

Conventional wisdom suggests that the marketing department for each brewer uses this analysis to compare consumers' attitudes about its beer relative to its competitors' beers; if meaningful gaps exist, they should be addressed by modifying the product or promotional effort.

In this example, consumers perceive national beer #2 as the highest-priced beer. If that perception poses a problem — especially if it's incorrect — the brewer's marketing department seemingly should either run ads that remind viewers that its beer is a reasonably priced, good-value-for-the-money beer, or reduce current prices.

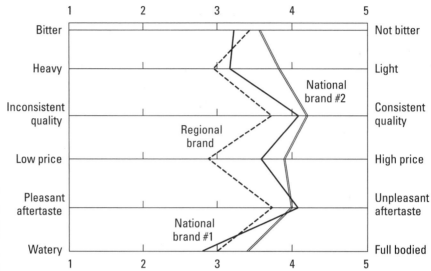

Profile Analysis of Three Beer Brands

Figure 8-8:
Profile
analysis for
three beers.

We include Figure 8-9 to show that a profile analysis can compare existing brands and consumers' ideal brand. In this example for large-screen LCD televisions, "I" represents the rating for a hypothetical ideal brand. Brand A is perceived as very expensive — far more expensive than Brand B — yet Brand B also is perceived as being too expensive relative to an ideal brand.

Figure 8-10 shows an image profile for a savings bank. The major gaps suggest that the present bank is perceived as being far more old-fashioned than the ideal bank, which is perceived as more modern. The ideal bank also is perceived as larger, more innovative, and a leader, relative to the present bank. This analysis suggests that the bank's managers should renovate their bank, update its procedures, and install new and more-modern equipment. Such changes seemingly would bring their bank into line with the ideal for their current customer base.

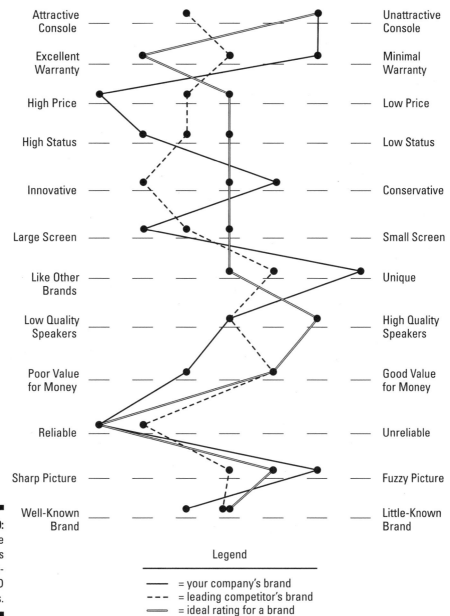

Figure 8-9:
Profile
analysis
for large-
screen LCD
televisions.

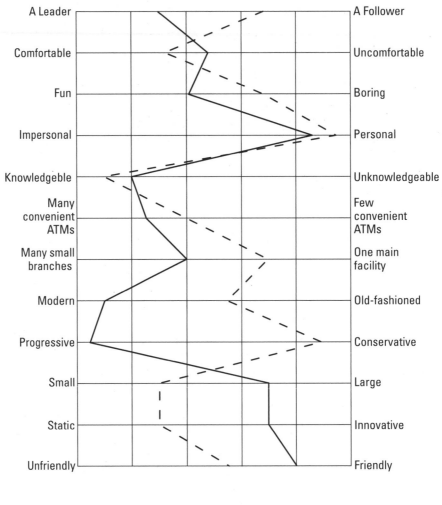

Figure 8-10:
Profile
analysis
for current
versus ideal
bank.

———————— "Ideal" Bank

– – – – – Present Bank

Although the preceding three examples suggest that profile analyses provide marketers with much useful information, we believe these analyses confuse decision-making about the best course of action for the following reasons:

- **Few brands can be depicted.** In the three previous examples, no more than three brands were compared. Admittedly, these are black-and-white graphs; with color, you may be able to compare as many as five brands. However, real markets tend to have more than four or five competitors, so such graphics would be incomplete. Alternative mapping procedures in marketing can depict far more than five brands. (Although these procedures are beyond the scope of this book, we briefly discuss and illustrate one mapping procedure in Chapter 21.)

- **Attributes may not be independent.** In the popular mapping procedures used by marketing researchers, you can guarantee that the underlying dimensions on which you're assessing things are independent (in the sense that the values for each dimension are uncorrelated; see Chapter 18). As typically created, profile analyses may include three or four items that relate to the same underlying notion. For the LCD television example in Figure 8-9, it's unclear that *innovative—conservative* taps into attribute than *like other brands—unique*. By not ensuring attribute independence, you may inadvertently overweight redundantly queried attributes.

- **Profiles may not be weighted by attribute importance.** Profile analyses don't indicate which attributes are of greater or lesser importance. In the earlier banking example, it seems that newness and innovation are major gaps that the bank managers should address. However, it's possible that the bank's customers view both gaps as trivial. Perhaps customers care about and therefore patronize this bank because it offers high-quality personal service. Without knowing which attributes are important or unimportant to customers, it's impossible to interpret these profiles meaningfully.

Chapter 9

Writing Good Questions

· ·

In This Chapter

▶ Comparing open-ended to close-ended questions

▶ Creating good questions

▶ Producing reliable and valid answers

▶ Working with comparative and non-comparative scales

· ·

A questionnaire is only as good as the questions it asks. You must ensure that your questionnaires are as well designed as possible (which we discuss in Chapter 10) and that your questions are as precise and as easy to answer as possible. Although it's easier to assume that respondents know what you mean by a certain question than to worry about its exact wording, that assumption is dangerous. You should care about the preciseness of your questions because respondents who interpret an imprecise question in different ways aren't answering the same question. In that case, differences in their answers can be due to either real differences in attitudes, preferences, and behaviors, or to bogus differences caused by various interpretations of the posed question. Because only meaningful responses and real differences between groups of respondents — for example, differences related to gender or income — truly can help you devise or revise your marketing strategy, you should strive for precisely worded questions.

In this chapter, we stress the importance of gathering reliable and valid answers from your respondents, which is essential for marketing research. Whether you use open or closed-ended questions, we discuss techniques that will help you acquire such data. For example, we discuss how to effectively measure consumer attitudes and purchase intentions using graphic, rating, and comparative scales.

Comparing Open-Ended and Close-Ended Questions

You can design questions so that any set of responses is feasible. With carefully biased wording, you could easily sway respondents into agreeing or disagreeing with almost any statement. That's never the goal of a marketing research study meant to help you choose among viable alternative courses of action (as we advocate in Chapter 1). Your survey should assess respondents' attitudes, preferences, and behaviors accurately. What you or anyone else does with those responses is up to you or them.

The first step toward ensuring that you ask good questions on your questionnaire is to plan what you'll measure. You must know what you need to learn (what are your research questions) and the targeted respondents (for example, who buys or has the potential to buy your product) for your questions. Different respondents have different abilities to answer different types of questions. After you identify and understand your targeted respondent, you'll have a better sense for how to write your questions. Then, you must choose the data collection method. You can ask far more complex questions in a self-administered mail questionnaire than you can in a telephone-administered questionnaire (for which response choices must be few and straightforward; more on that later in the chapter.) First, you need to decide how to structure your questions, starting with whether you prefer open-ended or close-ended questions.

Open-ended questions are analogous to the essay or short-answer questions you probably dreaded as a student, and close-ended questions are comparable to the multiple-choice questions you probably preferred. The reasons for your preferences parallel the advantages and disadvantages of both question types.

Looking at open-ended questions

By *open-ended question,* we mean a question that allows respondents to answer in whatever words they choose. For example, an open-ended question that a sports book operator may ask his patrons is, "Why do you like to bet on football games?"

The big advantage of open-ended questions is that they offer respondents an opportunity to provide a wide range of answers. Because some of these answers are unexpected, they spark revealing follow-up questions that can be used in person-to-person interviews.

However, the disadvantages of open-ended questions are many, including the following:

- **Articulate respondent bias:** To some extent, responses to open-ended questions are weighted unintentionally by respondent articulateness. Articulate respondents say more, and given the way responses are entered into a computer data file, more words will count more than fewer words.

- **Interviewer bias:** Open-ended questions don't lend themselves to self-administered questionnaires. They're best used with a live interviewer — either in person or via telephone. Unfortunately, interviewers aren't alike. Thus, interviewer differences can introduce additional response bias.

- **Hard-to-record answers:** Imagine asking people questions and then fully writing down what they say. Although audio or video recording may seem like a great alternative to reacquainting yourself with cursive writing, many people are reluctant to allow themselves to be audio or video recorded. As a result, the only record of their answers is whatever interviewers can scribble as quickly as they can scribble it. Often, these scribbles are incomplete and erroneous.

- **Coding inconsistency and difficulty:** Any post-data-collection numerical analysis would require you to examine every response to every question, develop basic categories that represent all possible responses, revisit all the answers, and then assign a numeric code to each answer. As you can imagine, such an effort requires much time and effort. (Refer to Part IV for more on collecting and analyzing data.) This disadvantage, more than any other, is the one that causes us to urge you to use close-ended questions if possible. They may take longer to write, but they'll make subsequent data analysis far easier.

- **Reduced cross-study comparability:** Open-ended questions are more difficult to use for cross-study comparisons because choices and contexts change over time. This problem is especially severe for cross-cultural studies. For example, the descriptions of similar behavior by Hispanic and Asian consumers may differ meaningfully, which would in turn obscure the similarity.

- **Complexity and costliness:** Open-ended questions are more costly because their best use requires live — and expensive — interviewers and additional costly data handling (associated with recording, coding, entry, and tabulation).

Explaining close-ended questions

By *close-ended question,* we mean a question that asks respondents to choose from a fixed set of alternative answers. For example, a close-ended question that a sports book operator may ask his patrons is, "Are you male or female?" Or, to gain more insight about patronage behavior, he can ask, "Are you more likely to bet on professional basketball or professional football games?"

Advantages of close-ended questions are

- ✔ **The communication skills of respondents are less critical.** Because close-ended questions merely require respondents to select from a set of alternatives, relatively inarticulate people won't struggle trying to answer them.

- ✔ **They allow for speedy responses.** Respondents can answer close-ended questions quickly, giving them the sense that they're making good progress toward completing the response task. Speedy response time per question also means you can ask more questions on a broader range of topics.

- ✔ **They're easier to answer.** It's easier for people to choose one option among several alternatives than it is for them to make an unstructured decision. Similarly, close-ended questions about attitudes, preferences, and behaviors are simpler to answer than open-ended questions. By easing the respondents' burden, you increase their enthusiasm for returning a completed questionnaire.

- ✔ **Data can be quickly coded, entered, and analyzed.** Close-ended questions are easily *pre-coded*. Specifically, each response category is assigned a number prior to data collection. That way, entering a respondent's answer into your response data file merely requires that you type a number corresponding with the answer provided. (You can read more about pre-coding in Chapter 10.) Subsequent basic analyses, like frequency distributions, are then straightforward in spreadsheet software like Excel (see Chapter 18 and the DVD).

- ✔ **Interviewing skills are less important.** Either little or no interviewing skill is needed to administer close-ended questions, which is why such questions dominate self-administered surveys.

Although close-ended questions have many advantages, they have some disadvantages relative to open-ended questions, including the following:

- ✔ **You can't obtain in-depth responses.** Respondents merely read through several options and pick the one that most represents their opinions or behaviors.

- ✔ **They're poor at providing new insights.** Such questions assume you already know the likely answers and you're merely asking respondents to pick one. Whether or not the response set includes many respondents' true answers, they're unlikely to volunteer insights about unlisted reply options.

✔ **They're more difficult to write.** It's more difficult to write good close-ended questions because you must anticipate all possible answers. Respondents who repeatedly fail to find suitable answer options for your questions will almost certainly abandon your questionnaire before they complete it.

✔ **Answers may not fully reflect respondents' attitudes.** You'll ask respondents to indicate the answer options that are most reflective of their attitudes, but you'll never know whether those options are spot on, vaguely appropriate, or something in between.

✔ **Categories hint at correct answers.** By providing the possible responses, you're suggesting the correct set of answers. Respondents may have answered differently, but once they read your answers, they sensed what comprised an appropriate answer and responded accordingly.

Writing Good Questions

Sound questions are critical to effective survey research. Such questions are unambiguous, concise, appealing, and relevant to the research problem. Although the process is seemingly simple, developing good questions taxes even seasoned researchers, so in the following sections we provide you with some critical rules of thumb.

Only write questions that address your research problem

A research proposal requires you to develop a research problem and a related set of research questions. (Chapter 2 helps you identify your research problem.) The following three guidelines can help you write effective survey questions that relate to your proposal:

✔ Create specific questions only after you've thoroughly thought through your research questions, which you've formalized in writing.

✔ When working on a questionnaire, constantly refer to your research questions. Otherwise, you'll find yourself writing interesting questions that may not help you make better marketing-related decisions.

✔ For each question you write, understand how responses to that question will help to answer your research questions. If you've written a question that's unrelated to your research questions, delete it from your questionnaire.

Write clear and precise questions

You may believe that a question is a question is a question. You also may believe that chewing gum takes seven years to pass through the human digestive system. However, both beliefs are false. Some questions are better — and more clear and concise — than others. If you don't believe us, consider these three versions of a candy bar consumption question:

#1: *How frequently do you eat a candy bar? (Circle number to the right of your answer.)*

Very frequently. 1
Often. 2
Not too often. 3
Never 4

#2: *How many candy bars do you eat during a typical week? (Circle the number to the right of your answer.)*

None. 1
1-2. 2
3-4. 3
5-6. 4
More than 6. 5

#3: *How many standard-sized candy bars–the roughly 2 oz. size you find in vending machines–did you eat last week? (Circle the number to the right of your answer.)*

None. 1
1-2. 2
3-4. 3
5-6. 4
More than 6. 5

Version 1 of the question asks how frequently the respondent eats a candy bar, from very frequently to never. Although seemingly straightforward, this version is ambiguous because "frequently" means different things to different people. One person may believe it means eating one candy bar daily, but another person may believe it means eating one candy bar weekly. Obviously, it's a problem when different people provide the same answer to describe vastly different behaviors or attitudes.

Version 2 is a bit better because it's more specific. Nonetheless, the question is ambiguous in several ways. What's a typical week? Is it five or seven days?

What's a candy bar? Are they the roughly 2-ounce versions found in many vending machines, or are they the 1-pound bars available in supermarkets? Again, your data are useless when respondents provide the same answers to describe different actions.

Version 3 is the clearest and most precise version because it defines what's meant by a candy bar and asks about a specific and recent time frame that respondents should be able to recall (last week rather than last three months or typical week).

Now consider these two versions of a question about watching Major League Baseball games on TV:

#1:   *How often do you watch major league baseball games on TV? (Circle number to the right of your answer.)*

> Never 1
> Rarely 2
> Occasionally 3
> Regularly 4

#2:   *How often did you watch at least half of a major league baseball game in the last month? (Circle the number to the right of your answer.)*

> Never 1
> Once or twice 2
> Roughly once a week 3
> Roughly twice a week 4
> More than twice a week 5

Version 1 suffers from imprecise questioning and poor wording. The wording of Version 2 is more specific in defining what's meant by watching a game — catching a few minutes of highlights on the new MLB channel doesn't qualify — and the time period.

Version 2 doesn't require respondents to recall behavior from more than one month ago or to develop a model of their behavior — neither of which people do well (as we discuss later in this chapter).

Although it's impossible to eliminate all ambiguity in a question — after all, natural language is inherently imprecise — you'll receive more reliable answers to questions that are less subject to respondent interpretation.

Include only mutually exclusive and exhaustive responses

Good close-ended questions provide respondents with answer options that are exhaustive and mutually exclusive. *Exhaustive* means all possible responses are represented, and *mutually exclusive* means that each answer precludes all other answers.

Exhaustive doesn't mean you should list every possible answer. For some questions, such a list would be needlessly detailed and may confuse some respondents. In creating an answer list, your goals should be to include the most likely choices and to capture rare responses with an "Other, please specify" category. That way, all respondents can find their answer to the question.

Consider this income question with choices that are exhaustive but not mutually exclusive:

Which of the following categories best describes your total household income before taxes in 2009? (Circle one answer only.)

$$
\begin{array}{ll}
\text{Less than \$20,000} \dots\dots\dots\dots\dots\dots & 1 \\
\text{\$20,000-\$40,000} \dots\dots\dots\dots\dots\dots & 2 \\
\text{\$40,000-\$60,000} \dots\dots\dots\dots\dots\dots & 3 \\
\text{More than \$60,000} \dots\dots\dots\dots\dots & 4
\end{array}
$$

The choices in the preceding list are exhaustive because all incomes from $0 and up are represented. The choices aren't mutually exclusive because there's no clear answer when the respondent's total household income before taxes is $20,000 or $40,000. In other words, if the respondent's income is $20,000, is the correct response Choice 2 or 3? If it's $40,000, is the correct response Choice 3 or 4? To fix this needlessly ambiguous question, you would change $40,000 to $39,999 in Choice 2 and $60,000 to $59,999 in Choice 3.

Your efforts to provide exhaustive choices may create a muddled list that mixes different types of things. One possible solution is to ask a series of questions that ask about one type of thing only. For example, consider these two versions of a question about the death of Michael Jackson:

In Version 1, the choices are muddled: radio and television are types of sources; while at work, home, and traveling to work are places (in other words, unparallel kinds of information). Instead of blurring sources and places, it's better to ask two distinct questions. In the revised version, the first question asks about the source and the second question asks about the place.

#1: *From which of these sources did you first hear about the death of Michael Jackson? (Circle one answer only.)*

> Radio 1
> Television 2
> Someone at work 3
> While at home 4
> While traveling to work 5

#2: *From which of these sources did you <u>first</u> hear about the death of Michael Jackson? (Circle one answer only.)*

> Radio 1
> Television 2
> Another person 3

Where were you when you first heard about it? (Circle one answer only.)

> At work 1
> At home 2
> Traveling to work 3
> Elsewhere 4

Use natural and familiar language

Using natural and familiar language requires more than avoiding sophisticated words; it also requires sensitivity to regional differences in words that mean the same thing. For example, people living in different regions of the United States refer to sandwiches you pile high with meat and veggies by five different descriptors. In some regions, those sandwiches are called grinders; in other areas, hoagies. In Chicago, they're called hero sandwiches; in New York, they're called submarine sandwiches; and in Texas and Louisiana, they're called po' boys.

You'll collect more reliable data if you use regionally accepted terms in your questions. Alternatively, your questionnaire can include descriptions of critical terms to help your respondents understand what you mean.

Here's an example in which the word "intoxicated" is problematic:

In the last twelve months, how often did you become intoxicated while drinking any alcoholic beverage? (Circle only one answer.)

Never 1
Once 2
Every few months 3
Once a month 4
Every few weeks 5
Once a week 6
Several times a week 7
Daily 8

A questionnaire is meant to assess respondents' attitudes and behaviors; it's not intended as a vocabulary test. Although the choices in the preceding question also may be problematic, the major issue with the question is the word *intoxicated*. People tend to mean vastly different things by that word. Many people mean the legal limit, which in many states is a 0.08 blood-alcohol level. Other people may mean falling-down drunk or totally out of control. Clearly, that latter state of drunkenness differs markedly from being ever-so-slightly over the 0.08 blood-alcohol level. Rather than assume that all respondents will interpret the word *intoxicated* similarly, you could rephrase the question as follows:

> *Sometimes people drink so much beer, wine, or hard liquor that they act differently than usual. In the last 12 months, how often did you drink enough of these beverages that you acted differently than usual?*

By defining intoxication in terms of a modified behavior, people are more likely to think about the same consumption level when responding to a question about consumption frequency. Also, the revised wording eliminates any confusion about what qualifies as an alcoholic beverage.

Avoid leading questions

Unless you have a political agenda — you want to document that people agree or disagree with a certain position or candidate — your questions should provide data to help you make more informed marketing-related decisions. Thus, you should avoid questions that lead to a certain conclusion. For example, this question initially seems reasonable:

> *What did you dislike about the product you just tried?*

Even if respondents didn't dislike anything about the product, the question encourages them to think of some aspect that they found less than totally satisfactory. Such a question may lead you to believe that your customers are far less satisfied with the product than is the case. As a result, you may try to fix something that isn't broken. Instead, divide the question into two parts:

> *1. Did you dislike any aspect of the product you just tried?*

> *2. If yes, then what aspect and why?*

Here's another leading question and a revised version that eliminates the bias:

> **Leading version:** *Do you believe private citizens have the right to own firearms to defend themselves, their families, and their property from violent criminal attack?*

> **Revised version:** *Do you believe a ban on private ownership of firearms would significantly reduce the number of murders and robberies in your community?*

Firearm ownership is an emotional issue for many people, and the original version's phrasing encourages a biased emotional response. After all, who wouldn't answer yes to the implied question, "Do I have the right to protect my family?" In contrast, the revised version eliminates the family defense issue, so its emotional overtone is reduced markedly (but not completely).

Ask one question at a time

A question that asks more than one question at a time is called a *double-barreled question.* These questions are problematic because respondents don't know which inquiry to focus on, so their answers (and your data) end up muddled. Here's an example of a double-barreled question:

> *Do you believe the service at our coffee shop is fast and courteous?*

How does a respondent who believes the service is fast yet rude — or slow but reasonably courteous — answer this question? Because two questions are present, respondents won't know which question to answer.

Here's a double-barreled question and a revision that eliminates the problem:

> **Double-barreled version:** *Should the city use tax revenue to build a new community swimming pool that includes lanes for swimming laps but isn't enclosed for winter use?*

> **Revised version:** *(1) Should the city use tax revenue to build a new community swimming pool that includes lanes for swimming laps? (2) If you answered yes, should the city enclose this pool for winter use?*

The following example shows a problem akin to the double-barrel problem. To reduce the number of questionnaire pages — and hence the postage costs — for a mail questionnaire, you may be tempted to format questions like the upcoming original version. Unfortunately, efforts to save photocopying and postage costs in this way are pennywise but dollar foolish.

Here's the original version:

Please indicate how important each of our online banking services is to you. For each service you rated 'very important', please indicate how frequently you used it during the last three months. (Please circle your importance answer and write the number of times you used this type of service in the space provided.)

Banking Service	How Important?			Times Used in Last Three Months
Automatic drafts	Very	Somewhat	Not	_____
Buying CDs	Very	Somewhat	Not	_____
Bill paying	Very	Somewhat	Not	_____
Funds transfers	Very	Somewhat	Not	_____
Overdraft protection	Very	Somewhat	Not	_____

Here's the revised version:

How often have you used each of our online banking services during the last three months? (Write number in space provided.)

Automatic drafts .... _____
Buying CDs .... _____
Bill paying .... _____
Funds transfers .... _____
Overdraft protection ...... _____

How important is each of these online services to you?

Online Service	Very Important	Important	Somewhat Important	Not Important
Automatic drafts	1	2	3	4
Buying CDs	1	2	3	4
Bill paying	1	2	3	4
Funds transfers	1	2	3	4
Overdraft protection	1	2	3	4

Soften the impact of potentially objectionable questions

People are reluctant to answer questions about sensitive attitudes and behaviors; for example, their attitudes toward legalizing marijuana and their use of medical marijuana. So if you're a California politician who's both desperate for tax revenues and worried about voter backlash for supporting an unpopular bill, then you want truthful answers from voters surveyed about their marijuana-related attitudes and behaviors. How do you overcome people's tendency to give socially desirable responses (as we discuss in Chapter 7)?

You can follow this simple procedure when your sensitive question is a yes or no question: Present respondents with two questions — one innocuous and one sensitive — and a random mechanism, such as flipping a coin, for selecting which of the two questions to answer. Because only the respondents know which question they answered, they won't worry about giving a socially undesirable answer.

Here's an example to illustrate our point. To assess the popularity of a bill supporting the legalization of marijuana, you mail a questionnaire to 2,000 likely voters. Here's a possible pair of innocuous and sensitive questions:

> **Innocuous question:** *Is the last digit of your Social Security number odd?*
>
> **Sensitive question:** *Would you support a bill legalizing marijuana?*

To choose which question they'll answer, you instruct the respondents to flip a coin; heads requires them to answer the innocuous question, and tails requires them to answer the sensitive question. Of the 1,000 people who returned a completed questionnaire — a respectable 50 percent response rate (see Chapter 12) — 550 answered yes, and 450 answered no. If they all used a fair coin, roughly 500 of them answered the innocuous question and 500 of them answered the sensitive question. The odds are 50/50 that the 500 people who randomly selected the innocuous question answered yes; hence, roughly 250 yes answers are attributable to that question. If you received 550 yes answers, then roughly 300 of the 500 people (or 60 percent) who responded to the sensitive question answered it yes. Thus, you wouldn't jeopardize your re-election by supporting a bill to legalize marijuana.

Alternatively, you can simply soften potentially objectionable questions as much as possible. For example, if you believe that higher-income households are more likely than lower-income households to prefer your product, you'll need household income data for classification purposes. Unfortunately, people often refuse to answer a fill-in-the-blank income question like "In 2009, what was your total household income, before taxes, from all sources?" Instead, you may ask this somewhat softer version:

For 2009, which category best describes your total household income,
before taxes? (Circle number to the right of your answer.)

Less than $20,000 1
$20,000 to $39,999 2
$40,000 to $59,999 3
$60,000 to $79,999 4
$80,000 to $99,999 5
$100,000 or more 6

People are far more likely to report the range in which their household income falls than to report an exact income figure.

Suppose you're a retailer who's considering an expensive surveillance system to curtail shoplifting. You want to know whether the system will pay for itself in reduced thefts. If many of your customers are shoplifters, the answer is yes; otherwise, the answer is no. As part of a larger self-administered questionnaire, you can ask one of these two questions to estimate how many of your customers are shoplifting:

#1: *Have you ever shoplifted anything from a store? (Circle number to the right*
       of your answer.)

Yes 1
No 2

#2: *Have you ever taken anything from a store without paying for it? (Circle number to*
       the right of your answer.)

Yes 1
No 2

Understandably, many people are reluctant to admit that they've committed a crime. So instead of using the word "shoplifting," which is a jarring word, you can substitute the softer phrase "taken anything . . . without paying for it." Although Versions 1 and 2 are synonymous, Version 2 doesn't seem to ask about past criminal behavior. As a result, respondents are more likely to answer the second version honestly.

Generating Reliable and Valid Answers

Because your marketing research findings will influence your business decisions, it's imperative that you obtain reliable and valid answers from respondents.

Attending to several psychological issues — such as memory effects, need-lessly complex calculations, overly specific questions, order bias, and man-ageable comparison tasks — will help you to obtain such answers.

Consider memory effects

People have faulty memories that can be stressed beyond the point where they can give reliable answers. As a result, people who are asked questions that overtax their memories may experience any of the following memory effects:

- ✔ **Omission:** *Omission* is forgetting that you have done something. Many behaviors of great interest to marketers barely register in consumers' consciousness. For example, unless you're a health fanatic or have an iron will, it's unlikely that you'd accurately recall all your purchases from food vending machines in the past two weeks. Obviously, any pur-chase you forgot would be omitted from a self-reported total.

- ✔ **Telescoping:** People tend to recall memorable events, and with *telescop-ing* they remember such events as having occurred more recently than was the case. If you ask people the last time they dined at a high-end restaurant, they may recall having done so in the last few months, when in fact they may not have done so in the last half year.

- ✔ **Creation:** Like eyewitnesses who after repeated questioning by police eventually believe they saw a specific person commit a crime, consum-ers can construct false purchase or consumption memories. This behav-ior is called *creation.* Unintentionally erroneous responses to questions about previous behavior are called *demand artifacts;* the demands of the questioning process can cause people to create false memories. Self-reports about socially desirable behaviors, such as the number of times you exercised for 30 minutes or more during the last month, are espe-cially susceptible to this effect.

Consider these problematic and improved versions of two questions:

> **Faulty version:** *In the last five years, how many times have you visited with a doctor about your health?*

> **Improved version:** *In the last six months, how many times have you visited with a doctor about your health?*

People are unlikely to recall accurately routine events that occurred years ago. Instead, the improved version asks about the same behavior over a shorter period of time.

Unlike physician visits, dining out is a relatively common and generally for-gettable occurrence. In reporting the frequency of such behaviors over an extended period, people tend to construct personal models and answer consistently with those models. For example, people who believe they, on average, eat at a restaurant twice per week will calculate that they've dined at a restaurant 52 times in the last six months ($2 \times 26 = 52$). That number may or may not be representative of the true number.

Your intuition may suggest asking people to model their behavior over a shorter period. Regardless of time frame, people's personal models tend to be inaccurate. Although counterintuitive — because idiosyncratic events would seem to meaningfully influence the short-term variability of common behaviors — it's best to limit your questions to recent behaviors, which people are most likely to recall accurately. Hence, the third version in the following list of questions is best:

> **Worst version:** *How many times in the last six months did you eat at a restaurant?*

> **Improved version:** *On average, how many times per week do you eat at a restaurant?*

> **Best version:** *In the last month, how many times did you eat at a restaurant?*

Don't ask respondents to make unnecessary calculations

Many people lack good mental math skills, so you shouldn't ask them to make unnecessary mental calculations. To do so will either frustrate them — which will discourage them from continuing to answer your questions — or produce erroneous responses that may be indistinguishable from accurate responses. For example, here's a needlessly difficult question:

> *In the last 12 months, what percent of the time did you stay overnight at a hotel or motel while on a business trip? (Write your answer in the blank space provided.)*

> _____ percent

To answer this question, respondents must first think about how many nights they stayed overnight at a hotel or motel in the last year. Then, they'd need to estimate the percent of those nights related to business-related travel. For frequent business travelers, who also tend to be frequent leisure travelers, a question that requires such counting and dividing is excessively complex to answer meaningfully. Here's a better multi-question version:

These answers provide the raw data for researchers to calculate the percent of nights stayed at a hotel or motel due to business-related travel. Although a shorter time frame would reduce memory effects, most people travel on business fewer than four times per year; thus, a longer time frame is needed to capture differences in people's travel frequency.

In the last twelve months, how many nights did you stay at a hotel or motel? (Write answer in blank space below.)

_____ nights

How many of those nights were due to business-related travel? (Write answer in blank space below.)

_____ nights

Steer clear of impossibly specific questions

Don't ask respondents such specific questions that they couldn't possibly have an accurate ready-made answer. The results of asking such questions include erroneous responses and respondents frustrated by attempting to formulate a difficult answer. Consider these two versions of a question about watching commercial films:

#1: *Roughly how many movies–either broadcasted or on electronic media–did you watch at home during the last twelve months? (Write answer in blank space below.)*

_____ movies

#2: *In the last twelve months, roughly how many movies–either broadcasted or on electronic media–did you watch at home? (Circle number to the right of your answer.)*

    Fewer than 10 1
    10-29 2
    30-59 3
    60-89 4
    90 or more 5

It's almost impossible for respondents, unless they've watched very few movies during the last 12 months, to recall the number watched with a reasonable degree of accuracy. Instead, Version #2 provides broad categories that offer ready-made answers. Of course, the choices suggest the nature of an appropriate answer; in this case, somewhere between 10 and 90 movies. So, you must pretest such questions (see Chapter 10) to ensure that the response options don't hint either *too low* or *too high* relative to typical movie-watching frequency.

Control for order bias

At first blush, you may think that the order in which you present possible responses to a close-ended question shouldn't pose a problem. After all, order isn't an issue on multiple-choice exams administered to students. However, the same isn't true for survey research.

Independent of the question, response style influences people's answers. Some people prefer initial response options, and other people prefer later response options. (Psychologists refer to the undue influence of initial and most recent experiences as *primacy* and *recency* effects.) To overcome order bias, which is a tendency to favor questions or objects because of their position in a sequential list, for non-naturally-ordered categories you should field multiple questionnaires with items listed in different orders. To ease respondents' effort, you should list naturally-ordered categories — like the multiple categories that range from *strongly agree* to *strongly disagree* — in logical sequence.

Always provide equal comparisons

To increase sales, ads often include unequal comparisons, which require respondents to compare two vastly different things. For example: *This pile of clothes was washed with detergent alone, but this other pile was washed with detergent plus our wonderful laundry additive. See how much cleaner this second pile looks.* Because the same detergent is common to both piles of clothes, the ad essentially asks you to compare the efficacy of the laundry additive with nothing! Unequal comparisons tend to bias responses, especially to questions about socially charged issues like public school education, tobacco and alcohol usage, decriminalization of marijuana, and the like.

Here's a survey question that asks respondents to make an unequal comparison:

Which one of the following do you believe is responsible for the growing obesity of people in the U.S.? (Circle number to right of answer.)

> Irresponsible parents 1
> Food producers 2
> Ineffective government regulations 3

Unlike irresponsible parents and ineffective government regulations, food producers are a non-emotionally-charged choice. To create equal choices, the question can be revised as follows:

Which one of the following do you believe is responsible for the growing obesity of people in the U.S.? (Circle number to right of answer.)

Parents 1
Food producers 2
Government agencies 3

State both sides of an attitude scale in question stems (lead lines)

Presenting only one side of an *attitude scale* (see Chapter 8) will bias responses in that direction. So, you shouldn't ask "To what extent do you agree with this statement?" Instead, you should ask "To what extent do you agree or disagree with this statement?"

In the following examples, Version 2 provides both sides of the scale and discourages *acquiescence bias,* or yea-saying (which we discuss in Chapter 7):

#1: *To what extent do you agree with this statement? 'Buying a new car is easier now than it was last year'. (Circle number to right of answer.)*

Strongly agree 1
Agree 2
Neither agree nor disagree 3
Disagree 4
Strongly disagree. 5

#2: *Do you believe buying a new car now is much easier, somewhat easier, neither easier nor harder, somewhat harder, or much harder than it was last year? (Circle number to right of answer.)*

Much easier 1
Somewhat easier. 2
Neither easier nor harder 3
Somewhat harder 4
Much harder. 5

Ask questions as complete sentences

If self-administered questionnaires are surrogates for face-to-face or telephone interviews, then respondents are participating in pseudo-conversations. Your questionnaire should avoid questions phrased as incomplete sentences; complete sentences are preferred. Consider these two sets of open-ended demographic questions:

#1: Number of years at current residence: _____ years

Current city of residence: _____

Current occupation: _____

#2: How many years have you lived in your current residence? _____ years

In what city is your full-time residence? _____

If you earn income from a job, what is your main occupation?

_____

By making the questionnaire more conversational — as in Version 2 — you encourage respondents to think more carefully about their answers and treat their effort more like a conversation with you.

Distinguish undecided responses from neutral ones

As we discuss in Chapter 8, *response scales* (scales that contain a mutually exclusive and exhaustive set of response choices) can be either balanced or unbalanced and present either a forced or nonforced choice. A nonforced choice scale clearly differentiates the *neutral point* (typically the *neither agree nor disagree* option) from the *no opinion* option. If you provide a *no opinion* or *don't know* option, it should be the last response option and visually set apart from the scale (as much as possible). These options should be last and somewhat apart because they aren't part of the continuum represented by the scale (for example, a degree of agreement continuum or a degree of satisfaction continuum). Consider these two scales:

#1: *To what extent do you agree or disagree with this statement? 'Pix are for kids'. (Circle number to right of answer.)*

Strongly agree 1

Agree 2

Don't know 3

Disagree 4

Strongly disagree. 5

#2: *To what extent do you agree or disagree with this statement? 'Pix are for kids'. (Circle number to right of answer.)*

Strongly agree 1

Agree 2

Neither agree nor disagree 3

Disagree 4

Strongly disagree. 5

Don't know 6

In Version 1, *Don't know* is the midpoint. In this position, you don't know if it represents "I have no opinion?" or "I've thought about the issue but I neither agree nor disagree?" To avoid this ambiguity, you should use scales like the one shown in Version 2. Also, by offsetting the nonsubstantive *Don't know* response from the substantive responses, you're making the conceptual (how it's processed) and visual (how it looks) scale midpoints identical.

Formatting a Purchase Intent Scale

At times, people may be poor predictors of their eventual purchases; yet, the format of your *purchase intent* scale can improve its predictive power.

Here are two effective formats for a purchase intent scale. Both formats include an odd number of response categories. In the first example, the scale is balanced and has a neutral point; in the second example, the scale is balanced without a neutral point. (Refer to Chapter 8 for more on neutral scale points.)

Five-point Purchase Intent Scale

_____ Definitely would buy

_____ Probably would buy

_____ Might or might not buy

_____ Probably would not buy

_____ Definitely would not buy

Eleven-point Purchase Intent Scale

_____ Certain (99 in 100 chance)

_____ Almost sure (9 in 10 chance)

_____ Very probable (8 in 10 chance)

_____ Probable (7 in 10 chance)

_____ Good possibility (6 in 10 chance)

_____ Fairly good possibility (5 in 10 chance)

_____ Fair possibility (4 in 10 chance)

_____ Some possibility (3 in 10 chance)

_____ Very slight possibility (2 in 10 chance)

_____ Almost no chance (1 in 10 chance)

_____ No chance (0 in 100 chance)

Designing Effective Graphic Rating Scales

Graphic rating scales present respondents with a graphic continuum and ask them to rate an attribute by placing a check or _x_ at the appropriate point on a line that runs from one attribute extreme to the other. These scales can take many forms and can measure a host of phenomena, such as consumer perceptions, beliefs, and behavioral intentions.

Figure 9-1 shows a graphic purchase intent scale, which is used to assess a person's willingness to buy something. (You can read more about nongraphic purchase intent scales in the earlier section "Formatting a Good Purchase Intent Scale.")

Figure 9-1:
Graphic
purchase
intent scale. (Place an "X" in a position on the line that indicates your likelihood of buying Product X.)

Would _____ Would
not buy   Might or might not buy   buy

Figure 9-2 shows a series of graphic scales for assessing respondents' beliefs about the similarities of different diet colas. (You can substitute any product category or brand you wish; we chose diet colas arbitrarily.) To enter respondents' answers into a computer data file, you'd need to measure the distance between the left-most point on the line and the x. That distance, in inches or centimeters expressed in decimal form (for example, 2.5 inches), is the number you'd enter for each response.

Here are several pairs of carbonated soft drinks. Please indicate your beliefs about the similarity of each soft drink pair by marking the line anchored by the phrases 'Identical' and 'Totally Different'. For example, if you believe that Diet Pepsi and Diet Coke are extremely similar, your response might look as follows:

Diet Pepsi versus Diet Coke

Identical--X - Totally Different

Diet Pepsi versus Tab

Identical - Totally Different

Tab versus Coke Zero

Identical - Totally Different

Coke Zero versus Diet Pepsi

Identical - Totally Different

Diet Coke versus Tab

Figure 9-2:
Series of
graphic
scales for
diet colas.
Identical - Totally Different

Tab versus Diet Coke

Identical - Totally Different

Graphic rating scales are useful when respondents' language capabilities are deficient. Language isn't an issue when it comes to the ladder scale shown in Figure 9-3, which serves as an analogy for the way people think about life and climbing the ladder of success. The top rung of the ladder (one end of the continuum) represents the best possible life and the lowest rung (the other end of the continuum) represents the worst possible life. Respondents indicate their opinion by placing an *x* on the rung that best represents their response. This scale is especially effective because it symbolizes the underlying construct you're trying to assess.

Best Possible Life

Figure 9-3:
Ladder
scale.

Worst Possible Life

Figure 9-4 shows a thermometer scale for evaluating the quality of food served at the Chow Down diner. As most diner food is meant to be served hot, cold diner food is a negative. So, this scale also symbolizes — although less comprehensively — the underlying construct; in this case, food quality, but you can substitute any product characteristic.

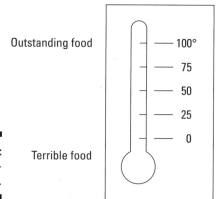

Figure 9-4:
Thermom-
eter scale.

Outstanding food — 100°
— 75
— 50
— 25
— 0
Terrible food

As mentioned about the ladder scale, you can use graphic scales on children or adults with language limitations. Often, the verbal abilities of younger children are minimal. Even if they're interviewed by an expert in communicating with children, a scale like the one shown in Figure 9-5 may provide a more accurate attitude assessment than a simply phrased question.

Interviewer's question and instruction:

Please circle the picture that shows how much you like Yummy-Yummy fruit snacks.

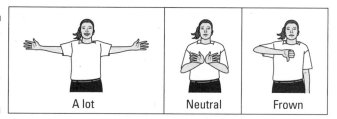

Figure 9-5:
Graphic
response
scale for
children.

A lot   Neutral   Frown

Figure 9-6 shows a smiling-face scale that can work for either young children or language-challenged adults. Such scales may prove especially effective when surveying customers who speak English as a second language, because all people understand what a smiley face denotes.

Interviewer's question and instructions:

Show me how much you like Super-Duper candy bars by circling the face that best shows how much you like them. If you don't like Super-Duper candy bars at all, then you should circle Face #1. If you liked them very much, then you should circle Face #4.

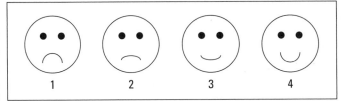

Figure 9-6:
Smiley-face
scale.

Working with Comparative Scales

Noncomparative scales, like the ones discussed in Chapter 8, require respondents to consider the characteristics of a single object or person. In contrast, *comparative scales* require respondents to compare multiple objects or persons according to a specific characteristic. In the following sections, we provide information on several different types of comparative scales.

Ranking scales

Ranking scales are a type of comparative scale in which objects (or people) are ranked on a single characteristic (like cost, size, speed, or beauty). Ranking provides a direct comparison of objects (or people) from best-to-worst/highest-to-lowest/most-to-least on each of several important characteristics, which combined with the relative importance of those characteristic can reflect respondents' overall preferences.

Here's an example of a ranking scale for toothpaste:

*Please rank these six toothpaste brands from best to worst. For each characteristic,
the best brand should be ranked '1' and the worst brand should be ranked '6'.
(Write each number in the space provided.)*

	Freshens breath	Pleasant taste	Whitens teeth
Aim	_____	_____	_____
Aquafresh	_____	_____	_____
Crest	_____	_____	_____
Colgate	_____	_____	_____
Gleem	_____	_____	_____
Ultra Bright	_____	_____	_____

This scale allows respondents to rank six different brands on three different characteristics. It presents as complex a rating task as we'd recommend you ask respondents to perform. Ranking more than a half-dozen objects on a given characteristic is beyond many respondents' abilities. Although such scales can indicate the most preferred (or highest ranked) and the least preferred (or lowest ranked) object reliably, the rankings for all other objects will be unreliable.

Table 9-1 represents data collected from ten people asked to rank four brands.

Table 9-1	Raw Rank-Order Data			
Person	*Brand #1*	*Brand #2*	*Brand #3*	*Brand #4*
1	1	2	4	3
2	4	2	1	3
3	2	1	3	4
4	4	2	1	3
5	3	1	4	2
6	2	1	3	4
7	2	1	3	4
8	3	1	2	4
9	1	3	2	4
10	2	1	4	3

As we discuss in Chapter 18, you must analyze rank-order data properly. Because they aren't metric (interval or ratio-scaled) data, they shouldn't be analyzed with traditional statistics; doing so violates basic statistical assumptions and produces misleading analyses.

For the results reported in Table 9-1, you shouldn't compute mean ranks and then conclude that Brand 2 is ranked best *on average*. Instead, you must create a table like Table 9-2, which summarizes the raw data in Table 9-1 by showing the number of times each brand is ranked first, second, third, and fourth. This second table illustrates a meaningful and statistically correct way to summarize rank-order data.

Table 9-2		Summary of Raw Rank-Order Data		
Brand	*Times Ranked 1st*	*Times Ranked 2nd*	*Times Ranked 3rd*	*Times Ranked 4th*
1	2	4	2	2
2	6	3	1	0
3	2	2	3	3
4	0	1	4	5

Paired-comparison scales

A *paired-comparison scale* is a ranking scale in which respondents are presented with two objects at a time and asked to pick the one they prefer. This is a relatively simple task that almost all respondents can perform properly, so it's quite reliable.

Here's a paired-comparison scale that can help you plan ads for a restaurant. Restaurants have different characteristics, such as price level, location, service, and atmosphere. To design the most effective ads, it would help to know the most important characteristics people consider when selecting a restaurant.

Here are some characteristics of restaurants. Please indicate the characteristic in each pair that's most important when you choose a restaurant for a relaxing meal with friends. (Place an 'x' in the space provided.)

_____ Moderate prices ..... or.... _____ Convenient location

_____ Convenient location .. or.... _____ Good service

_____ Warm atmosphere ... or.... _____ Moderate prices

_____ Good service .... or.... _____ Warm atmosphere

_____ Warm atmosphere ... or.... _____ Convenient location

_____ Moderate prices ..... or.... _____ Good service

Assume you want respondents to rate ten brands from most to least preferred. If you used a ranking scale (see the preceding section), the ten items would be listed, and respondents would place a number 1 through 10 next to each item according to how they rank it from most to least preferred. Although this is a seemingly straightforward task, people's responses will be unreliable because they're comparing an excessive number of items. We recommend that you never ask people to rank more than a half-dozen items at once.

Instead, you can pose this ranking question as a series of paired comparisons: Which do you prefer: Brand 1 or Brand 2? Brand 1 or Brand 3? Brand 2 or Brand 3? And so on. From such data, you can construct a table like Table 9-3, which for illustration purposes was constructed from only one person's hypothetical responses. Each column indicates whether the brand heading the column was preferred to the brand listed for each row; a *1* indicates the brand named at the top of the column is preferred to the brand named at the left of each row, and a *0* indicates the reverse preference. (Because a person can't prefer a brand to itself, all the diagonal entries are noted as "–.") Table 9-3 shows that this person preferred Brand 3 to Brand 1 and Brand 3 to Brand 2.

Although people's paired-comparisons across more than three items won't always be consistent, they'll be sufficiently consistent that you'll be able to determine general preferences from a table like Table 9-3.

Table 9-3	Brands Preferred in Paired Comparison		
	Brand 1	*Brand 2*	*Brand 3*
Brand 1	–	0	1
Brand 2	1	–	1
Brand 3	0	0	–

You can't assess an excessive number of items at once with paired-comparison scales. Returning to the ten-brand example from earlier in the section, if you asked about all possible combinations, you'd be posing 45 ($10 \times 9 \div 2$) brand-pair questions. Rather than writing ten numbers, respondents would indicate their preferred brand in 45 brand pairs, which would be tiring. After they become fatigued, respondents won't carefully discriminate between brands, thus negating the advantage of paired-comparison scales over rank-order scales. If you must rank more than ten things, check out the method we discuss in the section under the heading *Q-sort*.

Constant-sum scales

Constant-sum scales have one especially favorable property as comparative scales: They generate ratio-scaled data. As we discuss in Chapter 18, scales can yield nominal, ordinal, interval, or ratio-scaled data. Because ratio-scaled data makes possible statements like, "X is twice as much as Y," they allow for the strongest comparisons.

Here's an example of a constant-sum scale. In this example, respondents are asked to allocate 100 points across five characteristics of golf shirts.

Below are five characteristics of golf shirts. Please allocate 100 points among these characteristics such that your allocation represents the importance of each characteristic to you. Assign more points to characteristics that are more important to you and fewer points to characteristics that are less important to you. For example, you should assign twice as many points to a characteristic that is twice as important as another characteristic. Assign zero points to a characteristic that is unimportant to you. When you have finished, please check that you have assigned all 100 points.

Characteristic	Number of Points
Contemporary style	_____
Good value for the money	_____
Made in the U.S.	_____
Won't show sweat stains	_____
Looks good after repeated washings	_____

If "contemporary style" receives 15 points, and "good value for the money" receives 30 points, the first characteristic is only half as important as the second characteristic. That level of analysis is unavailable with nominal- or interval-scaled data.

One limitation of constant-sum scales is that most respondents will be unfamiliar with them. As a result, respondents who fail to read your instructions may just *check off* those characteristics they believe are most important. Such responses are unusable. Also, be certain not to ask respondents to assign points among an excessive number of characteristics. After you exceed ten characteristics, respondents will be unable to allocate points in a way that reliably represents their beliefs about the relative importance of those characteristics.

A weighted-paired-comparison scale combines the features of a constant-sum with a paired comparison scale. Such data reveals which brand is preferred and the degree to which it's preferred.

Please allocate a total of 10 points to each pair of shampoo brands listed below. Allocate those points so that they represent how much you prefer one brand to the other brand. Some possible allocations are 11-0, 1-10, 9-2, 3-8, 7-4, and 5-6. (Write those point allocations in the space provided.)

Suave.............. _____ .... Finesse............ _____

Pantene............ _____ .... Herbal Essence ..... _____

Suave.............. _____ .... Pantene .... _____

Finesse .... _____ .... Herbal Essence ..... _____

Herbal Essence ...... _____ .... Suave............. _____

Pantene............ _____ .... Finesse............ _____

Q-sort

Q-sort is a method for ranking many items without taxing people's abilities to provide meaningful responses. Suppose you want respondents to rank 70 magazines from most to least preferred. A traditional ranking approach would produce highly unreliable rankings for all but the several most and least preferred magazines. Because of the enormous number of pairs — $(70 \times 69) \div 2$, or 2,415 pairs — a paired-comparison approach is ruled out.

One workable alternative is to give respondents a mechanical sorting task. You can provide them a deck of cards, with each card showing a cover from one magazine. Your instructions to them could be as follows:

> *Please choose the 10 magazines you most prefer from the 70 magazines depicted in this set of cards. After you select the 10 cards corresponding to your 10 most-preferred magazines, place those cards in the envelope marked #1. Now select the 10 cards that depict your next 10 most-preferred magazines and place those cards in the envelope marked #2. Continue this process until you've placed all 70 cards into the 7 envelopes.*

Respondents can perform this mechanical sorting task, but asking them to identify a set of ten most-preferred magazines and then a set of ten second-most-preferred magazines, and so forth, is moderately difficult. As a result, their placement of cards in the middle envelopes — marked #2 through #6 — may be somewhat unreliable. To produce a more reliable preference ranking of magazines, you can use a less taxing Q-sort approach.

The main difference between the first sorting approach and a Q-sort is your sorting instructions. It's relatively easy for people to place an item into one of two categories; after all, they merely need to make a binary decision. In essence, a Q-sort requires respondents to make a series of binary decisions. For the aforementioned Q-sort, you could give these instructions:

In Step 1, please divide the 70 cards depicting 70 different magazines into two piles of more-preferred and less-preferred magazines. When you've completed Step 1, you should have two piles containing 35 cards.

In Step 2, take each pile and divide it into two piles of more-preferred and less-preferred magazines. When you've completed Step 2, you should have four piles containing 17 or 18 cards. Pile 1 should correspond with your most-preferred magazines, pile 2 should correspond with your next-most-preferred magazines, and so forth.

In Step 3, divide the four piles into eight piles using the same procedure as Steps 1 and 2. When you've completed Step 3, you should have eight piles of eight or nine cards.

Finally, place the pile representing your most-preferred magazines in the envelope marked #1, the pile representing your next-most preferred magazines in the envelope marked #2, and so forth.

Asking people to place cards into one of two piles — the more-preferred versus less-preferred pile — essentially requires them to make repeated paired comparisons. Relative to other ranking procedures, this Q-sort procedure is far more likely to produce reliable respondent preferences for many items.

Dollar-metric scale

The *dollar-metric scale* can help you to make product feature decisions based on the cost of including a feature versus the money consumers are willing to pay for a feature. This scale is an extension of the paired comparison method (discussed earlier in this chapter) that provides high-quality data because it doesn't unduly tax respondents.

Here's an example of a dollar-metric scale:

Which type of fruit juice container do you prefer? (Place an 'x' next to your preferred container type.)		How much more would you be willing to pay for fruit juice in your preferred container? (Write in that amount.)
_____ glass bottle	_____ aseptic box	_____ cents
_____ can	_____ glass bottle	_____ cents
_____ aseptic box	_____ plastic bottle	_____ cents
_____ plastic bottle	_____ glass bottle	_____ cents
_____ can	_____ plastic bottle	_____ cents
_____ aseptic box	_____ can	_____ cents

You can use the preceding question to assess people's willingness to pay more or less for different fruit juice containers, or any product category for that matter. Respondents must indicate which of each pair of container types they most prefer and then how much more they'd be willing to pay for juice delivered in that container type (relative to the type they didn't choose).

If you sold packaged fruit juice, the information gleaned from this study could help you to make a maximally profitable packaging decision. For example, suppose people (on average) prefer a glass bottle over a can by $0.10, and glass bottles cost $0.05 more than cans. If you switch from cans to glass bottles, but only increase your price by $0.07 per container, many juice consumers would buy your glass-enclosed juice because they believe it's a bargain. (In essence, they're paying $0.07 for something they believe is worth $0.10.) You, of course, are netting $0.02 more on each container sold, so you're happy to offer this bargain. Thus, dollar-metric data combined with cost data can help you to optimize the design of your product.

Chapter 10

Designing Good Questionnaires

*I*n addition to the issues surrounding the creation of good survey questions, which we cover in Chapter 9, you also have to consider the issues surrounding the creation of good questionnaires, especially questionnaires used to capture data for unusual research questions.

Case in point: one of Mike's marketing professors at Purdue conducted a survey to study people's willingness to donate human body parts, either before or after death, and the extent that willingness related to compensation. In essence, the professor's research question was, "Would some people be willing to donate certain body parts before death in return for money, and if so, how much money for each part?"

Although this research question sounds macabre, at the time there was interest in creating a national organ bank in the United States, and the issue was how to stock it. If people were willing to exchange money for body parts they could donate while alive (like a kidney or bone marrow) or after death, then adequately stocking an organ bank was merely an economic (supply versus demand) issue. However, if most people resisted donating on religious grounds, then it was necessary to alter their attitudes about organ donation (to increase the supply and thus lower the inventory-creation costs) before trying to establish a price schedule for body parts. Both identifying an optimal pricing schedule and designing public-service messages meant to change people's attitudes are marketing problems; hence the value of this marketing survey.

For more generic research problems, designing a good questionnaire may seem like a relatively simple and straightforward task. However, it requires surprisingly long and painstaking work, often by several researchers. In this chapter, we give you the information you need to design an effective questionnaire regardless of the research topic.

Unlike the old joke about a camel being a horse designed by a committee, a good questionnaire typically requires multiple authors. Because each author will be blind to certain limitations or idiosyncrasies in formatting and wording, several authors working individually and jointly can eliminate such shortcomings.

What's in a Good Questionnaire?

Because questionnaire design is an art rather than a science, there are basic formatting and content guidelines rather than rules for creating an effective questionnaire. For example, good questionnaires should be as brief as possible, well organized, appealing to the eye, clear and easily answerable, and cordial with professional overtones. The guidelines we discuss in this book (primarily in this chapter and in Chapter 9) revolve around five questions:

- ✔ What should you ask?
- ✔ How should you phrase questions?
- ✔ How should you sequence questions?
- ✔ What's an effective questionnaire layout?
- ✔ How should you pretest the questionnaire?

In the following sections, we provide you with all the information you need to design an effective questionnaire. We discuss screeners to filter out the unqualified respondents, skip patterns, organization, and formatting.

Finding qualified respondents with screeners and filter questions

Screeners are designed to filter out all but qualified survey respondents. Figure 10-1 is a page from an example screener questionnaire for a study on leisure travelers who stay overnight at hotels (check the DVD for the entire document). Because these travelers tend to be nonrepresentative of the general population, the screener questionnaire is designed to exclude people who are knowledgeable about the research domain and have participated recently in another marketing study. The screener also qualifies respondents as overnight hotel guests when traveling on leisure.

Name: _____

Address: _____

Telephone: _____

Interviewer: _____

Date: _____   Time Start: _____   Time End: _____

Hello, my name is _____ , and I'm calling for Researcher 'R Us, a national market research company. We're conducting a study on traveling habits in the United States and would like to include your opinions. May I please speak with *(Name Above)*?

> *(If speaking with designated respondent, continue.)*

> *(If not speaking with designated respondent, ask to speak with him or her, reintroduce yourself, and continue.)*

> *(If designated respondent is not available, or does not have time to be interviewed now, arrange for callback.)*

If Respondent Refuses at Introduction

I understand your concern; however, your opinions are important and you may find the survey of interest. If now is not a good time for you to complete the survey, I will gladly call you back at a more convenient time. (*If necessary, record time and date of callback on the respondent call sheet.*) Please remember that this is a national opinion poll and not a sales call. Your answers will be confidential and no one will contact you in any way as a result of your participation in this study.

Screener and Trip Count Measures

1. Is any family or close friend employed in any of the following occupations? *(Read list) (Circle one number)*

> A travel agency. 1
> An advertising agency. 2
> A hotel 3
> A marketing research company 4
> None of the above. 5

(If answer other than "5," terminate interview.)

Figure 10-1: Sample page from a telephone screener for leisure travel study.

In contrast to screeners meant to ensure that only qualified respondents participate in your study, *filter questions* are meant to ensure that respondents receive the correct questionnaire out of multiple questionnaires they may receive. Figure 10-2 represents a study in which three types of consumers are queried. Each type can provide useful but different information. Here are the three types of consumers queried:

- ✔ **Aware nonusers:** From people who recognize but have never used the brand, you can discover why they've chosen not to try it.

- ✔ **Trier-rejecters:** From people who've tried but no longer use the brand, you can discover why they stopped using it.

- ✔ **Current users:** From people who currently use the brand, you can determine what they like and dislike about it, which can help you discover ways to retain them as customers.

The filter questions represented by Figure 10-2 can ensure that the appropriate questionnaire is administered to each of the different types of consumers of interest in this study.

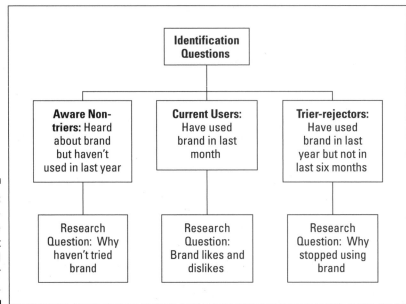

Figure 10-2:
Question-
naire
assignment
based
on filter
questions.

Familiarizing yourself with skip patterns

Skip patterns reflect a series of instructions that questionnaire respondents receive to answer or ignore certain questions based on their answers to previous questions. For many questionnaires, all respondents won't be qualified to answer every question. As such, you don't want unqualified respondents answering questions that don't pertain to them because their answers are likely to distort your findings and suggest inappropriate and costly strategy changes.

If respondents answer questions they should have skipped, and you fail to exclude those answers during data cleaning (as we discuss in Chapter 17), you may be introducing meaningful error into your statistical analyses and other data summaries.

Here's a series of questions with a skip pattern:

Q #1: *Have you heard of Never Miss a Shot brand golf clubs?*
(Mark answer in space provided)

    ____ Yes   →   **(If "Yes," answer Question #2.)**
    ____ No   →   **(If "No," skip to Question #4.)**
    ____ Not sure → **(If "Not sure," skip to Question #4.)**

Q #2: *Have you ever tried Never Miss a Shot brand golf clubs?*
(Mark answer in space provided)

    ____ Yes   →   **(If "Yes," answer Question #3.)**
    ____ No   →   **(If "No," skip to Question #4.)**
    ____ Not sure → **(If "Not sure," skip to Question #4.)**

Q #3: *The first time you tried the clubs, who provided them?*
(Mark answer in space provided)

    ____ A fellow golfer
    ____ A golf pro who works at a course I play
    ____ A salesperson at a sporting goods store
    ____ Someone else

Asking golfers who have never heard of this brand — which Jeremy and Mike would buy without hesitation if name and performance matched — about their attitudes toward it is nonsensical.

Following skip patterns properly isn't an issue for computer-assisted telephone and self-administered browser-based surveys. In both cases, the questionnaire-administering PC can run software programmed in such a way that only appropriate questions are displayed. Skip patterns are a bigger problem for self-administered pencil-and-paper questionnaires. Despite efforts to ensure that respondents read instructions and only answer relevant questions, they often answer questions that don't pertain to them.

For a self-administered pencil-and-paper questionnaire, multiple visual elements can increase the likelihood that respondents recognize the need to skip questions that don't pertain to them. Arrows directing respondents to the next appropriate question — based on their answer to the current question — are especially effective.

Organizing your questions

All questionnaires — even self-administered ones — simulate conversations between researchers and respondents. Like conversations, questionnaires should have a logical flow. We provide helpful hints about the most logical flow in the following sections.

Going from general to specific

In general, your questionnaire should flow from general to specific. The big-picture questions come first, and the more detailed ones follow. Starting respondents with specific questions can unsettle them and fail to prime their memories sufficiently to answer your questions accurately. Starting them with general questions — as a warm-up for the specific questions they'll answer subsequently — is preferred.

Figure 10-3 illustrates a skip pattern with questions sequenced from general to specific, which is called a *funnel organization*. In work mode, a funnel is broad at the top and narrow at the bottom, which is analogous to proceeding from general to specific. In this example, the question sequence moves from a general question about auto ads to a specific question about the content of a television ad for a specific model of Toyota automobile.

Here's a question that's far too complex to ask early in a questionnaire:

Please think about all the aspects of your automobile that make it enjoyable to drive. Then, please write down the five most important aspects and rank them from 1 (the most important aspect) to 5 (the least important aspect). **(Write those aspects and your ranking in the space provided.)**

In the same way that a difficult first question on an exam can spook even a well-prepared student, the mental gymnastics required to answer this question will discourage respondents and make them wonder about the difficulty of your entire questionnaire. As an alternative to this question, you may consider a set of easier-to-answer close-ended questions like the following (which, as we discuss in Chapters 9 and 17, are easier for data entry):

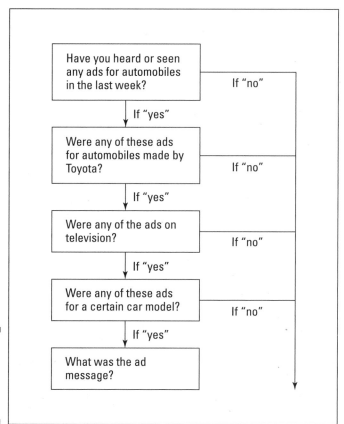

Figure 10-3:
Example
of a funnel
organization
skip pattern.

If you don't own an automobile, or you don't drive one at least once per week, please skip to the next question.

When you drive your automobile, how important are each of the following aspects to your enjoyment? **(Circle one number for each aspect.)**

Aspect	Very Important	Important	Somewhat Important	Barely Important	Unimportant
Smooth ride	1	2	3	4	5
Comfortable driver's seat	1	2	3	4	5
Effective air conditioning	1	2	3	4	5
Good road visibility	1	2	3	4	5
Responsive steering	1	2	3	4	5
Effective breaks	1	2	3	4	5
Good sound system	1	2	3	4	5
Little road noise	1	2	3	4	5

Deciding on the general sequence of questions

Start with screener or filter questions that help you ensure that your respondents are qualified and receive the correct questionnaire (if you're fielding multiple questionnaires). Next ask several warm-up questions that encourage respondents to begin thinking about the topic of interest. After that, your next set of questions should be simple and straightforward. Then, you can begin to ask more challenging and sensitive questions.

Carefully consider the placement of your mentally challenging and sensitive questions. If you need to include these types of questions, here are the general guidelines for placement:

- **Mentally challenging questions:** If you must ask mentally challenging questions — for example, questions that require respondents to recall past behaviors and outcomes in detail — you should place them after the midpoint of your questionnaire. Otherwise, respondents faced immediately with tough questions may become frustrated and decide not to complete your questionnaire.

  Several years ago, Mike participated in those quarterly surveys the Bureau of Labor Statistics uses to calculate the Consumer Price Index. After 90 minutes of answering questions about everything he'd purchased during the last three months, he was exhausted. Had he known responding carefully would be so taxing, he may have reconsidered his participation in the survey.

- **Sensitive questions:** You should place sensitive questions — classification questions about age, income, occupation, family configuration, and the like — toward the end of the questionnaire. If sensitive questions appear at the beginning, respondents may become suspicious about the goals of your research. After completing most of your questionnaire, respondents have bought into cooperating, so they're unlikely to discontinue their efforts or refuse to answer those questions.

Providing clear instructions

Clear and concise instructions increase the likelihood that respondents answer your questions properly, especially with self-administered questionnaires. When you receive a questionnaire from a respondent, it's often difficult to assess whether he followed the instructions and answered the questions as intended. The clearer and less ambiguous your instructions, the more likely respondents will understand them and answer each question appropriately.

Because respondents often are less than highly motivated to complete your questionnaire, it's best to put instructions exactly where needed rather than providing a lengthy list of instructions to introduce your questionnaire. If an instruction is important for responding properly to a question on Page 5, but appears on Page 1, respondents are less likely to follow that instruction.

To make questionnaires more conversational, include special instructions as part of the question and not as a free-standing entity. Here's an example to show you what we mean:

Original version:

> **Please be as specific as possible in answering the next question. Include any areas of work-related expertise and specialization; for example, marketing professor at a state university. If you currently have multiple jobs, then answer about the job from which you earn the most money.**
>
> *What is your current occupation? (Fill in space below.)*
>
> _____

Revised version:

> *What is your current occupation? Please be as specific as possible. Include any areas of work-related expertise and specialization; for example, marketing professor at a state university. If you currently have multiple jobs, then answer about the job from which you earn the most money. (Fill in space below.)*
>
> _____

Creating an effective layout

Just as a job candidate's personal appearance affects a job interview, a questionnaire's appearance affects respondents' beliefs about research quality and researcher professionalism. Layout issues pertaining to binding, color schemes, question numbering, and page formatting affect such perceptions. These factors, along with question coding, also affect data-entry efficiency. We discuss these issues in the following sections.

Provided your questionnaire has a professional appearance, none of the layout considerations we discuss in the following sections are likely to boost your response rate. Nonetheless, they may affect the quality of the responses you receive.

Booklets

Using a booklet, instead of a series of sheets stapled in the upper left-hand corner, may make questionnaires appear more professional, thus increasing the thought respondents put into their answers. You can include more questions per page in a booklet format as well. As a result, the inbound and outbound postage for self-administered mail questionnaires may be reduced. That said, if you're word-processor challenged, you may find creating a booklet outside your skill set (and hiring someone to lay out and print your questionnaire is likely to consume much of your research budget).

Color coding

Eliminating order bias (a problem we discuss in Chapter 9) requires multiple questionnaire versions with question items sequenced differently. Color coding may help you organize those multiple versions. By color coding, you'll be less likely to enter the wrong number into your response data file. For example, if a *3* response on the blue questionnaire, a *5* response on the yellow questionnaire, and a *1* response on the white questionnaire indicate the same answer to a question, then all three responses should be coded identically in your data file.

Question numbering

Numbering questionnaire items is somewhat arbitrary. You can number each question separately (1, 2, 3 . . .), or you can number questions by logical groupings (1a, 1b, 1c . . .). Regardless, numbering questions on paper-and-pencil questionnaires can facilitate data entry by providing checkpoints. In essence, numbering lets the people transferring data from questionnaires to a data file check that they're entering a response to each question into the correct column in the data file (see Chapter 17). Also, when you design your questionnaire with skip patterns, numbering the questions makes the skipping process easier for respondents to follow.

For a long paper-based questionnaire that respondents can skim before starting, question numbering can reduce response rate (an important issue we discuss in Chapter 7). Seeing a large number for your last question will dissuade some people from responding to your questionnaire because they'll conclude it's not worth the time and effort to complete.

Fitting questions on a page

For paper-based questionnaires, resist the urge to save paper by jamming every square centimeter with small font text. Crowded questionnaires are ugly and daunting for respondents. People appreciate a visually appealing questionnaire, so they're more likely to respond carefully to it. In contrast, they're more likely to rush through or discard a poorly designed one.

The trade-off is questions per page versus number of pages. More pages make your questionnaire appear longer, which may discourage some respondents from completing it. Conversely, fewer pages with smaller print may make your questionnaire unreadable to people with poor vision; as a result, they may decide not to respond. Thus, you should design your questionnaire with your typical respondents' visual acuity in mind.

Pre-coding

Pre-coding assigns a number to each possible response to a close-ended question. This coding method is useful because it enhances data-entry efficiency. You can pre-code any close-ended question.

Figure 10-4 shows several pre-coded questions that rely on marking a space rather than circling a number to the right of a response option (like many of the questions in Figure 10-1). Either format is acceptable.

Using Figure 10-4 as a reference, here's how coding works: Codes 1 through 5 are listed to the right of the response options for the question "How many years have you played at least 10 or more rounds of golf?" Inputting this type of data isn't difficult; if the respondent checked "11 to 20 years," which is a "4," you enter a "4" into your data file.

Formatting consistently to guide respondents through your questionnaire

You can boldface your questions, italicize your response categories, place all your extended instructions in shaded boxes, and use arrows to indicate skip patterns. However, you should use such conventions consistently. You reduce the response burden by formatting each questionnaire element similarly because respondents will quickly adapt, either consciously or subconsciously, to your pattern. For example, you should invariably identify the beginning of each question and section of your questionnaire.

How many years have you played at least 10 or more rounds of golf?

Less than 2 years	___ -1
2 to 5 years	___ -2
6 to 10 years	___ -3
11 to 20 years	___ -4
More than 20 years	___ -5

What is your level of play?

Novice	___ -1
Lower intermediate	___ -2
Upper intermediate	___ -3
Advanced	___ -4
Expert	___ -5

In the last twelve months, has your level of play increased, remained the same, or decreased?

Increased	___ -1
Remained the same	___ -2
Decreased	___ -3

Do you have an annual membership at a public golf course or country club with a golf course?

Yes	___ -1
No	___ -2

Why do you play golf? (Place "X" under "Yes" or "No" for each reason.)

Reason	Yes	No
For the exercise	___ -1	___ -2
It's fun	___ -1	___ -2
Opportunity to be with friends	___ -1	___ -2
To make business contacts	___ -1	___ -2
The challenge of improving my game	___ -1	___ -2
To compete against other players	___ -1	___ -2

In the last twelve months, have you purchased instructional or practice materials to improve your game?

Yes	___ -1
No	___ -2

Figure 10-4:
Sample
pre-coded
questions.

WARNING!

To increase the likelihood that respondents notice key words in your questions, use bolding, all upper-case letters, italics, or underlining. However, use these attention grabbers sparingly because excessive highlighting is visually distracting.

Figure 10-5 contains so many inconsistently used bolded and specialty characters that it's a chore to read these four questions. In contrast, the first four questions in Figure 10-4 have a consistent typeface and clean appearance, which makes them easier to read and answer.

Even if your word-processing skills are modest, you can adjust question elements to encourage respondents to see things in the right order. Such elements include the size and boldness of the font and type of script. How you alter these elements affect the order in which respondents read through your questionnaire.

The original version of the following question is a bad example that draws initial attention to the response options rather than the question or instructions. The revised version is superior because the instruction "Begin here" is in large font and all uppercase, the question is bolded and in a smaller but upper- and lower-case font, and the choices aren't bolded and in a still smaller font.

---

(1) **How many years have you played at least 10 or more rounds of golf?**
(*Check one answer.*)

▶ Less than 2 years .... ____
▶ 2 to 5 years. .... ____
▶ 6 to 10 years .... ____
▶ 11 to 20 years .... ____
▶ More than 20 years .... ____

B. What is your level of play? (*CIRCLE ANSWER.*) ☺

Novice   Lower   Upper   Advanced   Expert
          Intermediate   Intermediate

3. In the last twelve months, has your level of play increased, remained the same, or decreased? (Mark one answer only.)

Increased............................. ____
Remained the same.................. ____
Decreased............................. ____

4. Do you have an ANNUAL MEMBERSHIP at a public golf course or country club with a golf course? **(Check right answer.)**

____ Yes ✎
____ No

Figure 10-5:
Inconsistent questionnaire formatting (to be avoided).

Original version:

> Begin here:
>
> *What's your favorite flavor of ice cream?* (Choose only one flavor.)
>
> ___ Vanilla
> ___ Chocolate
> ___ Strawberry
> ___ Other flavor (SPECIFY BELOW)
>
> _____

Revised version:

> ► BEGIN HERE ◄
>
> **What's your favorite flavor of ice cream?** *(Choose only one flavor.)*
>
> ____ Vanilla
> ____ Chocolate
> ____ Strawberry
> ____ Other flavor (SPECIFY BELOW)
>
> _____

Choosing simple answer formats

Even a well-crafted question can be undermined by a poor answer format. When respondent confusion and frustration surface as a result of confusing answer formats, measurement error increases. In the following sections, we offer do's and don'ts of formatting the answer options. To reduce complexity, we also suggest ways to lower the number of options you give respondents.

Best practices

To avoid confusing respondents, it's best to run all your scales in one direction — such as from negative to positive — throughout your questionnaire. For example, when asking respondents to answer using a seven-point Likert scale, all 1s would mean "strongly disagree" and all 7s would mean "strongly agree." That way, they're more likely to provide an answer consistent with their true opinion.

The placement of check boxes or numbers or blank lines to either the left- or right-hand side of the page is arbitrary. However, that placement should be consistent throughout your questionnaire.

See the sample questionnaires on the DVD for various placement examples.

Practices to avoid

Regardless of the questionnaire format you choose, avoid needlessly complex formats. Doing so will help keep your respondents in a good frame of mind and motivate them to complete your questionnaire.

As an example, consider these three questions:

When you drive your automobile, how important is a smooth ride?
(Circle number to right of your answer.)

       Very important 1
       Important 2
       Somewhat important. 3
       Barely important 4
       Unimportant 5

When you drive your automobile, how important is a comfortable driver's seat?
(Circle number to right of your answer.)

       Very important 1
       Important 2
       Somewhat important. 3
       Barely important 4
       Unimportant 5

When you drive your automobile, how important is effective air conditioning?
(Circle number to right of your answer.)

       Very important 1
       Important 2
       Somewhat important. 3
       Barely important 4
       Unimportant 5

Although you should avoid complex and crowded question matrices, the preceding format wastes paper without improving readability meaningfully.

You also should avoid using check-all-that-apply formats. The problem with this format is that it's impossible to know whether people meant not to check a choice, meant to check it but failed to do so, or didn't see it. The positive confirmation provided by the yes/no version in Figure 10-4 is preferred.

Here's an example of a check-all-that-apply question format:

Why do you play golf? (Check all answers that apply.)

For the exercise. . . . . ____
It's fun . . . . ____
Opportunity to be with friends. . . . . ____
To make business contacts . . . . ____
The challenge of improving my game. . . . . ____
To compete against other players. . . . . ____

Reducing complexity by offering fewer response options

For questions with many response options, self-administered mail questionnaires work better than telephone questionnaires. If a telephone interviewer reads a response list with more than four or five choices, respondents will likely forget the initial choices by the time they've heard the last one. In contrast, all the choices are readily available with a self-administered mail questionnaire, so it's far easier to pick among a larger set of options.

Reviewing Guidelines for Cover Letters

Cover letters are important for encouraging people to respond to your questionnaire. In essence, the cover letter is your sales pitch; you're trying to convince people to expend the time and effort needed for responding care-fully to your questionnaire. Regardless of promised compensation, if your cover letter doesn't sell your cause, then most people won't respond.

Be mindful of the following guidelines when creating a cover letter:

- ✔ **It must provide enough information for potential respondents to make an informed decision about participating in your study.** Due to exten-sive *sugging* and *frugging* by unethical marketers (see Chapter 4), you should indicate that you're conducting a bona fide survey. (In essence, you only want their answers and not their money — at least not yet!) You should describe the survey's purpose clearly and simply and indi-cate how that person was chosen to participate in your study.

- ✔ **It should answer all likely questions.** Be sure to include all contact and procedural information. If your questionnaire includes profile ques-tions for classification purposes (for example, questions about age and income), respondents may contact you to ensure that their personal data doesn't fall into the hands of an identity thief.

- ✔ **It should be concise and include only essential facts.** People don't read more than one page — especially to introduce a commercial study — so you need to convince them of your study's value and to respond within that single page.

- ✔ **It should be easy to understand on the first reading.** If your cover letter is difficult to read, potential respondents will assume your entire ques-tionnaire will be the same. As a result, they're less likely to respond. Replace all ten-dollar words with simpler synonyms.

- ✔ **It should be accurate.** Verify that all contact and procedural information are correct. Respondents who have clarification questions will wonder about the authenticity of your survey if they dial the telephone number you list and a bookie answers.

- ✔ **It should be proofread by a qualified person for grammatical, spelling, and punctuation errors.** Potential respondents will infer the quality of your questionnaire from your cover letter, so it should appear profes-sional. Grammatical, spelling, and punctuation errors suggest otherwise.

If you follow this checklist, your cover letter will be of similar quality to the one in Figure 10-6.

University of _____

Marketing Department
College of Business Administration

August 8, 2009

Dear Consumer:

The College of Business at the University of _____ is studying consumer attitudes and lifestyles in the _____ area. We have undertaken this study because a comprehensive understanding of consumer attitudes is of substantial interest to researchers, businesses and the government. We hope to publish the findings of this research in professional journals.

Yours is one of a small number of households that are being asked for their opinions. It was drawn in a random sample of _____ households. Hence, in order for the results to truly represent all of them, your participation in this effort is critical. ***The enclosed questionnaire should be completed and returned by the male or female head of your household in the postage-paid return envelope.*** You may keep this cover letter for your records.

While developing this questionnaire, we asked several people to try it out, helping us improve its content and clarity. Most of them reported taking about 30 minutes to fill it out; further, none reported any major difficulty with any of the questions.

You can be assured of complete confidentiality. The number stamped on the back of the return envelope is for mailing purposes only. This is so that we may check your name off the mailing list when your questionnaire is returned and save some mailing costs. We will destroy the return envelopes and the mailing list at the conclusion of the survey and your name will **never** be placed on the questionnaire.

Your participation is voluntary. If you prefer not to answer a question, just skip it and go on to the next one. We do hope to get all of your answers, but we would rather have some than none.

We would like to show our deep appreciation of your participation in this survey, by sending you a "bird's eye view" summary of the results of this research. If you would like to receive this summary, please write "copy of results requested" on the back of the return envelope and print your name and address below it. Please do not put this information on the questionnaire itself. You might find it interesting to compare your views with those of others!

This project has been reviewed and approved by the _____.
If you have questions, you may call them directly at (817) 565-3940.

In closing, we sincerely hope that you would participate in this effort. If you have any other questions about the survey, please call me at the University of _____. Thank you for your assistance. We are very grateful for your cooperation.

Sincerely,

_____

_____
Associate Professor of Marketing
Project Director

Figure 10-6:
A sample
cover letter.

Cover letter appeals

Depending on the research sponsor, different cover letter appeals will be relatively more or less effective for encouraging people to participate in a survey. Appeals tend to fall into the following four categories:

✔ **Social-utility appeal:** A *social-utility appeal* encourages people to respond because it will help to make the world a better place. Example: *Your assistance is needed. Your attitudes and opinions can provide information that will help us understand how we can improve service to all of our customers. Your cooperation is truly appreciated.*

✔ **Help-the-sponsor appeal:** A *help-the-sponsor appeal* encourages people to respond because it will help the researcher, who would really appreciate the assistance. Example: *We really need your assistance! Your attitudes and opinion are very important to our successful completion of this study. We truly appreciate your cooperation!*

✔ **Help-yourself appeal:** A *help-yourself appeal* suggests that participating in the study benefits the respondent in some way.

Example: *Your opinions are important. It's important for you to express your opinion so we can know the types of services you would like us to offer. Thanks for expressing your opinions.*

✔ **Combined appeal:** A *combined appeal* would meld all three appeals. Example: *Your attitudes and opinions are important for three reasons. First, they can provide information that will help us understand how we can improve service to our customers. Second, they'll enable us to offer the types of services you prefer. Third, they'll help us successfully complete this study. Thank you for your cooperation.*

Which appeal is likely to boost response rates most? If the survey sponsor is a university or a government agency, a social appeal or help-the-sponsor appeal should be most effective. In contrast, if the survey sponsor is a commercial entity, a "make the world a better place" appeal likely would be ineffective. In this case, you should use a help-yourself appeal. A combined appeal will be equally effective regardless of survey sponsor.

Using Browser-Based Questionnaires

Internet browsers, computer-based graphics, and online bandwidth have improved markedly during the last few years. As a result, many alternative browser-based survey platforms are now available to you. The advantages of such platforms include the following:

✔ They make it simple to create browser-based versions of previously created paper-and-pencil questionnaires. With question templates readily available, you can use a copy-and-paste procedure to expedite the transfer of your paper-based questions (in a Microsoft Word or comparable file) to an online questionnaire.

✔ They have advanced audio and video capabilities, which allow a level of visual excitement that's unavailable in traditional self-administered questionnaires. By increasing respondent involvement, these capabilities boost response rate and response quality.

✔ Their data collection and storage are reliable and efficient. For example, data can be stored on the operator's server or sent via e-mail to your PC and saved to a Microsoft Access file. This makes for easy data retrieval and eliminates the excuse that "your dog ate your data."

✔ They allow you to eliminate data-collection middlemen — such as field services and their interviewers — thereby reducing your cost per completed questionnaire.

We explain the basics of Internet surveys in the following sections, including the reasons they're so effective as well as their layout and display options.

Understanding the advantages of browser-based questionnaires

There are definite advantages to using browser-based questionnaires as opposed to self-administered mail questionnaires. These advantages include the following:

✔ **Boolean skip and branching logic:** Browser-based questionnaires can be programmed so that appropriate skips and logic are followed. As a result, people only answer the questions intended for them, either based on their profile or previous responses.

✔ **Hidden skip logic:** With hidden skip logic, respondents don't see skip traces. In other words, skips are transparent to them — which saves respondents reading time and eliminates skip errors.

✔ **Variable piping software:** *Variable piping* means that text can be inserted within a question based on one or more previous responses or the respondent's profile. (The junk mail you've received with your name inserted into the cover letter is an example of variable piping.)

✔ **Error trapping and forced answering software:** It's possible to evaluate answers as they're entered. Because browser-based survey software can identify errors during the interview process, it can inform respondents that they've answered improperly and should try again.

✔ **Interactive help desks:** Browser-based questionnaires can include online help, which you can't provide for self-administered mail questionnaires. If respondents have problems with mail questionnaires, their only recourse is to e-mail or call the researcher, which is likely to take more than a few minutes and create an additional barrier to questionnaire completion. As a result, these respondents are more likely to withdraw their cooperation before completion. With browser-based surveys, interactive help is available immediately, so respondents are more likely to continue once it's received.

Visualizing browser-based questionnaires

Boosting response rates, increasing respondent involvement, and obtaining accurate responses are essential goals of survey research. When data collection occurs online, these factors can be influenced by graphical user interfaces, page layouts, and status bars.

Rather than text-based interfaces like MS-DOS, *graphical user interfaces* (GUIs) rely on graphic icons (for example, images, colors, and sounds) and pointing devices (arrows) to create screen displays. Although people typically navigate a GUI-based software with a pointing device like a mouse or trackball, they also can navigate with a keyboard (for example, the arrow and shortcut keys).

Browser-based questionnaires with *screen-to-screen paging* restrict viewing to one or a few questions at once. Such paging helps respondents to focus their attention and prevents them from peeking ahead. Previewing an entire questionnaire, which a *scrolling layout* allows, can reduce response rates for longer questionnaires and increase bias responses by hinting at the research problem (also called *hypothesis guessing*).

That said, informed consent to participate in a survey requires an accurate estimate of completion time. Furthermore, answers may become unreliable after respondents have exceeded their self-imposed time allocation. Although it may boost the cost per completed interview, a peeking-induced drop in response rate may improve overall response quality.

As a compromise, a status bar indicating the percentage of the questionnaire that's completed can provide a realistic estimate of the remaining time to completion. If combined with a pause feature — which allows respondents to complete the questionnaire later — a status bar can reduce respondent frustration and improve data quality.

Reviewing some common on-screen display options

The tone of your research, which starts with your welcome screen and continues with your answer display options (radio buttons, check boxes, drop-down boxes, and open-ended boxes) are important decisions you'll make when creating an online questionnaire.

Here are a few display elements that are effective for Internet questionnaires:

✔ **Radio buttons and check boxes:** These elements allow you to present all choices simultaneously. To answer a question, respondents click on the button or check the box that's adjacent to their corresponding choice. These types of questions are easy to read and complete; they can be used for nominal, ordinal, and interval data (see Chapter 18).

✔ **Drop-down boxes:** These are analogous to the drop-down menus prevalent in most current software. Rather than have respondents click on a button, answer options are displayed in sequence and respondents choose one by moving the cursor to it and left-clicking their mouse.

✔ **Open-ended boxes:** As the name implies, open-ended box questions allow respondents to embellish their thoughts. For example, a restaurant operator may ask patrons to describe their experience during their last visit. Their answer requires them to elaborate, which makes it well-suited for a question of this form. As respondents type, the response box scrolls downward. You can limit the number of characters allowed in a response; by forcing succinct answers, you ease future data coding and analysis.

✔ **Welcome screens:** Browser-based questionnaires have welcome screens in the same way that self-administered mail questionnaires have cover letters. The welcome screen provides the relevant information about the sponsor and the purpose of the research; it's meant to encourage people who have reached that screen to complete your questionnaire.

Creating an Internet survey

Creating and fielding an online survey is a relatively straightforward process. You can either opt to outsource this process or do it yourself (see the nearby "Browser-based survey providers" sidebar for more). To get started, you need to identify your research questions, create well-crafted questions, and secure a reliable Internet connection.

Browser-based survey providers

Whether you decide to outsource or create your own survey, the browser-based survey providers we mention here can handle your research needs. Their user-friendly services and interfaces are meant to expedite your research program, leading to timely and appropriate strategy adjustments. To show you the types of services available, we include five providers of online survey research. Their appearance here shouldn't be interpreted as an endorsement.

✔ **Constant Contact** (www.constant contact.com): Among other foci, Constant Contact can help you to assess customer satisfaction, customer shopping experience, new products, and event planning.

✔ **Cvent Web Surveys** (www.cvent.com): Among other services, Cvent can provide templates and questions to assist with (1) creating questionnaires (including 18 pre-built surveys, a question library, and more than 50 survey templates), (2) distributing (through e-mail, website, telephone, and snail mail), scoring (for metric and non-metric data), and reporting survey results (including 50 standard reports, longitudinal analysis, and exporting results in seven formats), and (3) providing data security (with data encryption).

✔ **Survey Monkey** (www.surveymonkey.com): Survey Monkey offers a tiered (basic, pro, unlimited annual) service model for creating online surveys. The basic package is free and offers 10 survey questions from 15 survey themes for 100 respondents per survey.

✔ **The Survey Professionals** (www.surveypro.com): Survey Professionals specializes in concept tests, consumer satisfaction, preference analysis, and price/demand studies. Its services include designing surveys (which are developed, tested, and evaluated in real-time), sampling, storing data, analyzing data, and writing managerial reports.

✔ **Zoomerang** (www.zoomerang.com): Zoomerang offers a tiered (basic, pro, premium) service model for online surveys. The basic package is free and offers 30 survey questions and 100 respondents per survey; the pro and premium packages allow unlimited questions and respondents. The basic package supports 15 types of questions, including open-ended (one or more lines with prompt), matrix-formatted rating-scale, and ranking questions.

Pretesting: Ensuring Your Questionnaire Is a Good One

Fielding a survey is an expensive proposition. Mike's consulting experiences suggest that data collection costs often exceed 50 percent of the total research budget. Because of this substantial cost, you should pretest your questionnaire before you field it to ensure that it's properly constructed. Here are questions you should consider when formulating your pretest:

✔ **What items should be pretested?** You should pretest all items that haven't been used in previous studies. If you're using battle-tested items, pretesting is of lesser importance, unless the context is entirely different than in the previous studies.

✔ **How should a pretest be conducted?** Your pretest should mimic the conditions under which respondents will answer your questions. If respondents will be in a noisy and distracting environment, you should conduct your pretest in that type of environment.

✔ **Who should conduct a pretest?** Because you're in the best position to modify the questionnaire based on the pretest results, you should conduct the pretest yourself. In particular, be sensitive to any informal comments from pretest respondents about ways to improve your questionnaire.

✔ **Who should be the respondents in a pretest?** Pretest respondents should be as similar to the ultimate respondents as possible. If you're conducting a study in which many respondents will be elderly, it's non-sensical to pretest your questionnaire on college students with vastly different predispositions, behaviors, vocabularies, and reading abilities.

✔ **How large a sample is needed for a pretest?** You don't need an expensive pretest with many respondents; a small pool of 20 people will suffice in most cases. You shouldn't waste "real" respondents on a pretest. Instead, people who are readily available at low cost and who are relatively similar to your ultimate respondents — what we call a *convenience sample* (see Chapter 11) — are preferred.

✔ **How should you evaluate the pre-test results?** If you choose to mimic actual survey conditions, then debriefing the interviewers who conduct the pre-test is essential. These people can tell you how easy it is to administer the questionnaire and which questions caused trouble for respondents.

Chapter 11

Deciding on a Sample Type

*W*hen you *sample* something, you examine a part of *that something* to reach a conclusion about all of that something. In marketing research you sample part of a population to determine how the entire population thinks about a new or existing product or service. Only when you've sampled effectively can you safely generalize your research results to the population of interest; depending on your research question, you need to select a certain type of sample, because some types of samples are more suitable for certain research problems.

In this chapter, we discuss the importance of sampling to effective marketing research; in doing so, we delve in to sampling terminology, differentiate between nonprobability and probability sampling, lay out the steps for selecting a sample, and discuss strategies for collecting samples for online research.

Introducing Basic Sampling Terms

You'll believe this chapter is gibberish unless you're familiar with the following sampling terminology:

▸ **Population or universe:** A *population,* or *universe,* is any complete group of entities, such as people, sales territories, or stores. It's the total group about which you want information. Although popular usage suggests otherwise, a population doesn't need to be huge. For example, all the people in your household represent the population or universe of people in your household. In marketing research, current customers or households newly in the market for a product — such as diapers and baby wipes for first-time parents — represent typical populations.

✔ **Census:** To take a *census* means to study all the elements comprising a population. The U.S. Government attempts a population census every ten years. Of course, that's a colossal census; a census need not be that large. A university instructor who surveyed all students enrolled in her course would be taking a census as well. In marketing research, a census might entail all of a company's major corporate clients or salespeople.

✔ **Sample:** A *sample* is a subset of a larger population. Cost and time are the main reasons for drawing a sample instead of conducting a census. A census is expensive unless the population is small and accessible. In marketing research, populations typically are large and not readily accessible; therefore, selecting a representative sample is the only cost- and time-effective way to assess a population's attitudes, preferences, and behaviors.

Figure 11-1 shows the same photo at four different resolutions. Photo 1 is at standard photo resolution and the subsequent three photos are at progressively lower resolutions. Although the pooch in the photos remains recognizable in Photo 2, by Photo 4 it's almost impossible to discern a snout and floppy ears. This photo analogy hints at issues about sample size and representativeness.

Photo 1 represents the population of interest to you. Assuming you've designed an otherwise good study, an adequate and appropriate sample — analogous to Photo 2 — should allow you to properly understand that population. As your sample size decreases and/or your respondents become less representative of your target population, your understanding will become increasingly muddled — analogous to Photo 3. Eventually, your sample can become so small and nonrepresentative that you learn nothing about your target population — analogous to Photo 4. Hence, there's no substitute for an adequate and representative sample; without one, you're wasting your research time and money.

✔ **Probability and nonprobability samples:** For a *probability sample,* every population member has a known and nonzero probability of selection. For a *nonprobability sample,* the probability of selecting each population member is unknown. This known versus unknown probability of selecting population members differentiates the two types of samples; an unknown probability makes extrapolating from a sample to the population risky. Much of the remaining chapter addresses these types of samples and how they're used by marketing researchers.

✔ **Sample frame:** A *sample frame* is the list of elements from which a sample may be drawn. For example, a list of customer e-mail addresses can provide a sample frame for an online retailer. Only probability samples are drawn from a sample frame.

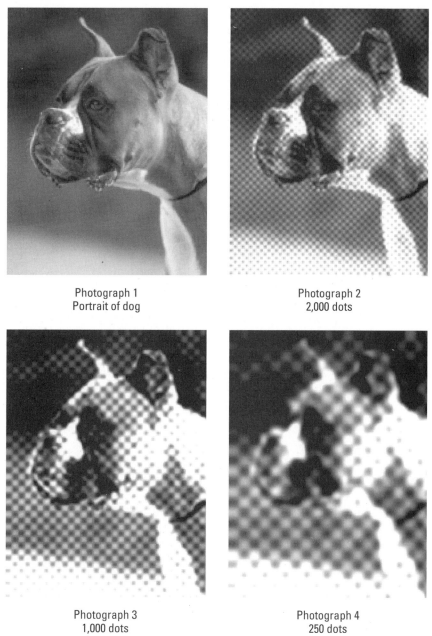

Photograph 1
Portrait of dog

Photograph 2
2,000 dots

Photograph 3
1,000 dots

Photograph 4
250 dots

Figure 11-1:
Photo-
graphs at
decreasing
resolution.

Getting Familiar with Nonprobability and Probability Samples

Depending on your research goals and budget, you can choose from several different types of nonprobability and probability samples. In essence, they can all be used to help answer research questions, although some types are more appropriate for some situations. Understanding the various sample types will help you identify the most suitable sample for your research needs. In the following sections, we show you the differences between the two categories of samples and how to select the right one for your circumstances.

Examining the different types of nonprobability samples

Different types of nonprobability and probability samples exist. Figure 11-2 shows the four types in each category. The nonprobability samples are convenience, judgment, quota, and snowball. The following sections cover each of these nonprobability samples in more detail.

Figure 11-2:
Types of nonprobability and probability samples.

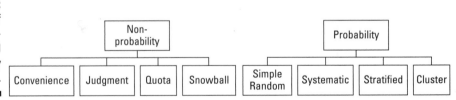

Convenience sample

Convenience sampling is a procedure for selecting people or units that are convenient to the researcher. Although not recommended for many contexts, convenience sampling is desirable in some cases. In particular, convenience samples are useful for pretesting questionnaires because they're inexpensive and can help identify poorly worded questions and poorly formatted questionnaires. (Visit Chapter 10 for more information on creating effective questionnaires.)

The likely sampling error introduced by convenience sampling is twofold:

✔ Certain elements of the target population will be systematically excluded.

✔ Elements that aren't members of the target population will be included.

As a result of these errors, the sample will contain a biased subset of the target population, which in turn will bias your findings.

Judgment sample

Judgment samples, which also are called *purposive samples,* are samples that an experienced researcher selects based on his judgment about appropriate characteristics required of sample members.

Unlike convenience samples, which include people who are and aren't members of a population, judgment samples include only relevant members of a population. However, survey results may be biased when judgment samples systematically exclude certain members of the population.

Here's an illustration of judgment samples that's probably familiar to you: Television broadcasters use judgment sampling to forecast election-day winners before all votes are tallied. These forecasts are based on exit interviews of voters as they leave polling locations. Obviously, it's cost prohibitive for these broadcasters to place interviewers at every polling location. However, historical voting data indicate which districts' voters tend to vote for the winner. Armed with this data, broadcasters can concentrate their interviewers at key polling locations. In this case, the judgment is informed by historical voting patterns. If conducted properly, exit polling provides the accurate forecasts that networks tout to gain viewers. (You can't blame the misleading exit polls for the Bush-Kerry presidential election on poor sampling; instead, they were a byproduct of poor questioning.)

Judgment samples can help a clothing store manager predict the clothing styles his customers will prefer next season. The manager can ask his best customers — based on expenditures during the last two years — to participate in a preference study. In this case, the manager chose to exclude occasional buyers and include only high-spending customers. Likewise, a golf course manager can ask regulars about proposed course changes, such as relocating tee boxes, adding out of bounds stakes on certain holes, and renumbering the holes.

Quota sample

A *quota sample* is a sample in which various population subgroups are representative of characteristics critical to the research problem. To fill a quota, interviewers screen people based on key characteristics. After enough people with those characteristics have participated, no more like them are solicited.

For example, if you manage the pro shop at your local golf course, you may want to determine which brands of clubs you should carry to maximize sales. To ensure that you consider the preferences of enough golfers who use each major brand, you decide to survey 50 Callaway users, 50 Nike users, 50 Taylor Made users, 50 Titleist users, and 50 Ping users. Before handing customers a questionnaire, you ask them which brand of golf clubs they used most often during the last 12 months. (We discuss such screener questions in Chapter 10.) After you receive 50 completed questionnaires from the users of a brand, you stop asking additional users of that brand to participate in your survey.

Sex and age are two characteristics often controlled with quota sampling. For example, a magazine publisher who knows the male-to-female ratio of subscribers is 2-to-1 may survey them in that proportion. Similarly, a movie theater operator who knows that 30 percent of patrons use senior citizen discounts would collect a sample in which 30 percent of respondents are 60 years of age or older.

Snowball sample

With *snowball samples,* a few initial respondents are selected with a probability method (like simple random sampling; discussed in the next section) and then additional respondents are recommended by these initial respondents. If you want to survey a group that's rare in the general population and you can't find a good mailing or phone list, a snowball sample can be effective.

To collect a snowball sample, you can randomly dial telephone numbers until you find a person who qualifies as a member of the target population. If you dial enough numbers, you'll eventually find such a person. Given the nature of social groups, it's likely that person knows similar people. So, you'd close the interview by asking that person for the names and contact information of three other people who are qualified to participate in your study due to similar interests, predispositions, and behaviors.

Describing the different types of probability samples

In contrast to nonprobability samples, probability samples are drawn from an exhaustive list of population members. In other words, all that's needed for a probability sample is a sample frame that lists all population members. Here, the probability of selecting each population member is known, but not necessarily equal. As shown previously in Figure 11-2, the four types of probability samples are simple random, systematic, stratified, and cluster, which are covered in the following sections.

Simple random sample

In a *simple random sample,* each population member has an equal, known, and nonzero chance of selection. To draw one, you simply select members from your sample frame at random. Often, this sample is ideal for marketing research.

Suppose, for example, that you want to study the promotional strategies of Major League Baseball teams but only have time to study 15 of the 30 teams. You could write each team name on a slip of paper, place those slips in a New York Yankee cap, and then draw 15 slips from that cap. (No peeking!) In this case, the probability of selecting each team is 50 percent.

The advantage of simple random samples is this: They allow the strongest inferences to the general population. From a statistical standpoint, a simple random sample is most preferred. However, they're expensive and cumbersome to collect.

Systematic sample

A *systematic sample* is an easy and inexpensive way to draw the operational equivalent of a simple random sample, which we discuss in the preceding section. To collect a systematic sample, you pick every nth name from your sample frame, where *n* depends on the size of the sample you wish to draw.

For example, assume you must draw a sample of 100 persons from a list of 1,000. To draw a systematic sample, all you must do is pick a random name within the first ten names and then select every tenth name from that starting point. If the random starting point is the 7th name, for instance, you'd select the names that are 7th, 17th, 27th, and so on from that list.

Stratified sample

A *stratified sample* and *quota sample* (which we discuss earlier in this chapter) attempt the same goal: to sample a sufficient number of members from each subgroup of interest. However, a stratified sample draws from a sample frame for each subgroup, whereas a quota sample has no sample frame. You would use a stratified sample when your research question requires you to determine differences between subgroups, such as ethnic subgroups (Blacks, Hispanics, and Whites) or fans of different baseball teams (New York Yankees and Boston Red Sox).

For example, to stratify respondents into low, medium, and high income subgroups, you would first construct a sample frame for each income subgroup and then randomly select people from each list. This process would guarantee a sufficient number of respondents from each subgroup — like a quota sample — but it would create a probability sample because respondents in each stratum would be selected from a sample frame.

Cluster sample

Cluster sampling is a multistage probability sampling approach; after clusters are randomly selected, elements within each cluster are randomly selected. The single purpose of a cluster sample is to sample economically while retaining the characteristics of a probability sample.

Marketers often search for groups of consumers who are similar to one another but different from other consumers. In contrast, the groups used in cluster sampling must be as similar as possible to one another; otherwise, the study results will depend on the clusters selected.

As an example of cluster sampling, consider face-to-face interviews conducted with a geographically scattered sample. The cost of transporting interviewers to physically dispersed respondents would be prohibitive. However, if you can identify similar clusters of people, select a few clusters at random, and then select people within each cluster randomly, your respondents will be more geographically proximate and interviewing costs would drop markedly.

Balancing probability samples

What if, despite using a probability sampling method, you drew a sample nonrepresentative of the population along one or more characteristics? Although unlikely, it's possible; after all, a fair coin can come up heads on ten consecutive flips despite the odds against it. Similarly, probability sampling only reduces the odds that you'll draw a nonrepresentative sample. In the unlikely case of such a sample, it may be necessary after the fact to balance it for the relative propensity of respondents in the population.

For example, suppose you drew a probability sample of your customers. If people younger than 25 years old comprise 10 percent of your sample but 20 percent of your customers, and people older than 55 years old comprise 30 percent of your sample but 15 percent of your customers, you can weigh the former 200 percent (count each answer twice) and the latter 50 percent (count each answer ½) to achieve balance.

Selecting a Sample: The Eight Steps

To choose a sample for your research project, you must be familiar with the sample selection steps that researchers follow. If you skip any of the steps or perform them poorly, your sample is likely to be less representative of the population. Here are the steps:

1. Decide whether to use a probability or nonprobability sampling method.

2. Define the target population.

3. Select a sample frame.

4. Identify the sample unit.

5. Plan the procedure for selecting sample units.

6. Determine the sample size.

7. Draw the sample.

8. Conduct the field work.

The following sections address the first five steps of the process. Determining the sample size is the focus of Chapter 12; drawing the sample is a strictly mechanical task based on the previous steps; and conducting field work is the focus of Chapter 17.

Choosing either a probability or nonprobability sample

Here are some important considerations when deciding whether to draw a probability or nonprobability sample:

- ✔ **Operational considerations:** Nonprobability samples are easier and faster to collect, more accessible, and less expensive. Probability samples, on the other hand, tend to require great care in selection and are more expensive because creating a sample frame is an expensive proposition.

- ✔ **Available resources:** Nonprobability samples are much cheaper than probability samples. As for probability samples, simple random samples are more expensive than cluster samples, and stratified samples typically make better use of data-collection budgets.

- ✔ **Timeliness:** Nonprobability samples can be collected faster. For instance, simple random samples take longer to collect than convenience samples because of the time required to generate a sampling frame.

- ✔ **Needed degree of accuracy:** Nonprobability samples tend to be less representative of the population, so estimates based on those samples tend to be less accurate. For exploratory research, nonprobability samples often are pragmatic. For conclusive research — from which you would draw conclusions and act accordingly — probability samples are more representative and hence more reliable.

✔ **Dominant error type:** If nonsampling error is a major error component in your research, a nonprobability sampling is acceptable because sampling error is a lesser error source. Alternatively, if sampling errors are the largest error component, a probability sample is preferred. (Refer to Chapter 12 for more on these error types.)

✔ **Similarity of population members:** If the population is relatively *homogeneous* — members are relatively similar to one another — intra-population variability is low and a nonprobability sample may be sufficiently representative of the larger population. In other words, it may be possible to draw a fairly representative sample without probability sampling. Alternatively, if the population is highly variable, or *heterogeneous,* a probability sample is preferred because it's far more likely to be representative of the population.

Think about boxes of cookies, for example. (We apologize if you're now hungry, but this is a good example.) How many cookies from a box of chocolate chip cookies would you need to sample to determine whether the box contains delicious cookies? Only one; they are the same flavor, come from the same box, and were produced by the same manufacturer at the same time. Alternatively, how many cookies from a box of mixed cookies would you need to sample to determine whether the box contains delicious cookies? If the box contains many types of cookies, you'd need to sample at least several cookies. (Perhaps the ginger snaps are wonderful but the coconut creams are awful.)

✔ **Statistics needed:** If statistics — which are invalid for nonprobability samples — are needed to extrapolate from a sample to the population, probability sampling is required.

✔ **Sample scope:** Deciding whether to draw a local or national sample also influences the sample design. If it's a local sample, cluster sampling won't be cost effective. If it's a national sample, cluster sampling may be critical to cost management.

✔ **Statistical analysis requirements:** Statistical analyses are only appropriate for probability samples because those are the only samples that can be projected reliably onto the larger population. For the most part, nonprobability samples are inappropriate in that regard.

Nonprobability samples are appropriate for exploratory research when nonsampling errors are larger than sampling errors, the members of the population are similar, statistical analyses aren't required, and operational considerations are critical. In contrast, probability samples are preferred when business decisions will be made based on the research, sampling error is the largest component of total error, population members tend to differ markedly from one another, statistical analyses are important for extrapolating to a larger population, and unfavorable operational considerations are less critical.

Defining your target population

Members of your target population are qualified to participate in your study. In many cases, these people are potential patrons of your business. To define a target population, you need look no further than your research question. The answer to that question strongly suggests who should participate in your study.

For example, if you want to test different advertising appeals for netbooks or fine-tune a new questionnaire scale, an appropriate target population is students. Alternatively, if you're a marketing manager interested in adding a product to your existing line of luxury automobiles, the appropriate population is unlikely to be students.

To identify a target population like Whatsamatta University alumni, you may contact the alumni office and request a complete list of alumni. If the population is marketing majors at Whatsamatta University, you may acquire a list of those students from the business college or the marketing department. Although such a list won't be perfect — it will include some nonmajors (and nonstudents) and exclude some current majors because student populations are always in flux — it's acceptable to assume that all current marketing majors appear on that list.

When selecting a target population, you should consider the convenience and cost of alternative samples. All else being equal, a population that's less expensive to access should be used, because the savings per completed questionnaire can be put toward collecting a larger sample.

Selecting your sample frame

Selecting a sample frame (a list of elements from which a sample may be drawn) is only relevant for probability samples. This frame consists of appropriate respondents who are eligible to participate in your study. Your research question determines the sample frame from which you solicit respondents. For example, to examine bettor behavior, a casino operator is likely to use a list of the casino's loyalty or rewards program members as a sample frame.

Possible sample frames include mailing and commercial lists, but they can be problematic if they're not representative of the target population (as we discuss in Chapter 7).

For example, Mike once needed to survey people who had relocated within the last six months. At the time, R.L. Polk maintained a new movers list, so he paid $4,000 for contact information on 40,000 households. Unfortunately, the list wasn't as advertised; specifically, 80 percent of the households hadn't relocated in the last six months. In fact, one woman hadn't changed her residence in 57 years! Given the distribution of new movers, he would have been better off randomly phoning people. Although other commercially available lists may perform better, such lists can be problematic.

Identifying sample units

A *sample unit* is any element that comprises a sample, such as people, households, and businesses; these units provide the data you seek. Your research question determines your sample unit selection.

Several years ago, Mike conducted a study to assess the skills of undergraduate marketing majors at his home university. (A sample questionnaire from that research program is included on the DVD.) He surveyed several groups, including current and recent students. He also surveyed Fortune 500 companies to identify desirable skills for new hires. Of course, you can't survey companies, but you can survey personnel directors; hence, the sample unit in that case was personnel directors.

Sometimes, the primary sample unit is of interest; other times it's the secondary sample unit (as per cluster sampling).

Planning the procedure for selecting sample units

If you're collecting a probability sample, the procedure for selecting sample units is relatively straightforward: You just select names from the sample frame. If that frame includes many more members than you need to sample, you select every nth one as described in the previous section "Systematic sample." Otherwise you have to contact every member listed in that sample frame.

You need to exercise additional care when collecting nonprobability samples. Although there's a greater chance of nonrepresentativeness for nonprobability than probability samples, you should prevent avoidable biases in nonprobability samples.

For example, mall-based interviewers may be instructed to approach every tenth person who passes them, regardless of race, gender, age, apparent busyness, or anything else. That way, they — in theory — will be sampling a somewhat representative group of people who visit the mall. However, these clipboard holders may be tempted to approach people who are younger or seem less busy because such people may provide more entertaining answers or be more willing to participate in the survey. Such a practice would create unnecessary sample bias because people who are younger or who are more willing to participate are likely to differ from mall visitors in general. Minimal interviewer supervision can prevent this problem.

Another important problem is selecting unqualified respondents. As we discuss in Chapter 17, interviewers are motivated to complete interviews because they receive incentive pay per completed interview. As a result, interviewers are encouraged unintentionally to interview people who are willing to participate but aren't qualified.

Suppose, for example, you're conducting a study about parents with preschoolers and a father with only teenagers is willing to participate. The interviewer you hired may want to survey that person to earn additional money; however, that father should be disqualified, regardless of interest, because he isn't a member of the target population.

Collecting Samples for Online Research

Despite the growing pervasiveness of the Internet, not all people are equally enthusiastic users. As a result, collecting a probability sample of customers for online research remains a challenge. That said, you have many methods at your disposal. The typical methods for collecting online samples can be divided into nonprobability and probability methods.

Here are the nonprobability methods:

- **Entertainment:** Entertainment methods pertain to polls. For example, ESPN solicits viewers to visit its Web site and vote for the team they believe will win the Big 12 football championship. Other media companies, like CBS and *USA Today,* run similar polls.

  You can gather opinions with the increasingly popular social media Web sites like YouTube, Twitter, and Facebook. On these sites, consumers can voice their opinions about brand-related issues and experiences. For example, students who receive an unexpected poor grade in a course sometimes vent their frustrations on Web sites like www.ratemy professors.com, which can be a bummer for Mike and Jeremy.

- **Unrestricted self-select:** With this method, potential respondents can choose to participate in a survey often solicited through a banner ad or Web site. Although it's an efficient way to collect a large respondent sample, issues pertaining to repeat responders may arise.

  For example, fan votes determine the starting position players for the Major League Baseball All-Star game. Unlike political elections, Major League Baseball encourages fans to vote early and often. This voting process overweighs less knowledgeable fans whose main interest is to see their favorite player make the team. (Players with a contract bonus for making the team and lots of unemployed friends also have a motive and means for skewing the vote.)

✔ **Volunteer opt-in:** Similar to the unrestricted self-select method, opt-in respondents volunteer to participate over time in a survey research panel. Panel operators tailor online survey strategies to attract such respondents. For example, panelists may see a banner ad soliciting survey participation each time they visit a certain Web site.

Probability methods include the following:

✔ **Intercept:** The intercept method captures shoppers' attitudes before, during, and after their online shopping experience. A randomization process solicits shoppers, and a cookie-based monitoring system minimizes repeat responders. (Don't forget that cookies are tied to PCs rather than users, so such monitoring won't identify people who respond from multiple PCs. Also, browser-savvy respondents can block or delete cookies.) Web sites like www.bizrate.com provide data about online shoppers' retail experiences.

✔ **List-based:** Web sites that require user registration can rely on a list-based method to collect data. Although site users are solicited at random through intercept or e-mail, which encourages a somewhat diverse sample, only registered users can be queried. Thus, such samples are representative of registered site users but may not be representative of other populations.

✔ **Prerecruited:** Although similar to volunteer opt-in — because people volunteer to participate in both cases — prerecruited sampling differs in that the panel operator controls sample recruitment; as a result, the probability of selection is known. Nielson Media Research engages in prerecruitment for its online surveys on television viewership.

Chapter 12

Selecting a Sample Size

*O*ur goal in this short chapter is to show you the issues associated with selecting a sample size, including the approaches you can take to determine the appropriate one. As any marketing researcher can attest, adequate sample size is a prerequisite to meaningful data analysis.

For some advanced statistical procedures, a sample size of roughly 200 is ideal; in contrast, determining whether the difference between the average score for two groups is statistically significant requires a sample only one-fourth that size. Unfortunately, businesspeople often rely on faulty common sense ("500 sounds like a good number.") or budget constraints ("We can only survey 200 people because that's all the money we have.") when choosing a sample size. Such decision criteria are bound to waste some (in the case of excess sample size) or all (in the case of insufficient sample size) of their research dollars.

Examining the Relationship between Sample Size and Random Sampling Error

Even if you've identified the right people or things (like other businesses) to sample — in the sense that they can provide the information to help you make a more informed marketing decision — it's possible that a small sample may contain enough "atypical" people or things to skew your findings. With a sufficiently large sample, the other people or things you survey should counterbalance these atypical people or things, which should reduce your sampling error and make you more confident about your estimates of the population.

Sampling error relates directly to sample size: The larger the sample, the smaller the error. Figure 12-1 depicts the relationship between sampling error and sample size. The graph indicates that returns to increasing sample size are diminishing. With a very small sample, the random sampling error will be large.

Initial increases in sample size cause marked decreases in random sampling error. As sample size increases further, random sampling error decreases at an ever-slower rate. So, you have an opportunity to identify the optimal sample size relative to an acceptable error and your data-collection budget.

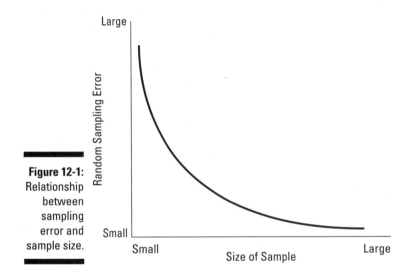

Figure 12-1: Relationship between sampling error and sample size.

Practical Criteria for Determining the Size of a Probability Sample

As we discuss in Chapter 11, nonprobability samples have no statistical properties. As a result, you don't need to worry about sampling errors for those types of samples because you shouldn't use statistics to generalize from such samples to larger populations. In contrast, you use statistical analyses to generalize from a probability sample (also discussed in Chapter 11) to a larger population.

The following three practical criteria are related to determining the ideal size for a probability sample:

✔ **Financial:** Data are a resource, and each completed questionnaire has a prorated cost. Figure 12-1 shows that sampling error declines at a slowing rate as sample size increases. You must weigh the prorated cost of additional data against the reduced error associated with that cost.

✔ **Statistical:** Estimates based on samples will differ from true values based on populations. Recall any recent election; pollsters always state their results as $x \pm y$ percent. Newscasters typically indicate whether the leading candidate's edge is within the margin of error. If within that margin, estimates based on a different sample of voters can even be opposite the reported results. From a statistical standpoint, knowing that the sample-based estimate can be lower or higher than the true score (for the population) raises issues about the acceptable plus or minus range. The larger the sample, the closer the endpoints of the range to the sample-based estimate; it can be ± 10 percent for a small sample but only ± 1 percent for a large sample.

✔ **Managerial:** Consider the preferred level of confidence about the outcome. How much does additional data reduce uncertainty? (We discuss this issue in Chapter 1.) Is a high degree of confidence in the estimates necessary, or will ballpark estimates suffice?

Approaches for Determining Sample Size

You may use one of several approaches to determine a sample size for a probability sample. Some are better than others. A few of the most common — but less wise — methods are as follows:

✔ **Blind guess:** Guessing that 200, 300, 500, or 1,000 respondents seem sufficient is a terrible way to determine sample size. Such a guess probably would be wrong.

✔ **Available budget:** You may budget $10,000 for a study and guess that 60 percent is a reasonable proportion to spend on data collection; so, your sample would be as large as $6,000 permits. That's a poor way to decide the size of your sample. Because advertising should achieve a goal — for example, to increase brand awareness — advertisers should spend whatever is necessary to achieve it. Spending too much is a waste, and spending too little dooms them to fail.

✔ **General rules of thumb:** One standard rule of thumb is 100 cases for every main group and between 20 and 100 cases for every subgroup. For example, in a study on gender differences, the main group would be 100 males and 100 females. That same study also can examine differences by gender and age, so age would be the subgroup. Typically, such a sample would include enough respondents to avoid major random sampling error. However, general rules ignore study context, which may demand larger or smaller samples to achieve an acceptable error level. For example, if respondents in a main group tend to be very (dis)similar, then 100 cases is too (few) many.

Here are two better ways for you to identify an appropriate sample size:

- **Standards for comparable studies:** Many clever people have already examined the statistical and cost implications of different sample sizes and have identified the appropriate sizes for different types of studies. Following conventional wisdom doesn't require learning extensively about statistics, making assumptions, or doing calculations. Table 12-1 lists minimum and typical sample sizes for several types of studies.

- **Statistical precision:** A more sophisticated approach, statistical precision considers the acceptable plus or minus percent for sample-based estimates.

Table 12-1	Minimum and Typical Sample Sizes for Different Types of Studies	
Study Type	**Minimum Size**	**Typical Size**
Name tests	100 per name tested	200–300 per name and respondent category (for example, males versus females)
Package tests	100 per package tested	200–300 per name and respondent category
Radio commercial tests	150 per commercial	200–300 per commercial
Television commercial tests	150 per commercial	200–300 per commercial
Print ad tests	150 per ad	200–300 per ad
Concept/product tests	200	200–300 per concept/product and respondent category
New-product-market-penetration test	200	300–500
Market studies	500	100–1,500

Assuming you have an appropriate level of statistical sophistication and certain types of available information, we suggest you use the statistical precision approach. This approach is preferred because it will select a sample size that can provide estimates of sufficient accuracy. Here's what you need to use this approach:

- **Variability of the total population and subgroups:** To use your data-collection budget most efficiently, you should draw relatively more of your sample from subgroups with people who differ markedly from one another and draw relatively less of your sample from subgroups with people who tend to be similar to one another. Overall variability of the population also is important; to reduce random sampling error, the sample size should be larger if the population tends to include people who differ markedly from one another.

✔ **An acceptable level of random sampling error:** This level can be high or low, depending on the needed level of confidence (± percent) in your estimates.

✔ **How data are distributed:** If data are normally distributed (in a roughly bell-shaped curve), a sample of a certain size is needed to ensure a minimal random sampling error. If your data aren't normally distributed — for example, bi-modally (two peaks) or uniformly distributed (no peaks) — you need a larger sample, relative to normally distributed data, to ensure minimal random sampling error.

Using Sample Size Formulas and Calculators

The assumption in the statistical precision and sample calculator approach is that there's one key variable on which to base your sample size. That variable can be the most important question on your questionnaire. Figure 12-2 shows the equations for calculating sample size.

If you're uncomfortable with performing the calculations required to use preceding formulas, you can try an online calculator from one of the following Web sites instead:

✔ www.surveysystem.com/sscalc.htm

✔ www.raosoft.com/samplesize.html

✔ www.macorr.com/ss_calculator.htm

✔ www.dssresearch.com/toolkit/sscalc/size.asp (also does proportions)

✔ americanresearchgroup.com/sams.html

✔ www.custominsight.com/articles/random-sample-calculator.asp

✔ 74.220.224.110/longbow_1x1/samplesizer/rightsizer.aspx

✔ www.gmi-mr.com/resources/sample-size-calculator.php

✔ www.ginns.info/ssc.htm

✔ www.nss.gov.au/nss/home.nsf/pages/
sample+size+calculator

To calculate the sample size for a proportion, you can use the sample calculator like the one shown in Figure 12-3. Scale A indicates the percent of favorable responses, or p-level. Scale C indicates the percent error that's acceptable at a confidence level, either 95 percent on the left side of the scale or 99 percent on the right side of the scale. In order to find the appropriate sample size, take a straight edge, move it on the left-hand Scale A to the desired p-level, move the other edge to the right-hand Scale C, and line up with the percent error of favorable responses (where the straight edge crosses Scale B). The point at which your straight edge crosses Scale B is the appropriate sample size.

Sample Size Formula

$$n = \left(\frac{zs}{E}\right)^2$$

where

n = sample size

z = confidence interval in standard error units

s = standard error of the mean

E = acceptable magnitude of error

Sample Size Formula for Proportion

$$n = \frac{Z^2 pq}{E^2}$$

where

n = number of items in samples

Z^2 = square of confidence interval in standard error units

p = estimated proportion of success

q = (1-p) or estimated the proportion of failures

E^2 = square of maximum allowance for error between true proportion and sample proportion, or zs_p squared.

Figure 12-2:
Sample size
formulas.

To use the chart, lay a straightedge to connect known values on any two of the scales. Read the unknown value where the straightedge intersects the third scale.

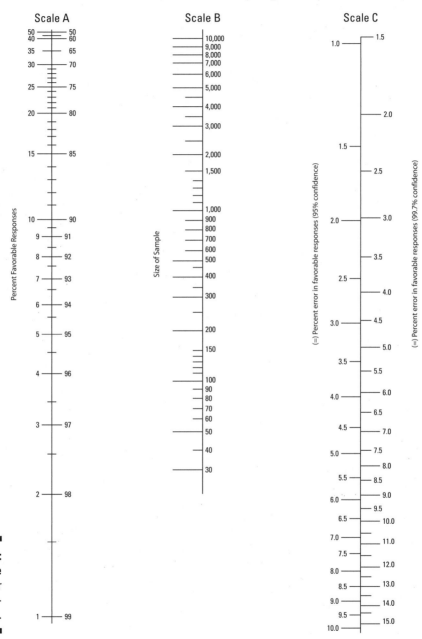

Figure 12-3:
Sample size calculator for proportions.

Part III
More Methods to Meet Your Needs

The 5th Wave   By Rich Tennant

SALES &
MARKETING
PICNIC

"Get names!"

In this part . . .

The chapters in this part cover different types of marketing research methods and how to use them. Chapter 13 presents secondary data, with attention to online sources and sites. For an overview of qualitative research, with emphasis on in-depth interviews and focus groups, see Chapter 14. Chapters 15 and 16 give you the basics on observational research and experiments, with multiple examples of experiments retailers may run to determine the best price points, promotional efforts, and more.

Chapter 13

Secondary Data: What Is It and How Do You Use It?

*U*nlike primary data (for example, survey data), which are collected for a specific and immediate research need, *secondary data* are data that already exists and can be used to uncover facts and build business-related models. Such data often are historical and in a form suitable for your research purposes. Before conducting an original marketing study, you should consult secondary sources either to inform that study or to provide data that the study would duplicate at a substantially higher cost.

You can rely on many valuable secondary data sources and search mechanisms. For instance, you've probably used Google's, Yahoo!'s, or Microsoft's search engines to scan the Web. You also may be familiar with government databases, library catalogs, and other resources available online. However, there are many other sources of secondary data that you may find helpful. Fortunately, a friendly neighborhood librarian — either working at a local public library or university — can help you identify and access such data. In this chapter, we show you how to acquire secondary data and evaluate them for your own use.

Understanding Uses for Secondary Data

Secondary databases come in four flavors:

> ✔ **Bibliographic:** For bibliographic sources, think bibliographies or listings; although not self-contained, bibliographic databases suggest possible sources for further query.

✔ **Numeric:** Numeric sources contain numbers; for example, national governments create many meaningful reports based on census data.

✔ **Directory:** A directory can list relevant information by national newspaper, type of business, or people by profession.

✔ **Full text:** For full text, think online databases of professional publications, like EBSCO's Business Source Complete or Proquest's ABI/INFORM. Although some works listed in these sources are limited to article abstracts, titles, authors, and keywords, most works are available in complete form. Full-text databases exist for newspapers as well, because many of these and comparable information sources have moved online.

You can use secondary data for both exploratory and confirmatory purposes. These data can help refine research objectives or questions. Alternatively, they can confirm previous research results; for example, to assess the accuracy of the models you use to forecast industry sales.

Secondary data sources can be useful in locating important facts related to your research problem. They also can provide the raw material you — or more likely your researcher — can use to create forecasting models of future sales or revenues.

Using secondary data for fact-finding

Whether you're trying to understand consumers' latest buying tendencies or competitors' latest successes and failures, secondary data sources can provide the needed information. In other words, these sources are great for fact-finding. Here are three typical fact-finding uses of secondary data:

✔ **Identifying consumption patterns:** You may want to identify consumption patterns within a region, a town, a zip code, or an area code. For example, if you want to introduce a product into a region, local consumption patterns for similar products should influence your warehouse location and distribution decisions. A bar operator interested in revamping the happy hour menu should consider historical sales data to identify poor-selling items and avoid discontinuing popular items. Historical sales data also can indicate coupon promotions — if any — that boosted sales.

You can create a database of current customers — which would include customers' names and addresses — and use it to identify purchase patterns or responses to past marketing efforts.

✔ **Tracking trends:** Consumers' behaviors are affected by trends in both controllable (advertising and product assortment) and uncontrollable (local economic conditions) factors. Secondary data can help you identify industry-specific trends in both domains. Data collected over time — especially government-collected data — can help you anticipate rather than merely react to changes in consumers' preferences and purchase tendencies.

✔ **Scanning the environment:** Scanning the competitive landscape can reveal business opportunities and threats. Whether through online sources (like LexisNexis and Factiva) or conventionally published reports, such scanning can help you improve your business strategies. Because timeliness is critical, online push technology like electronic smart agents can filter, sort, prioritize, store, and promptly deliver pertinent secondary information to your PC.

Regression-type model building

Secondary data are the foundation for *regression-type models,* which are used to estimate market potential, forecast long-run sales, and select new trade areas. In statistics, regression analysis includes methods for determining the relationship between the variable you want to predict (dependent variable) and the variables that might help you to make that prediction (independent variables). In essence, regression analysis can identify which set of candidate predictor (independent) variables relate significantly to the predicted (dependent) variable and the nature of that overall relationship. (See Chapter 21 for a brief introduction to simple regression-type models.) Here are more details about each type of usage:

✔ **Estimating market potential:** Secondary data can help you estimate the sales potential for a large geographic area, which also can be further parsed to predict subregion potential. For example, determining the number of frequent golfers in southern New Mexico can help a golf course developer decide whether Las Cruces needs an additional golf course. Similarly, a microbrewer contemplating expansion into a nearby city can use that city's per capita beer consumption to predict likely sales.

✔ **Forecasting sales:** You can use historical sales data to forecast future sales. Consider a hotel operator's need to forecast revenue. A simple forecasting model may multiply previous sales by some growth rate published in a reliable industry source. A more sophisticated model may rely on a *moving average* — a weighted sum of previous sales that weights more-recent periods more and less-recent periods less — to predict future sales. An even more-sophisticated regression model may forecast annual room revenue as a function of room revenue per capita, number of travelers per capita, number of available rooms per capita, and average number of nights stayed per capita.

✔ **Selecting trade areas and sites:** You've almost certainly heard the real estate mantra "location, location, location." Secondary data can help you make location decisions. Mom-and-pop establishments, franchise outlets, and corporate conglomerates can use the *retail saturation index* to help identify an ideal store location. By dividing local market potential (which is an area's population multiplied by annual per capita sales for a product category) by local market retail space, you can calculate the retail saturation index; values that exceed 200 predict a ripe opportunity.

In addition, trade area analysis data can be obtained from the following Web sites:

- www.mappinganalytics.com/trade-area-analysis/
  perform-trade-area-analysis.html

- www.businessdecision.info/mapsreportsdata/maps
  andreports.asp

- www.businessinfomaps.com/applications/trade_area.htm

Recognizing Internal Secondary Data

Internal secondary data are data that already have been collected by a company for some other purpose. You can use these data, regardless of the original collection reason, for making marketing decisions.

Sources of internal secondary data include

- Accounting reports that contain inventory, cost, and sales figures
- Global positioning satellite data for monitoring employee and product locations
- Salesperson self-reports for customer complaints, competitor behavior, and new product opportunities
- Scanner data for sales and coupon redemptions
- Web-based information for Web site tracking

Typically, the original purpose of collecting internal data is to satisfy accounting, sales-tracking, backorder-logging, and customer-complaint-monitoring needs. Each purpose creates a specific type of data. Consider the following:

- **Accounting information:** For obvious reasons — like to avoid tea and crumpets with IRS agents — you (or your company) collect accounting data. In turn, you (or your company) also can apply such data to marketing decisions. For example, you can relate sales force costs to sales per region. Here, costs may include travel expenses (air fare, hotel, food), promotional items (brochures, free stuff), and task-related necessities (netbook, cellphone, software, presentation materials). If sales exceed overhead costs, you may consider allocating additional selling resources to that region.

✔ **Sales information:** Sales data can inform marketing strategies. Identifying the cyclical nature of your sales — if they routinely shift during certain times — should help you set promotions, staffing, and pricing. In addition, you can relate sales data to other expenses; for example, if price promotions boost volume but not profit, you may reconsider future price promotions.

✔ **Backorders:** Backorder data can help identify supply chain inefficiencies. If you discover that certain suppliers are repeated backorder offenders, you have good reason for switching suppliers.

✔ **Customer complaints:** These data often are captured via telephone, browser-based, e-mail, or on-premises customer satisfaction surveys. You can monitor such surveys continually to identify operational deficiencies. For example, hoteliers who solicit guest feedback — both negative and positive — are better able to improve service quality. During his resort days, Jeremy asked important guests to critique each new entree before he added it to the menu. Likewise, a manager who strolls the restaurant floor and converses with patrons can discover ways to improve the dining experience.

Looking at the advantages

There are two main advantages to collecting internal secondary data:

✔ **Suitable geographic and product breakdowns:** Although internal secondary data have been collected for other purposes, they likely have been organized according to business operations. As a result, these data should be structured along suitable geographic and business/product lines.

For example, companies operating in different locations can analyze sales and cost-related data to allocate resources more effectively and alter strategies appropriately. Likewise, product line comparisons across geographic regions can inform promotional, supply chain, and product assortment decisions.

✔ **Minimal time lags:** Data ought to be relatively fresh. Sales data should be available from recent months as well as from the previous year. In service settings like restaurants — where customers' preferences can change rapidly — data timeliness is critical.

Noticing the disadvantages

Although internal secondary data have advantages, they also have disadvantages, including the following:

- ✔ **A hard-to-handle volume of information:** Companies often collect so much internal secondary data that their handling and analysis become difficult. In other words, information overload is a possibility.

- ✔ **Inputs tied to compensation:** Inputs to a company's internal secondary data often are tied to compensation. For example, salespeople who meet their quota within the first three days of a month may try to smooth the entry of those orders into the ordering system. As a result, they may withhold booking those orders for a week or ten days, which may confound analyses about newly introduced products.

- ✔ **Data in accounting format:** Much company-related data are collected for accounting and financial purposes. Data formatted for accounting purposes may not be ideal for marketing decision-making.

Improving Efficiency with External Secondary Data

External secondary data are data that have been collected by some entity — for example, a newspaper, journal, trade association, or government — exclusive of your organization. Such data often are available from online data archives, which should improve your search efficiency. After all, which is easier: running a Web search engine on your home or office PC, or wandering down to a large public and/or university library (assuming there's a local one) and either searching through the catalog or asking a librarian for help? Also, many library-stored data archives are in hard copy rather than electronic form, which necessitates entering the data you want into a spreadsheet or database file. Unless you prefer inconvenience, limited availability, and typing practice, the first option clearly dominates.

Examining sources

Governments collect secondary data as part of their mandate; for example, many federal governments must conduct a population census each decade. Trades associations often collect and share secondary data to promote their industry. Private organizations like news agencies and research firms may sell such data for profit. In essence, different entities collect secondary data for good but different reasons.

Here are some sources of external data:

- **Government agencies:** Government agencies are a rich and accurate source of secondary data. The U.S. Census of Population (for demographic data), Federal Reserve Bulletin (for financial data), Current Housing Report (for housing data), and the Statistical Abstract of the United States (for socioeconomic data) can answer many marketing questions. Web sites such as `www.fedworld.gov` and `www.stat-usa.gov` also may prove helpful.

- **Syndicated research services:** Syndicated research services provide clients with important and relevant information in return for a fee. The information they provide is reported in standardized form; in other words, it's not customized to your needs.

  For example, J. D. Power and Associates (`www.jdpower.com`; automobile quality and satisfaction data) and the Nielson Company (`en-us.nielsen.com`; retailing, consumer behavior, and media data) offer syndicated data reports. Vendors like Dow Jones Factiva (`factiva.com/index_f_w.asp`) and D&B's Hoovers (`www.hoovers.com/free`) sell financial and operational-related company data to interested parties.

- **Trade and professional associations:** Trade and professional associations often collect useful data about industry practices. Mike once helped collect data for the now World Floor Covering Association; `www.wfca.org`). Mike surveyed association members and created a report that members can use as a baseline for comparing their previous year's performance. In addition to customized, computer-generated reports sent to every self-identifying survey participant, the association created an annual report for public consumption.

  Web sites for professional associations offer a wide range of marketing information (see below for a sample list). For example, the AMA Web site offers its' members access to webcasts, podcasts, reports on industry trends, and several professional and academic publications.

  - American Marketing Association (AMA), `www.marketingpower.com`)
  - Direct Marketing Association, `www.the-dma.org/index.php`
  - Chartered Institute of Marketing, `www.cim.co.uk/home.aspx`
  - Business Marketing Association, `www.marketing.org/i4a/pages/index.cfm?pageid=1`
  - Sales & Marketing & Executives International, `www.smei.org`
  - Society for Marketing Professional Services, `www.smps.org/AM/Template.cfm?Section= Body_of_Knowledge1`
  - Hospitality Sales & Marketing Association International, `www.hsmai.org/Americas.cfm`

✔ **Custom research firms:** Some research firms publicize their activities (in newspapers, magazines, and the like) as well as publish reports in professional journals and other outlets. For example, Green Book (`www.greenbook.org`) has compiled a directory of marketing research providers that can ease your search for a vendor. Likewise, GfK Custom Research North America (`www.gfkamerica.com`) provides data on brand management, customer satisfaction, and new product development.

✔ **Books, newspapers, and periodicals:** Although available in hard copy, you often can access these types of sources via electronic means. For example, you can identify journals (like those noted in Chapter 3) and book excerpts through indexing services such as Business Source Complete or ABI/INFORM, which are available through university libraries. Through simple Web searches, you can identify data pertaining to the stock market, industry sales, and consumer behavioral patterns.

✔ **Internet:** In addition to individual Web sites, directory sites like `www.business.com` and `www.allbusiness.com` can suggest relevant secondary data. Social media Web sites like `www.twitter.com` and `www.facebook.com` can reveal vital information about consumers and brands. For example, advertisers can use Twitter-posted critiques of commercials aired during a Super Bowl broadcast to inform future ad campaigns. Companies with a Facebook page that offers customers a venue for venting dissatisfaction about a recent purchase experience can use such complaint data to improve business operations and increase customer satisfaction.

Noting the advantages

The advantages of external secondary data are as follows:

✔ **Inexpensive relative to primary data:** Consider the large direct costs of fielding a study, collecting data, and analyzing that data in a meaningful way. These costs cause us to argue that marketing research is an asset best regarded in terms of cost-versus-benefit (or net value). Secondary data are less expensive to you because each entity that collected them either did so for another purpose or will sell them repeatedly to recover its' direct costs over a sufficient number of buyers.

✔ **Can be obtained rapidly and are readily available:** Fielding a research study means designing it, fielding it, and analyzing the data it yields — all which take time. Luckily, you may be able to avoid that time. Government data often are readily available free of charge, online, at public libraries, and at archival facilities like university libraries.

✔ **Provide information that may not otherwise be accessible:** Given the scope and expense, such data would be unavailable to you otherwise. As such, you should tap secondary data when it's appropriate to your research question and within your budgetary constraints.

✔ **Aid in the design of primary research:** Secondary data can indicate the questions that you should ask and the ways you should ask them. For example, they can help you determine the suitable vocabulary for your questionnaires.

✔ **Enhance existing primary data:** Primary data can provide some information and secondary data can provide complimentary information. Jointly, they offer a sharper picture of your business environment.

Staying mindful of the disadvantages

Although external secondary data have many advantages, you should be mindful of these disadvantages and discount any implications accordingly:

✔ **They may not be consistent with your needs.** Secondary data may rely on incompatible units of measurement. For example, people may be grouped in an unsuitable way. Media reports often group people according to key demographics, such as 35- to 50-year-olds. That age classification may be too broad for your purposes.

✔ **They may be dated.** In many cases, relevant secondary data are collected over relatively long periods. For example, the U.S. Government collects census data continually — rather than only once every decade — and in particular conducts a mid-census assessment. Yet, even these data may be as much as 5 years old, which is ancient for some research needs. The same can be said of data from the Economic Census of the U.S., which are collected roughly every half decade.

✔ **It may be difficult to assess their trustworthiness.** You may be unable to assess the trustworthiness of such data because the researchers failed to describe their methodology in sufficient detail.

Evaluating External Secondary Data

Taking secondary data at face value can cause problems. Failing to ensure the trustworthiness of secondary data can lead to incorrect analyses and poor business decisions. To evaluate external secondary data, you should assess the provider's purpose, the data collector, how data were collected, what data were collected, when data were collected, and the consistency of these data to data from other sources. We discuss these and other assessment criteria in the following sections.

Asking the right questions

Like any rumor you hear or any article you read on the Web, you should assess the credibility of any secondary data you access. Here's a list of six questions you should ask yourself about data before you decide to trust it:

- **What was the research provider's purpose?** It matters greatly whether the research was conducted for public policy purposes or a commercial venture. Because commercial and politically-oriented entities often promote their vested interests, assessing the research provider's intent can help you weigh the data by their trustworthiness.

- **Who collected these data?** Was it a government agency? Was it a highly reputable commercial firm? Was it a fly-by-night research organization? Data quality relates to the abilities and credibility of data collectors.

- **What data were collected?** Do these data truly fit your research needs? Just as conjoint analysis (a powerful data analysis method that we discuss in Chapter 21) isn't appropriate for every research problem, you should avoid secondary data that don't address your research needs. For example, beverage sales aren't beer sales, so a microbrewer shouldn't expect beer sales to mirror beverage sales.

- **When were data collected?** Knowing when data were collected helps assess their adequacy and timeliness. For example, in rapidly changing Las Cruces, New Mexico, data timeliness is critical. Five-year-old U.S. Census Bureau data may be useless for identifying a location for a new restaurant or apparel boutique.

- **How were data collected?** The data-collection method relates to quality, and quality relates to credibility. If data were collected haphazardly from a convenience sample (which we discuss in Chapter 11), they're likely meaningless to your research needs.

- **Are these data consistent with data from other sources?** If a government report, several commercial reports, and a newspaper-sponsored report converge on the same assessment, you'd be more comfortable trusting that assessment than you'd be if different sources drew different conclusions.

Assessing Web sites

Evaluating Web sites is important to help find a good fit between the online source and your research needs. When evaluating Web sites as sources of secondary data, you should ask questions related to the following:

- **Purpose:** Is it a vanity site or a trustworthy source? Examining the mission statement or company description should help answer this question. If such detail is obscure or missing, you should search elsewhere.

✔ **Authority:** You should examine the sponsor's credentials, sources, and contact information for additional insight.

✔ **Scope:** For example, data age and frequency of data updates should be available. Obsolete data are irrelevant at best and harmful at worst to your forecasts and business-related decisions.

✔ **Audience:** Just as you selectively target some consumers, you should avoid Web sites that cater to people unlike you. For example, trying to use a Web site meant for research professionals may be more damaging than helpful.

✔ **Format:** A poorly formatted Web site suggests a lack of professionalism that may reflect untrustworthy data.

Being leery of non-U.S. secondary data

We would be remiss if we didn't alert you to potential problems with secondary data collected outside the United States. In addition to the usual limitations of secondary data from the United States (which we discuss earlier in this chapter), non-U.S. data may suffer from two additional problems:

✔ **The data you want may be unavailable.** Although we'd like to believe that all governments collect the diverse types of high-quality data collected by the U.S. government, some governments don't collect such data because it's cost prohibitive. For example, governments of lesser-developed countries with low per capita income may decide that collecting data about consumers' spending habits is a waste of limited tax revenue.

✔ **The data may lack sufficient accuracy.** Non-U.S. data may be improperly collected and poorly tabulated. The data also may be far more dated than what's available in the United States. In other countries, the equivalent of census data may be far less timely.

Nonetheless, you may have no choice but to rely on non-U.S. secondary data. If so, then here are a few Web sites that may help satisfy your international data needs:

✔ **Demographic and census data:** www.marketresearch.com

✔ **Attitude and public opinion data:** www.worldpublicopinion.org/pipa/about.php?nid=&id

✔ **Consumption and purchase behavior data:** www.marketresearch.com/browse.asp?categoryid= 1591&sortby=dd&page=5

✔ **Advertising data:** www.warc.com/LandingPages/Data

Taking care with percentages and index numbers

Be careful when secondary data are presented as either percentages or index numbers. (The U.S. Government's Consumer Price Index and the Housing Market Index — an index based on data from hundred of home builders that show the demand for new homes in the United States — are two examples of frequently cited indices.) Percentages can be based on large or small populations and on large or small samples. With small populations or samples, apparently large percentage differences may not be statistically significant, let alone managerially meaningful. Be careful that percentages, if judged meaningfully different, are based on sufficient samples or populations.

As for index numbers, they're often computed relative to a base year or a base period, and those bases can shift over time at the data reporters' convenience. When comparing index numbers — especially government index numbers — be careful that they're computed from the same base year. Otherwise, you'll need to convert those index numbers before comparing them.

Chapter 14

Using In-Depth Interviews and Focus Groups

*Q*ualitative methods allow researchers to discover peoples' deep-seated beliefs, experiences, attitudes, preferences, and behaviors without relying on numerical measures. Two well-known qualitative methods of inquiry are in-depth interviews and focus groups. After a brief overview of exploratory research, this chapter focuses on in-depth interviews and focus groups.

Seeing How Qualitative Methods Can Help You

At the beginning of the research process, qualitative methods can help you better understand your marketing problem. Here are several reasons for using this type of research:

✔ **To diagnose a situation or to help better define the problem area:** You can use exploratory research for both analysis of a situation and for problem definition. However, it's not useful for symptom detection or for a formal statement of research objectives. You don't need have to conduct exploratory research, but often it's advisable to further define your research problem and specify your research questions.

✔ **To screen alternatives:** You may consider dozens or even hundreds of strategy alternatives; researching them all extensively would be cost prohibitive. As an affordable alternative, you can use qualitative research, which is typically less expensive and faster than quantitative research, to reduce an initial large set of alternatives into a more manageable set that's suitable for descriptive or causal research.

✔ **To discover new ideas:** Quantitative research (see Chapter 3) tends to be more structured; as a result, it may be less able to identify new possibilities. In contrast, qualitative research can reveal consumers' subconscious attitudes and preferences, which can suggest new products and ways to promote them.

The open-ended questions needed for in-depth interviews and focus groups are relatively easy to write (as we discuss in Chapter 6.). However, such questions demand careful thought by respondents, are more slowly answered, and are in respondents' own words (so answers are more varied and require more effort to evaluate). Because response categories aren't hinted, memory-related problems are more pervasive when answering such questions. Consider aided versus unaided recall; a person is more likely to recall having seen a commercial when prompted. (See Chapter 9 for more on recall.)

Given the nature of qualitative data, analysis is slow and subjective. Although it's impossible to run a statistically meaningful analysis on qualitative data, such data are more flexible, require smaller samples, usually precede quantitative methods, and are useful for exploratory research.

Figure 14-1 shows typical research problems and related research questions answerable with qualitative research.

Qualitative versus quantitative research

Although you can use qualitative research to further explain the results of a *quantitative* (or numerically measureable) study, qualitative and quantitative research differ from one another in several ways:

✔ Qualitative studies intended for exploratory research provide initial understanding; in contrast, quantitative research typically is descriptive or conclusive and intended for recommending courses of action.

✔ Researchers engage in dialogue with participants in qualitative research, but they have limited interaction with participants in quantitative research.

✔ Qualitative research relies on smaller and nonrepresentative samples rather than the larger and more representative samples needed to extrapolate statistically to larger populations. (We discuss such samples in Chapter 11.)

✔ Qualitative research relies on flexible questioning methods rather than highly structured ones (as is the case with quantitative research). That flexibility is needed to explore unanticipated responses. Structured questions, by their nature, are more focused and therefore provide insufficient flexibility for pursuing the unexpected.

✔ Qualitative research data require subjective interpretation. In contrast, quantitative research, with its highly structured questions, often provides numerical scores that easily are subjected to subsequent statistical analysis.

In general, qualitative methods are less structured than quantitative methods — in large part because they're supposed to be flexible and allow you to pursue directions you didn't anticipate. More structured quantitative methods don't permit such flexibility. Qualitative methods also tend to be more intensive in the sense that you query fewer respondents in far more detail. Due to small and nonrepresentative samples, you must be careful when generalizing results to a larger population, which is the purview of quantitative research. Instead, you should mine this small number of people extensively for their opinions and potential behaviors.

Research Problem	Related Research Questions Answerable with Qualitative Research
Improve ads	What image should my ads convey? What message will be most memorable and convincing?
Understand key customer groups	What are the lifestyles of my key customer groups? How does my product fit into the lifestyles of our core customers?
Develop new products	What product features are most important to targeted customers? What do targeted customers believe are the strengths and weaknesses of my competitor's products?
Increase sales	Why are my previously most loyal customers buying elsewhere? How can I modify my merchandise assortment to attract new customers?
Improve package design	How will alternative packaging redesigns affect customers' perceptions of my product? How do customers use the current packaging?
Improve brand image and positioning	How does my brand image compare with competitors' brand image? What's the best way to differentiate the image of my brand from the image of competitors' brands?
Understand how customers use product	How do different groups of customers use my product? For what different purposes do my customers apply my product?
Improve retail (brick-and-mortar and online) store design	Why do my customers prefer to shop at my store? What physical changes can I make in my store to enhance my customer's shopping experience? How can I improve the aesthetics of my online store?

Figure 14-1:
Typical research problems along with related qualitative research questions.

Conducting In-Depth Interviews

An *in-depth interview* is used to gather rich insight from respondents, which is essential to understanding your customer's behavior. Whether the interview is nondirected or semistructured, as we discuss later, the data captured can help you develop more effective business strategies.

Consider this example that shows how in-depth interviews can be helpful: Mike belongs to a generation that enjoyed occasional cigarette smoking, especially when driving long distances on interstate highways. He once drove regularly from Houston to Dallas or Austin. He thought of those drives in terms of the number of cigarettes consumed. The Austin drive, which was roughly three hours, was a two-cigarette drive for him, and the Dallas drive, which was closer to four hours, was a three-cigarette drive. Typically, he smoked a bit less than one cigarette per hour when driving long distances.

Why are we telling you about Mike's previous smoking habits? Here's why: It's unlikely that a researcher using a structured questionnaire would ask respondents whether they equated the number of cigarettes they smoked per hour with the number of hours they had driven. However, this type of unexpected finding may be revealed through an in-depth interview because rich insight — rather than the numerable close-ended responses characteristic of quantitative research — is sought.

Describing two types of in-depth interviews

In-depth interviews can be classified as nondirected or semistructured. Although both types are highly flexible, they differ by their degree of structure and ease of administration.

Here's the rundown on the two types:

- **Nondirected:** Think of *nondirect interviews* as conversations with a dominant speaker (the respondent) that proceed in a general direction preplanned by the other speaker (the interviewer). Although the interviewer has identified what should or needs to be asked, the ultimate direction of any conversation is unknowable; thus, the interviewer must be able to adapt instantaneously. Given this unpredictability and need for rapid accommodation, seasoned interviewers are better suited than novices to conduct such interviews.

    You've probably seen thousands of nondirected interviews on television. If you're a news junkie or talk-show enthusiast, you've probably seen tens of thousands! Television reporters and talk-show hosts (or their staffs) typically prepare a small set of broad questions in advance of an interview. If these questions are astute and the interviewee's answers are thoughtful, an interviewer with keen listening skills will be able to concoct good follow-up questions on the fly.

✔ **Semistructured:** Think of *semistructured in-depth interviews* as quasi-non-directed in-depth interviews for less experienced interviewers. In other words, consider them the type of interview you can conduct success-fully.

Relative to a nondirected interview, a semistructured interview relies on a more detailed and organized set of open-ended questions. Although this additional structure doesn't preclude follow-up questions (in fact, it encourages them), it relieves some of the multitasking stress you'd experience with nondirected interviews. In addition, such interviewing typically requires interviewers to record answers longhand, because most interviewees will resist mechanical recording to retain plausible deniability ("I never said that!"). A more detailed set of questions will reduce your anxiety about conceiving each question while conversing.

Reporters and talk-show hosts are intelligent, personable, highly skilled, and highly practiced questioners. You may possess the first two qualities, but most people lack the skill and practice to be good nondirected in-depth interviewers. The point is, you probably should avoid nondirected interviews (unless you hire out the job) and opt for semistructured interviews.

Seeing how in-depth interviews should be conducted

If you have the skills necessary to be an in-depth interviewer, then you should conduct your interviews in ways that encourage the best or highest-quality responses from interviewees.

The most important thing to remember when conducting in-depth interviews is to encourage interviewees to do the talking. You may know the questions, but they have the answers!

As you proceed through an interview, you should do the following:

✔ **Provide a comfortable environment.** For instance, schedule the inter-view for a setting that will ease the interviewee, such as her home, work place, or quiet cafe. Also, providing food and beverage may create a relaxed setting. Such environments will encourage interviewees to answer as completely as possible and minimize the degree that they censor their thoughts.

✔ **Allow interviewees to express their opinions and thoughts in their own words.** That's not to say you shouldn't rely on a set of prepared questions that you can adapt as the interview progresses. Rather, you should be as unobtrusive as possible and allow respondents to volunteer their opinions and determine the direction in which to take the interview.

✔ **Reflect interviewees' feelings as summary statements.** After an interviewee has spoken for a minute or two, you may say something nondirective, such as "Let me see if I understand what you're saying," and then you can summarize what you believe the interviewee said. If you misunderstood and your summary is inaccurate, the interviewee can clarify.

Although it's natural in everyday conversation, you should never express your own opinion. Otherwise, respondents' answers are more likely to reflect your opinion rather than their opinions. Think about your first conversation with someone you've just met. Without a long history, social etiquette encourages you to avoid confrontation by not disagreeing with this person regardless of your true opinions. Instead, use the summarizing technique to make the interview process seem more conversational and to ensure that you interpreted answers properly.

✔ **When appropriate, ask probing questions so interviewees can expand on their comments.** The ability to ask probing questions is a major strength of in-depth interviews because it's impossible to anticipate how interviewees may answer your initial questions. When interviewees provide answers that are interesting and unexpected, you can ask follow-up questions to further develop those answers.

✔ **Use a discussion outline to ensure that all pertinent topics are covered.** After developing the 20 to 30 related questions you want to ask, you can anticipate the most logical sequence for asking them. An organized list minimizes the likelihood that you'll forget to ask a key question. Nonetheless, interviewees may jump to answering questions you planned to pose much later in the interview. Write those answers as they're given, and, if it doesn't seem unnatural, try returning to your original question schedule.

✔ **Avoid evaluative comments or other behaviors that may inhibit interviewees.** To allow interviewees time to think, you should remain silent during extended pauses. Inexperienced interviewers may have trouble with this requirement. After all, it takes skill and experience to wait out interviewees while they contemplate answers. Jeremy has found sipping on coffee or biting into a snack — especially of the chocolate variety — can encourage patience. To Mike's chagrin, this technique doesn't work well with his children, who seemingly can remain silent indefinitely when asked "Who broke the . . ."

Customer insights from an in-depth interview

Here's a verbatim comment from a dissatisfied customer about a shopping experience. The level of detail is far greater, and the emotion expressed is far more intense than would be revealed by the typical customer satisfaction questionnaire (see Chapters 9 and 10). Also, the (occasionally colorful) language used and topics covered may suggest questions for a subsequent self-administered questionnaire. We disguised the store name to protect the guilty (and thus avoid a defamation lawsuit):

I was a little bit cranky (imagine that) when I went to Stuff 'R Us this morning and got even more cranky when I saw that they were in the final stages of rearranging the locations of about ⅓ of the products in the store. I found a manager and yelled at him. I told him that I love Stuff 'R Us because it has such a wide assortment of products but that counts only when I have a clue about where to find them. I said that I'm sure that they thought they had a good reason for the major rearrangement but whatever that was I was sure that it wasn't as compelling as the logic of not changing it so people knew where to find products. He started to say something, and I said "STOP changing stuff around" in a manner that was much stronger than I intended, and he stopped

talking because I think he may have been seriously concerned that I was going to go postal if he didn't. It was too funny.

As I was checking out, my cashier asked me if I was able to find everything okay like they always do. I said I'm so glad you asked that. I was very nice to her (as always) but complained to her as well. I believe the primary purpose of their change was to put their pharmacy in the middle of the store so it would be much more visible to those few total clueless shoppers who were oblivious about Stuff 'R Us having a pharmacy. Of course, that change necessitated numerous other changes and so on until they really got carried away. So the bottom line is that I (and I'm guessing the vast majority of regular customers) receive no benefit from the change but now have to find where previously regularly purchased products are now located. I'm sure they had some academic do a traffic analysis and are trying to drag grocery customers by their pharmacy or pharmacy customers by their groceries, or both, but they made it a huge hassle to their regular customers. It took me twice as long as usual to do my weekly shopping.

Carrying Out Focus Group Interviews

A *focus group interview* is an unstructured, free-flowing, laid-back, group interview that helps researchers define problems, reveal subconscious motivations for behaviors, and expose product or brand attitudes. In this section, we discuss the basics for running your own focus group.

Characterizing focus group interviews

Focus group interviews, which take between one and three hours to complete, are conducted by a moderator who works from a somewhat structured script (to ensure that all topics are covered) and, as with in-depth interviews, manages conversation flow. Typically, the scripts start with a broad topic and gradually shift to more specific issues.

Interview sessions always are audio- and video-recorded. Observers who watch a session from behind a two-way mirror may have an assistant hand-deliver notes with follow-up questions to the moderator. If a session is streamed in real time over the Internet to remote observers, they can text such questions to the moderator.

You can choose from three types of focus groups. Although the last type is far more typical for marketers, all three are useful for marketing research:

- ✔ **Exploratory focus groups** help to define research problems and generate *hypotheses* (formal statements to be tested). Concept testing and pilot testing require such focus groups.

- ✔ **Clinical focus groups** can probe deeply into participants' psyches and reveal subconscious motivations for their behaviors.

- ✔ **Experience focus groups** can reveal product or brand usage attitudes and beliefs.

Focus groups typically are conducted with groups of six to ten people who have been prescreened, which ensures that the prospective interviewees are qualified to speak on the topic of interest. (See the later section "Knowing what to include in a recruitment screener" for more on prescreening.) Interview sessions should continue until they've revealed almost everything that can be revealed by the interviewees; usually, three to four sessions allow sufficient opportunity to hear different viewpoints and learn enough about different behaviors.

Although people recruited for these sessions may differ markedly from each other socio-demographically, behaviorally, and attitudinally, people within a given session should be as similar to one another as possible. Consider the difficulty of managing substantive conversations between people who have little in common or who don't use the same words to describe the same things. A successful focus group requires participants to converse meaningfully with each other, and intra-group similarity — at least in terms of the product or service in question — maximizes the potential for such conversations. The prescreening process can help you group participants according to lifestyles and experiences.

The typical cost of a professionally-conducted focus group

Focus groups are expensive; hiring a professional to run three or four sessions can cost $10,000. Regardless of the moderator or venue, the cost of an additional session typically exceeds the incremental benefit once three or four sessions have been conducted. Surprisingly — given the personal nature of focus groups and the rising cost of human services — the nominal cost of these group interviews has remained stable during the last 15 years. Perhaps the cost stability is due to technological improvements that reduce the time needed to generate summary reports; for example, low-cost, high-quality video recordings can replace verbatim transcripts from low-fidelity audio-only recordings.

Nonetheless, the moderator's fee, preplanning expenses, rent for a facility with a two-way mirror (for unobtrusive live viewing and video recording), reasonable food service and respondent incentives (because people are unlikely to show up at 6 p.m. on a Tuesday unless they're promised free food and money), the analysis of participant comments, and written and oral reports, cost roughly $2,500 per session for four sessions, or $10,000. Although videotaping may now cost less, increased travel costs more than compensate.

Without the ability to amortize costs over multiple sessions, a single session is likely to run roughly $4,000; hence, you'll find it worthwhile to run three or four sessions on consecutive nights at a given facility.

Focus groups with experts are even more costly. For example, a free deli sandwich, soft drinks, and $40 are unlikely to induce physicians to participate in a focus group. Instead, remuneration for physician participants is likely to reach hundreds of dollars, which drives up the total cost of each session considerably.

Many factors encourage and discourage people from participating in focus groups. The positive factors include ego enhancement, personal validations, personal growth, socialization, and extrinsic rewards for participating. In contrast, the negative factors include ego threats, political correctness, memory decay, inarticulateness, reticence, and time constraints. These negative factors tend to inhibit participation by stopping people from attending a session or speaking during it.

 Allowing consumers to chat about their product usage and attitudes can help advertising agencies develop new ads and establish consumer vocabulary, which is an important precursor to descriptive research. After all, it's important that you write questions that respondents fully understand; and you're most likely to write such questions if you use the same words that respondents use (see Chapter 9).

Here are some uses for focus groups:

✔ Uncovering basic consumer needs and attitudes

✔ Identifying new product concepts

✔ Generating new ideas about established products

✔ Helping to interpret the results of previously conducted quantitative studies

Although focus groups are appropriate for studying consumers' attitudes, they're also useful for studying experts' attitudes, beliefs, and knowledge bases. In the late 1970s, Mike conducted a focus group with automotive and battery experts. At the time, the United States was experiencing an oil price shock, and automotive companies intensified their efforts to develop viable electricity-powered cars. (The more things change, the more they stay the same!) The experts revealed important product information unavailable from consumers.

Reviewing the advantages of focus groups over in-depth interviews

Focus groups have many important advantages over in-depth interviews. Here they are:

✔ **You benefit from the synergy of the group.** When six to ten people participate in a coordinated group discussion, rather than one person at a time responding to an interviewer, the resulting give and take produces synergy. That's why focus groups are so successful. One person's comments can trigger thoughts and comments by other people that wouldn't have occurred otherwise.

✔ **Groups make people feel more secure.** Often, people are more willing to speak in a larger group with people who may confirm their beliefs. Focus groups tend to be unperturbed affairs that encourage open and occasionally unexpected responses.

✔ **They cost less.** Conducting six to ten in-depth interviews costs far more than speaking with those same six to ten people simultaneously; as a result, focus groups are a more efficient use of trained interviewers. (However, they're still fairly pricey; see the nearby sidebar "The typical cost of a professionally-conducted focus group.") The cost per hour for an in-depth interviewer and the number of hours required to interview that many people would cause interviewer costs to exceed focus group costs, like site and food costs.

✔ **Focus groups are conducted in a centralized location and in a more controlled way.** Typical in-depth interviews occur at respondents' workplaces or homes, and such interviews aren't monitored. Focus groups are audio and video recorded, so you gain more control over the interviewing process.

✔ **They can be conducted more quickly.** A series of focus groups can be scheduled for two days; in contrast, one person trying to conduct in-depth interviews would complete, at best, two per day. As a result, interviewing 40 people may require a month or more.

Knowing what to include in a recruitment screener

A *recruitment screener* allows you (or your hired moderator) to ensure that your prospective focus group participants are qualified to participate in your focus group. For example, when Mike conducted several focus groups for a Las Vegas casino interested in the motivations of local slot machine players, the Las Vegans invited to participate in those groups were screened to ensure that they played video slots. Although not a requirement, recruiting and screening usually occur over the telephone.

The sample telephone screeners included on the DVD and in Chapter 10 require roughly five minutes to administer.

What should you include in a screener? Here's a reasonable list:

✔ **A heading and the screening requirements:** This information entails something comparable to a title and the minimum qualifications for participants, such as type of shopper or minimum age.

✔ **Contact information:** Such identifying information may include home/work address, phone number, and e-mail address.

✔ **Introduction to the research:** Without this background information, it's impossible for people to assess whether they're interested in the research and qualified to participate.

✔ **Questions to reveal overparticipation or conflict of interest:** *Professional respondents* — people who participate regularly in marketing research — should be avoided. Because focus group participants are fed, paid, and socially engaged, people who are lonely, bored, and of lower-income — who may be atypical of the targeted population — would participate excessively in focus groups if unchecked.

✔ **Key demographic questions:** A successful focus group requires participants who can converse meaningfully with one another. Demographic information facilitates the formation of groups with similar people.

✔ **Questions about the frequency of product use, purchase history, or brand loyalty:** Such questions ensure that people are qualified to participate. You also should ask pertinent lifestyle, attitude, and knowledge questions.

✓ **Questions to assess whether a potential participant is sufficiently articulate:** Willingness to participate is a necessary but insufficient condition; participants must be able to express their thoughts adequately during a one- to three-hour session. Asking potential participants to answer a relevant open-ended question or two should be ample to ensure sufficient articulateness.

✓ **Reasons that people should participate:** Without good reasons, many potentially good respondents may decline your invitation. ("Sorry, but I'd rather watch the New York Yankee game that night.")

Acting as a focus group moderator

An important part of a successful focus group is an effective moderator. A *moderator* is the person who directs and focuses the group's discussion. Before a focus group interview begins, a moderator writes a loose script to ensure that all relevant topics are covered during the discussion. He exerts relaxed control through his attempts to follow the script. One of his goals is to encourage rapport among the six to ten people who have opted to participate in the session.

During the group interview, a moderator interacts with participants, listens carefully to what they say, and often — as with in-depth interviews — summarizes what someone has said and then asks other group members to comment. (Refer to the earlier section "Seeing how in-depth interviews should be conducted" for more on summarizing an interviewee's comments.) Ultimately, a moderator tries to hear equally from all group participants, which may be difficult when groups contain both reticent and highly talkative speakers.

Figure 14-2 shows a sample page from a focus group script. You can view the entire script on the accompanying DVD.

Although conducting a focus group isn't rocket science, successful moderators share certain characteristics:

✓ **Kind but firm:** Although sessions should be informal and fun, they're not parties. Disruptive participants who insist on speaking out of turn or in secondary conversations must be controlled.

✓ **Permissive but alert to signs that the group's cordiality or purpose is disintegrating:** Rather than merely answering a moderator's questions, focus group participants must converse cordially about the topic of interest — and the moderator must ensure that those conversations begin and stay on task. Poor moderators fail to placate heated discussants and drift without good reason from the question schedule.

✔ **Acts engaged, enthused, and involved:** Even if the focus group topic is dull — like deodorant, laundry soap, or other mundane products — a successful moderator will convince all participants they're involved in an interesting and important task.

✔ **Encourages specific and substantive comments and discourages glib, vague, and ambiguous comments:** Comments of the latter type won't help reduce uncertainty about your best course of business action, so the moderator must encourage informative answers. (We suspect a focus group with politicians is doomed to fail!)

✔ **Encourages everyone to participate:** When one or two people dominate a discussion, some interesting opinions won't be expressed, causing the group to suffer from "group think."

✔ **Flexible and able to improvise:** No matter how carefully a moderator plans a session, it never unfolds as planned. Once people are involved, the process becomes unpredictable. As a result, the moderator must be flexible about the flow of each session.

✔ **Sensitive:** A successful moderator must have good intuition about people and their comfort levels, and he must be capable of relating to people on an emotional level.

Planning and executing your focus group

Much planning and preparation go into conducting successful focus groups. But don't worry; we provide the following step-by-step guide to help you conduct a successful focus group:

1. **Identify the objectives of your research and define the problem.**

   If you don't know what you want to know and why you want to know it, then you're wasting your time.

2. **If your focus groups are intended as exploratory research (see Chapter 3), specify objectives relevant to your research program.**

   Is your goal to write the best possible self-administered questionnaire by learning the words consumers' use when discussing your product? Alternatively, do you want to discover consumers' attitudes toward your advertising to suggest new ads for testing? Again, you're wasting your time if you don't know how your focus groups fit into your overall research plan.

3. **Write a screening questionnaire to identify and recruit participants.**

   See the earlier section "Knowing what to include in a recruitment screener" for more details.

4. **Write a script to guide the sessions.**

   Use the sample script in Figure 14-2 as an example.

"RECENT MOVER" FOCUS GROUP SCRIPT

1. Introductory comments
2. Warm-up discussion: Best and worst aspects associated with moving
3. Leaving the prior community
   a. Trauma associated with separation from prior community
   b. Move induced tensions and stresses at home
      i. Causes
      ii. What would have reduced
   c. Disposal of previous residence
      i. If owned
         1. Employer support
         2. Most troublesome aspects in general
         3. Specific difficulties inherent to present market and economic environment
      ii. If rented
4. The move: The transition stage
   a. Criteria for selecting overall community (SMSA)
   b. Criteria for selecting specific neighborhood/suburb
   c. General attitudes toward housing
      i. What one is looking for in a residence
      ii. Rent versus buy decision: Barriers and reasons
      iii. Is purchase of house/condominium still a "good buy"?
      iv. Purchase of residence as an investment: Expectations of future value
      v. Desirability of buying an "old place" and "fixing it up"
   d. Residence search process: Description
      i. Employee support
      ii. Alternative types of residences considered
      iii. Information sources most relied upon in search process
   e. Mortgage financing
      i. Available types of financing assistance and type of financing chosen
      ii. Preferred type of financing assistance
         1. Preferential rates
            a. Information about service to handle paperwork on loan
            b. Actual mortgage: Should employer help to find mortgage money?
      iii. Magic interest rate or monthly house payments
      iv. Impact of present mortgage rates on
         1. Housing package settled on
         2. Life style in new community
      v. Who managed the physical move?
         1. Employer, outside supplier, yourself?

Figure 14-2:
A sample
page from a
focus group
script.

5. **Recruit qualified participants.**

   Although screening and recruiting typically occur via telephone, you also can recruit on-site customers. If you're interested in the opinions and behaviors of different groups of people, recruit accordingly.

6. **Choose the site for your focus groups.**

   Rent a focus group facility if available locally and within your budget. A dedicated facility can provide proper seating, lighting, audio and video recording capability, and the like. Using a lower-budget alternative, such as a meeting room at a local hotel, will require additional time and effort; for example, you'd likely need to acquire and arrange all the recording equipment.

7. **Order food and beverages for each session and prepare remuneration.**

   People prefer cash, so prepare envelopes that you'll distribute to participants upon session completion.

8. **Conduct the sessions.**

   Anticipate subtle script changes based on what did and didn't work and what was and wasn't interesting in earlier sessions. Take notes on participant responses.

9. **After the sessions are completed, analyze the audio and video recordings.**

   If necessary for a lender or for prospective investors, write a summary of the sessions. Figure 14-3 contains a page from a standard focus group summary. You can see the entire write-up on the DVD.

10. **Consider follow-up research suggested by the sessions.**

Classifying online focus groups

Focus group objectives can be achieved entirely online if you can't or aren't interested in gathering participants in a centralized location. You can choose from two types of online focus groups:

✔ **Videoconference-based:** Videoconferencing permits people at two or more locations to interact through two-way audio and video programming. Managers can view the focus group without traveling to the focus group location; as such, they can communicate with the moderator from a remote location when necessary.

✔ **Text-based:** Participants can enter ideas, comments, opinions, and remarks on an Internet display board of some sort, including chat-room postings or focus blogs.

SUMMARY OF "RECENT MOVER" FOCUS GROUP SESSIONS

Given the rapid changes in the "relocation market" during the past two years, there was a strong possibility that even the most current literature would be badly dated. Thus, the long distance relocation process was examined through a series of focus group interviews. Although a series of six interviews was planned initially, budgetary constraints necessitated no more than two sessions be conducted. One session with exclusively unmarried individuals and another with exclusively married couples were conducted in Chicago during late January.

Both sessions followed the schedule (which appears in Figure 14.1). The "game plan" was to follow the session participants chronologically through their most recent move, with an emphasis on:

(1) the dynamics of the moving process,

(2) the hardships/barriers associated with exiting the last and entering the new community, and

(3) the process of acclimating to the new community of residence.

A summary of the two sessions follows.

General Characteristics of the Focus Group Participants

Given the somewhat idiosyncratic fashion in which participants were recruited, reporting some basic generalizations about the groups is possible. In both sessions, group members were typically under 30 years of age, recent college graduates, white collar professionals early in their careers, and past and current apartment dwellers. Career advancement was the primary motivation behind their relocation decision. The only sytematic difference between the two groups was intentional: Group #1 participants were single, and Group #2 participants were married.

Physical Move

There were two basic scenarios associated with the physical move: (1) the employer only reimbursed moving costs, and (2) the employer selected the moving van line company and financed the move. In the first scenario, the individual households managed their own move. The van line was chosen on the basis of prior experience, with a prior negative experience removing a company from consideration in subsequent moves.

Figure 14-3:
A sample page from a focus group write-up.

Although both online focus group methods provide important insights, we suggest you use videoconferencing, when feasible, because this venue affords dialogue. After all, it's easier and more efficient for respondents to state why they dislike the Boston Red Sox than it is for them to type their opinions on a keyboard or texting device.

The advantages of using online focus groups include the following:

✔ They're relatively inexpensive and they can bring together participants from a diverse geographic area.

✔ Participants in text-based focus groups can be anonymous, unlike participants in traditional focus groups.

✔ Transcripts are created automatically in the process of running text-based focus groups, and thus data analysis is more efficient.

✔ Interpretive software, such as ATLAS.ti and NVivo, is readily available, making the identification of common themes in answers more efficient than pen-and-paper transcription.

Of course, online focus groups also have some disadvantages, including the following:

✔ They're less interactive than traditional focus groups. Ten people in a chat room texting one another or conversing via videoconference lacks the synergy of ten people sitting face-to-face and enjoying a meal.

✔ Because it may occur at ten different computing stations, online focus groups lack vital visual feedback. For example, it's impossible for participants or the moderator to sense people's facial expressions or body language during text-based sessions. Similarly, the small Webcam images available in videoconference sessions provide limited visual feedback at best.

✔ The moderator's job differs markedly for an online focus group. In addition to the social skills discussed in the earlier section "Acting as a focus group moderator," the moderator may need technical skills to encourage people in physically remote places to participate openly.

✔ Typing on a keyboard is more taxing than talking; as a result, answers provided during text-based sessions may lack the thoroughness evident in traditional focus groups.

Chapter 15

Projective Techniques and Observational Methods

*W*hen people are reluctant — for social reasons — to express their opinions (especially when they're identified with those opinions), you can't use direct questioning like that found in self-administered questionnaires. Instead, you can use *projective techniques,* which provide a safer avenue for people to reveal their opinions because those opinions seemingly aren't reflective of themselves.

You can acquire useful information — the type that can help you make better decisions — by querying consumers directly through conventional surveys or indirectly through projective research. However, the act of asking consumers to report what they're thinking, how they behaved previously, or how they may behave in the future, can distort those reports relative to truly held attitudes and either previous or possible future behaviors.

As an alternative, you can use observational methods. *Observational methods* permit a researcher or fieldworker (see Chapter 17) to systematically record people's behaviors as they occur. Hence, the data are captured in real time with or without respondent knowledge. As a result, the researcher can capture true respondent behaviors and reactions to marketing stimuli; such data are unattainable with conventional survey methods. In this chapter, we give specific examples of both projective techniques and observational methods and their applications.

We intend this chapter more for research consumers than research doers. We describe methods that research consultants (and academics) may use but that would likely exceed the skill set of most research novices. Nonetheless, an understanding of these approaches will help you decide whether to hire a research supplier who'll conduct a study that includes these methods. Should you decide to do so, this understanding also will help you execute your study and interpret its findings.

Putting Projective Techniques to Work

Many little boys believe that they shouldn't fear the dark, so they're unwilling to express those feelings to their parents. Instead, they say that a favorite plush toy fears the dark and that they're merely trying to abate their toy's fright by sleeping with the bedroom light on. Because plush toys aren't little boys and don't need to be brave, little boys are comfortable assigning their problematic feelings to those toys. In essence, projective techniques work the same way; people project their attitudes, preferences, and behaviors onto a safe person or object.

Projective techniques require people to respond to ambiguous, unstructured stimuli. Because there's no right or wrong way to respond to such stimuli, they're especially useful for controversial topics. For example, asking employees directly, "Why would you steal from your employer?" is sure to inspire a social-desirability-biased answer like "I would never steal from my employer!" Instead, asking respondents to project their attitudes onto ambiguous stimuli is safer for their self esteem and thus more likely to elicit an honest response. Users of projective techniques assume that people can't know their subconscious buying motives, and these techniques allow people to reveal these motives in a way that isn't personally threatening.

Projective techniques were inspired by the motivation-research binge of the 1950s. During that period, Ernest Dichter and other then-famous marketing gurus advocated a Freudian perspective for studying consumers and their motivations.

In the following sections, we discuss a variety of projective techniques; these include thematic apperception test (focuses on picture interpretation), word association (focuses on response time), sentence completion (focuses on word combinations), and third-person role playing (focuses on projective answers in the third person). These indirect methods can provide meaningful insight into your customers and lead to better marketing strategies.

Exploring the thematic apperception test

The *thematic apperception test* (T.A.T.), which psychologists use for personality assessment, relies on a standardized series of socially ambiguous pictures. (Marketing researchers also refer to it as the *picture interpretation technique.*) People taking the T.A.T. are asked to concoct a dramatic story based on each picture. That story should include the following:

- ✔ Important precursors of the depicted event
- ✔ A description of the depicted event

> ✔ The cognitions and emotions of the depicted person
>
> ✔ A conclusion

Psychologists assume that these stories reveal people's conscious and subconscious needs, motives, emotions, and conflicts, which in turn influence people's behaviors. Knowing consumers' needs, motives, and the like would help marketers to create more desirable products and more effective ads. In the next sections, we give several examples that illustrate how researchers can use T.A.T.s to reveal consumers' true attitudes and preferences.

But first we want to show you the pros and cons of using thematic apperception tests. Here are pros:

> ✔ **Pictures are fun and easy to understand.** Respondents like to view pictures and find them easy to understand. Thus, they're likely to attend closely to each picture and provide genuine responses.
>
> ✔ **Pictures can be adapted to any research context.** No matter your business, a picture can be adapted to reflect your research needs.

Here are cons of using thematic apperception tests:

> ✔ **Pictures are fictional.** Because pictures don't represent reality per se, respondents may adopt a "who cares" mentality because depicted situations are imaginary.
>
> ✔ **Coding and interpreting data may be cumbersome.** Coding, analyzing, and interpreting T.A.T. data may be time consuming and expensive. Ensure the value of a T.A.T. study exceeds its cost (see the DVD for a Bayesian approach to assessing research value).

Example 1: Upgrading office software

The marketing variation of the T.A.T. in Figure 15-1 shows a manager asking an IT person whether the department should upgrade its networking software.

Respondents may have many opinions about upgrades and their necessity, but they may be reluctant to express them or unaware of them. By answering *as if* they were the IT person, respondents project their beliefs about networking software upgrades onto her, which is safer than admitting to those opinions. Respondents may project the woman saying something like, "Let's wait until the upgrade has been out a few more months, because new upgrades always contain bugs" or "It's critical to upgrade now to maintain compatibility." By projecting them onto a safe target, such *as if* answers reveal a respondent's true beliefs about software upgrades.

Figure 15-1:
An office
software
T.A.T.

Example 2: Reflecting on a sports car's image

Porsche 911s have a certain image, and so their drivers maintain a certain image as well. Direct questions about those images may not provide answers reflective of respondents' true attitudes and perceptions. Instead, asking respondents to guess huge-smirking Joe's (in Figure 15-2) reply about where he's going in his new car allows them to indicate their true impressions. A response like "I'm going for a ride in the country to enjoy the fall colors" suggests far different underlying attitudes than "I'm going to tool up and down Main Street until some hot chick asks for a ride. Then I'll show her the ride of her life!"

Example 3: Reinforcing milk's healthy image

Consider the long-running and award-winning *Got Milk?* ad campaign. What would have inspired milk producers to promote the idea that milk is a beverage consumed by young, active people? It's possible that their researchers used a projective device like the one shown in Figure 15-3 and received responses that indicated it was wise to convince younger, active people to consume more milk.

For example, it's possible that many respondents answered "Ms. Smith" to the question, "Do you believe that Ms. Smith or Ms. Jones drinks more milk?" Respondents may have answered this way because Ms. Smith appears older, less active, dowdy, and out of shape. If such responses were typical, milk producers may have chosen to reposition their product so it would be more attractive to younger and more active consumers (who constitute a meaningful group of consumers).

Figure 15-2:
A sports car
T.A.T.

Example 4: Understanding spousal differences over automobiles

The T.A.T. in Figure 15-4 requires respondents to project comments onto a married couple. The projected dialogue between them should reflect respondents' beliefs about the typical dynamic between spouses who are considering a new automobile.

In the 1960s, respondents of both sexes may have projected the following conversation onto a traditional couple:

> *Wife: Our mechanic told me our car is breaking down and will soon need a new transmission. Do you think we should trade it in for a new one?*

> *Husband: Yes, and I know exactly what we should buy.*

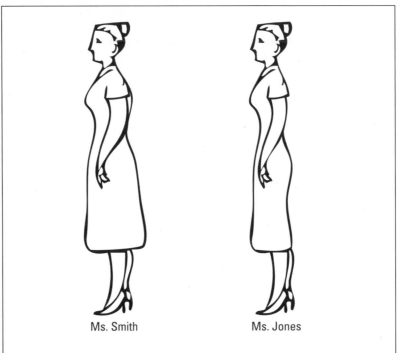

Figure 15-3:
A milk T.A.T.

Do you believe that Ms. Smith or Ms. Jones drinks more milk? If you believe that either one drinks more milk, why do you believe this is true?

Respondents today may project this very different conversation onto a traditional couple:

> *Wife: I just took my car in for maintenance. The mechanic said the transmission is shot, and I'll need to replace it soon. Frankly, my car looks worn, and it makes a bad impression on my clients and business associates. After studying the recent Consumer Reports issue on new cars, I've decided to buy a Toyota Highlander hybrid. You know I mostly drive in town, so good in-city gas mileage and high reliability are vital to me. Also, I need an SUV's spaciousness for the many clients I typically haul around. What do you think?*

> *Husband: Sounds like you gave this a lot of thought. Do whatever you think is best.*

In many cases, the decision-making dynamic between spouses has shifted markedly during the last half century, and unstructured stimuli like the one shown in Figure 15-4 may reveal that shift. Also, identifying the key spouse in a couple's decision to buy a new automobile can help manufacturers design and place their ads more effectively.

Figure 15-4:
An auto
purchase
T.A.T.

A married couple is discussing the possible purchase of a new automobile. What are they saying to each other?

Example 5: Comparing personal computers

Apple computers have competed with Microsoft-OS-based PCs since the early 1980s. Interestingly, the T.A.T. in Figure 15-5 allows respondents to project what the person on the right both says and thinks in response to the person on the left stating that he plans to buy an Apple MacBook Air. Respondents may project the person on the right saying something like this:

> *You're overpaying for hype and image. Also, you're stuck with Apple's operating system. It's much safer, and you'll save a few bucks, if you buy a notebook PC from Dell or HP.*

However, the same respondent may project that the person on the right is thinking something like this:

> *The MacBook Air looks so cool. I wish I could afford to splurge on one.*

By allowing respondents to imagine both the statements and thoughts of a person, you may discover far more about people's attitudes toward the MacBook Air (or any other product you research).

Figure 15-5:
A personal
computer
T.A.T.

Example 6: Determining perfume pricing

If you wanted to identify an acceptable price point for a new perfume, you could use a T.A.T. similar to the one in Figure 15-6, which depicts a woman shopping for perfume. The bottle of perfume costs $10 in the left-hand picture, but it costs $75 in the right-hand picture. When asked to create a story consistent with those pictures, a respondent may offer the following:

> *A woman goes to the store, sees a $10 bottle of perfume, and knows that such inexpensive perfume can't be any good. Later, she sees the $75 bottle of perfume and reluctantly acknowledges that good perfume is very pricey. She then buys the more expensive perfume.*

Alternatively, a respondent may offer this story:

> *A woman sees a $10 bottle of perfume and buys it because she believes all perfume is of similar quality, so if it smells okay, then you should buy it. Later, when she sees the $75 bottle of perfume, she wonders about women who would be silly enough to pay ten times more for the same thing in a slightly more attractive package.*

The two very different stories projected onto these two pictures reflect vastly different impressions about the appropriate price point for perfume. For perfume marketers trying to determine the optimal price for a newly package perfume brand, these data may prove useful.

Figure 15-6:
A perfume
T.A.T.

Example 7: Studying eyewear styles

Suppose you're the marketing director for an eyeglass manufacturer and believe that people associate different demographic tendencies with different styles of glass frames. If you asked people directly about the relationship between glass-frame style and the wearer's age, income, or education, they may report no connection. However, you believe that people unconsciously associate different demographic profiles with different glass-frame styles.

Instead of direct questioning, you could use the T.A.T. in Figure 15-7 to test your belief. Here's how the process would work in this case:

1. **Divide your respondent pool into three similar groups.**

2. **Show one group the left-hand picture, another group the middle picture, and the remaining group the right-hand picture.**

3. **Ask each person in the three groups to indicate the age, income, and education of the man in the picture.**

4. **Compare the average responses among the three groups to determine whether people believe that wearers of different glass-frame styles tend to differ demographically.**

If a relationship exists, then you'd re-design and re-target your ads accordingly.

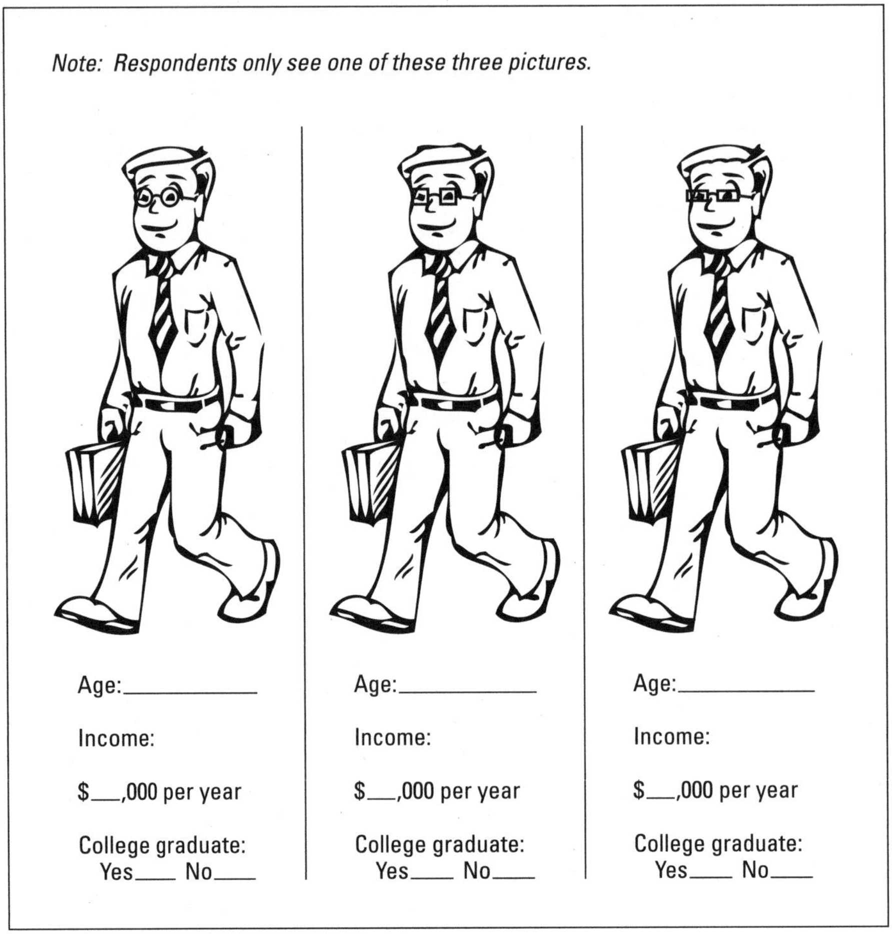

Note: Respondents only see one of these three pictures.

Age:_____

Income:

$___,000 per year

College graduate:
Yes____ No____

Age:_____

Income:

$___,000 per year

College graduate:
Yes____ No____

Age:_____

Income:

$___,000 per year

College graduate:
Yes____ No____

Figure 15-7:
An eyewear
T.A.T.

Using word association

Another projective device is *word association,* which asks respondents to reply to a series of preplanned words or statements with the first words that come to their minds. Unlike movie portrayals of a psychotherapist using word association during a therapy session, respondents' answers are irrelevant. Instead, the time needed to answer is of interest.

The assumption, according to psychologists like Jung — a student and later contemporary of Freud — is that the longer the response time, the more complex respondents' thoughts are about the named entity. Essentially, greater response time equates with being more conflicted about the named entity.

For example, an electronics store owner may want to decide which large high-definition TV brands to carry. He could ask respondents to agree or disagree with statements such as, "When watching football, I want to watch it on Sierra Vision rather than AJ Vision" or "Sierra Vision rather than AJ Vision provides the clearest picture for watching sports." These same questions can be reversed, with "AJ Vision" being named first in the statement. A longer pause for statements with "Sierra Vision" mentioned first would indicate that the owner should carry "AJ Vision" high-definition TVs.

Because conflicted people are less likely to be loyal buyers, first identifying conflicted consumers and then studying their related attitudes and behaviors can help you improve your product offerings and promotional efforts.

Here are pros of using word association:

- ✔ **It requires short answers.** Because you ask respondents to indicate their initial thought, it may be perceived as a simple task, thereby encouraging meaningful responses.

- ✔ **You can gather data for classifying customers.** Although you may not request it, you can easily capture demographic data (such as gender and approximate age) from your respondents and use these data along with the word association data to group your customers into useful segments.

Here are cons of using word association:

- ✔ **It may be onerous for respondents.** Some respondents may struggle to conceive what they believe is a relevant response. As a result, their response quality and willingness to complete the task will diminish.

- ✔ **Responses may be based on limited brand or product experience.** You can't control for respondent knowledge or experience. Thus, insufficient knowledge or mistaken beliefs may influence response latencies.

Understanding attitudes with sentence completion

Sentence completion tasks are totally unstructured and provide no hint about appropriate responses. Consider, for example, the statement, "People who drink beer are (fill in the blank)." There are thousands, if not millions, of word combinations that respondents can use to complete that sentence.

You could ask "A man who drinks light beer is (fill in the blank)." If respondents doubt the manliness of guys who drink light beer, then they may reveal that doubt in the way they complete that sentence. Similarly, you could ask "Imported beer is most liked by (fill in the blank)." Again, if respondents doubt that "real" men drink imported beers, then their words to complete that sentence may reveal that attitude.

Finally, this sentence can provide similar information: "A woman will drink beer when (fill in the blank)." Completions like "she's very thirsty, and there's nothing else to drink" or "at a sports event and wine is unavailable" suggest that respondents don't believe women like beer.

If the goal is to understand people's attitudes about beer drinkers in general, light beer drinkers, imported beer drinkers, and female beer drinkers, a sentence completion task can help assess these attitudes without asking direct questions that may trigger social desirability response bias. (Flip to Chapter 7 for more on this type of bias.)

An advantage of using sentence completion is that it can focus responses on research questions. While still ambiguous — in the sense you don't ask respondents to choose from a list of seemingly acceptable answers — the sentence roots can be fairly specific. For example, if you own a coffee shop and want to discover customers' attitudes about your muffins, you can ask respondents to complete this sentence: The muffins for sale here are (fill in the blank) _____.

A disadvantage of using sentence completion is that the method may become taxing to respondents. Some respondents may find sentence completion mentally challenging. As a result, they may provide quick and unintelligent answers.

Assessing participants' ideas with third-person role-playing

In *third-person role-playing exercises,* study participants either project their thoughts and behaviors onto a third person and respond accordingly, or they imagine they're a third person and then describe themselves. The value of this technique to marketers is evident in the following example.

Imagine trying to assess people's attitudes about instant coffee. Those Folgers Crystal ads — which seem to have run for decades — always depict an effort to convince a drip/ground-coffee drinker that Folgers Instant Coffee is so good that it would receive rave reviews if served at the finest restaurants. The claim is meant to convince ad viewers that instant coffee is suitable for special guests and as a treat for themselves. Why would then-Folgers coffee owner Procter & Gamble believe this ad campaign would be effective?

A classic motivation research study from the mid-1950s also typifies third-person role-playing. In this study, two similar samples of 50 housewives were randomly selected. Both sets of housewives received a shopping list, were told the list was written by a housewife, and then were asked to describe her. The lists were identical except for one product: one list included Nescafé Instant Coffee, and the other list included Maxwell House Coffee.

In the mid-1950s, respondents offered markedly different descriptions of a housewife who bought instant coffee versus a housewife who bought ground coffee: The former was perceived as lazy, a poor purchase planner, and a poor spouse; in contrast, the latter was perceived as hardworking, a good purchase planner, and a good spouse. Seemingly, people held lukewarm opinions about instant coffee in the mid-1950s.

Interestingly, this study was rerun in 1970, and the results were the opposite; the wife who bought instant coffee was seen as modern, thrifty, and a good spouse, whereas the wife who bought ground coffee was seen as old fashioned and a poor spouse. Thus, consumers' attitudes toward instant coffee changed markedly during the 15 years between studies. This finding would have been difficult to uncover through more structured questionnaires.

An advantage of using third-person role playing is that it encourages more elaborate projections. Although top-of-mind responses to words and sentence roots can be meaningful, those responses also can be superficial. In contrast, third-party role playing, because it requires more elaborate projection into another person, can provide richer insights into consumers' attitudes, preferences, and behaviors.

Here are some disadvantages of using third-person role playing:

- **Responses aren't seriously considered.** Because projecting oneself onto another person — with all that other person's thoughts, predispositions, and behaviors — is challenging, some respondents may be lazy and answer superficially.

- **When respondents choose, the third person still may trigger social desirability bias.** For some third-person methods — especially methods used in marketing ethics research — respondents are asked to answer as if a close friend. Such projections may reduce, but not eliminate, social desirability bias because respondents may prefer to depict their friends in a socially favorable light.

Scrutinizing Behavior with Observational Methods

As mentioned earlier in this chapter, observational methods allow researchers to record people's behaviors in real time, which is infeasible with traditional survey methods. However, observation is less straightforward than consumer self reports, as this quote from Sherlock Holmes implies: "You see, but you don't observe." The fictional Holmes knew that the smallest detail may reveal an important secret. (The lead characters in the detective shows *Psych* and *Monk* would believe similarly.)

Although researchers can observe many things in people's behaviors, they often don't recognize what's important and what's trivial. Knowing what to observe is an art and a science. Here are things you chould observe:

- ✔ **Physical action:** Physical action can mean shoppers' movements within a store. Each time Mike visits a supermarket, for example, he tends to begin in a certain aisle and wind his way through the store along a similar path. (He usually starts with produce and finishes with frozen products.) Clearly, the optimal placement of products within a store would depend on customers' movements through it.

- ✔ **Verbal behavior:** Researchers can observe consumer utterances in many contexts, such as statements made by airline travelers waiting in line. *Queuing behavior* — what people do while waiting to be served — can provide useful information about customers.

- ✔ **Expressive behavior (like body language):** Expressive behavior — which includes facial expression, tone of voice, or any sort of body language — can show that people's words suggest one thing but their nonverbal behaviors suggest a vastly different thing.

- ✔ **Spatial relations and locations:** You may observe how close people stand to paintings in art museums or how close salespeople stand to customers as they discuss a possible purchase. In Western cultures, people like their personal space; as a result, people conducting business in the United States tend to remain several feet apart. In other cultures, people crowd closely together; for example, restaurant tables in Europe are placed closer to one another than in the United States (except possibly in New York City). Thus, salespeople who stand an appropriate distance from customers are more likely to make a sale, and restaurateurs who know how closely to pack the tables in their restaurants can maximize sales.

- ✔ **Temporal patterns:** You may observe how long fast-food customers wait for food from the time they enter the restaurant until the time they receive their meal. (It's called fast food for a reason, and customers are buying that convenience.)

- ✔ **Physical objects:** You may observe the brand names of items stored in consumers' pantries. Such pantry audits suggest what people have in stock and therefore use.

- ✔ **Verbal and pictorial records:** Consider the bar codes on product packages and the scanner data that local supermarkets collect. With this data, you can match a brand to a person and observe the degree to which that person routinely buys that brand.

Classifying observation research

When putting your observations of consumers into practice, remember these three dichotomies:

✔ **Human versus mechanical:** In many cases, the observer is a human being. Alternatively, the observer can be a mechanical device, such as a scanner or video recorder.

✔ **Visible versus hidden:** Observers may be visible — in the sense that the people being observed know they're being observed — or hidden. Hidden observation has ethical implications, which we discuss in Chapter 4.

✔ **Direct versus contrived:** With *direct observation,* people are observed in their natural environment; with *contrived observation,* researchers create artificial environments that encourage people to behave in certain ways.

Weighing the pros and cons of observation

Regardless of the observation method, you must weigh the pros and cons of monitoring human beings. Here are the pros:

✔ **Direct communication with respondents is unnecessary.** You need not ask respondents about their behaviors if those behaviors are observable. Talking to an interviewer imposes on respondents; being observed is less taxing.

✔ **You collect data without the distortions caused by self-report bias.** Despite researchers' instructions to the contrary, respondents tend to clean up their act, cognitive and otherwise. When asked how they made a decision, respondents don't report all the wrong turns they took or the dead ends they followed. Instead, they report a straight reconstructed path from problem recognition to problem solution. In other words, they provide no indication of their true convoluted path. Similarly, they tend not to report behaviors that they believe are socially questionable.

✔ **You need not rely on respondents' memories.** As we discuss in Chapter 9, respondents' memories can be faulty, especially about relatively unimportant long-term behaviors. For example, respondents may not recall the brand of laundry detergent they bought three purchases ago. Observation means not relying on respondents' memories about mundane consumer acts.

✔ **You can access nonverbal behavior.** Observation allows researchers to track nonverbal behaviors, which may be far more indicative of people's true opinions than their verbal statements. For more information on nonverbal behavior, see the later section "Physiological observation."

✔ **You can obtain certain data more quickly.** Completing 100 or more face-to-face interviews or collecting several hundred self-administered questionnaires takes time. Even administered surveys (see Chapter 6) may take several days because researchers are imposing on supervisors and some subordinates will procrastinate. On the other hand, observing people's behaviors may be done relatively quickly.

✔ **Environmental conditions can be recorded.** In addition to observing people's behaviors, a researcher also can observe the environment in which they're behaving. This type of observation is impossible with traditional survey approaches.

✔ **You can combine the results with a survey to provide supplemental evidence.** Observation data can flesh out survey findings about what people may think and how they behave.

In addition to the pros, you should be aware of the cons of observing human beings, including:

✔ **Cognitive phenomena aren't observable.** You can ask people what they think and hope those self reports are reflective, but when you observe people's behaviors, inferences about their cognitive processes are indirect. As there may be an infinite number of reasons why people acted in a certain way, you may guess incorrectly.

✔ **Data interpretation may be problematic.** The scheme for coding behaviors may be faulty. Regardless of their observational skills, observers can't record all behaviors, so they selectively record behaviors according to researchers' theories. If those theories are incomplete or erroneous, the recording itself also will be incomplete or erroneous.

✔ **Not all activity can be recorded.** To some extent, observation is subjective, so you may be unable to infer what caused the behaviors you observed. Also, for privacy and ethical reasons, some behaviors shouldn't be recorded (see Chapter 4). If observers can't record all activity — and some of that activity informs marketing decisions — you can select a faulty business strategy.

✔ **Only brief periods can be observed.** Reality television notwithstanding, most people won't agree to being watched for long periods. As a result, observation often is limited to brief periods. For example, observing shoppers in a supermarket — when they approach an aisle and select a certain product — isn't a problem because those observations typically are limited to a minute or less. Because stores are a public arena, you shouldn't encounter any privacy issues with brief observation periods.

✔ **Observer bias possible.** Unlike identical printed questionnaires, each observer is unique, so observer bias is possible regardless of training efforts. In particular, some observers may focus more on some behaviors and less on other behaviors.

✔ **Invasion of privacy is possible.** Observing people's behaviors is an invasion of their privacy if they're unaware that they're being observed. (Flip to Chapter 4 for more information on ethical issues.)

Explaining the types of observation

Many types of observation techniques exist. We discuss the techniques you can choose from in the following sections.

Contrived observation

In contrived observation, researchers create an artificial environment. For example, this type of observation could entail an experiment in which people are first shown several ads for new soft drinks and then allowed to select one of those soft drinks for consumption. (Chapter 16 discusses such marketing experiments in detail.) If people select one soft drink most frequently, then its relative popularity likely was inspired by its ad.

Figure 15-8 summarizes a different type of contrived observation: mystery shopping. Retailers and other service providers often hire mystery shoppers to help assess service quality. Such shoppers follow a carefully scripted activity — for example, ordering a specific fast-food meal at a specific franchise location at a specific day and time — and then provide detailed reports about their experiences. The report in Figure 15-8 summarizes the experience of a mystery shopper who pretended to be a potential bank customer.

Good human observers must be sensitive to consumer behaviors that are relevant to the marketing problem of interest. A structured report form, like the one in Figure 15-9, can alert observers to focus their attention on specific behaviors. Such forms can reduce the level of expertise otherwise required for insightful observation.

Observation of physical objects

One type of observation that's free of ethical implications — because it doesn't require the observation of people and their behaviors — is the observation of physical objects. In this case, what's observed is how those objects change over time. For example, if you want to understand how people use books, then you may look at the wear patterns on library books. This type of measure is unobtrusive because you're not affecting the thing you're trying to observe.

You can use the following to measure physical objects:

- **Garbology:** Yes, we mean the study of trash! Suppose you're interested in people's consumption behaviors relative to fast food or alcohol. You can ask them in a survey, but their answers may be distorted by social desirability biases. In other words, if you ask people about their fast-food and alcohol habits and they believe that they consume either or both excessively, they may not accurately report their consumption habits. As opposed to asking consumers directly, you can sift through their garbage, systematically counting empty alcohol bottles or convenience-food packages. Don't worry; anything left on someone's curb is public domain.

Observer #001
Bank: Last National Bank at 1st and Main
Bank employee: Ms. Moneypenny
Date and time: 12/29/2009 at 11:27 am

After entering the bank lobby, I waited in line for two minutes until I could ask a teller (Mr. Nichols) if he could help me open a checking account. He pointed to Ms. Moneypenny, the new account manager, and told me to see her. As Ms. Moneypenny was busy with another customer, Mr. Nichols told me, "I'd go to the brochure rack near the front door and grab a brochure about the checking accounts we offer. That brochure gives lots of good information about our different types of accounts. You can sit in the waiting area near Ms. Moneypenny's desk and read it while you wait for her."

I thanked Mr. Nichols and did as he suggested. After roughly five minutes, Ms. Moneypenny became available, so I walked over, shook her hand, introduced myself, and told her I wanted to open a checking account. She saw the brochure in my hand and asked if I'd had a chance to read it. I told her I'd glanced over it but hadn't had enough time to study it carefully. She said, "Well, then perhaps we should review it together. That way, I can answer your questions along the way."

For roughly five minutes, we read through the brochure together. Ms. Moneypenny asked me several questions about my checking account needs; for example, "What level of balance would you be comfortable maintaining? How important is overdraft protection? Do you also want to open a savings account today, as we can link the accounts and offer you an extra 1% interest on your savings account balance?" She also told me that all checking accounts come with a free ATM card and that withdrawals were free from the bank's 22 ATMs around town.

Toward the end of our conversation, she said that "The Last National Bank is a full-service bank, so we can loan you money, sign you up for a credit card, and store your valuables in a safety deposit box." I thanked her for her time and effort, but told her I couldn't open an account until I received my first paycheck from my new employer. She thanked me for considering her bank for my banking needs.

Figure 15-8:
Report on
contrived
observation
at a bank.

✔ **Traffic counters:** To optimize the timing of traffic signals in a community, city managers sometimes place traffic counters at key spots on roads, such as near busy intersections. When a vehicle is driven over the censor strip, it counts as one vehicle. By analyzing the pattern or number of cars that pass a location at certain times of day or per hour, city managers can set traffic signals to minimize the time drivers spend in traffic, thus reducing gas consumption, air pollution, and other negative side effects associated with automobile travel.

What do traffic counters have to do with marketing? Actually, a lot! Retailers can use traffic counters to analyze how customers navigate their stores. By identifying crowded versus sparse spaces, retailers can rearrange merchandise displays to reduce crowding and increase shopping efficiency.

Store_____   Date_____
Location_____   Time_____
Salesperson_____   Transaction_____

Salesperson Description
         Sex: Male_____   Female_____
         Approx. height:_____
         Approx. age:_____
         Attire: Professional___Casual___   Other___
         Grooming: Neat___   Sloppy___   Other___
         Well spoken: Yes___   No___

Salesperson Behavior
         Chewed gum: Yes___ No___
         Had personal conversation
             With customer: Yes___ No___
             With other employee: Yes___ No___
             Via telephone: Yes___ No___
             Via texting: Yes___ No___
         Other non-selling behavior:

         _____
         _____
         _____

Transaction
         Waited on immediately   Yes___ No___
           If no, waited   _____ minutes
         Salesperson was
           Knowledgeable about products: Yes___ No___
           Asked the right questions: Yes___ No___
           Suggested suitable alternatives: Yes___ No___
           Positive (in demeanor):   Yes___ No___
           Friendly: Yes___ No___
           Pleasant: Yes___ No___
           Courteous: Yes___ No___
           Professional: Yes___ No___
           Confident: Yes___ No___
           Good listener: Yes___ No___
           Focused: Yes___ No___

Figure 15-9:
Structured
report form
for retailer.

✔ **Web site monitors:** Web site owners find it useful to monitor site visitors. For them, mechanical observation may be as simple as counting visitors or as complex as tracking how visitors navigate their site. The many metrics for assessing the behaviors of visitors to commercial sites include total time spent on the site, pages viewed, number of repeat visits per month, and dollars spent (if a retailing site).

Here's one key issue about virtual store visitors: They often select items to buy, put them in a virtual shopping cart, but never check out. If they don't check out, they can't generate profits for the site owner or product maker. Virtual store owners and designers can gain from understanding how visitors navigate their stores and what store modifications would increase sales.

✔ **Store scanners:** In-store scanners — those devices at checkout counters that scan universal product codes and now radio frequency tags on products — provide mechanical observations that ease inventory control and product assortment management.

Rather than rely on slower and less accurate pantry audits or purchase diaries (as we discuss in Chapter 6), home-based scanners can mechanically track customer purchases. Of course, shoppers must scan the items they've purchased once they return home, and often that's inconvenient. As a result, some purchases aren't recorded.

Your research question will help you decide which technique to use when observing physical objects. If you're having difficulty honing in on your research problem, turn to your local research consultant (as we suggest in Chapter 5) for advice.

Physiological observation

Asking people to indicate their thoughts about something is one way to learn their feelings and attitudes. However, direct questioning can trigger well-known response biases (see Chapter 7). Another way is to infer those thoughts with physiological measures. These types of measures include the following:

✔ **Eye tracking:** *Looker,* a very ordinary Hollywood movie released in 1981, featured eye movement technology (along with "looker" Susan Dey, Albert Finney, and James Coburn). In the movie, a marketing research company studied how people viewed and processed television commercials by tracking where test subjects looked as the commercial progressed. A good commercial encouraged viewers to focus on and around the advertised product. In contrast, a bad commercial failed to focus viewers' attention on the advertised product; instead, they focused on the background or the actors.

Eye-movement trackers can record the sequence of points that people focus on as they read or view an ad. Psychological evidence suggests that the focus of people's gazes is the thing about which they're thinking. People move their eyes subconsciously when viewing an ad. As a result, eye-movement data can't be tainted by social desirability bias or other ego-enhancing mechanisms.

✔ **Pupilometer:** *Pupilometery research* can assess people's interests in what they're viewing. You could ask consumers whether an ad is interesting or whether they're enthusiastic about viewing it, but they may be unable to respond meaningfully. People's pupils, however, dilate when they're viewing something of interest to them. A *pupilometer,* which views and records changes in the diameter of peoples' pupils, can determine whether what they're viewing is of greater or lesser interest. This technology can help advertisers improve their commercials by reducing the number of scenes to which viewers respond tepidly and increasing the number of scenes to which viewers respond excitedly.

✔ **Psychogalvanometer:** Galvanic skin response technology works like a lie detector. It's the same technology, but marketing researchers don't use it to assess the truthfulness of respondents' answers. Skin electrical conductivity changes with excitement level. People who are lying become excited; as a result, their skin conductivity changes. Similarly, the skin conductivity of people viewing an ad will change based on how exciting or unexciting they find that ad.

✔ **Voice pitch:** Another way to measure consumers' emotional reactions is through the physiological changes in their voices. The Israelis have developed a voice pitch analyzer that can assess the likelihood that a person on the other end of a telephone connection is lying. Although the Israeli device is of suspect reliability, it's based on sound principles: changes in the pitch of people' voices can indicate their emotional reactions. Because people are unable to consciously modify their voice pitch, voice pitch measures are uninfluenced by ego-enhancing mechanisms like social desirability bias.

✔ **People meters:** Television networks need to assess the popularity of their programming, especially with key demographic groups. If nothing else, that information is useful for optimally pricing advertising time. People meters are one way for companies like A.C. Nielsen to monitor people's television viewing behaviors.

The traditional Nielsen set-top box can monitor a broadcast playing on a household's primary television set. However, it couldn't determine whether anyone was present and watching that broadcast. People meters, on the other hand, record both what's playing on a television set and who's watching it. People meters have infrared sensors, so they can detect body heat and be calibrated to recognize household members. People meters also have input buttons, so household members can indicate when they've entered or exited the room. Thus, people meters provide a more accurate assessment, relative to traditional Nielsen set-top boxes, of ad viewers because many people actively avoid commercials by other means than channel surfing (for example, by temporarily leaving the room or muting the audio).

Naturalistic inquiry

When observations of people's behaviors aren't contrived (see the earlier section "Contrived observation"), naturalistic inquiry is possible. *Naturalistic inquiry* is a method used to observe people's behavior in a natural setting. In a contrived or survey-based study, you'll have research artifacts. People who know they're being studied will modify their behaviors or expressed attitudes. Naturalistic inquiry can avoid this laboratory bias problem because the setting is organic. For example, to truly understand collegiate and professional football fan tailgating behaviors, a researcher must tailgate with them rather than ask them about their tailgating behavior.

Ethnography — the study of cultures — is a type of naturalistic inquiry. In such studies, a researcher visits a culture, becomes part of that culture, and observes the rituals, behaviors, and lives of people in that culture. For example, to understand the behaviors and interests of people who joined a motorcycle group, several marketing scholars conducted an ethnographic study that required them to ride around the United States with such a group during one summer.

In general, the distinguishing characteristics of naturalistic inquiry include the following:

- ✔ **People's behaviors are studied in the environment in which the behavior naturally occurs.** It's often easier to understand people's behaviors in the appropriate environment. For instance, you can observe people's television viewing behaviors by inviting them into a laboratory room and asking them to sit in a hard-backed chair and view a 30-minute television program that's embedded with commercials. Afterward, you can question them about that program. However, in such an artificial environment, people may respond atypically. Alternatively, if you took an ethnographic approach, you can observe those behaviors in people's living rooms as they munch on a bowl of organic popcorn.

- ✔ **A fellow human being is the measurement instrument.** The human observer tries to check his expectations at the door when viewing behaviors or inferring reasons for those behaviors. Observers immerse themselves into the environment as a blank slate, try to observe others' behaviors uncritically, and then gradually infer the causes of those behaviors.

- ✔ **It relies on maximum variation sampling.** Most marketing research is conducted on a small but representative sample of people (as we discuss in Chapter 11). Researchers then extrapolate from data provided by such samples to the much larger population from which they were drawn. In essence, most marketing research requires representative samples of people or objects. In naturalistic inquiry, sample representativeness is unimportant; instead, researchers try to understand the range of people's behaviors and attitudes. Naturalistic inquiry relies on maximum variation sampling, which can reveal the broadest range of people's behaviors. There's no effort to find representative samples of people and behaviors.

- ✔ **It requires inductive rather than deductive data analysis.** For most marketing research, researchers first identify a research problem, then they develop a set of research questions, and then they develop a theory that they test by collecting data related to that set of questions. In other words, theory drives the analysis and conclusion-making process. In contrast, naturalistic inquiry doesn't start with theory; as a result, this data-driven rather than theory-driven technique works in reverse of most marketing research techniques. Because it starts with data rather than theory, it's inductive rather than deductive. Researchers examine their data for patterns, and through induction develop a theory consistent with their data.

Chapter 16

Conducting Experiments and Test Marketing

In This Chapter

▶ Reviewing experiment basics

▶ Developing effective marketing experiments

▶ Discussing the different types of test markets

*E*xperiments are studies conducted under controlled conditions. Such conditions allow alternative explanations for observed phenomena to be eliminated. Experiments allow research questions to be tested in the most rigorous way possible.

In marketing experiments, researchers manipulate at least one marketing element, such as price level or advertising message. They then measure the effect of that manipulation on peoples' responses — such as their willingness to buy a tested product.

In this chapter, we provide information on the basics of experiments and the types of experiments you may consider as well as a discussion on test marketing.

Discovering a Proper Approach to Experiment Basics

A basic objective of experimentation is to identify *causal relationships,* which are relationships that suggest one thing causes another thing. For example, if a brand's sales increase after the store shelf space allocated to that brand increases, then there may be a causal relationship between store shelf space and sales. Similarly, if a brand's sales increase after the price for that brand decreases, then there may be a causal relationship between price and sales. To ensure that such relationships are genuine, you must carefully design and execute any experiment.

Establishing causal relationships

When you're trying to establish a causal relationship, you may be asking questions like, "Is there a direct relationship between advertising expenditures and sales? When advertising increases, do sales increase? When advertising decreases, do sales also decrease?" To prove a causal relationship, you need to conduct an experiment that satisfies the following three conditions:

- ✔ **Concomitant variation:** *Concomitant variation* refers to two things that change in tandem. For example, many studies have shown that dollar or unit sales change when the amount spent on advertising changes.

- ✔ **Temporal ordering:** *Temporal ordering* means that a change in one entity always precedes a change in the other entity. In the context of sales and ad expenditures, temporal ordering would be evident if researchers could show that sales increase or decrease after ad expenditures increase or decrease, not vice versa. However, if managers spend some incremental sales dollars on additional advertising, sales increases would cause advertising increases. In this case, it's unclear whether advertising causes sales or sales cause advertising. Hence, the tenet of temporal ordering is muddled.

- ✔ **Control over other possible causes:** When you gain control over other possible causes, you know that the observed effect isn't due to something else. For example, to show that changes in ad expenditures cause changes in sales, researchers must exclude other causes, such as changes in sales force, product configuration, and competitors' strategies.

Experiments can establish a causal relationship, which requires concomitant variation of variables, temporal ordering of variables, and control over other possible causes that may influence the relationship between the variables.

Understanding design fundamentals

Certain features are fundamental to designing good experiments. For example, test units, studied variables, and control groups must be decided on before running an experiment. We describe these features in the following list:

- ✔ **Test units:** *Test units* are the participants in the experiment. Although test units in marketing experiments tend to be people, they need not be; test units also can be organizations or other entities. For example, suppose a textbook publisher wants to test alternative ways to promote its books. The publisher may ask sales reps at one set of universities to use one promotional approach and sales reps at another set of universities to use a different approach. The company then compares the textbook adoption rates. In this example, the test units are universities rather than people.

✔ **Independent variables and dependent variable:** The *independent variable* is the entity that researchers manipulate; in other words, they set the value of that entity in an experiment. For example, researchers conducting ad-copy experiments would manipulate the version of the ad copy that different study participants viewed. (Relative to experiments, frequently used synonyms for the term *independent variable* are *treatment* or *treatment condition*.)

Researchers expect the *dependent variable* — the variable you're trying to explain — to vary along with the manipulated independent variable. For example, researchers may believe that study participants will like some test ads more than other test ads. The criterion for assessing likeability is the dependent variable; the most likeable ad would receive the highest or best scores on an ad likeability measure.

✔ **Control group:** *Control groups* are the baseline groups that researchers compare to all other non-baseline groups. All true experiments have at least one control group. Although control group members aren't exposed to the researcher's manipulated independent variable, they're exposed to the same environment and respond to the same set of dependent variable measures as other study participants. If the control group is similar to the other experiment groups in all regards except exposure to the manipulated independent variable, response differences relative to other groups in the experiment can be attributed to that independent variable.

Controlling for extraneous variation

Something as simple as a researcher smiling or frowning can influence the way participants behave during an experiment. To eliminate extraneous variation, or alternative explanations for results, experiments must be controlled tightly. Be sure to take the following actions:

✔ **Hold conditions constant for each participant.** For example, participants in an ad-copy test should view test ads under similar lighting and seating conditions. If some people view ads while sitting on a comfy chair in a softly lit room, and other people view ads while sitting on a hard wooden chair in a harshly lit room, it's impossible to know whether different responses to the ads are attributable to differences in the viewing environment or differences in the ads.

✔ **Randomize your study.** Assigning study participants randomly to experimental treatments — different instances of the independent variable — ensures that groups of people exposed to different treatments differ systematically from one another. When they differ systematically, observed differences in their responses may be attributable to between-group differences rather than between-treatment differences. For example, if women tend to respond more favorably to a certain type of ad — and some test groups contain a larger percent of women but other test groups contain a larger percent of males — then differences in the responses to different test ads may be attributable to the dominant sex in each group rather than differences between ads.

✔ **Match your subjects across groups if randomization is difficult.** When randomization is difficult due to some environmental constraint, researchers try to approximate it by forming test groups with similar profiles on a few key profile variables, like age, income, occupation, and sex. For example, subjects can be matched by age, where each group would contain a similar percent of 20-to-35 year olds, 36-to-55 year olds, and 56-year-olds and older.

✔ **Present information in the same order to every study participant.** Order bias can affect your experimental results. For example, presenting test ads in different sequences may influence responses to those ads. Like order bias in questionnaires (see Chapter 10), researchers can control for order bias in experiments.

Understanding the differences between laboratory and field experiments

In a *laboratory experiment,* study participants who visit a centralized location that's carefully controlled by the researcher are exposed to a specific treatment and then their responses are measured. Laboratory experiments include concept tests, product taste tests, ad-copy tests, and package tests.

Field tests, as the name implies, occur in realistic settings. This type of test includes home-use tests, test markets (discussed in the later section "Getting a Handle on Test Marketing"), and on-air ad tests.

The relative advantages and disadvantages of laboratory and field experiments are the reverse of one another. Consider the following:

✔ The highly controlled environments in laboratory experiments can eliminate most alternative explanations for scores on the dependent variable. In contrast, if you ran a field experiment outdoors — for example, a soft drink taste test at an annual state fair — you couldn't eliminate extraneous factors like weather, sirens going off, and activity at nearby booths. Such factors can influence participants' responses.

✔ Laboratory experiments tend to be of lower cost and shorter duration than field experiments — a week or two versus multiple months for field experiments.

✔ Due to more extensive control relative to field experiments, laboratory experiments typically produce less noisy data; in other words, the data more reflect the relationship being studied and less reflect extraneous influences that may disguise that relationship. As a result, far fewer study participants are needed to detect the effect of an independent variable on a dependent variable. Fewer participants mean a lower cost and greater ease of running laboratory experiments.

✔ Field experiments often occur in a natural environment, which makes researchers more comfortable generalizing their results to what will occur in the "real world." Laboratory experiments, on the other hand, tend to cause participants to behave unnaturally because they know they're being observed.

The main concern with conducting laboratory experiments is the presence of demand artifacts. *Demand artifacts* are caused by experimental procedures that induce unnatural responses by study participants. Merely participating in a study and being asked to perform certain activities influences peoples' responses, which is a major problem with laboratory experiments. Because study participants know they're being observed, they tend to react in unnatural ways.

For example, participants in an ad-copy experiment may be more attentive to ads than under normal viewing conditions. Typically, viewing ads is a low-involvement activity; people aren't highly engaged, so they don't read every word. However, participants in an ad-copy experiment expect to be asked questions about the ads, so they view those ads carefully. As a result, participants' reactions — such as their attitudes about likeability and creativity — may be artifactual or unnatural, because they were encouraged inadvertently to view those ads more closely.

Examining internal validity and its threats

One major concern when running an experiment is its *internal validity,* which is the ability of the experiment to determine whether the treatment was the sole cause of changes in a dependent variable. In other words, did the researcher's manipulation do what it was supposed to do?

There are numerous threats to an experiment's internal validity, including the following:

✔ **History:** *History* refers to changes in the environment that are irrelevant to the effects of interest but may modify scores on a dependent variable. For example, if a major employer folded in a test market city, lower sales may be due to reduced worker incomes rather than a problem with the new or improved product.

✔ **Maturation:** *Maturation* refers to changes in study participants that occur during an experiment. For example, people asked to respond extensively about a series of test ads may grow weary. As a result, their responses about later-viewed ads may differ from their responses to early-viewed ads because they're tired (rather than because of some characteristic of the ads).

✔ **Testing:** *Testing effects* occur before study participants are exposed to an experimental treatment. Pre-exposure testing may sensitize your participants to the nature of the experiment; as a result, they may respond differently to subsequent post-exposure testing.

✔ **Instrumentation:** Changes in the instrument you use — for example, the specific questions you pose on a questionnaire — may cause differences in responses. Or, if the instrument is a human observer, one observer at one time and a different observer at a different time may judge participants' behaviors differently.

✔ **Selection bias:** *Selection bias* occurs when participants aren't randomly assigned or the experiments lacks a control group. We suggest you avoid conducting experiments in which participants self-assign their group. With that type of assignment, it's impossible to know whether observed between-group differences are due to the treatment or to systematic differences in the self-selection process.

✔ **Mortality:** By *mortality,* we mean people who drop out of an experiment over time for any reason. People who participate in a long-running experiment may differ systematically from people who quit. For example, one group in a hair-dye study may be women who moved to Florida after their husbands died. Widows from this group who withdrew from the experiment may have been the most successful hair dye users — they remarried and no longer needed the payment for study participation. Nonetheless, a researcher may conclude that hair dye doesn't alter older women's lifestyles positively because the most successful users withdrew from the experiment.

Simple Experiments for You to Consider

Although they may seem cumbersome, experiments can be run by seasoned and novice researchers alike. You don't need to run a complex experiment to discover something meaningful. The experiments in the following sections exemplify this notion. Using these examples (which are based on various professions) as a foundation, you can develop relevant experiments that may open the door to heightened business success. Refer to the preceding section, "Discovering a Proper Approach to Experiment Basics" if you run across unfamiliar terms.

Entrepreneur examples

If you're an entrepreneur — you own a business ranging from catering and retailing to landscaping and web designing, consider the following examples to generate ideas for your own experiment:

✔ **A customer support example:** Assume you own a CPA firm and you want to grow the business. You're toying with offering free tax counseling as an incentive for new customers. For two months, you hire a telephone solicitor to drum up new clients. The solicitor only offers free tax counseling to half of these potential clients.

In this example, the control group includes the potential clients who weren't offered free tax counseling, and the experimental group includes those potential clients who were offered this free service. The dependent variable is the number of new clients who switched to your firm.

✔ **A direct mail campaign example:** Say you own an auto repair shop. You want to determine which of two direct mail postcards will lead to a greater increase in routine oil changes. These postcards can be redeemed for $5 off a customer's next oil change. You mail each postcard to 1,000 randomly selected households within five miles of your shop. You track the number of postcards redeemed for the next two months.

Here, each group serves as the control for the other group. The number of redeemed postcards is the dependent variable.

Professional examples

Professionals are a broad category of folks. They include instructors, doctors, and financial advisors. If you're a professional, and you want some hints on conducting an experiment, consider the following examples:

✔ **A pricing example:** Imagine you're a chiropractor and you want to determine whether offering an additional service will lead your patrons to spend more money per visit. For 30 days, you offer an additional service of 10 minutes in the relaxation room, prior to the adjustment. The relaxation room has subtle lighting, ambient music, hot tea, and healthful snack foods.

In this experiment, the control group doesn't use the 10-minute pre-adjustment room, and the experimental group uses this room. The dependent variable is willingness to pay more for each visit, which is assessed by a traditional survey. An effective experimental condition — in this case, experiencing the relaxation room — would reveal itself as a willingness to pay more for services.

✔ **An example of offering additional services:** Assume you're a baseball instructor who's considering a few additional batting drills to increase batting averages. These drills will be incorporated into each session leading up to the start of the baseball season.

Players in the control group don't participate in these extra drills, and players in the experimental group partake in such drills. The dependent variable is batting average midway through the season. An effective experimental condition would reveal itself as a higher batting average for the experimental group.

Retailer examples

The folks who make up the retailer category include employees, managers, or owners of retail businesses that sell goods (for example, apparel and merchandise), services (for example, education and health), or a hybrid of both (restaurants and resorts). If you fall under this category, review the following examples to glean ideas for your own experiment:

✔ **A store layout example:** Instead of its current location in the middle of the sales floor, you wonder whether relocating your top-selling product to the rear of the floor will increase customers' browsing time. (It's well-known that browsing time and spending correlate positively.) To answer this question, you can alternate the position of the product (in the middle and at the rear of the floor) each week for six weeks and observe the browsing behaviors and times of systematically selected shoppers.

In this case, the control group consists of people who shop when the top-selling product is shelved in the middle of the sales floor, and the experimental group consists of people who shop when that product is shelved at the rear of the floor. If browsing time increased meaningfully for the experimental group, you can deem your experimental condition effective.

✔ **A merchandise assortment example:** Say you're interested in discovering whether carrying a certain brand will change the current image of your store. To promote the new brand you'll carry, you advertise it on your Web site. This ad campaign, which is the independent variable, will run for 60 days, followed by surveying a systematic sample of shoppers.

In this experiment, the control group includes shoppers who haven't visited your Web site in the past 60 days, and the experimental group consists of shoppers who have visited your Web site during that time. Perceived store image — measured with standard Likert-type attitudinal questions — is the dependent variable. (See Chapter 9 for more on Likert-type scales.) If perceived store image improved meaningfully for the experimental group, you can deem your experimental condition effective.

Restaurateur examples

The following folks fall under the restaurateur category: caterers, tavern operators, chefs, and the like. If you're a restaurateur who wants to run an experiment, browse these examples for inspiration:

✔ **An advertising example:** Suppose that your restaurant is in an ethnically diverse neighborhood. You wonder whether changing your print ad slogan from "Good Times" to the Spanish version "Bueno Tiempo" will increase patrons' frequency of dining at your restaurant, and whether any improvement is limited to Hispanic patrons. To answer these questions, you can run the Spanish version of your ad, which is the independent variable, in the local newspaper each week for one month and then survey a systematic sample of patrons.

In this case, the control group consists of people who only recall the English ad, and the experimental group consists of people who only recall the Spanish ad. (Of course, proper screening and filtering questions, as we discuss in Chapter 10, are critical for this experiment.) The dependent variable is predicted frequency of dining at your restaurant in the next month. An increase in restaurant patronage by the experimental group would indicate an effective experimental condition.

✔ **A couponing example:** As a restaurant manager, you want to boost the number of large-party tables at dinner. You believe that a two-for-one dinner coupon (the independent variable) will be effective, but you're undecided about how to distribute it. You can either post the coupon on your Web site or distribute it with current consumers' checks. To determine the most effective distribution method, for two weeks you have your wait staff inform half their tables about the online coupon; the other half receives the coupon, without instruction, with their checks. After these two weeks, you monitor large-party dinner tables and coupon redemptions for the next two months. To control for customers who browsed your Web site and found the coupon, but weren't given instructions to do so by your wait staff, you need to ask customers who redeem the coupon how they became aware of it. Customers who report no wait staff involvement must be discarded to avoid contaminating your experiment.

Here, the control group consists of patrons who received the coupons with their checks, and the experimental group includes patrons who received online instructions. The dependent variable is the number of large-party dinner tables that redeemed a coupon from each source during the two months.

Getting a Handle on Test Marketing

Test marketing is a type of field experiment. It's a field test of a new product or of marketing-related elements of a current product. Test markets are used to refine marketing strategies for new and established brands and to decide whether to discontinue newly introduced products. Pampers diapers is a well-known test marketing success story. These disposable diapers were doomed to marketing failure until test marketing revealed that P&G had set too high a price for them. P&G lowered the price prior to launching the product nationally and continues to skip and laugh all the way to the bank.

Test markets can provide the following information:

- **Estimates of market share and volume:** Test marketing can produce accurate sales forecasts, because you can track customer trial and repeat purchases.

- **Estimates of the cannibalization rate on an existing product line:** Sales of a new model in a product line typically draw sales from existing models. For example, Hewlett-Packard and Epson shrink sales for their current printer models when they introduce new printer models. Test market data allow you to estimate the net effect of these shifting sales on overall profits for a product line.

- **Competitor reactions:** Competitors may notice your test market efforts and adjust their strategies accordingly. By examining their efforts, you can anticipate their likely responses to your new or improved product and plan accordingly.

Test markets only provide behavioral data. For example, they can reveal that an ad campaign failed to stimulate sales, but they can't uncover why the campaign flopped. To determine how to fix a faulty ad campaign, it's necessary to ask people about their opinions of those ads. As a result, you need to supplement test market data with nonbehavioral (attitude and preference) data.

The four varieties of test markets are

- **Traditional:** With a *traditional test market,* sales are compared among multiple cities for 6 to 12 months. Initial repeat purchase rates tend to be overestimated because trial rates are higher than repeat purchase rates (and trial tends to dominate early purchases), so the timeframe is generally longer.

- **Simulated:** With *simulated test markets,* people are asked to walk through a simulated store (like a research facility inside a traditional mall) and purchase products with money they've been given. It sounds hokey, but the results of simulated test markets are highly predictive of ultimate market performance. Because only predictive accuracy is critical, the artificiality of this type of test market is irrelevant.

- **Controlled:** *Controlled test markets* rely on universal product codes, checkout scanning equipment (for recording shoppers' purchases), computers (for processing massive amounts of purchase data from many shoppers), and a marketing information system (for converting that data into a format that managers can use for decision-making).

- **Virtual:** *Virtual test markets* require consumers to log onto a Web site and participate in a shopping simulation. Data pertaining to product preference, store ambience, and browsing time are captured, enabling retailers to develop more effective strategies for their in-store and online operations.

We go into more detail about each variety in the following sections.

Traditional test markets

Traditional test markets offer you the opportunity to estimate sales potential under realistic conditions. They're also useful for finding and correcting product configuration, pricing, and promotional problems.

As a type of field experiment, the generalizability of the results for this type of test market to the "real world" is relatively high. Unlike other types of test markets, traditional test markets can assess both consumers' and distributors' acceptance of the product. By comparing sales across test cities, distributors can gauge the potential success of a product, which influences their willingness to distribute the product to certain cities.

However, such test markets suffer from the following limitations:

- ✔ **They can be cost prohibitive.** Traditional test markets aren't cheap; they often cost millions of dollars in direct and indirect costs (such as management time, diversion of resources from current products, and negative internal and external impacts of test failures). When likely costs exceed likely benefits, test marketing should be avoided.

- ✔ **They allow competitors time to respond.** Traditional test markets take time, and they can tip competitors about soon-to-be-released new or updated products. As a result, they allow competitors additional time to prepare a counterstrategy.

- ✔ **The cost of producing the product often is high.** Limited production runs to produce the small volume of product required for a test market may be costly.

- ✔ **Failure of a test product can damage a company's reputation.** The failure of a product in a traditional test market can negatively affect a company's reputation. For example, if Procter & Gamble conducts a test market and the product fails miserably, people who purchased that product may generalize negative attitudes about it to other Procter & Gamble products.

Finding acceptable markets for testing products isn't easy. The many criteria for screening possible test markets include the following:

- ✔ **A sufficient population for reliable projections:** Meeting this criterion is especially important for products with lower sales volume. Otherwise, the data will be insufficient to project sales accurately.

- ✔ **Proper representation:** Markets must be representative demographically and in terms of product consumption, behavior, media usage, and competition. A market with vastly different competitors makes cross-market comparison problematic.

✔ **Similarity among the various markets:** Test markets should be as similar as possible so that differences will be due to marketing differences rather than market differences. However, if regional differences are important, the chosen test markets should reflect those variations.

✔ **Little media spillover:** Test markets should have little media spillover to or from other markets; for example, Denton, Texas, would be a poor test market site because it receives extensive print and electronic media from nearby Dallas and Fort Worth. Otherwise, it's difficult to determine how advertising messages and advertising expenditures relate to sales.

✔ **Available auditing and marketing research services:** Without these services, you won't be able to collect needed measures like purchase frequencies.

✔ **A determination of whether your prospective market is an over-tested or idiosyncratic one:** Over-tested markets should be avoided because once consumers become wise to being tested frequently, they'll start to respond differently merely because they're frequently involved in testing. Idiosyncratic markets, by definition, aren't representative of the country or region as a whole; thus, you can't generalize the results from an idiosyncratic market to other markets.

Simulated test markets

In essence, a simulated test market is a research laboratory that mimics a brick-and-mortar store. Typically, consumers with the likely or known characteristics of test product buyers are recruited. Participants, who must visit a test facility, are first exposed to media messages — often one or more television commercials — for a test product. Next, they enter a room that resembles a supermarket and begin to shop. Days or weeks later — after they bought and had time to use the test product — they're contacted and asked to evaluate the product and predict their likelihood of purchasing it again.

Participants' in-facility search behaviors, brand choices, future purchase intentions, and post-usage evaluations are used to forecast test product sales and develop effective marketing strategies.

Advantages of simulated test markets include the following:

✔ **They create substantial time and cost savings.** Such tests can be conducted in a few months and are one-tenth or less the cost of traditional test markets.

✔ **They allow for the use of computer models to forecast sales.** Simulation software allows alternative combinations of marketing elements (for example, price and advertising) to be evaluated simultaneously.

✔ **They're reasonably accurate.** Typically, estimates of market share are ±20 percent of eventual values.

✔ **They don't tip off competitors.** Unlike traditional test markets, which are visible to competitors, simulated test markets can be conducted secretly. In this case, they don't compromise the competitive advantage associated with surprise launches of new or improved products.

However, there are some limitations to this type of test market, including the following:

✔ **They provide a highly artificial testing environment.** Although intended to mimic a real store, a simulated testing facility is an artificial shopping environment. As a result, searches and choices in such facilities may not correspond to searches and choices in real stores.

✔ **They induce unnatural behavior.** Because consumers know they're being monitored, they may act differently than in normal shopping situations.

✔ **They don't anticipate distributor acceptance.** A product can't appear on store shelves unless distributed by wholesalers and carried by retailers. If either group believes that the product is a loser, it won't appear in stores, so consumers' likely responses to it are irrelevant. In contrast, distributor acceptance is assessed easily in traditional test markets, as mentioned in the earlier "Traditional test markets" section.

✔ **They're cheaper, but still expensive.** Although less costly than traditional test markets, simulated test markets still cost from $75,000 to $150,000.

✔ **They're problematic for cross-country comparisons.** Because consumers in different countries don't respond similarly to simulated stores and aren't equally accurate in predicting their future purchases, cross-country comparisons may be dubious.

Controlled test markets

In essence, what's monitored in a controlled test market is a mostly closed shopping system in which most purchases are traceable. These test markets require two sets of participants in an electronic panel system:

✔ **Small-city grocers:** Smaller cities have fewer supermarkets, so it's possible to convince all owners to participate. The incentives to participate are free scanning equipment and free inventory data.

✔ **Consumers:** Consumers must be geographically isolated, so their shopping occurs locally and they're not influenced by out-of-market media. As incentives, they annually receive a small token gift and an opportunity to win larger prizes awarded by raffle.

With controlled test markets, each consumer panelist receives a bar-coded ID card that uniquely identifies him. Scanning that card at checkout allows the panelist to be linked to his purchased items. Products are labeled with universal product codes, which also are scanned at checkout. By recording panelists' purchases during each supermarket visit, it's possible to track household purchases over time.

Controlled test markets permit testing of television and newspaper ads. Here's how:

✔ **Television commercials:** Smaller cities often are dominated by a single cable operator. This operator's fiber optic network must maintain a parallel channel for each commercial channel it carries; that way it's possible, using uniquely addressable cable boxes (analogous to telephones), to electronically switch between the main and parallel channel. For example, suppose Procter & Gamble purchased 30 seconds on a commercial channel for a Crest toothpaste commercial. An alternative test commercial can be shown during that time to households targeted by socio-demographics or previous purchase behaviors. This process is transparent to viewers.

✔ **Newspaper ads:** Smaller cities typically have one local newspaper to which many households subscribe. As a result, it's possible to target specific subscriber households — again, selected for socio-demographics or previous purchases — to receive specific ads and coupons of a specific denomination in the customized newspaper they receive.

Here are some advantages to controlled test markets:

✔ **They provide complete store data.** Personally recorded reports of what consumers purchased — even those created by hand-held scanners — only reveal what they bought; they provide no indication of available alternatives. Knowing about the available alternatives (because you know all the brands the store stocked at time of purchase), as well as what was chosen, is valuable. Relative to traditional diary panels, controlled test markets provide more comprehensive purchase data.

✔ **They help you accurately track coupon use.** Coupon tracking data can help companies optimize coupon denomination; every unnecessary penny that companies rebate to induce a sale is a penny of foregone profit.

✔ **They allow you to experiment with groups matched on historical product usage.** Companies can expose one group of households known to purchase a certain type of product to one ad, a different set of households also known to purchase that product to a different ad, and then track the purchases of each group.

✔ **They provide faster feedback than traditional test markets.** Controlled test markets require weeks rather than months to collect data. For new and likely expensive promotions, the ability to make quick but minor tweaks is critical to boosting their effectiveness, so faster feedback is invaluable.

✔ **They're more accurate than traditional store audits.** Store audits require many people with electronic scanning equipment to check product quantities on shelves. Unfortunately, products disappear from shelves for reasons other than a purchase — for example, five-finger discounts and spoilage. A store audit accounts for items that have moved off store shelves regardless of reason. Because they only record purchases, controlled test markets provide far more accurate sales information.

✔ **They're more accurate than traditional purchase diaries.** As we discuss in Chapter 6, the burden of maintaining a purchase diary often exceeds panelists' patience; as a result, some purchases aren't recorded. Also, some panelists won't admit to buying less nutritious food; for example, they may omit high-fructose-corn-syrup and calorie-laden purchases.

The following are some limitations of controlled test markets:

✔ **They're limited to smaller markets.** For some products, people who live in bigger cities may differ meaningfully from people who live in smaller cities. For example, people who live in bigger cities have more opportunities than people who live in smaller cities or rural areas to find stores that carry new-to-the-market products. If smaller city and rural residents are more willing than bigger city residents to buy a new-to-the-market product just because it's new and different, then being limited to smaller markets can inflate test market sales.

✔ **They're limited to a few markets.** Setting up controlled test markets is an expensive proposition; thus, only a handful of cities are monitored. With so few cities being monitored, it's difficult to discern true geographical differences from specific-market idiosyncrasies.

✔ **They don't allow all retailing outlets to be represented.** It's possible to buy some grocery-type items — such as floor cleaners, light bulbs, and pet food — at outlets other than supermarkets. However, controlled test markets typically exclude drug or mass merchandise stores. As a result, purchases in those outlets are missed, which compromises sales data accuracy.

✔ **They make it difficult to track low-volume products.** Because purchases are recorded in a small sample of smaller cities, tracking low-volume products (like pickled pig's feet) is problematic.

✔ **They track TV and newspaper usage rather than ad exposure.** It's impossible to know whether anyone viewed the commercial or whether the television was running in an empty room. Similarly, it's impossible to know whether anyone read the newspaper ad or saw the coupon.

✔ **They can't track radio or magazine exposures.** Although such advertising can affect purchases, its influence is unknown.

Virtual test markets

An alternative to other types of test markets, virtual test markets have emerged as a way to monitor customer behavior. Web-based software enables shoppers to enter virtual shopping worlds, where they can browse a store, evaluate its ambience, participate in product evaluation, and make purchases.

Advantages of virtual test markets include the following:

- ✔ **They provide efficient store manipulation.** Virtual environments are more readily manipulated than actual retail settings.

- ✔ **They foster respondent participation.** Because technology is sexier than pen-and-paper questionnaires or interviews, getting respondents to participate in a virtual test market may prove easier than getting them to complete a questionnaire.

- ✔ **They accurately predict customer behavior.** A virtual environment is meant to mirror a real shopping setting; therefore, shopping behavior in such an environment may be representative of actual shopping behavior. As a result, forecasting precision may improve when running what-if simulations.

- ✔ **They're cheaper than traditional test markets.** Generating a shopping simulation with a URL link for access is cheaper than gathering test marketing data across several cities.

Here are some limitations of virtual test markets:

- ✔ **Virtual isn't real.** Although software attempts to mimic stores and shoppers (with avatars), a virtual shopping environment isn't real; therefore, how shoppers behave in the shopping simulation may not reflect their actual shopping behavior.

- ✔ **Consumers are more involved than normal.** Because consumers are interacting extensively in a simulation, their attentiveness is high. (Think about video game fanatics!) This heightened level of involvement may not be evident when actually shopping. As a result, a marketing strategy that works well in a simulated shopping environment may not work as well in the real world.

- ✔ **Some influencing factors are missing.** Although store factors like smell and size influence shopping behaviors, they can't be incorporated into shopping simulations.

- ✔ **Target market representativeness may be limited.** Because virtual test markets are considered high tech, it's possible that only a certain type of shopper (those who are tech savvy) will participate in such studies. In this case, data from other key demographics won't be captured.

Part IV

Collecting, Analyzing, and Reporting Your Data

The 5th Wave   By Rich Tennant

"I guess we have to ask ourselves how much marketing synergy we want between our snack cake and rat poison product lines."

In this part . . .

Chapter 17 provides information regarding strategies for increasing respondent involvement and avoiding respondent bias. This chapter also tells you what to look for when inputting data so you can identify both good and bad data. Data analysis is covered in Chapter 18. To get the scoop on creating research reports, visit Chapter 19, which includes a special focus on chart and table do's and don'ts.

Chapter 17

Collecting and Preparing Your Data

· ·

· ·

*W*hether you're conducting a survey or an observational study, some-one (either your in-house team or an outside service) needs to collect respondent data pertaining to that survey or study. The activity of collecting the data and monitoring their collection is called *fieldwork*. In this chapter, we provide you with information on who traditionally conducts fieldwork and what you do with the data once they're collected.

An untrained fieldworker can undermine your study, even if your research questions have been thoroughly developed and your survey questions effectively designed. How? A fieldworker who's lazy, preoccupied, or inattentive may collect invalid data from respondents who aren't members of the population of interest or fail to collect data from respondents who *are* members of the population of interest. If you collect a probability sample (see Chapter 10), then your fieldworkers must be conscientious throughout the data-collection process. If they aren't, your data are unlikely to represent the ideas, beliefs, and attitudes of the population of interest, which ultimately will prove detrimental to your business.

Determining Who Conducts Fieldwork

Fieldworkers are supplied either by a *field interviewing service* — a company whose mission is to provide fieldworkers — or through your own in-house interviewers. These in-house interviewers may be temporary or permanent employees who you hire to collect survey and observational data.

If you retain a field interviewing service, ensure that the person who's managing your study knows your research questions and understands the importance of your research. It's like public school education; teachers tend to expend more effort on children whose parents are engaged in their children's education. On the plus side, collecting reliable data for you makes good business sense for the field service, because having satisfied customers means repeat business and favorable recommendations to other potential clients. In contrast, using in-house interviewers can be cost effective and speed the data-collection process; that is, if they aren't already overworked and underpaid.

As Milton Friedman noted on many occasions, "There's no such thing as a free lunch." Thus, whether you use in-house or field service interviewers, someone must pay and train those fieldworkers to collect data properly; otherwise, the quality of the data they collect will be questionable.

Securing an interview requires skill. Getting one's foot in the door or getting the door slammed in one's face are two alternatives faced by fieldworkers conducting face-to-face interviews; obviously, the former is preferred. Experiencing that positive alternative only happens with good training.

Using professional fieldworkers

Fieldwork managers must select, train, supervise, and control fieldworkers. Field interviewing is a tedious task that requires reading and verbal skills that are on par with a high school or college education. Unfortunately, in good economic times — when other jobs are plentiful — people with that level of education often bore quickly of fieldwork and quit. Thus, fieldwork managers must continually identify new fieldworkers because turnover is high.

Fieldworkers must be monitored, because they have an incentive to cheat. Typically, fieldworkers are paid a small base salary plus a commission per completed interview. To grow that commission, they may fake answers or falsify entire interviews. As a result, most field service companies verify between 10 percent and 20 percent of interviews. That way, cheaters can be identified, their fake interviews deleted, and their employment terminated.

Monitoring in-house fieldwork

One advantage of using in-house fieldworkers is that you can train them exactly as you want them to perform in the field; in contrast, you can't control field interviewing service employees. Rather than selling shoes or a "sure-fire" winner at a Las Vegas sports book, your in-house fieldworkers are selling the importance of your research to respondents who typically would prefer to spend their time on other pursuits. In essence, your fieldworkers must convince potential respondents that the data they provide are of more value than their time, which is a hard sell. Friendly, efficient, and witty fieldworkers can help promote this value perception.

Regardless of whether you collect data via face-to-face or telephone interviews, successful interviewing requires you (or your interviewers) to do certain things, which we cover in the next few sections.

Make initial contacts pleasant so you can secure interviews easily

For many purchases, a meet-and-greet session determines the likelihood of a sale. If you like the person who's trying to sell to you, then you're more inclined to buy from him. The same is true of respondents' willingness to participate in surveys; they're more inclined to cooperate with interviewers they like. As such, training programs for fieldworkers must emphasize their need to be affable and professional.

After an interview date is set, promptness and efficiency are paramount. A well-executed interview can lead to snowball sample compliance (as we discuss in Chapter 11) and willingness to participate in future research.

Ask questions properly

You (or your interviewers) should ask every question exactly as worded on the questionnaire. Respondents may occasionally indicate that they don't understand a question posed by an interviewer. They may assume, as in normal conversation, that the interviewer will rephrase the question. Unfortunately, to do so would add variability associated with asking different, although similar, questions.

In this situation, you (or your interviewers) should repeat the question exactly as worded. If the respondent still doesn't understand, the interviewer can note that failure on the questionnaire so the answer subsequently can be ignored or addressed during the data coding and entry process. For example, the respondent can be contacted again via telephone and asked the question again in a controlled way.

Also, you (or your interviewers) should read questions slowly. Although you may be familiar with the questions after conducting a 50th interview, respondents are hearing the questions for the first time and may not be listening carefully. Questions must be read in the proper order. You (or your interviewers) shouldn't modify the question sequence, because order effects may be present (as we discuss in Chapter 9). Also, you (or your interviewers) shouldn't omit questions unless the respondent isn't qualified to answer them.

Use proper probing tactics

As we discuss in Chapter 6, the real value of face-to-face and telephone interviews is the option to probe further. You must prepare yourself and your fieldworkers to construct adequately probing questions. What we mean is that you must ask questions that encourage respondents to clarify and detail their initial answers.

Although this list isn't exhaustive of all probing techniques, here are four useful tactics:

- ✔ **Effective silence:** In normal conversation, a person who's asked a question will respond and then stop. If you (or the interviewer) remain silent, the respondent often feels pressured to elaborate on the initial response.

- ✔ **Summarizing respondents' comments:** You (or the interviewer) may say "What I hear you saying is . . ." and then summarize what you heard. Then you allow respondents to either acknowledge a properly understood answer or elaborate further.

- ✔ **Repeating the question:** Asking the same question a second time usually signals to respondents that their initial answer was incomplete.

- ✔ **Asking a neutral question:** A question like "Why do you believe that?" usually encourages respondents to elaborate further.

Make recording responses easy

Given today's audio and video technology, recording respondents' answers would seem to be a straightforward task. Reality television programs aside, many people resist electronic recording of their voices and images; as a result, longhand remains the universal way to record answers during face-to-face interviews. Although somewhat archaic in today's world of high-tech communications, answers written on a piece paper can still prove effective. For example, because telephone questionnaires are relatively short and tend to rely on close-ended or short fill-in-the-blank questions (see Chapters 8 and 9), interviewers easily can record responses with either a PC or pen-and-paper.

If you're mistaken for a physician based on your penmanship and you're uncomfortable entering respondents' answers directly into a data file, then you can turn to computer-aided telephone interviewing (CATI) software when collecting data over the telephone. For more information on CATI software, visit Sawtooth Software's Web site at `sawtooth.com/products/cati/index.htm`. (Note: Although we have used Sawtooth Software in the past with great success, this is not an endorsement of the company or its services.)

As we discuss in Chapter 14, the multiple tasks that interviewers must perform — like maintaining eye contact and looking engaged — tax even experienced interviewers. Performing such tasks while jotting paraphrased versions of respondents' answers may prove overwhelming, especially for amateur interviewers. To minimize this problem, you can conduct interviews with an assistant; one person can ask a question and maintain the conversational aspects of the interview while the other person jots down the answer. Of course, if you're paying interviewers for their services — you haven't volunteered good friends and family members to donate their time — then using two interviewers per interview can drive up your costs.

One way to ease your recording burden is to develop standard abbreviations for typical words used in responses. These standard abbreviations are akin to those used in modern texting. For example, if u cant imagin a day w/o txtng, u r alredy well prepared 2 breviate respndnts answrs. (Translation: If you can't imagine a day without texting, you're already well prepared to abbreviate respondents' answers.) Ask your children or your neighbor's children to help if you aren't sure what we're talking about here.

End on a good note: Terminate the interview properly

For the same reason that it's important to solicit interviewees' cooperation, it's also important to terminate interviews properly. You may need to contact interviewees again for clarification and elaboration of their answers. If you end an interview badly, you may find it difficult or impossible to recontact the interviewee.

Taking Care of Data Preparation and Entry

After you or your interviewers have collected all your data (see the earlier section "Determining Who Conducts Fieldwork"), you have to prepare that data for analysis. Part of the preparation includes data entry. Simply defined, *data entry* is the process of transferring data from sources like questionnaires to a computerized data file. Often those data are numeric — for example, scores on a 7-point attitude scale or number of children in a household — in which case subsequent analysis is statistical. When data are in word form, subsequent analysis is facilitated by specialized programs that perform word counts, identify common themes, and so on. In the following sections, we provide the information you need to prepare your data.

Knowing the basic terms

When researchers discuss data entry, they often use jargon that can baffle the best and the brightest. Becoming familiar with the basic terms can help you to avoid confusion. Here are a few such terms:

✔ A *file* is a complete data set.

✔ A *record* is a summary of the responses by one person or data about one object.

- ✔ A *field* is the individual variables within a record, such as questionnaire number, street, city, or response to question.

- ✔ The end product of the data preparation process is a *data matrix*. If you're familiar with spreadsheets software such as Quattro or Microsoft Excel, you've probably created at least a few data matrices. In marketing research, each record is a row, and the different fields, which correspond to the different variables in a data set, are the columns.

Beginning with pre-entry preparation

To prepare data for analysis — *pre-entry preparation* — you follow a two-stage validation and then editing process. We describe each stage in the following sections.

Validation

During the validation stage, you (or the fieldwork manager) should check that interviews occurred as specified and that all respondents were qualified to participate. For face-to-face interviews, fieldworkers should be monitored for professional behavior and appearance. You also should ensure that interviews transpired in the specified environment; in-office or in-home interviews shouldn't occur at a local tavern! For telephone interviews, you (or the fieldwork manager) should eavesdrop intermittently, especially if the phone bank contains multiple extensions. Finally, no matter what type of interview you conduct, you should check that all appropriate questions were asked.

Editing

When editing data, it's essential that clarity is achieved and the data are collected in a timely fashion; in other words, the data must be recognized and appropriately entered into a data file. Just as books need editors — to which Jeremy and Mike grudgingly can attest — completed data files typically require some editing.

Recognizing inconsistent data patterns or inappropriate responses is critical to meaningful data interpretation. If you allow such problematic data to remain in your data file, you risk "findings" that aren't representative of your target population. The items you (or the fieldwork manager) check during the editing stage differ by type of interview.

During personal interviews, you should check for:

- ✔ **Omissions:** These are improperly unanswered questions.

- ✔ **Ambiguities:** These are vague responses to open-ended questions, such as "I thought the resort experience was interesting."

✔ **Inconsistencies:** These are incompatible answers to different questions. For example, the answer to one question indicates a person is childless, but the answer to another question indicates that he's a parent of several children.

✔ **Improper skip patterns:** You should delete answers to questions that should have been skipped and try to acquire answers to questions that should have been answered.

✔ **Answers that weren't recorded properly, especially to open-ended questions:** Clearly, it's difficult for interviewers to record extensive answers. Nonetheless, some completed interview forms may contain only one- or two-word answers when it's obvious that interviewees provided far more detail.

During self-administered questionnaires, check that:

✔ **All key questions were answered:** For example, if an important aspect of the data analysis phase is to compare the responses of males versus females, but a respondent failed to indicate sex, that questionnaire is useless.

✔ **Respondents understood the instructions and took the questionnaire seriously:** This isn't always an easy call. Sometimes respondents circle an identical answer on a 7-point scale all the way down a page. You have to decide whether those answers are truly reflective of that respondent's opinions, or whether that respondent was merely providing meaningless responses.

✔ **No pages are missing:** Although missing pages could be pages omitted from the questionnaire, in most cases respondents skipped those pages either intentionally or unintentionally.

✔ **The questionnaire was returned after the cutoff date:** Events that occur in the world can influence people's responses, so questionnaires returned after a submission cutoff date may differ due to environmental changes.

The editing process is subjective. How do you know that a respondent took the task seriously? How do you know what was meant by an ambiguous response? There's no right or wrong way to cope with such editing problems, but here are several general solutions:

✔ If respondents aren't anonymous, you can contact them again to resolve response ambiguities or inconsistencies.

✔ You can discard the questionnaire. However, given the cost per completed questionnaire, that isn't a preferred solution.

> ✔ If the questionnaire seemed to be taken seriously, but some responses are problematic and the respondent is anonymous, you can use only the given responses. This practice has implications for advanced data analysis, but it has minimal implications for the basic data analysis you're likely to perform.

Coding your responses

Coding is the process of grouping and assigning numeric codes to different question responses. Coding data permits efficient data analysis. Rather than tabulate responses by hand — which is grossly inefficient — you can code your data, create a data file, and let your PC do the work. As we discuss in Chapter 9, close-ended questions are pre-coded, and so they greatly simplify the data-entry process.

Coding an open-ended question is a bit trickier; and exploratory research may require one or more open-ended questions. The steps for coping with such questions are as follows:

1. **Generate a complete list of all reasonable responses.**

   Compiling a list of this sort will help you identify bad data (unreasonable responses can be easily recognized and discarded) and better understand responses (because an exhaustive list will help you recognize the range of responses).

2. **Ask multiple judges to devise response categories that are mutually exclusive and exhaustive.**

   Creating such categories is a subjective process, so each judge is likely to devise a unique set. The judges, the coders, and you must resolve differences between those sets because only one consolidated response list can be used for coding the data. See Chapter 9 for more on mutually exclusive and exhaustive categories.

3. **Assign a numeric code to each response on the consolidated list.**

   For classification purposes, you need to develop a coding scheme for each response on the list of responses. You should use the simplest possible coding scheme; number the first response on the list *1,* the second response *2,* and so on.

4. **Coders return to the completed questionnaires, read each response, and assign one or more numeric codes that correspond to the consolidated response list.**

   Using coders in this way helps to ensure the reliability of your data and provide an efficient means for data analysis.

Clearly, this process is involved and complex. That's why we recommend that you use close-ended questions for nonexploratory surveys; coding open-ended questions is more taxing than writing good close-ended questions.

Creating and cleaning data files

It's far more accurate and efficient to go directly from questionnaires to data entry and storage, as opposed to transcribing data onto coding sheets and then entering the content of those sheets into a data file. The middle step can introduce additional error, which undermines your results.

If you use specialized forms, like the ones for standardized exams that require a #2 pencil, it's possible to scan responses directly into a computer data file. Similarly, optical scanners — similar to technology the U.S. Postal Service uses to scan the address on each piece of mail — can be used to read completed questionnaires. Regardless, a mechanical or human agent must transfer data from questionnaires to a computer data file.

Prior to data analysis, you must ensure that your data file is clean; that is, after your data file has been created, you can't just begin running statistical analyses without checking for data-entry errors and the like. So, double-check your data entries before delving in to data analysis.

The data-entry process can be either dumb (what you type is what you get) or intelligent (the computer won't accept obviously bad data). If you've ever omitted a key decimal point in a financial spreadsheet, you know that software like Microsoft Excel relies on dumb data entry. In other words, it can catch some errors — such as circular references — but it can't spot that 10000 should have been 100.00.

Because dumb data entry lacks error-checking protocols, you must identify and remove erroneous data from your data file. One standard file-cleaning approach uses *marginal reports* — tables of response frequencies for each question (which we discuss in Chapter 18) — to identify invalid keystrokes and improper skip patterns. Such reports indicate the number of responses to each question. If one report indicates that your data file contains an excessive number of seemingly valid responses to a question that could legitimately be skipped, you could have a skip pattern problem.

In contrast, you can program intelligent data-entry software to recognize inappropriate responses. For example, if the response to a question can be only 1, 2, or 3, and the data-entry person types a 4, the computer won't accept that keystroke as a valid response. Similarly, with *machine cleaning of data,* you can program software such as SPSS (which we mention in Chapter 18) to identify and suggest fixes for logical errors. For example, it's illogical for a respondent to answer "single and never married" to a marital status question but also answer questions about a spouse's preferences. You can program SPSS or similar software either to delete or merely flag such inconsistent answers.

Controlling missing responses

Respondents may skip certain questions, like those deemed overly personal or threatening. Of the socio-demographic questions, sex and income are the least likely to be answered. So how should you handle missing responses? The possibilities include the following:

- ✔ **Leave the response blank and allow Microsoft Excel (or other data analysis software) to treat it as a missing response.** To ensure that blanks aren't misinterpreted as zeros in your analyses, enter an impossibly large negative number (like −99999). Even one such number will have an obvious influence on statistics like means and standard deviations (as we discuss in Chapter 18), making this error easy to catch.

- ✔ **If data for any question are missing, delete that record.** However, given the expense of data collection, this option is wasteful and should be avoided if possible.

- ✔ **If a correlation between two variables is of interest, and data on either variable are missing, exclude that record from the calculation of that correlation.** A detailed discussion of correlation appears in Chapter 18.

- ✔ **Substitute the mean response for the missing value — either for the entire sample or the subgroup from which the respondent was drawn.** This method assumes that the overall or group mean is the best guess for a person's response had she opted to answer the question.

- ✔ **An imputed response — in which the respondent's answers to questions that are most highly related, in a statistical sense, to the question without data — can be calculated and substituted for the missing response.** In this sense, missing responses are replaced with data from provided responses.

Each of these approaches has pros and cons, and many have statistical implications. Nonetheless, for basic analyses we recommend that you represent missing data as blanks.

Chapter 18

Tools for Analyzing Your Data

. . . .

In This Chapter

▶ Summarizing data with descriptive analysis

▶ Converting data to a more usable form

▶ Using cross-tabulation tables

▶ Seeing what correlation can do for you

. . . .

W.A. Wallis defined statistics as "a body of methods for making wise decisions in the face of uncertainty." Sadly, many people are either afraid of statistics or think about them in the wrong way. The latter think of statistics along the lines of these famous quotes:

> *There are three kinds of lies — lies, damned lies, and statistics.*
>
> —Benjamin Disraeli

> *Torture numbers, and they'll confess to anything.*
>
> —Gregg Easterbrook

> *Statistics have shown that mortality increases perceptibly in the military during wartime.*
>
> —Alphonse Allais

> *If you want to inspire confidence, give plenty of statistics. It does not matter that they should be accurate, or even intelligible, as long as there are enough of them.*
>
> —Lewis Carroll

These humorous quotes imply that statistics either show the obvious or can be twisted to show almost anything. If you're of this persuasion, our goal in this chapter is to convince you otherwise; that's because you need a basic understanding of statistics to analyze your data. In this chapter, we give you the basics that you need to know for marketing research. If you want a more in-depth view of statistics, we recommend that you pick up *Statistics For Dummies* by Deborah Rumsey (Wiley).

Working with Descriptive Analysis

Descriptive analysis is the transformation of raw data — for example, demographic data like age, ethnicity, and income — into a form that make them easy to understand and interpret. This type of analysis entails rearranging, ordering, and manipulating data to generate descriptive information. In essence, it summarizes data in a more meaningful and reduced form.

In the following sections, we discuss techniques you can use to summarize your data, including tabulation and frequency tables. Although descriptive data summarized in paragraph and tabular forms are equally accurate, the latter form is more visually appealing and easier to read.

Summarizing data with tabulation

One of the simplest ways to summarize data is with *tabulation,* which is the orderly arrangement of data in a table or other summary format. The most common type of table is the easy-to-read frequency table that includes both counts and percentages. In the following sections, we discuss frequency tables.

Using frequency tables

A *frequency table* contains numerical data, arranged in a row-and-column format, and shows the counts and percentages of responses or observations for each category assigned to a variable. Those categories are preselected by you. The *coding number* is the category in which each study participant can fall, and you enter those numbers into your data file.

The coding numbers are for classification purposes only; they carry no meaningful value. For example, if you assign respondents to one of four income categories, those categories are predetermined, and the coding numbers 1 to 4 are meant for classification only.

Frequency tables can be created in Microsoft Excel or in a standard statistical package like SPSS (Statistical Package for the Social Sciences). The accompanying DVD provides a detailed account for generating a frequency table with Excel.

Figure 18-1 shows an example of a frequency table. The table summarizes the propensity of respondents to fall into different income categories. Here's an explanation of the different columns you see in the figure:

✔ **Column #1:** This column indicates the coding scheme for the income categories: *1* represents households earning $19,999 or less, *2* represents households earning from $20,000 to $39,999, and so on. The six income categories are *mutually exclusive* and *exhaustive;* in other words, all possible incomes are represented by a unique category. (Refer to Chapter 10 for more on these terms.) The *missing* category represents the respondents who didn't answer the question.

✔ **Column #2:** This column indicates the number of respondents — out of 203 total respondents — who fell into each category.

✔ **Columns #3 and #4:** These columns indicate the percentages for each income category. *Missing* responses cause the percentages to vary between these columns. For example, in Column 3 the percentage of respondents in the "$19,999 or less" income category is 13.8 percent, which is 28 of all 203 respondents. In contrast, the corresponding percentage in Column 4 is 14.7 percent, which is 28 of the 191 respondents who answered the question. When there's missing data, the percentage in the *Valid Percent* column will exceed the percentage in the *Percent* column.

✔ **Column #5:** This column contains adjusted cumulative percentages, which are a running total of the valid percentages in the column immediately to the left. Take 14.7 and add it to 24.1; the sum is 38.8. Take 23.0 and add it to 38.8; the sum is 61.8. This summation procedure continues until 100 percent is reached.

The raw numbers and percentages refer to all respondents, whether or not they answered the question; the adjusted cumulative percentage, on the other hand, is a running total of the percentages adjusted for nonrespondents.

Gross annual income 1=19,999 or less; 2=20,000-39,999; 3=40,000-59,999; 4=60,000-79,999; 5=80,000-99,999; 6=100,000 or more

		Frequency	Percent	Valid Percent	Cumulative Percent
	1	28	13.8	14.7	14.7
	2	46	22.7	24.1	38.8
Valid	3	44	21.7	23.0	61.8
	4	37	18.2	19.4	81.2
	5	19	9.4	9.9	91.1
	6	17	8.4	8.9	100.0
	Total	191	94.1	100.0	
	Missing	12	5.9		
Total		203	100.0		

Figure 18-1: A frequency table.

Choosing a possible base for your percentages

A percentage is a fraction of something larger. Seemingly straightforward to identify, the most suitable "larger thing" isn't always obvious. For example, if you want to examine your customers' credit card usage, you can compute the percentage of customers who used credit cards or the percentage of credit card transactions. Although both percentages provide useful information, the first percentage conceals customers who often pay for small purchases with cash and larger purchases with a credit card.

The issue of valid (non-missing) cases (respondents who gave a valid answer) entails the base for comparison. A *base* is the number of respondents or observations in a row or column that you use for computing percentages. You can choose from several alternative bases that make more or less sense depending on what you're summarizing. Here they are:

✔ **Using all respondents:** If you decide on a base of all respondents who answered the question, you must take the number who provided each answer and divide by the total number of respondents.

✔ **Using only respondents who were asked the question:** This base pertains to questions that all respondents weren't qualified to answer. If only a subset of respondents answered a question they could have appropriately skipped (as we discuss in Chapter 10), it's more meaningful to divide the number of responses in each category by the number of respondents who were asked that question.

✔ **Using only respondents who answered the question:** Regardless of your instructions or the professionalism of your survey, some respondents won't answer some questions. You can ignore their nonresponses or code them as missing; if you decide on the former method, your base is only respondents who answered the question.

The major issue about bases relates to multi-response questions — those "check all that apply" questions. For such questions, either the number of respondents or the number of responses can be the appropriate base. For example, you can present respondents with a list of magazines and ask them, "To which magazines do you currently subscribe?" Obviously, most if not all respondents will subscribe to a subset of listed magazines. Thus, you analyze multi-response data in two ways:

✔ **Using the percentage of respondents who subscribe to each magazine:** To calculate these percentages, you divide the number of subscribers by the total number of respondents.

✔ **Using the degree to which each magazine comprises the universe of magazines people read:** To calculate these percentages, you divide the number of subscriptions for each magazine by the total number of subscriptions for all magazines that all respondents indicated they read.

Both are a reasonable approach for analyzing such data; however, remember that your chosen approach should depend on your research question.

Measuring central tendency

Frequency tables provide an excellent way to summarize survey data, but such tables contain many numbers. Is there a more efficient way to summarize survey data? (By *efficient,* we mean that survey responses are summarized by fewer numbers.) Fortunately, the answer is yes! The *measures of central tendency* can help. There are three such measures:

- ✔ **Mode:** The *mode,* which is the value that occurs most often, can summarize nominal or categorical data, (For such data, values are assigned to objects for classification or identification purposes. Hence, the numbering scheme is arbitrary, like 1 = male and 2 = female.) For example, if more Hispanics than Caucasians, African Americans, or Asians responded to an ethnicity question, the mode on that question is Hispanic.

- ✔ **Median:** The *median,* which is the midpoint of scores ordered from lowest to highest, can summarize ordinal-scaled variables (For such data, values are assigned so that objects can be ranked from most to least on some characteristic.) The median is the same as the 50th percentile.

- ✔ **Mean:** The arithmetic *mean,* which is the sum all of scores divided by the number of respondents (or objects), can summarize metric — interval or ratio-scaled — data. (For interval scales, the scale points have equal width [like a thermometer]. For ratio scales, the scale points have equal width and there's a natural zero point [like dollars or euros].)

A sample mean isn't a population mean. The population mean pertains to a census, and the sample mean pertains to a sample, or part of a population. (We discuss census and sample in Chapter 11.) The sample mean is your best guess of the population mean.

Increasing understanding with measures of dispersion

Although measures of central tendency (see the preceding section) provide the best single summary number for a set of responses to a survey question, that single number lacks information about the degree to which people's responses differed. It also helps to know whether respondents answered a question similarly or dissimilarly to one another. As a result, you need both a best single summary measure (mode/median/mean) and a measure that indicates how well that single measure captures all responses. This second measure detects *dispersion,* or spread, in the data.

The following represent the five standard measures of dispersion:

- ✔ **Range:** This measure is the difference between the smallest and largest values in a set of numbers. Although range is a relatively primitive measure of spread, it's easy to compute and easy to understand.

- ✔ **Interquartile range:** This range is the difference between the 75th percentile and the 25th percentile.

- ✔ **Mean absolute deviation:** This measure is the average difference, either plus or minus, from the mean. It's often used as a measure of forecasting accuracy; in other words, it indicates the difference between a forecasted value and the value that occurred.

- ✔ **Variance:** This measure is the sum of the squared differences between each value and the mean divided by a slightly adjusted sample size (sample size − 1). Like sample population mean, sample variance is an estimate of population variance.

- ✔ **Standard deviation:** This measure is the square root of a variance. It also captures the distance of all observations from the mean.

The range provides a useful approximation for standard deviation. Often, the lowest score in the range corresponds to three standard deviations below the mean and the highest score in the range corresponds to three standard deviations above the mean; hence, the range often is roughly six standard deviations. Dividing the range by six typically provides a good estimate of the standard deviation.

Interquartile range is a good approximation of ±1 standard deviation from the mean. The interquartile range is the middle 50 percent of the distribution; for normally distributed data, ±1 standard deviation from the mean is a bit more than 68 percent of the distribution.

Figures 18-2 and 18-3 illustrate low versus high dispersion for answers to a Likert-type question. In both figures, the mean value is roughly 4. All answers tend to cluster around 4 in Figure 18-2, but they range from 1 to 7 in Figure 18-3. In the first case, the mean is an excellent summary of all respondents' answers; in the second case, the mean isn't reflective of some respondents' answers.

Computing deviation scores

If you collect metric data, you can compute *deviation scores*. For each measure you take, these scores are the difference between each observed value and the mean.

Deviation scores reveal the extent that observed values on a measure differ from one another. Such information can help you identify the best measures for differentiating people — most likely your customers — from one another.

For example, if your customers tend to earn similar incomes, then income is a poor measure for classifying customers into groups.

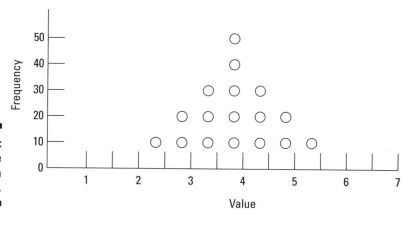

Figure 18-2:
An example
of low data
dispersion.

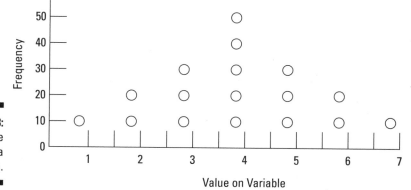

Figure 18-3:
An example
of high data
dispersion.

In addition, deviation scores can reveal the presence of outliers — values that differ greatly from the mean value. Although outliers may be legitimate, outliers often are caused by data-entry error. Thus, large deviation scores can indicate data-entry mistakes that you can fix by checking the original data source.

The *mean* is the best single summary number for metric data. If you take the mean, subtract it from each response or observation, and then sum all those positive and negative differences, the total is *0,* which indicates that the mean is an unbiased estimator of central tendency. (Refer to the earlier section, "Measuring central tendency," for more information.) In other words, the responses or observations less than the mean equal the responses or observations greater than the mean weighted for difference from that mean.

Making Your Data More Useable

You can make your data more amenable to analysis with data transformation or recoding. In this section, we discuss both methods.

Converting with data transformation

Data transformation converts data from its original form into a new form that may be more appropriate for a specific analysis. In doing so, a new variable is created. For example, you may wish to convert your data to linear form. Although many marketing relationships are nonlinear, many frequently used statistical analyses assume linear relationships.

Normally distributed data can be converted from raw scores into Z scores, which are scaled from +3 to –3. That score indicates the extent a score is above or below its mean. When dealing with raw metric data, it's important to know the mean and difference from that mean. All that information is contained within a Z score. When dealing with multiple Likert-scaled items that address the same underlying construct, it's often useful to sum the Z scores across all those related items. For example, assume you asked respondents three questions about the same underlying attitude and scaled them in a similar direction (so reverse coding, mentioned in the next section, isn't needed). It's reasonable to sum the scores on those three questions to create a total score. Researchers often use multi-item scales because responses to single questions tend to be less reliable than the sum of responses to multiple related questions. (We discuss reliability in Chapter 7.)

Consider index numbers a type of data transformation. With an index number, the score or observation is recalibrated to indicate how it relates to a base number. For example, the Consumer Price Index (CPI) relates current prices to a base year.

The problem with index numbers, especially in secondary data reports, is that the base year can change. Comparing CPI numbers reported in 1971 to index CPI reported in 1995 can cause confusion because the base year changed. Index numbers are a useful way to transform data, but you should use such numbers cautiously if acquired from secondary sources.

Knowing when to recode your data

Recoding data means using your PC to convert original codes used for the raw data into codes that are more suitable for subsequent analysis. Here are some reasons you may need to recode data:

✔ **You need to reverse code questionnaire items.** For instance, some related questions may be posed positively (for example, "I like . . .") and other related questions may be posed negatively (for example, "I dislike . . ."). In that case, you first identify each question that's worded in reverse. For example, the response is subtracted from 8 for a 7-point scale. As a result, the 7s are now 1s, the 6s now 2s, and so on. Then, you either replace the original number in your data file or create a new column in your data file for the recoded values.

✔ **You need to assign values to complex socioeconomic variables.** For example, social class is comprised of several components: level of education, income, occupational status, and other indicators. To create a social class measure — and to assign a value for social class to each respondent — you'd need to combine these components appropriately (using a weighted sum to calculate an overall value).

✔ **You need to reduce or collapse the number of response categories.** For example, the scale for a Likert-type item may have five possible responses: strongly agree, agree, neither agree nor disagree, disagree, and strongly disagree. It's possible to collapse this scale from five points to three points by combining the *strongly agree* and *agree* answers and combining the *strongly disagree* and *disagree* answers. Such collapsing of variables may be necessary for valid cross-tabulation statistics if some categories contain few responses. (See the next section for more on cross-tabulation.)

Considering More Than One Variable: Cross-Tabulation and Banner Tables

Frequency tables, although of great value, only allow you to consider one variable at a time. Often, the real story emerges when you consider more than one variable at a time. Cross-tabulation and banner tables are two basic approaches for evaluating two or more variables at a time. We discuss both approaches in the sections that follow.

Examining the basics of cross-tabulation

Cross tabulation allows you to organize data by groups or categories, thus facilitating comparisons. It provides *joint frequency distributions,* which summarize the relationships between observations on two or more sets of variables.

For example, if you want to understand the relationship between a person's sex and car ownership, sex is *male* or *female,* and car ownership is *yes* or *no.* A percentage is male, a percentage is female, a percentage is car owners, and a percentage isn't car owners. A cross-tabulation allows you to look at males who are and aren't car owners separately from females who are and aren't car owners.

Figure 18-4 shows a cross-tabulation table that relates respondents' sex to their full-time employment. It shows that 54 of the 81 males (66.7 percent) are employed full time, whereas 59 of the 85 females are (69.4 percent) are employed full time. The table is formatted similarly to the tables generated by SPSS (a popular statistical software package). The numbers in each cell refer to the following:

✔ The first number is the *count,* or frequency.

✔ The second number is the percent of the row total represented by that count.

✔ The third number is the percent of the column total represented by that count.

✔ The fourth number is the percent of all respondents represented by that count.

Sex	Full-time Employment		
	Yes	No	Row Total
Male	54	27	81
	66.7%	33.3%	100.0%
	47.8%	50.9%	
	32.5%	16.3%	48.8%
Female	59	26	85
	69.4%	30.6%	100.0%
	52.2%	49.1%	
	35.5%	15.7%	51.2%
Column Total	113 (68.9%)	53 (31.9%)	166 (100.0%)

Figure 18-4:
A cross-tabulation table.

Key: 1st number in cell = count (frequency)
        2nd number in cell = percent of row
        3rd number in cell = percent of column
        4th number in cell = percent of total

Interpreting cross-tabulation tables

The best way to explain how to interpret cross-tabulation tables is by example. In the following sections, we provide two examples that show you how to analyze cross-tabulation tables.

Example #1: Interpreting a home ownership survey

Pretend that you surveyed 200 people with the goal of determining whether annual household income is related to home ownership. Figure 18-5 shows the histogram for the household incomes of that sample. These annual incomes are grouped in $10,000 increments from "Less than $20,000" to "$90,000 or more." The histogram suggests that roughly half the households earned less than $40,000 annually and roughly half earned $40,000 or more annually.

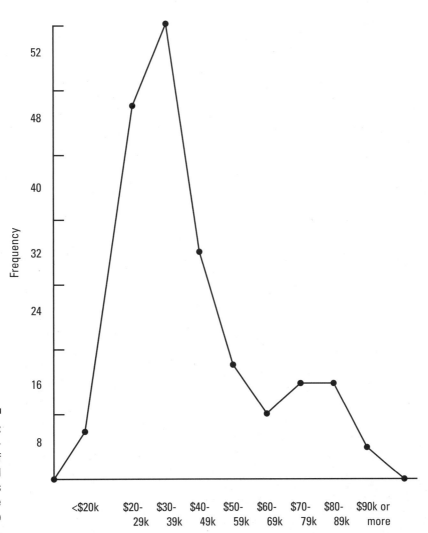

Figure 18-5:
A histogram of household incomes in a home ownership survey.

Figure 18-6 shows that 108 of 200 households have incomes less than $40,000 annually, and that 92 of 200 households have incomes of $40,000 or more annually. Of those 108 households in the lower-income category, 96 didn't own a home, and 12 owned a home. The 92 higher-income households show a 60/40 split, with 54 of the 92 not owning a home and 38 owning a home.

You can sum across rows, look at the marginal figures (those figures in the rightmost column and bottom row), and consider just the 108 cases. You also can sum down columns and look at the 150 non-home-owning households; roughly 64 percent had incomes less than $40,000, and 36 percent had incomes of $40,000 or more. In contrast, the home-owning households show a reversal, with a roughly 1-to-3 split (12 to 38). Only 24 percent of home-owning households earn less than $40,000, but 76 percent of home-owning households earned $40,000 or more.

You can examine cross-tabulation tables in total, or you can look across the rows or down the columns. The way you extract information from a cross-tabulation table depends on your research question.

Annual Household Income	Own Home		
	No	**Yes**	**Row Total**
Less than $40,000	96 88.9% 64.0% 48.0%	12 11.1% 24.0% 6.0%	108 100.0% 54.0%
$40,000 or more	54 58.7% 36.0% 26.0%	38 41.3% 76.0% 19.0%	92 100.0% 46.0%
Column Total	150 (75.0%)	50 (25.0%)	200 (100.0%)

Figure 18-6: A cross-tabulation table for household income versus home ownership.

Key: 1st number in cell = count (frequency)
2nd number in cell = percent of row
3rd number in cell = percent of column
4th number in cell = percent of total

Figure 18-7 shows that home ownership also is related to household size. Households are divided into "four or fewer" members or "five or more" members. In this sample of 200 households, 156 have "four or fewer" members, and 44 have "five or more" members.

The table shows that for households with "four or fewer" members, 90 percent didn't own a home, meaning that only 10 percent owned a home. In contrast, for households with "five or more" members, 23 percent didn't own a home, and 77 percent owned a home.

Household Size	Own Home		
	No	**Yes**	**Row Total**
Four or fewer members	140 89.7% 93.3% 70.0%	16 10.3% 32.0% 8.0%	156 100.0% 78.0%
Five or more members	10 22.7% 6.7% 5.0%	34 77.3% 68.0% 17.0%	44 100.0% 22.0%
Column Total	150 (75.0%)	50 (25.0%)	200 (100.0%)

Figure 18-7: A cross-tabulation table for home ownership versus household size.

Key: 1st number in cell = count (frequency)

2nd number in cell = percent of row

3rd number in cell = percent of column

4th number in cell = percent of total

Relating only two variables at a time (as done in Figures 18-4 and 18-6), both income and household size seem related to home ownership. In contrast, Figure 18-8, which relates income, household size, and home ownership to one another simultaneously, gives a better perspective.

If you divide the sample into the 156 smaller households and the 44 larger households, only 4.3 percent of the smaller households with income less than $40,000 own a home; 18.7 percent of the smaller households with an income of $40,000 or more own a home. Of the 44 larger households, only 50 percent with income less than $40,000 own a home; in contrast, 93 percent of larger households with $40,000 or more in income own a home.

Thus, it seems that household size is the primary determinant of whether or not a household owns a home because larger households are willing to invest in a residence. However, income is a constraint, so households earning less than $40,000 annually may want to purchase a home but often can't afford one.

Annual Household Income	Four Members or Less Own Home			Five Members or More Own Home		
	No	Yes	Row Total	No	Yes	Row Total
Less than $40,000	88	4	92	8	8	16
	95.7%	4.3%	100.0%	50.0%	50.0%	100.0%
	62.9%	25.0%		80.0%	23.5%	
	56.4%	2.6%	59.0%	18.2%	18.2%	36.4%
$40,000 or more	52	12	64	2	26	28
	81.3%	18.7%	100.0%	7.1%	92.9%	100.0%
	37.1%	75.0%		20.0%	76.5%	
	33.3%	7.7%	41.0%	4.5%	59.1%	63.6%
Column Total	140 (89.7%)	16 (10.3%)	156 (100.0%)	10 (75.0%)	34 (25.0%)	44 (100.0%)

Figure 18-8: A cross-tabulation table for home ownership by household income and size.

Key: 1st number in cell = count (frequency)
2nd number in cell = percent of row
3rd number in cell = percent of column
4th number in cell = percent of total

Example #2: Age and PDA usage

Suppose you surveyed different-aged folks about their PDA usage. Figure 18-9 summarizes respondent age and PDA usage data from such a survey. Out of 300 respondents, 183 answered "yes," and 117 answered "no" to a question about current PDA usage. The respondents' answers about their age ran as follows: 66 were less than 21 years old, 99 were between 21 and 35 years old, and 135 were more than 35 years old.

So, the question is, "Are a consumer's age and PDA usage related?" You may think that the answer is *yes* because older people are less adept at and inclined to use high-tech products. Confirming this relationship may encourage PDA manufacturers to develop extensive Web sites for educating more mature consumers about PDA usage.

Each cell in the cross-tabulation table in Figure 18-10 includes the following numbers:

✔ The count of people who answered both questions a certain way.

✔ The expected count if there's no relationship between answers to these questions (more about this later in the chapter).

✔ The row percent, which is the percent of people who answered the PDA question a certain way in each age category.

PDA Usage	Frequency	Percent	Valid Percent	Cumulative Percent
Yes	183	61.0	61.0	61.0
No	117	39.0	39.0	100.0
Total	300	100.0		

Figure 18-9: Frequency distribution tables for PDA usage and age.

Age	Frequency	Percent	Valid Percent	Cumulative Percent
Under 21	66	22.0	22.0	22.0
21-35	99	33.0	33.0	55.0
Over 35	135	45.0	45.0	100.0
Total	300	100.0		

✔ The column percent, which is the percent of people who answered the age question a certain way for each PDA usage category.

✔ The total percent of people who answered both questions a certain way.

Figure 18-10: A cross-tabulation table for PDA usage versus respondent's age.

PDA Usage	Age			
	Less than 21	21-35	36 or more	Row Total
Yes	60	69	54	183
	40.26	60.39	82.35	100.0%
	32.8%	37.7%	29.5%	
	90.9%	69.7%	40.0%	
	20.0%	23.0%	18.0%	61.0%
No	6	30	81	117
	35.74	38.61	52.65	100.0%
	5.1%	25.6%	69.2%	
	9.1%	30.3%	60.0%	
	2.0%	10.0%	27.0%	39.0%
Column Total	66 (22.0%)	99 (33.0%)	135 (45.0%)	300 (100.0%)

Key: 1st number in cell = count (frequency)

2nd number in cell = expected count (if no relationship)

3rd number in cell = percent of row

4th number in cell = percent of column

5th number in cell = percent of total

How many people less than 21 years old hadn't used a PDA? The answer is "6." For that first age column, 6 of 66 is 9.1 percent, and 6 of 300 (for the total sample) is 2 percent. Clearly there's a pattern in the row and column percents; PDA usage declines with respondents' age. In other words, respondents in the "less than 21 year old" age category are almost all PDA users. In contrast, more than half of respondents age 36 or older haven't used a PDA.

Running a chi-square (χ^2) test on a cross-tabulation table

The χ^2 test is used to determine whether observed counts significantly differ from counts that are expected by chance. It also can be used to assess differences between two or more samples, like between samples of New York Yankees and Boston Red Sox fans. Hence, the χ^2 test is used to determine whether a statistically meaningful relationship exists between two variables.

Although a χ^2 test can determine whether a statistically meaningful relationship exists between the two variables, a statistically significant finding may not be a managerially relevant finding. As a result, after you find a statistically significant difference, you must ask "Does that difference make a difference?" As one of Mike's professors often said, "A difference that makes no difference is no difference."

Typically a χ^2 test is used with nominal data, like gender or ethnicity, to determine differences between two independent groups. However, you may want to use a χ^2 test for ordinal data, like ranking brands. Doing so is okay, but you'll lose a bit of information because the χ^2 test is designed for nominal data, and you lose information when you treat ordinal data as nominal data. (Refer to the earlier section "Measuring central tendency" for more information.)

Figure 18-11 shows a cross-tabulation table on which you can run a χ^2 test. This table summarizes responses by men and women about awareness of a PC manufacturer's brand. In this case, the question that you can answer using a χ^2 test is this one: "Is the difference between the distribution of answers between men and women statistically significant?"

As the figure shows, of 300 respondents, 195 are men and 105 are women. Of the men, 150 were aware of the brand, and 45 were unaware; for the women, only 30 were aware, and 75 were unaware. These numbers produce a more than 3-to-1 ratio of aware to unaware men and a 2-to-5 ratio of aware to unaware women. Although seemingly different, you can't know whether these ratios differ significantly until you run a χ^2 test. We show you how to perform this test (using the example from Figure 18-11) in the following sections, and on the DVD as well.

	Men	**Women**	**Total**
Aware	150 (No relationship = 117)	30 (No relationship = 63)	180 (60%)
Unaware	45 (No relationship = 78)	75 (No relationship = 42)	120 (40%)
Total	195 (65%)	105 (35%)	300 (100.0%)

Calculation for Expected Count in a Cell for Unrelated Variables

$$E_{ij} = \frac{R_i C_j}{n}$$

R_i = total observed frequency for the i th row

C_j = total observed frequency for the j th column

n = sample size

Chi-square (χ^2) Test

Figure 18-11:
A cross-tabulation table and χ^2 test for the aware-ness of a PC manufactur-er's brand.

$$\chi^2 = \sum \frac{(O_i - E_i)^2}{E_i}$$

O_i = observed frequency for the i th cell

E_i = expected frequency for the i th cell

$\chi^2 = \{[(150 - 117)^2 / 117] + [(30 - 63)^2] / 63 + [(45 - 78)^2 / 78] + [(75 - 42)^2 / 42]\} / 300$

$= [9.31 + 17.29 + 13.96 + 25.93] = 66.49$

Calculating χ^2 value

A χ^2 test assesses cell-by-cell differences between the observed count (in this case, numbers based on a survey) and the count you'd expect if no relation-ship exists between the answers to these questions. Figure 18-11 shows the formula for the χ^2 test and the formula for calculating the expected count in each cell if no relationship exists between a person's sex and PC brand awareness.

To calculate a table with two unrelated variables, you take the following steps (this calculation is represented by the second formula in Figure 18-11):

1. **Multiply the observed percent in the row by the observed percent in the relevant column.**

2. **Multiply that fraction by the sample size.**

If the answers to two questions are unrelated, the probability of giving a certain answer to one question and the probability of giving a certain answer to the other question are unrelated to one another. When probabilities are unrelated, you multiply them to calculate a joint probability.

Imagine flipping a coin; the odds of flipping heads are ½. If you flip it twice, the odds of two heads are ¼, which you calculate by multiplying ½ by ½. The first flip is independent of the second flip; and independent means unrelated.

Here are the two reasons that the "observed minus expected" difference for the χ^2 test is squared:

✔ The absolute mean differences sum to zero if they aren't squared; hence, squaring eliminates the "sums to zero" problem.

✔ From a practical perspective, you'd like bigger differences to count more and smaller differences to count less; squaring differences is one way to weight them accordingly. The square of a small number also is a small number, but the square of large number is a huge number.

Consider taking "observed minus expected" differences for a small sample. Even if those differences are large percentage-wise, they're relatively small in absolute terms, so the squared differences are small. In contrast, "observed minus expected" differences for large samples are much larger in an absolute sense, and the square of a large difference is a huge number. Because it must adjust for sample size, the χ^2 test divides the sum of squared differences for each cell by the expected count for each cell.

Controlling for the number of categories

Even if you control for overall sample size, you also need to control for the number of cells. If you're trying to relate a variable with five categories to another variable with five categories, your cross-tabulation table will contain 25 cells. Squaring 25 differences is likely to produce a large number regardless of sample size.

How do you control for the number of categories in each cell? You calculate something called the *degrees of freedom,* which is (the number of rows – 1) × (the number of columns – 1). For example, assume there are three numbers that must sum to 100. If you choose 10 as the first number and 40 as the second number, you have no choice for the third number; it must be 50 for the sum to equal 100. In other words, the last number isn't free to vary. In this case, the degrees of freedom are 2.

Because Figure 18-11 shows two rows (aware versus unaware) and two columns (male versus female), the first count in a row or column can equal any number, but the last count in each row or column must allow the sum to equal the count indicated in the margin. In this case, the degrees of freedom equal $(2 - 1) \times (2 - 1)$, or 1.

To complete the χ^2 calculation for Figure 18-11, the expected count of aware males is 117, aware females is 63, unaware males is 78, and unaware females is 42. The cell-by-cell calculation at the bottom of Figure 18-11 shows that the χ^2 value is 66.49. With 1 degree of freedom, this value is significant at the 0.001 level, which is technical statistics talk for, "It's all but guaranteed that a person's sex and awareness of this PC brand are related."

Example: PDA usage revisited

If you look to the PDA usage example in Figures 18-9 and 18-10 earlier in the chapter, you can see that a relationship exists between consumers' PDA usage and age. As a result, younger consumers are more likely and older consumers are less likely to use a PDA. What does a χ^2 test on this data reveal?

For PDA usage versus age, the observed counts are 6, 30, and 81 for no usage, and 60, 69, and 54 for usage. For the cell "less than 21" who said yes to PDA usage, you'd expect 40.26 if no relationship exists between PDA usage and age. By summing the "observed minus expected" differences for each cell, squaring them (so bigger differences count more and little differences count less), and adjusting for sample size, the χ^2 value is 62.61. With 2 degrees of freedom ($2 - 1$ rows $\times$ $3 - 1$ columns), a χ^2 value of 62.61 is significant at the 0.001 level. Thus, you can confirm that a statistically significant relationship exists between PDA usage and age.

Exploring the effect of moderator variables

A *moderator variable* is a third variable that alters the relationship between two other variables. In particular, the moderator may indicate that there's a spurious relationship between the other variables.

Figure 18-12 depicts the rules for deciding when and how to introduce a third variable into a cross-tabulation analysis.

Figure 18-13 shows the spurious association revealed by introducing a third variable. For this example, suppose that a marketing manager for a transit company wants to assess the efficacy of a recent ad campaign to boost intentions to use mass transit. The manager assumes that unseen ads can't boost intentions to use mass transit; it then follows that a positive relationship should exist between recalling the ads and intentions to use mass transit. In essence, the question is, "Do potential riders' abilities to recall a mass transit ad increase their intentions to use mass transit?"

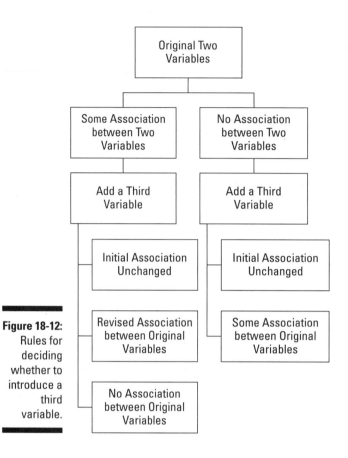

Figure 18-12:
Rules for deciding whether to introduce a third variable.

	Recall Ad	Don't Recall Ad	Users		Non-users	
			Recall Ad	Don't Recall Ad	Recall Ad	Don't Recall Ad
Intend to Use	190 (65%)	150 (36%)	170 (85%)	96 (80%)	20 (20%)	54 (18%)
Don't Intend to Use	110 (37%)	270 (64%)	30 (15%)	24 (20%)	80 (80%)	246 (82%)
Total	300 (100%)	420 (100%)	200 (100%)	120 (100%)	100 (100%)	300 (100%)
Statistically Significant χ^2	Yes		No		No	
Implied Relationship	Ad Recall $\longrightarrow$ Intend to Use		Previous Usage $\longrightarrow$ Intent to Use Previous Usage $\longrightarrow$ Ad Recall			

Figure 18-13:
A cross-tabulation table showing the introduction of a third variable.

To answer this question, 720 people were surveyed. The leftmost of the three cross-tabulation tables in Figure 18-13 relates their intentions to use mass transit to their ad recall. The table and χ^2 test strongly suggest a positive relationship. Of the 300 people who recall seeing the ad, 63 percent indicated that they intend to use mass transit in the next month; of the 420 people who didn't recall the ad, only 36 percent indicated that they intend to use mass transit in the next month.

The percentages for the first column are the reverse of the second column. The χ^2 value is 25; with 1 degree of freedom, that value is statistically significant at the 0.001 level. At first blush, the marketing manager would be overjoyed that the ad campaign stimulated demand so dramatically.

However, the second and third cross-tabulations in Figure 18-13 suggest a different interpretation. The original table has been divided into two sub-tables: current users of mass transit and current nonusers of mass transit. Of the 720 people sampled, 320 are current users and 400 are nonusers. Again, the numbers in parentheses are the counts. The cell "recall the ad/intend to use" for transit contains 170 people, and the cell "recall the ad/intend to use" for nonusers contains 20 people, which sums to 190 people. The sub-tables are equivalent in the sense that the "matching cell numbers" (in other words, the matching pairs of counts in each of the four pairs of cells) sum to the numbers in the original table.

By dividing the sample further and considering a third variable, the picture changes. The table in the center, for users, shows that roughly 80 percent intend to use mass transit in the next month whether or not they recalled the ad. For nonusers, roughly 20 percent intend to use mass transit whether or not they recalled the ad. The χ^2 value for both these sub-tables isn't significant, which suggests that the ad campaign didn't boost intentions to use among either current users or nonusers. Instead, current use is related to ad recall; people who use mass transit are more likely to recall ads for mass transit. Current users also are more likely to use mass transit in the future, so user status is related to ad recall and user status also is related to future use intentions. Thus, in this case the ad campaign is unrelated to intended usage. Instead, current user status relates positively to both variables; it's the third variable that's causing the apparent relationship between the first two variables.

By assessing only two variables at a time — "intentions to use" and "ad recall" — the marketing manager can erroneously conclude that the ad campaign stimulated intentions to use and may be encouraged to spend more on advertising. Adding current user status to the analysis shows that advertising isn't creating additional intentions to use; hence, the money spent on it is wasted. Both the manager and the public would be better off if fares were lowered, which would encourage more people to ride mass transit.

Avoiding banner tables

A *banner table* is a batch of cross-tabulation tables smashed together. You can see an example of one in Figure 18-14. Although banners make more efficient use of paper and are easier to read, we don't recommend them for these two reasons:

✔ **Most banner software doesn't include statistical tests of significance like the χ^2 test.** As a result, percentages and totals may seem to reflect meaningful differences that don't exist. Statistical tests are important because they show you whether a statistically significant relationship exists between the variables in question; if so, you can eyeball the cross-tabulation to discern the nature of that relationship.

✔ **They lack important information.** Banners include totals, counts for individual responses, and column percentages, but they don't include row percentages and the total percentages, which provide useful information about the nature of a relationship between variables.

Notebook PCs Owned by Household

| | Total | ---- Sex ---- | | ------- Age ------- | | | ------- Income ------- | | |
		Male	Female	<30	30-45	45+	<$30k	$30k-$50k	$50k+
0	64	30	30	42	4	18	20	4	16
	24.2	22.4	26.8	30.9	7.4	25.7	33.3	13.3	15.4
1	106	56	46	52	28	24	22	10	52
	40.2	41.8	41.1	38.2	51.9	34.3	36.7	33.3	50.0
2 or more	80	42	36	40	16	22	16	12	28
	30.3	31.3	32.1	29.4	29.6	31.4	26.7	40.0	26.9
No Answer	14	6	--	2	6	6	2	4	4
	5.3	4.5	--	1.5	11.1	8.6	3.3	13.3	7.6
Total	264	134	112	136	54	70	60	30	104
	100.0	100.0	100.0	100.0	100.0	100.0	100.0	100.0	100.0

Figure 18-14: A banner table.

Becoming Familiar with Correlation

In this section, we explore correlation, which is a statistical measurement of the relationship between two variables. Such relationships are especially important in marketing when one variable can be used to predict the value of another variable.

Understanding the difference between correlation and causation

Many folks often mistake correlation (how things relate to each other) with causation (one thing has to happen first for a second thing to happen next). The confusion between these two terms is due to the common usage of the terms "correlation" or "correlated." (See Chapter 16 for more about causation.)

The following examples illustrate how correlation doesn't mean causation:

✔ The rooster crowing at dawn doesn't mean the rooster causes the sun to rise.

✔ Teachers' salaries and liquor consumption tend to correlate positively. The increase in liquor consumption associated with an increase in salaries doesn't mean that reducing teachers' salaries will reduce their liquor consumption; rather, there's a third variable — the economy — that co-varies and influences these two variables. When the economy is booming, teachers' salaries rise, so they have more disposable income and can better afford to buy liquor. It's not that raising teachers' salaries causes increased liquor consumption; instead, both teachers' salaries and liquor consumption correlate positively with the state of the economy. (Check out the earlier section "Exploring the effect of moderator variables" for more on how third variables affect data results.)

Associating between measures with the correlation coefficient (r_{xy})

The *correlation coefficient* (r_{xy}) is a statistical measure of the covariation, or association between two measures that are typically interval or ratio-scaled. (See the earlier section "Measuring central tendency" for definitions of these terms.) It indicates two things: How strongly two variables are related and direction of that relationship.

A question that you can answer using r_{xy} is "Are my sales associated with my advertising expenditures?" To answer that question "yes," you'd need to show that the correlation coefficient differs significantly from zero, which occurs when two variables are statistically related either positively or negatively.

One advantage of r_{xy} is that it's standardized; its value ranges from +1 to –1. If r_{xy} is +1, a perfect positive linear relationship exists; if it's –1, a perfect negative linear relationship exists. If r_{xy} equals 0, x and y are unrelated linearly. The strength of a linear relationship between two variables is reflected by the proximity of r_{xy} to ±1.

The eight correlation patterns in Figure 18-15 depict the linear nature of correlations. Correlation can indicate whether two variables are related linearly; however, it can't detect nonlinear relationships. These patterns illustrate the range of possible correlation patterns; they depict the strength of the relationship between two (non-nominal) variables. The more the points — for each point, which represents a single respondent, the x coordinate reflects the value on one variable and the y coordinate reflects the value on the other variable — seem to follow a straight line, the closer r_{xy} is to either +1 or –1. The positive or negative slope of the line indicates whether the relationship between the two variables is positive (r_{xy} = +1) or negative (r_{xy} = –1).

The r_{xy} in Graph 1 is +1; x and y are linearly related in a positive way. Graph 2 shows that x and y are linearly related, but in a negative way. Graph 3 shows points that are aligned but not perfectly; the r_{xy} is close to, but not at +1. For Graph 3, x's value is a good predictor of y's value. In contrast, for both Graphs 1 and 2, x's value is a *perfect* predictor of y's value. The r_{xy} in Graph 4 is close to –1, with x as a good but not perfect predictor of y. A straight line drawn through the points in Graph 4 would provide a good summary of the relationship between x and y. Graph 5 shows a positive but close-to-zero correlation between x and y. Graph 6 shows a close-to-zero negative correlation between x and y.

Linearity comes into play with Graphs 7 and 8. For Graph 7, knowing x's value doesn't help to predict y's value; as a result, x and y are uncorrelated (r_{xy} = 0). The same is true of Graph 8 (r_{xy} = 0). However, you may recall from your algebra class that Graph 8 depicts a parabolic function; x's value perfectly predicts y's value. In this case, a strong relationship exists between x and y, but the r_{xy} is zero.

The *coefficient of determination* (R^2) is r_{xy} multiplied by itself. As r_{xy} ranges from –1 to +1, R^2 ranges from 0 to 1 because multiplying a negative number by a negative number produces a positive number. R^2 is useful in data analysis because it indicates the percent of the variation in one variable explained statistically by variation in another variable.

Setting up a correlation matrix

Correlation examines the relationship of a single variable to another single variable. You may want to study a set of those relationships. For example, you may want to study how Variable 1 relates to Variable 2; how Variable 1 relates to Variable 3; how Variable 2 relates to Variable 3; and so on. A *correlation matrix* provides an efficient summary of those correlations. This matrix also is important because it can be used as a first step in multivariate statistical analyses (like exploratory factor analysis, which we discuss in Chapter 21).

Figure 18-16 shows a correlation matrix. This matrix shows that Variable 1 correlates perfectly with itself, as do Variables 2 and 3; hence, the 1s on the upper-left-to-lower-right diagonal. (When something correlates perfectly with something else, the correlation between the two things is 1.0.) The off-diagonal elements indicate the degree that each variable correlates with every other variable. This matrix is symmetric in the sense that the correlation between Variable 1 and Variable 3 is identical to the correlation between Variable 3 and Variable 1.

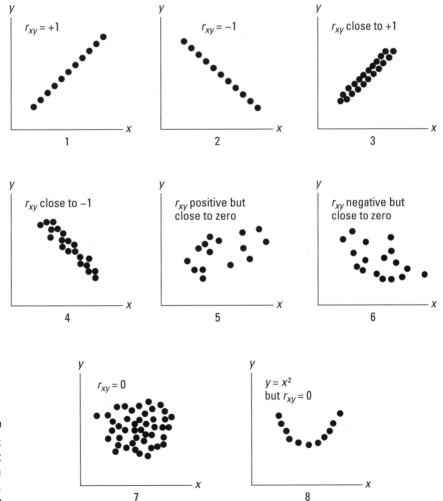

Figure 18-15:
The eight correlation patterns.

	Measure #1	Measure #2	Measure #3	Measure #4
Measure #1	1.00	0.39	0.54	–0.13
Measure #2	0.39	1.00	0.22	–0.35
Measure #3	0.54	0.22	1.00	–0.04
Measure #4	–0.13	–0.35	–0.04	1.00

Figure 18-16:
A correlation matrix.

It's possible to use nonparametric statistics (a special kind of statistics) to compute correlations between ordinal-scaled measures (see the section "Measuring central tendencies"). Although not often used in marketing research, such statistics are available in most statistical packages like SPSS. If you compute correlations, be certain that you first check whether your data are metric (interval or ratio-scaled) or ordinal. Otherwise, you'll be applying the wrong statistical method.

Chapter 19

Creating Effective Research Reports

. . . .

In This Chapter

▶ Determining the main objectives of a research report

▶ Developing an effective research report

▶ Becoming familiar with the writing process

▶ Presenting your research to an audience

▶ Using visuals to add value to your report

. . . .

According to Ralph Waldo Emerson, "It is a luxury to be understood." So, effectively communicating research results is an essential component of the research process. Clear, concise, and cogent reports enable informed decision-making. For people to benefit fully from your research efforts, they must be able to understand your report or presentation.

In this chapter, we discuss the goals and components of a research report. Obviously, if your research report is deficient, you won't obtain your research project goals. Although a thorough and well-written research report is important, failure to present your study effectively will undermine your efforts; therefore, we also discuss strategies for preparing your research presentation.

Understanding the Objectives of a Research Report

Just as a golfer needs a platform (golf course) to display his skills, marketing researchers need a platform (report) to communicate their findings (and display their research skills!). In this sense, your report is the only permanent medium for conveying all research-related processes, findings, and implications.

A well-designed and executed study will be for naught if your written report lacks necessary detail or is incoherent. Writing an effective research report requires an understanding of its objectives. Without a sound understanding of what a research report should achieve, it's impossible to write an effective one. Here are five main objectives:

- **Explain why the research was conducted.** Unless you explain the need for research, people won't take the time to read your report. In other words, you must clearly communicate the value of your research.

- **State the specific research objectives.** In addition to your underlying problem, you must indicate the specific research objectives and questions that the research addressed. These objectives and questions are essential because they reinforce the reasons you conducted the research. As a result, you need to alert the reader to those reasons.

- **Explain how the research was conducted.** For example, specify the methodology you used and the population you queried. Without such details, readers won't be able to assess your report's credibility.

- **Present the research findings.** Without findings, your research has been strictly a learning exercise and a waste of time and money.

- **Provide both conclusions and recommendations.** Conclusions are helpful because they provide readers a venue that efficiently summarizes your research. Recommendations are essential because they suggest the best course of action for your business.

Your recommendations may not be as definitive if the research you conducted was meant to provide information needed to make a more informed decision. In that case, the decision-makers — for example, lenders, potential investors, and business partners — will examine the conclusions and formulate their own recommendations.

Crafting Your Research Report

A comprehensive marketing research report consists of the following components:

- Prefatory parts
- Main body
- Appendixes

We cover each of these components in more detail in the following sections.

Although you should include all these components in formal research reports, some — such as certain prefatory parts — may be omitted when a less formal report will suffice.

The DVD includes six examples of marketing research reports written by the student groups we mention in Chapter 5. Although none of these reports is perfect, they generally are well-done and can give you realistic expectations about the quality of report you should write or receive from lower-cost research suppliers.

Introducing your research with the prefatory parts

The *prefatory parts* of a research report include a title page, a letter of transmittal, a letter of authorization, a table of contents, and an executive summary (which includes goals, findings, and recommendations). Here's a description of each part:

- ✔ The *title page* indicates the title of the report, for and by whom the report was prepared, and the date of report submission. The title should be brief (roughly ten words or less) and suggest the research project's objectives. For confidential reports, the title page may indicate the recipients.

- ✔ A *letter of transmittal* delivers your report to the recipients. You should exclude details about the research findings, but a broad overview is acceptable. This letter can be omitted in less formal reports.

- ✔ A *letter of authorization* is addressed to the researcher (if not you) and discusses issues such as project approval, parties responsible for the report, and resources used to support the research. In many cases, authorization can be mentioned in the letter of transmittal.

- ✔ The *table of contents* lists sections of the report (for example, methodology, findings, and recommendations) as well as figures, tables, survey instruments, interview transcriptions, and so on.

- ✔ An *executive summary* indicates why the research was conducted, what was discovered, what the findings mean, and the actions suggested by those findings. This roughly one page of text must be persuasive because it will be read by most relevant parties (unlike the entire report). It should be self-contained; if detached from the report, the executive summary should present the research effectively.

Using the main body to explain your research

The main body includes the introduction, a thorough discussion of the methodology, the results, the limitations, the conclusions, and the recommendations. The following list details each of these:

✔ The *introduction* provides an overview of the project, including relevant background information, the project value, and an explanation of the research problem and questions. Its extensiveness depends on audience needs. Both excessive and insufficient introductions will prove ineffective.

✔ The *methodology* section includes four components:

- **Research design:** Describes the type of study (exploratory, descriptive, or causal), the data sources (primary or secondary), and the means of data collection (survey, observations, or experiment). For survey-based studies, the questionnaire is included in an appendix.

- **Sample design:** Describes the target population, sampling frame, sample unit selection, sample size, and response rate. (See Chapters 11 and 12 about sample design.) If extensive calculations are required to make design decisions, they can be included in an appendix.

- **Data collection and fieldwork:** Describes the number and type of fieldworkers, their training and supervision, and the method for validating their work (see Chapter 17).

- **Analysis:** Offers a general outline of the statistical methods. This section shouldn't overlap with information provided in the results section (see Chapters 18 and 21 as well as the DVD).

If decision makers aren't convinced that the appropriate methodology was used, they'll discount the findings heavily; hence the importance of a sound methodology and its corresponding discussion.

✔ The *results* section is the "guts" of a report; this detailed discussion includes the findings and answers to the questions posed at the onset of the research. You can use summary tables, figures, and charts to clarify the discussion. However, if these visuals are highly detailed, you should move them to an appendix. (The later section "Charts and Graphs: Depicting Your Data" provides more information on incorporating such content into your report.)

✔ Despite your best efforts, no research project is perfect. Research *limitations* — such as a small sample size, data-collection efforts that mistakenly lead to biased responses, poor design of survey questions, and the like — sometimes are unavoidable. Limitations may arise due to the types of errors we discuss in Chapter 7. The intent of this discussion isn't to discount the findings of your research. Instead, you use this section to offer a pragmatic perspective for interpreting the results.

✔ The *conclusions and recommendations* section summarizes the study and offers insight as to how decision-makers can apply the findings. In essence, these report components comprise informed opinions about appropriate responses to the findings.

Presenting supplemental information in appendixes

Appendixes prove handy when a report includes material that's highly technical, complex, or detailed. For example, appendix materials can include the following:

- ✔ Data-collection forms, such as surveys and interview questions
- ✔ Detailed or unique calculations
- ✔ Visuals, such as tables, graphs, and figures
- ✔ Primary materials, such as interview transcripts
- ✔ Secondary materials, such as journal articles
- ✔ A bibliography, if appropriate

It's not rare for appendixes to comprise more than 50 percent of a report. However, don't let the appendixes overwhelm the body of your report. After all, readers will prefer to read what you've written more than a bibliography or a complex statistical formula!

Exploring the Writing Process

Just as golfers who want to putt well must practice for many hours, good writing comes from extensive practice. There's no substitute for the building, demolishing, and remodeling of your own paragraphs. In addition to the sample reports we include on the DVD, you should visit the following Web sites to help hone your report-writing skills.

- ✔ **StatPac:** www.statpac.com/research-papers/research-proposal.htm
- ✔ **All About Market Research:** www.allaboutmarketresearch.com/articles/art080.htm
- ✔ **Social Science Research & Instructional Center (SSRIC):** www.ssric.org/node/144

Because a poorly written report will undermine sound research design and execution, it's imperative that your report reflect the care, time, and effort that went into your study design and execution. The writing stages you'll work through include outlining, gathering, and organizing all report-related materials; writing a first draft; and editing (rewriting) the report until it's polished.

A professional research report usually requires multiple rewrites to improve its readability, correct grammatical or spelling errors, assess its appropriateness, and evaluate its content. For example, it's common for us to go through 10 to 15 rewrites before we deem a manuscript ready for journal submission (and weer reel good righters).

Steps to a winning report

Organization and lucidity are essential to writing a winning report. You must organize the report components so that your reader can easily follow your research process. You write, rewrite, and rewrite again to make your report clearer to readers. Having a few trusted colleagues review your report will help you identify any additional problems that need fixing. Be sure to write with passion and excitement to keep your audience interested.

Here are four steps you should follow to ensure a winning report:

1. **Organize your report components before you begin writing.**

   A research report has many components that contribute meaningfully to its overall value. Prior to writing your report, develop a game plan to organize the components and related discussions. A disorganized report will only confuse readers. (Refer to the earlier section "Crafting Your Research Report" for more information on the necessary components.)

2. **Write a first draft.**

   When writing the first draft, be as thorough as possible. Avoid jargon and long-winded explanations; effective business writing is cogent and terse. Don't become married to discussions or paragraphs at this stage. This draft sets the foundation for the editing process.

3. **Revise your first draft.**

   Think of the revision process as a refinery. Your objective is to distill your first draft into a concise and powerful final version. Although the revision process may be trying at times, focus on the incremental improvement you see in subsequent versions.

4. **Have a set (or two) of fresh eyes review your final report.**

   Although modern word processors (and your own eyes) can catch many errors, don't be shy about asking friends and colleagues to review your work. It may cost you a few dinners out or some future favors, but these are small prices to pay for an improved and polished report.

Do's and don'ts of report writing

In addition to the four steps covered in the previous section, here are some report-writing do's you should keep in mind:

- ✔ **Say what you mean in as few words as possible.** Length doesn't equal quality; long reports can be highly redundant or stuffed with superfluous content. Eliminate needless words to enhance readability. Instead of wordy paragraphs, rely on bullet points, charts, and figures. These visually appealing elements can be more persuasive (and easier on the eyes) than endless pages of prose.

- ✔ **Feed information to clients in sound bites.** When trying to capture the essence of a discussion or point, use sound bites (short and easily remembered tidbits of information), which are more likely to grab a reader's attention than a long paragraph. Sound bites can be presented in quotation form.

- ✔ **Use present tense verbs and active voice.** When developing arguments, making points, and drafting paragraphs, present tense verbs and active voice are more effective than past tense and passive voice. Our Wiley editors certainly believe this recommendation!

Following the preceding do's is important when writing your report, but you also must be careful to avoid these don'ts:

- ✔ **Don't provide insufficient explanation.** You must explain the technical details of your research — even if that information is relegated to an appendix. Although many readers may lack the knowledge needed to understand such detail fully, its absence will constitute a huge red flag to technically-versed readers.

- ✔ **Don't fail to connect with your objectives.** A research report's objective is to provide answers to your initial research questions. A report that sways from its intent by not linking results to objectives lacks focus, credibility, and value.

- ✔ **Don't indiscriminately use quantitative methods.** In other words, don't try to dazzle readers with needless statistical sophistication and jargon. If your research requires quantitative analysis, use the simplest methods that are appropriate. Your authors' consulting experiences suggest that decision-makers prefer simple graphics, frequency tables, and cross-tabulation tables. Anything beyond those visuals and simple t or χ^2 tests (see Chapter 18 and the DVD) are likely to overload and possibly confuse readers.

✔ **Don't provide a sense of false accuracy.** For example, if your data are scaled from 1 to 7, it's nonsensical to report mean scores to 1/10,000th of a unit. If people can respond with only single-digit accuracy, reporting means in more than tenths is false accuracy and gives the impression that the results are more precise than is the case.

✔ **Don't offer single-number research.** Provide *confidence intervals* (or ranges for the likely mean) rather than single-point estimates. Although researchers can calculate mean scores, those scores summarize data from only one study. If the study were to be repeated, the odds of identical mean scores are close to zero. It's more honest to present the range in which the "real' score is likely to fall.

Preparing Your Presentation

The goal of a presentation is to emphasize important findings and offer viewers an opportunity to ask questions about your research. Presentations can be made either in-person or through video conferencing, and tend to last 20 to 30 minutes (excluding the question-and-answer period). Common presentation tools include Microsoft PowerPoint-type software or flip charts.

Be prepared to answer likely questions and to defend your research. As legendary UCLA basketball coach John Wooden says, "Failing to prepare is preparing to fail."

Although you should anticipate audience needs and preferences, you also should try to match your presentation to your preferred presentation style. For example, if you're naturally enthusiastic and gregarious, encourage audience interaction. Alternatively, if repeated interruptions throw you off your game, ask audience members to hold their questions until you've completed your presentation. In addition, graphic and visual aids (which we discuss later) can increase your presentation's effectiveness.

Just as a grocery list helps expedite shopping for household necessities, you also should write a presentation checklist. Besides focusing on many mundane (but important) things — such as not forgetting the USB drive with your PowerPoint file, shining your shoes, and remembering the time and location of your presentation — you also should include the following materials, which will support an effective presentation that enhances your credibility:

✔ **A presentation outline:** For presentation rehearsal, you can review this outline, which must include relevant points from the main body and appendix of your report. Attendees who receive a copy of this outline can quickly determine the gist of your overall presentation, which may help them better understand your research story.

✔ **Visuals:** In addition to showing visuals during your presentation, you may print and distribute copies of the most important ones to attendees.

You can refer attendees to such handouts during relevant discussion. We cover visuals in more detail in the following section.

- ✔ **An executive summary:** This is the one document that live-presentation attendees would like to read before and during your presentation. See the six sample research reports on the DVD for examples of executive summaries. Bring enough copies for everyone in attendance and print them on professional stock paper.

- ✔ **Copies of the final report:** Just in case, you should bring several copies of your report because some attendees may want a copy (see "Crafting Your Research Report" earlier in this chapter). In place of a hard copy, you may ask whether those in attendance would like a copy sent electronically.

Charts and Graphs: Depicting Your Data

Charts and graphs are powerful tools for communicating your research results. If designed properly, such pictorials are easy to comprehend and can summarize extensive information efficiently.

In addition to the survey-building Web sites we mention in Chapter 10, Web sites like www.corda.com, www.smartdraw.com, and www.origramy.com can help you build appropriate charts and graphs. Also, the sample research reports on the DVD include examples of charts and graphs. Details on how to build such visuals are provided in the Microsoft Excel template.

In the following sections, we include examples of the most common types of charts and graphs used in research reports. All charts and graphs should include a number (for easy reference), a descriptive title, explanatory legends (which labels your axes and offers a key to values), and a list of secondary sources used for development.

Cutting your info into slices: Pie charts

Pie charts are useful for depicting, sometimes in colorful fashion, what percent of all responses is comprised by each response category. For example, pie charts can be used to depict the ethnic diversity, in percentages, of your sample. See Figures 19-1 and 19-2 for pie chart examples.

If all data are accounted for, including missing data, your pie chart percentages should total 100 percent. If your slice percentages sum to more or less than that, your audience will assume you're a math idiot and will discount all your subsequent empirical claims.

Research Question: Are golfers aware of our new driver and putter?

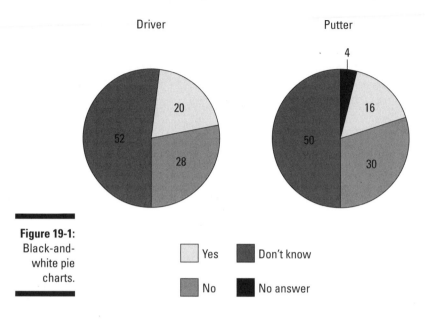

Figure 19-1:
Black-and-white pie charts.

Yes Don't know

No No answer

Times per week that members of a
country club typically play golf

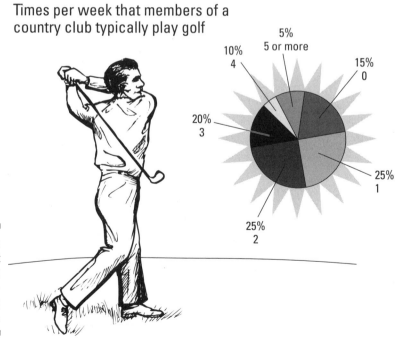

Figure 19-2:
A pie chart
with
attention-
getting
graphics.

Showing changes in variables with bar charts

Bar charts show changes in a dependent variable (plotted on the vertical axis) at specific intervals (for example, time and percent) of the independent variable (plotted on the horizontal axis). See Chapter 14 for a description of independent and dependent variables. When you want to depict several dependent variables at once, you can use either clustered column charts (as in Figure 19-3) or stacked bar charts (as in Figure 19-4).

In most cases you want to use clustered column charts, because they're easier to read. Avoid the 3-D effects used in Figure 19-4 because the slight improvement in aesthetics is outweighed by the greater likelihood of misreading.

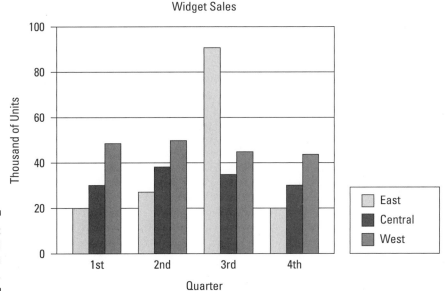

Figure 19-3: A clustered column chart.

Comparing relationships over time: Multi-line graphs

Multi-line graphs, like the one shown in Figure 19-5, are used to indicate relationships between multiple dependent variables (in this example, sales by region) and time (first through fourth quarter).

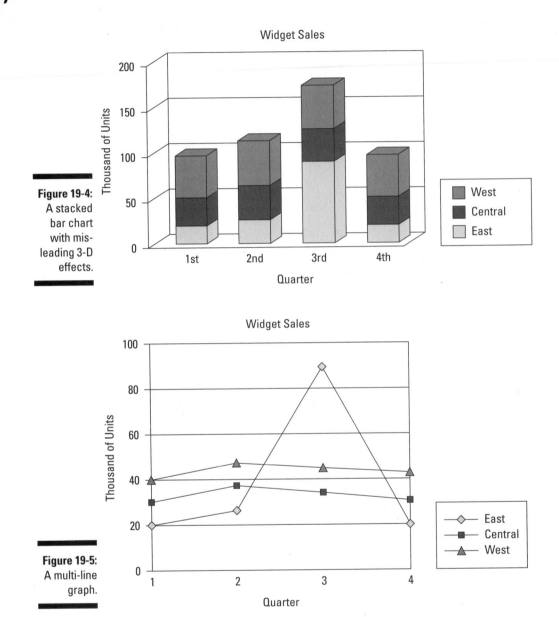

Figure 19-4:
A stacked bar chart with misleading 3-D effects.

Figure 19-5:
A multi-line graph.

Plotting many data points with scatterplots

You can use *scatterplots,* like the one shown in Figure 19-6, when many data points must be shown. In such cases, a series of bar charts won't work, because they can show only so many data points meaningfully; imagine a bar chart with 150 bars! Scatterplots show the joint values of people or objects on two measures.

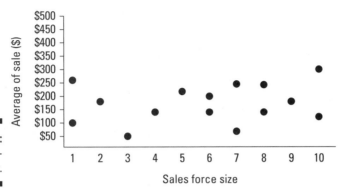

Figure 19-6:
A scatter-plot.

Applying area graphs when bar charts aren't enough

An *area graph* is a continuous version of a bar chart that's often used to depict trends in the same measure; for example, average household income in Indianapolis from 1980 to 2010. If data aren't discrete — and measures are continuous — an area graph, like the one depicted in Figure 19-7, is useful because it makes trends more obvious.

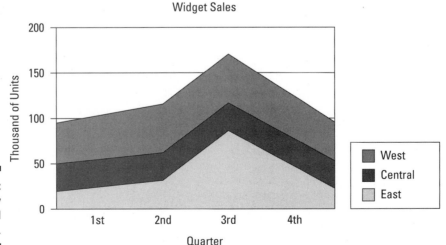

Figure 19-7:
A poorly constructed area graph.

You must follow some rules of thumb about which items are stacked first versus last or bottom versus top in area graphs. To minimize confusion, you should place the least-varying items at the bottom and the most-varying items at the top. Otherwise, you create the illusion that all items above the highly varying one also vary highly, when in fact they're relatively stable. Figure 19-7 shows the problem of placing the most varying item at the bottom.

Depicting data with box and whisker plots

Box and whisker plots are an effective way to depict data generated by descriptive statistical analysis (see Figure 19-8). They can be used to indicate the mean, median, inter-quartile range, and standard deviations for a particular measure and are easy to interpret.

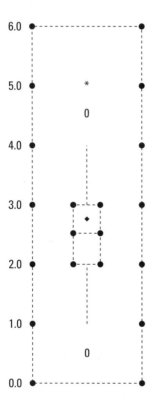

Figure 19-8: A box and whisker plot.

Mean	2.75
Median	2.50
75th percentile	3.00
25th percentile	2.00
Standard deviation	0.50

Part V
The Part of Tens

The 5th Wave   By Rich Tennant

In this part . . .

This quick (but important) part is a tradition in *For Dummies* books. In Chapter 20, we offer ten essential tips for business operators. In Chapter 21, we list ten statistical methods that a marketing research supplier may use to analyze data. Also included in this part is an appendix that covers the specifics of the DVD that accompanies this book.

Chapter 20

Ten Useful Research Tips for Business Operators

Tips, in general, are meant to benefit listening ears or attentive eyes. Here we are ready to benefit you. The tips we offer in this chapter are meant to improve your efficiency as a researcher, to enhance the value of your research program, and to reinforce the wisdom of inviting your constituents into your research process.

Look to University Help First

Before soliciting independent marketing research firms, turn to the marketing faculty and students at your local university. As we discuss in Chapter 5, these academics often can fulfill your research needs satisfactorily and at a greatly reduced price relative to commercial suppliers. Because they're keen to explore business phenomena, provide community service, and earn a few extra dollars, their research expertise often is available to you (unless they have a book or project deadline to meet).

In particular, marketing instructors can help you formulate your research problem and questions, develop a data collection strategy, design your questionnaire, and guide your data analysis and interpretation. They also can introduce you to practitioner-friendly marketing and business journals (see Chapter 3), which can inform your study design. Finally, instructors can assign enthusiastic and well-trained students who'll work with you.

For efficiency, we recommend that you contact the marketing department chairperson when trying to solicit research help, as opposed to contacting marketing faculty directly. Pursuing the latter may land your e-mail in more than one spam folder. The chairperson will evaluate your situation and pass your request to the appropriate faculty member.

Take a Statistics or Research Class

Take an introductory statistics or marketing research course at your local community college or university to heighten your skills. Even though budgets are tight and school administrators lust after tuition dollars, some professors may allow you to sit in free of charge if they have empty seats in their classrooms.

A needless fear of statistics can inhibit your ability to understand and thoroughly examine your data. Although Chapter 18 presents useful basics, teasing meaning out of respondent data is as much art as it is science. A complete statistics or marketing research course can develop your data analysis knowledge and intuitions. After you gain confidence in your data analysis skills, you can rely on yourself more to conduct a study from start to finish; thus, you can become the research assistance you seek (and spend less money hiring help to boot).

View Research as an Ongoing Process

Your business success depends on having the proper information to make informed decisions. Conducting one well-designed study can improve your odds of success in the short run, but business environments are dynamic and ever-changing. The wisdom of Satchel Paige notwithstanding ("Don't look back. Something might be gaining on you."), you continually need new information — especially about rapidly changing consumers and their preferences — to make new decisions.

Important environmental changes can occur gradually or suddenly. As stock analysts contend: "The trend is your friend" when trying to anticipate ongoing or cyclical change. To identify trends in your customers' attitudes, preferences, and behaviors, you need to monitor them regularly. Ongoing analysis of primary and secondary data can reveal new competitive threats. A thorough understanding of consumers and competitors can help you cope with unexpected changes.

Avoid Research Method Myopia

When trying to answer your research questions, don't limit yourself to one method, such as a survey or a focus group. Because each research method provides unique insight, it's appropriate to use several methods jointly to develop a detailed picture of your business situation.

For example, to understand consumers' perception of your brand, you can design and field a survey with multiple close-ended questions. Although answers to such questions can help to identify basic differences in the brand perceptions of various consumer groups, these answers can't fully capture consumers' attitudes and preferences toward your brand. A more in-depth method, such as in-depth or focus group interviews, can reveal deep-seated beliefs and emotions critical to the success of your brand.

Start Researching Only After You Know What You Want to Know

Before collecting data, ensure that you clearly define and carefully formulate your research questions. These questions are the guiding force behind any research effort. Designing a study around ill-advised questions is at best a waste of time and money. You can formulate these questions without help, but your employees and customers represent a font of wisdom from which you can draw.

Here's an example of why appropriate questions are important: Pretend you own the Fashion 'R Us Boutique, a high-end clothing store meant for middle-aged and older women. You suspect a substantial sales decline during the last six months is due to a newly opened store that offers comparable apparel and accessories at lower prices. In response, you plan to lower prices, but you're uncertain how much to lower them. To answer this question, you design and field a survey, and based on the responses you lower prices accordingly. Nonetheless, your sales continue to plummet. Little do you know that poor customer service and ambience, rather than relatively higher prices, have caused the sales decline. It seems that several new salespeople would text message friends — rather than attend to customers — and switch the store music to contemporary hip-hop whenever the manager left the sales floor. If you'd considered alternative causes for the sales decline, rather than assumed that noncompetitive pricing was the sole cause, you may have discovered the true solution.

Don't Ignore Opportunity Costs

Opportunity costs are profits or advantages foregone due to missed opportunities. Avoiding and overcoming internal and external business-related threats aren't the only goals of research; missed opportunities can be as damaging — but more insidious — than realized threats. Just as a retailer may earn less by forgoing a satellite store across town or not adding a product line, you can lose sales by failing to conduct a timely study that reveals an important customer need or preference.

Perhaps, for example, your store's sales are holding steady despite an economic downturn. Meanwhile, several competitors have shuttered their operations. You believe all is well. However, you could have boosted sales markedly during this time had you updated your store's product assortment, layout, and ambience. By failing to research employees' and customers' attitudes and preferences about these store characteristics, you missed a golden opportunity to firmly establish your market dominance and reduce (or at least delay) future threats to profitability.

Pretest Everything

Like a boy who can't wait to tear into his presents on Christmas morning, you'll want to field your study as soon as you finish designing it. Resist that temptation, and pretest your methodology and questionnaire prior to actual data collection.

For example, pretesting your questionnaire can be invaluable (see Chapter 10). Despite what you may think, the process isn't cumbersome; you simply can ask a few employees and customers to comment on questionnaire layout, understandability, and completion time. Based on their feedback, you can design a greatly improved questionnaire.

Pretesting also can help you recognize the best approach for data collection. For example, you may need research results to make a decision within the next two weeks. Although a telephone interview seems ideal, a pretest may reveal that in-house interviewing — all you can afford — can't produce an adequate set of responses in less than one month. To overcome this problem, you can switch to a browser-based survey (as we discuss in Chapter 10), with its much faster response time.

Pretests may prove useful when conducting experiments as well (as we discuss in Chapter 16). Suppose you need to choose one of two ads to run in a local magazine. The only difference between the ads is that your brand name appears at the bottom of one but at the top of the other. Prior to testing the ads on several hundred people, a pretest may reveal that the background color used in both ads makes seeing the brand name difficult, thus making brand name location irrelevant. By altering the background color in the test ads, your research results would go from meaningless to meaningful.

Study Your Customers Thoroughly

It's insufficient to ask customers about their attitudes and household characteristics. Customers aren't robots who calculate the value of each alternative before making a purchase. Like all human activity, purchase decisions are an artifact of interacting beliefs, opinions, preferences, recognized and unrecognized emotions, behavioral tendencies, and socio-demographics.

To fully understand your customers — which is critical to anticipating their responses to planned changes in your business — you must study their rational (cognitive) and irrational (emotional) thoughts. For example, a diner may patronize a restaurant because the food is healthful and tasty (cognitive) and he enjoys harmless flirting with a certain server (emotional).

Assuming your customers buy from you based strictly on rational grounds (such as the acceptability of selling price and merchandise assortment) and ignoring emotional drivers (such as happiness with their treatment by service providers) may lead to ineffective marketing strategies. (See Chapters 14 and 15 for qualitative research approaches to studying customers.)

Make Incentives a Part of Your Research

To motivate respondents about your research and thus secure their thoughtful participation, you must compensate them in a meaningful way; after all, their time isn't free! Although marketing research excites us (perhaps we live dull lives), we know this isn't true for most people. Whether you offer a monetary token of appreciation or a gift certificate, reciprocity — and higher quality data — dictates that you offer *something* in return. Consider respondent reward a form of enlightened self interest.

Independent of other incentives, convincing potential respondents that your research is important likely will increase their compliance. (See Chapter 7 for the use of incentives to minimize survey error.)

Share Research Results with Employees

Upon obtaining and understanding your research results, strategy changes may follow. Making changes without sharing your reasons with employees is a recipe for failure, however; they may believe the changes are impulsive rather than carefully considered and substantiated by trustworthy research results. Communicating research findings with employees can help them recognize the value of research, which may encourage them to solicit and attend to customer feedback.

You personally can't interact with every customer who enters your facility. So, your employees represent a priceless conduit for relaying the customer's voice to you. Your employees are as critical as your customers to your company's success. Employees who believe that they're valuable contributors to your research efforts are more likely to take customer surveys seriously.

Chapter 21

Ten Statistical Methods that You (or Your Research Consultant) May Use

In This Chapter

▶ Examining compiled data using difference and correlation tests

▶ Introducing advanced statistical techniques

Although the data analysis approaches discussed in Chapter 18 (and included on the DVD) often will be sufficient for answering your research questions, some research problems may require more sophisticated methods. If you plan to conduct or purchase marketing research regularly, consider enrolling in (or at least auditing) a marketing research or statistics class at your local university. (See Chapter 20 for more on the benefits of enrolling in a college class.)

In the interim, we've selected ten data analysis methods that you or a research consultant may use to analyze your data. For each method, we provide a basic description. The information provided in this chapter is meant to increase your knowledge of statistical methods that are available to answer your research questions. Such knowledge is sure to come in handy throughout your ongoing research efforts. The topics are loosely organized by the number of variables they handle; the further into the chapter you go, the more variables the method can handle. Please note, though, that each method comes with drawbacks, so be certain to research a method carefully before you decide to use it.

We intend for this chapter to be directed more at current consumers rather than future doers of marketing research. We chose methods based on their popularity, value, and ability to accomplish your likely research goals. If you want to know more about statistical methods, check out *Statistics For Dummies* by Deborah Rumsey (Wiley).

The DVD includes Excel-related output for independent samples t-tests, paired samples t-tests, ANOVA, and multiple regression analysis.

Independent Samples T-Test

You use an *independent samples t-test* to examine mean differences between two exclusive or independent groups on a ratio-scaled (measure that has a natural zero point, like selling price) or interval-scaled (measure that has intervals of comparable length but an arbitrary zero point, like attitudes) measure. For example, if you want to determine whether males or females have stronger intentions to buy your product — based on a survey in which you measured purchase intentions with a Likert-type scale (like the ones in Chapter 9) — you'd run an independent samples t-test.

The following are situations in which you may use an independent samples t-test:

- To determine whether current customers' and noncustomers' beliefs about your brand differ
- To determine whether higher-income or lower-income consumers are more loyal to your brand
- To determine whether people with active or inactive lifestyles view your ads more favorably

Paired Samples T-Test

You use a *paired samples t-test* to compare the means of nonindependent or nonexclusive samples; for instance, you may want to determine whether males and females differ in their pre-purchase versus post-purchase beliefs about your brand. In essence, you use this statistical test to compare multiple answers to the same questions by two groups of respondents.

Here's how you may use a paired samples t-test:

- To determine whether respondents differ in their attitudes toward print and television ads
- To determine whether Caucasians or Hispanics respond more favorably to banner or pop-up ads
- To determine whether younger or older customers are more likely to dine in or order takeout from your restaurant

One-Way Analysis of Variance (ANOVA)

You use *one-way analysis of variance* (ANOVA) to examine the mean differences in how respondents answer an interval or ratio-scaled question (dependent variable). For ANOVA, respondents must be part of a demographic that has three or more independent groups, such as ethnicity (independent variable). This technique is referred to as a *one-way* analysis because it uses only one independent variable. Chapter 18 provides more information on this method.

Here's how you can use ANOVA:

- ✔ To determine how customers' brand perceptions vary by service quality (specified as high, average, and low)
- ✔ To determine how customer loyalty varies by selling price (specified as expensive, reasonable, and cheap)
- ✔ To determine whether marital status influences buying intentions
- ✔ To determine whether return policies (measured by easy, typical, and difficult) influence customers' beliefs about your store

Linear Multiple Regression (LMR)

You use *linear multiple regression* (LMR) to explain variance in a dependent variable with multiple independent variables (see Chapter 18). With LMR, the dependent variable is interval- or ratio-scaled, and the independent variables can be of any scale type (but you must code nominal and ordinal data in a special way). Although academic researchers often use LMR to "explain" the variability in a measure over time — in other words, to test models that deduce "how the world works" — you'd only use LMR to generate important forecasts (for example, sales next quarter or customers' purchase intentions).

Different predictors anticipate different aspects of the "something" you want to predict. For example, future sales of your product will depend on consumers' disposable incomes, your marketing expenditures, competitors' marketing expenditures, technological changes, and so on. Combining all these predictors, so that the unique sensitivity of each one is captured, should produce a more accurate sales forecast than is possible with any one predictor. Think of LMR as producing the optimal weights for combining multiple predictors.

In addition to predicting a dependent variable, LMR provides an R^2 *value,* which denotes the percent of variance in the dependent variable explained by the independent variables; the more jointly predictive the independent variables, the larger the R^2 value.

Here's how you may use LMR:

- ✔ To identify marketing strategies that influence purchases by targeted customers
- ✔ To identify profit-maximizing marketing strategies
- ✔ To forecast future sales

Conjoint Analysis

Conjoint analysis can determine how people value the different components of a good or service. Toothpastes have different features, such as teeth whitening, breath freshening, and the like. Hotels offer different amenities, such as free continental breakfast, free newspaper, free phone calls, and pay-per-view television programming. To design the profit-maximizing version of a product, you must discover the monetary value that customers assign to each component.

Although you can choose from alternative approaches to conjoint analysis, all the approaches require respondents to indicate their relative preferences for different combinations of product attributes. Those overall preferences are then decomposed into preferences for different levels of each critical attribute; for example, consumers interested in a new automobile value a fuel efficiency of 20 mpg less than a fuel efficiency of 30 mpg. Because the same unit of measurement — a *utility score* — is used to express the relative value of each attribute level, it's possible to compare apples to apples when designing a product.

Here are ways you can use conjoint analysis:

- ✔ To design a new product (provided it shares features with existing products)
- ✔ To fine-tune your marketing strategy, especially as it relates to pricing
- ✔ To identify groups of consumers who have similar product preferences
- ✔ To evaluate new products (For example, if a new brand is introduced, how might it compete against current and likely competitor brands?)

Because of the popularity of conjoint analysis, several software companies have developed easy-to use conjoint analysis software. As a result, it's possible for a researcher without true expertise to sell conjoint analysis studies. Like all marketing research, a valid and reliable study requires a good design and sufficient high-quality respondent data. So beware who you hire.

Exploratory Factor Analysis (EFA)

You use *exploratory factor analysis* (EFA) to identify a reduced number of factors from a larger pool of measures. In other words, EFA allows you to summarize your data efficiently by reducing the number of characteristics you need to analyze. As such, you can use it to assess the reliability and validity of your survey questions. Also, by revealing basic underlying constructs, EFA can help you extract additional meaning from your data.

You can use EFA in the following ways:

✔ To identify defining characteristics for grouping consumers

✔ To determine product evaluation and acceptance based on brand attitudes

✔ To understand media viewing habits of targeted consumers

Multidimensional Scaling (MDS)

Multidimensional scaling (MDS) is a statistical technique for mapping objects (typically products or retailers, like on the map shown in Figure 21-1) based on respondents' perceptions of either specific object attributes or overall object similarity. In essence, MDS can help you identify the characteristics that consumers use to differentiate products or retailers. These visual depictions can help you to identify saturated and unaddressed niche markets, which in turn can inform your product positioning strategies.

Here's how you may use MDS:

✔ To identify the product aspects that consumers use to evaluate different brands

✔ To develop new products that satisfy consumers' currently unmet or unsatisfactorily met preferences

✔ To assess the efficacy of marketing strategy changes to shift consumers' perceptions of your brand in a desired direction

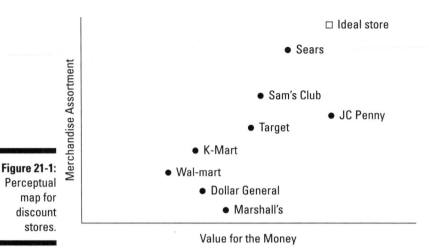

Figure 21-1:
Perceptual
map for
discount
stores.

Cluster Analysis

You use *cluster analysis* to assign people or objects to groups so that intra-group similarity and intergroup dissimilarity are maximized. In essence, your goal is to identify naturally occurring (rather than predefined) group-ings of people or objects based on their characteristics. Web sites like www.mybestsegments.com and www.gis.com target clusters of consumers based on zip code and lifestyle preferences.

Unlike regression techniques, cluster analysis includes no predicted (depen-dent) or predictive (independent) variables (see Chapter 16). Also, cluster analyses rely on computer algorithms rather than statistical formulae, so you can base groupings on nonmetric (for example, sex, race, and religion) and metric (for example, age and household size) data.

You can use cluster analysis in the following ways:

- ✔ To help select test markets (see Chapter 16)
- ✔ To help identify new product opportunities
- ✔ To identify customer groups seeking certain combinations of product benefits (for example, toothpaste that freshens breath and whitens teeth)

Discriminant Analysis

You use *discriminant analysis* to determine which characteristics discriminate between two or more naturally occurring groups; for example, males versus females, or nonusers versus light users versus heavy users of a product. The goal is to assign new people, households, or businesses to a group — to predict group membership — based on characteristics that accurately assign known group members to the proper group.

Credit-scoring schemes rely on discriminant analysis. Lenders, such as banks and credit card companies, collect detailed customer profiles. Over time, some customers never miss payments, and other customers rarely make payments. By weighing and summing the characteristics that differentiate reliable from unreliable payers — creating a model that generates predictive credit scores — creditors can reduce their costs by denying new credit to likely financial deadbeats.

You may use discriminant analysis

- To determine whether targeted customer groups view different media

- To identify the distinguishing characteristics of consumers who often, occasionally, and never respond to online solicitations (for example, e-mail and banner ads)

- To identify lifestyle preferences that differentiate loyal from nonloyal customers

- To identify demographic characteristics that differentiate highly price-sensitive, somewhat price-sensitive, and price-insensitive customers

Logistic Regression

You use *logistic regression* to predict the probability of an event. It models a binary response (dichotomous) outcome variable (for example, will happen or will not happen), which is coded as 1 (probability of success θ) or 0 (probability of failure $1 - \theta$) as predicted by continuous and/or dichotomous independent variables.

Logistic regression is comparable to discriminant analysis (with only two groups) and multiple regression. However, unlike these other methods, logistic regression requires no data distribution assumptions on the predictor variables; that is, the predictors don't have to be normally distributed, linearly related, or have equal variance in each group.

Here's how you may use logistic regression:

- ✔ To forecast which salespeople are likely to quit in the next six months
- ✔ To forecast who will purchase a home in the next 12 months
- ✔ To forecast the regular customers who will switch to a new provider

Large sample sizes are required for logistic regression. Small sample sizes — less than several hundred — will produce unstable and inaccurate models.

Appendix

About the DVD

side from increasing your knowledge and understanding, one goal of *Marketing Research Kit For Dummies* is to improve your ability to conduct sound marketing research, which, like hitting golf balls straight, requires practice. The DVD accompanying this book provides templates, discussions, samples, and analyses that are meant to support key research-related skills. In all, there are 50 documents on the DVD, to aid you with your marketing research. This chapter summarizes the DVD's content.

Many of the sample questionnaires and research reports — as well as the two sets of focus group materials — on this DVD are derived from the types of low-cost research suppliers we recommend in Chapter 5. We intend this content to reflect the quality of the questionnaires, reports, and materials you should expect from such suppliers. In essence, we want to keep your expectations realistic by resisting the urge to boost production values.

System Requirements

To run the files and audio and video components on the DVD, make sure your computer meets the minimum system requirements shown in the following list. If your computer doesn't match up to most of these requirements, you may have problems using the files on the DVD. For the latest and greatest information, please refer to the ReadMe file located at the root of the DVD.

- ✔ A PC running Microsoft Windows or Linux with kernel 2.4 or later
- ✔ A Macintosh running Apple OS X or later
- ✔ An Internet connection
- ✔ A DVD-ROM drive
- ✔ A sound card for PCs; Mac OS computers have built-in sound support
- ✔ A media player, such as Windows Media Player or Real Player

If you need more information on the basics, check out these books published by Wiley Publishing, Inc.: *PCs For Dummies* by Dan Gookin; *Macs For Dummies* by Edward C. Baig; *iMac For Dummies* by Mark L. Chambers; *Windows XP For Dummies* and *Windows Vista For Dummies,* both by Andy Rathbone.

Using the DVD

To install the items from the DVD to your hard drive, follow these steps:

1. **Insert the DVD into your computer's DVD-ROM drive. The license agreement appears.**

   Note to Windows users: The interface won't launch if you have Autorun disabled. If you do have Autorun disabled, choose Start⇨Run. (For Windows Vista, choose Start⇨All Programs⇨Accessories⇨Run.) In the dialog box that appears, type **D:\Start.exe**. (Replace *D* with the proper letter if your DVD drive uses a different letter. If you don't know the letter, see how your DVD drive is listed under My Computer.) Click OK.

   Note to Mac users: The DVD icon will appear on your desktop. Double-click the icon to open the DVD, and then double-click the "Start" icon.

2. **Read through the license agreement, and then click the Accept button if you want to use the DVD.**

   The DVD interface appears. The interface allows you to install the programs and view the content with just a click of a button (or two). After you click Accept the first time, the license agreement window won't appear again.

What You'll Find on the DVD

The following sections are arranged by category and present lists of the related files and software you'll find on the DVD. If you need help with installing the items provided on the DVD, refer to the installation instructions in the preceding section.

For each program listed, we provide the program platform (Windows or Mac) plus the type of software. The programs fall into one of the following categories:

✔ *Shareware programs* are fully functional, free, trial versions of copyrighted programs. If you like particular programs, register with their authors for a nominal fee and receive licenses, enhanced versions, and technical support.

✔ *Freeware programs* are free, copyrighted games, applications, and utilities. You can copy them to as many computers as you like — for free — but they offer no technical support.

➤ *GNU software* is governed by its own license, which is included inside the folder of the GNU software. There are no restrictions on distribution of GNU software. See the GNU license at the root of the DVD for more details.

➤ *Trial, demo,* or *evaluation* versions of software are usually limited either by time or functionality (such as not letting you save a project after you create it).

Cost-and-benefit analysis for marketing research

As part of the research process (discussed in Chapter 1), you must assess the research value relative to its costs. Obviously, the value must exceed its cost; if not, you shouldn't conduct the research. To help you objectively assess the cost/benefit relationship for conducting marketing research, we provide two files on the accompanying DVD. One file summarizes Bayesian analysis in this context and provides two detailed examples. The other file contains a Microsoft Excel spreadsheet to help you perform a Bayesian cost/benefit analysis for marketing research. This template is meant to expedite your analyses by saving you the spreadsheet creation time.

Bayesian analysis discussion and examples: 520680bc01.doc

Excel (2007) template for cost/benefit Bayesian analysis: 520680bc02.xlsx

Marketing research ethics

Ethics are essential for any business-related decision, and marketing research is no exception. (See Chapter 4 for an extensive discussion on marketing research ethics.) To help you use the ethics checklist presented in Chapter 4, we provide several practice vignettes with answers (like in your grade-school textbooks) on the DVD.

Applications of the Hyman, Skipper, and Tansey (1990) ethics checklist: 520680bc03.doc

Sample telephone screener questionnaire

Not every shopper who walks by those clipboard-holding interviewers at the local mall is qualified — due to socio-demographics, previous purchases, current product knowledge, and so forth — to participate in the researcher's survey. Similarly, if you're trying to collect data from a probability sample of respondents, not everyone included on your list of potential respondents (also known as a *sample frame;* see Chapter 11) will be qualified to participate.

To avoid wasting their time — by gaining their cooperation but then ignoring their responses — or inadvertently analyzing inappropriate data, you should screen potential study respondents by telephone before inviting them to participate in your study. The sample telephone screener questionnaire that we include on the DVD was designed for a travel industry study, but it can work for your research as well. It indicates the number and types of questions you can use to qualify participants.

Leisure traveler: 520680bc04.doc

Sample telephone questionnaires

On the DVD, we provide three examples of telephone surveys, which all pertain to the travel industry. Although face-to-face interaction is lacking in telephone surveys, it doesn't limit the type of data you can collect or the type of questions you can ask. As you'll see, the sample questionnaires include a variety of closed- and open-ended questions. For more information about using telephone surveys to collect data, see Chapter 6.

Business traveler: 520680bc05.doc

Leisure traveler: 520680bc06.doc

Travel agent: 520680bc07.doc

Sample self-administered questionnaires

Properly designed questionnaires are essential to collecting accurate survey responses. To help you be successful, the DVD includes nine sample self-administered questionnaires that you can use as a framework for your own questionnaires. The business contexts from which these questionnaires were taken include education, conference registration, human resource management, and the golf industry. To discover more information on developing questionnaires, turn to Chapters 8, 9, and 10, which discuss measuring consumer attitudes, writing good questions, and designing effective questionnaires, respectively.

Assessment of current undergraduate students: 520680bc08.doc

Assessment of past undergraduate students: 520680bc09.doc

Conference registration: 520680bc10.doc

Driving range: 520680bc11.doc

Employee assistance program: 520680bc12.doc

Executive golf course: 520680bc13.doc

Golf equipment and clothing: 520680bc14.doc

Golf pro shop: 520680bc15.doc

Professional Golf Management program: 520680bc16.doc

Focus groups

As we discuss in Chapter 14, focus groups are a rich source of insight into consumers' thoughts and behaviors. To help you to conduct a focus group, we include two sample focus group scripts on the DVD — one for the casino resort industry and one for the restaurant industry.

Additionally, we provide a 65-minute recorded focus group that Jeremy moderated about restaurant customer behavior; an executive summary of that focus group's findings are included as well. We also include an edited, roughly 15-minute presentation of the results from several focus groups as well as the associated Microsoft PowerPoint slides (which are difficult to read from the video).

The 15-minute presentation (and the focus groups it was based on) was conducted by Ms. Sarah Fischbach, a PhD candidate under the supervision of Dr. Colin Payne at New Mexico State University (NMSU). The research focused on ways to increase community awareness and funding of the NMSU Center for the Arts. Specifically, three focus groups with local community members helped to hone a new marketing campaign for the center. Sarah made her presentation of the research findings and recommendations to the center's board of directors.

Sample focus group script (for resort and casino): 520680bc17.doc

Restaurant customers focus group script: 520680bc18.doc

Restaurant customers video recorded session: 520680bc19.mov

Restaurant customers executive summary of findings: 520680bc20.doc

Center for the Arts video presentation: 520680bc21.mov

Center for the Arts presentation PowerPoint slides: 520680bc22.ppt

Data analysis

To expedite your Microsoft Excel data analysis efforts, on the DVD we provide a tip sheet along with multiple video files that illustrate the techniques summarized on that sheet. All these files show a step-by-step approach for creating histograms, scatterplots, pivot (contingency/cross-tabulation) tables, correlation analyses, simple regression analyses, paired samples t-tests, independent samples t-tests, and analyses of variance (ANOVA). We briefly discuss these data analysis techniques in Chapters 18 and 21.

The video file tutorials were created by Dr. Vaidotas Lukosius of Tennessee State University.

Tip sheet for data analysis with Excel (2007): 520680bc23.doc

Data file (Excel 2007) (data collected with Employee Assistance Program questionnaire): 520680bc24.xlsx

Basic set-up: 520680bc25.avi

Descriptive statistics: 520680bc26.avi

Histograms: 520680bc27.avi

Scatterplots: 520680bc28.avi

Correlations: 520680bc29.avi

Contingency (cross-tabulation) analyses: 520680bc30.avi

T-tests: 520680bc31.avi

Analysis of Variance (ANOVA): 520680bc32.avi

Regression: 520680bc33.avi

Sample research reports

To help you write your own research reports — or at least properly set your expectations for reports written by the research suppliers we discuss in Chapter 5 — on the DVD we include six reports derived from reports written by undergraduate students enrolled in a marketing research course. They aren't perfect, but they're reflective of the quality of reports either you or such research providers can write. The reports reflect a wide range of business contexts, including retail, food service, sports, healthcare, and entertainment industries. For a basic overview of report content and report do's and don'ts, refer to Chapter 19.

Attendance at school sporting events: 520680bc34.doc

Cafeteria: 520680bc35.doc

Dog biscuits: 520680bc36.doc

Golf practice facility: 520680bc37.doc

Student health center: 520680bc38.doc

Movie theatre: 520680bc39.doc

Miscellaneous resources

The DVD includes a few more miscellaneous marketing research resources: a sample coding sheet (for conference registration), a face-to-face interview question guide, a research framework (for the hotel industry), and a marketing research proposal letter.

The coding sheet provides an example of how nominal data can be coded (Chapters 17 and 18 provide information on coding data and nominal data, respectively). The interview question guide indicates how data can be collected during an interview (refer to Chapter 14 for interviewing strategies). The research framework suggests the amount of detail needed to address a particular research problem and associated set of research questions. The proposal letter shows how such a letter should be drafted and what it should include.

Coding sheet (for Conference Registration questionnaire): 520680bc40.doc

Consent letter template: 520680bc41.doc

Face-to-face interview question guide: 520680bc42.doc

Research framework for hotel industry: 520680bc43.doc

Research proposal letter: 520680bc44.doc

Chapter figure documents

Chapters 6, 10, and 14 contain figures that display samples from questionnaires, a self-administered electronic survey, a focus group script, and more. To see these documents in their entirety, please refer to the chapter figure files contained on the DVD. The figure files are in Adobe's Portable Document

Format (PDF). You can read and search through the files with the Adobe Acrobat Reader (also included on the DVD).

Figure 6-1 from Chapter 6: Sample telephone questionnaire: 520680bc45.pdf

Figure 6-3 from Chapter 6: Sample self-administered questionnaire: 520680bc46.pdf

Figure 6-4, from Chapter 6: Self-administered electronic survey: 520680bc47.pdf

Figure 10-1, from Chapter 10: Sample telephone screener for leisure travel study: 520680bc48.pdf

Figure 14-2, from Chapter 14: A sample focus group script: 520680bc49.pdf

Figure 14-3, from Chapter 14: A sample focus group write-up: 520680bc50.pdf

Troubleshooting

We tried our best to compile programs that work on most computers with the minimum system requirements. Alas, your computer may differ, and some programs may not work properly for some reason.

The two likeliest problems are that you don't have enough memory (RAM) for the programs you want to use, or you have other programs running that are affecting installation or running of a program. If you get an error message such as Not enough memory or Setup cannot continue, try one or more of the following suggestions and then try using the software again:

- **Turn off any antivirus software running on your computer.** Installation programs sometimes mimic virus activity and may make your computer incorrectly believe that it's being infected by a virus.

- **Close all running programs.** The more programs you have running, the less memory is available to other programs. Installation programs typically update files and programs; so if you keep other programs running, installation may not work properly.

- **Have your local computer store add more RAM to your computer.** This is, admittedly, a drastic and somewhat expensive step. However, adding more memory can really help the speed of your computer and allow more programs to run at the same time.

Customer Care

If you have trouble with the DVD-ROM, please call Wiley Product Technical Support at 800-762-2974. Outside the United States, call 317-572-3993. You also can contact Wiley Product Technical Support at `http://support.wiley.com`. Wiley Publishing will provide technical support only for installation and other general quality control items. For technical support on the applications themselves, consult the program's vendor or author.

To place additional orders or to request information about other Wiley products, please call 877-762-2974.

Index

Wiley Publishing, Inc.
End-User License Agreement

READ THIS. You should carefully read these terms and conditions before opening the DVD packet(s) included with this book "Book". This is a license agreement "Agreement" between you and Wiley Publishing, Inc. "WPI". By opening the accompanying DVD packet(s), you acknowledge that you have read and accept the following terms and conditions. If you do not agree and do not want to be bound by such terms and conditions, promptly return the Book and the unopened DVD packet(s) to the place you obtained them for a full refund.

1. **License Grant.** WPI grants to you (either an individual or entity) a nonexclusive license to use one copy of the enclosed DVD track(s) (collectively, the "DVD") solely for your own personal or business purposes on a single computer (whether a standard computer or a workstation component of a multi-user network). The DVD is in use on a computer when it is loaded into temporary memory (RAM) or installed into permanent memory (hard disk, DVD-ROM, or other storage device). WPI reserves all rights not expressly granted herein.

2. **Ownership.** WPI is the owner of all right, title, and interest, including copyright, in and to the compilation of the DVD recorded on the physical packet included with this Book "DVD Media". Copyright to the individual tracks recorded on the DVD Media is owned by the author or other authorized copyright owner of each program. Ownership of the DVD and all proprietary rights relating thereto remain with WPI and its licensers.

3. **Restrictions on Use and Transfer.**

   (a) You may only (i) make one copy of the DVD for backup or archival purposes, or (ii) transfer the DVD to a single hard disk, provided that you keep the original for backup or archival purposes. You may not (i) rent or lease the DVD, (ii) copy or reproduce the DVD through a LAN or other network system or through any computer subscriber system or bulletin-board system, or (iii) modify, adapt, or create derivative works based on the DVD.

   (b) You may not reverse engineer, decompile, or disassemble the DVD. You may transfer the DVD and user documentation on a permanent basis, provided that the transferee agrees to accept the terms and conditions of this Agreement and you retain no copies. If the DVD is an update or has been updated, any transfer must include the most recent update and all prior versions.

4. **Restrictions on Use of Individual Programs.** You must follow the individual requirements and restrictions detailed for each individual program in the "About the DVD" appendix of this Book or on the DVD Media. These limitations are also contained in the individual license agreements recorded on the DVD Media. These limitations may include a requirement that after using the program for a specified period of time, the user must pay a registration fee or discontinue use. By opening the DVD packet(s), you agree to abide by the licenses and restrictions for these individual programs that are detailed in the "About the DVD" appendix and/or on the DVD Media. None of the material on this DVD Media or listed in this Book may ever be redistributed, in original or modified form, for commercial purposes.

5. **Limited Warranty.**

   (a) WPI warrants that the DVD and DVD Media are free from defects in materials and workmanship under normal use for a period of sixty (60) days from the date of purchase of this Book. If WPI receives notification within the warranty period of defects in materials or workmanship, WPI will replace the defective DVD Media.

   (b) **WPI AND THE AUTHOR(S) OF THE BOOK DISCLAIM ALL OTHER WARRANTIES, EXPRESS OR IMPLIED, INCLUDING WITHOUT LIMITATION IMPLIED WARRANTIES OF MERCHANTABILITY AND FITNESS FOR A PARTICULAR PURPOSE, WITH RESPECT TO THE DVD, THE PROGRAMS, THE SOURCE CODE CONTAINED THEREIN, AND/OR THE TECHNIQUES DESCRIBED IN THIS BOOK. WPI DOES NOT WARRANT THAT THE FUNCTIONS CONTAINED IN THE DVD WILL MEET YOUR REQUIREMENTS OR THAT THE OPERATION OF THE DVD WILL BE ERROR FREE.**

   (c) This limited warranty gives you specific legal rights, and you may have other rights that vary from jurisdiction to jurisdiction.

6. **Remedies.**

   (a) WPI's entire liability and your exclusive remedy for defects in materials and workmanship shall be limited to replacement of the DVD Media, which may be returned to WPI with a copy of your receipt at the following address: DVD Media Fulfillment Department, Attn.: *Marketing Research Kit For Dummies,* Wiley Publishing, Inc., 10475 Crosspoint Blvd., Indianapolis, IN 46256, or call 1-800-762-2974. Please allow four to six weeks for delivery. This Limited Warranty is void if failure of the DVD Media has resulted from accident, abuse, or misapplication. Any replacement DVD Media will be warranted for the remainder of the original warranty period or thirty (30) days, whichever is longer.

   (b) In no event shall WPI or the author be liable for any damages whatsoever (including without limitation damages for loss of business profits, business interruption, loss of business information, or any other pecuniary loss) arising from the use of or inability to use the Book or the DVD, even if WPI has been advised of the possibility of such damages.

   (c) Because some jurisdictions do not allow the exclusion or limitation of liability for consequential or incidental damages, the above limitation or exclusion may not apply to you.

7. **U.S. Government Restricted Rights.** Use, duplication, or disclosure of the DVD for or on behalf of the United States of America, its agencies and/or instrumentalities "U.S. Government" is subject to restrictions as stated in paragraph (c)(1)(ii) of the Rights in Technical Data and Computer DVD clause of DFARS 252.227-7013, or subparagraphs (c)(1) and (2) of the Commercial Computer DVD - Restricted Rights clause at FAR 52.227-19, and in similar clauses in the NASA FAR supplement, as applicable.

8. **General.** This Agreement constitutes the entire understanding of the parties and revokes and supersedes all prior agreements, oral or written, between them and may not be modified or amended except in a writing signed by both parties hereto that specifically refers to this Agreement. This Agreement shall take precedence over any other documents that may be in conflict herewith. If any one or more provisions contained in this Agreement are held by any court or tribunal to be invalid, illegal, or otherwise unenforceable, each and every other provision shall remain in full force and effect.